Surface Design for Fabric

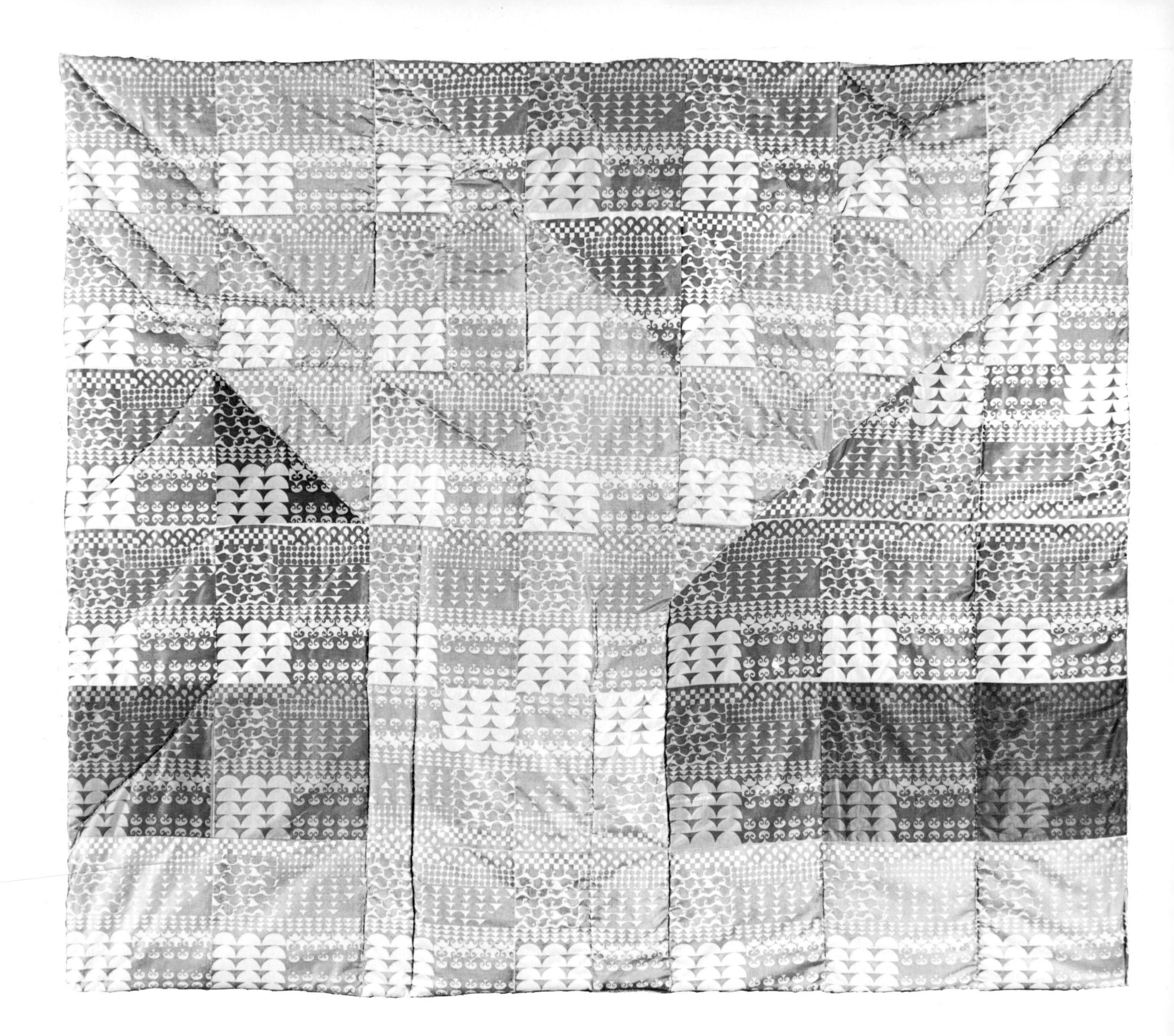

Surface Design for Fabric

Richard M. Proctor and Jennifer F. Lew

University of Washington Press   Seattle and London

To our parents

Kathryn M. Proctor and the late Edgar E. Proctor
Rose W. Lew and the late Bong Wing Lew

Printed in the United States of America

Library of Congress Cataloging in Publication Data

Proctor, Richard M.
Surface design for fabric.

Bibliography: p.
Includes index.
1. Textile design. I. Lew, Jennifer F.
II. Title.
TS1475.P76 677'.022 81-7420
ISBN 0-295-95874-X AACR2

Page 2: *Jennifer F. Lew. Screen printed quilt. Small squares of different colored polished cotton were printed with Inko prepared vat dye, then cut and pieced for the quilts. Hand-quilted with polyester fiber fill and polyester/cotton backing, top skin, ca. 6′ x 8′ (183 x 244 cm).*

Page 3: *Japanese hand painted and paste resist stencil printed fabric. Blue and white. Costume and Textile Study Collection, University of Washington.*

Embroidered collar. China, 19th century. Belonged to young boy and was worn with a robe of state. Shows fish turning into dragons. Gift of Fenton Jacobs. Courtesy of the Seattle Art Museum.

Contents

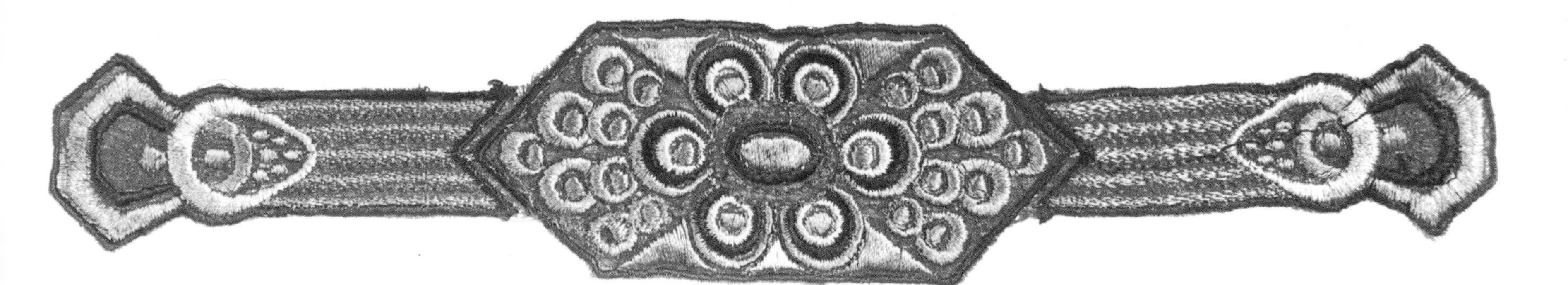

Acknowledgments

This project has had the support and encouragement of many people. Although it is impossible to name everyone here, a few key figures to whom we wish especially to extend our thanks are Nancy C. Newman, for editorial suggestions and technical assistance in the early phases of this book; Karen Ableson, Mrs. E. Sam Dick, Mary Hardin, Janie Kelley, and Jean Sevelle, for clerical work beyond the call of duty; Jack Lenor Larsen, for several valued suggestions, including the title of our book; Hazel Koenig and Spencer Moseley, for artistic assistance and continued encouragement; Ann Marie Patterson and Ronald Granich of Cerulean Blue Ltd., for their generous technical help, and especially to the latter for manuscript suggestions and for permission to quote freely from his own technical papers; and finally Ronald Childers for his personal support, encouragement, and an occasional but all too necessary shove.

Credits

Photographs not otherwise credited are by William Eng, Don Ruple, and Paul Meyer of University of Washington, Instructional Media Services.

Field Museum of Natural History: 96 right, 129 bottom
Ragnhild Langlet: 8, 179
Jack Lenor Larsen: 156, 157, 187
Lowie Museum of Anthropology, University of California, Berkeley: 71 left, 111 left
National Museum of History and Technology, Smithsonian Institute: 169 left
Seattle Art Museum (photo by Earl Fields): 9, 72, 113 both

Drawings are by Jennifer F. Lew.

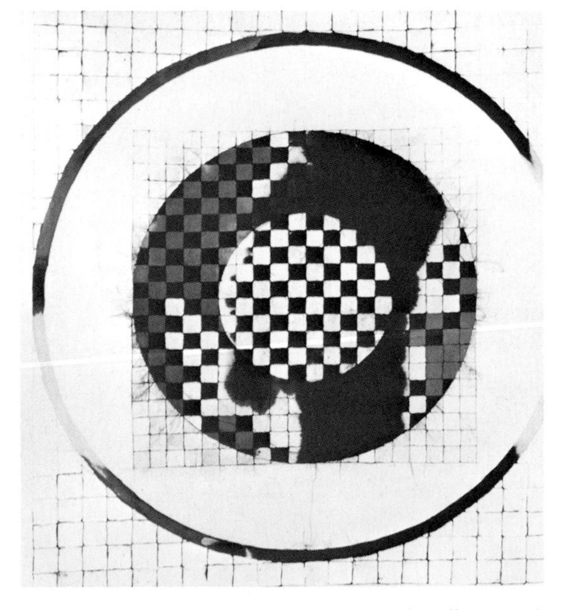

Trina Hoof. Batik with acid dyes on silk noil. Collection of Louise McCready, Seattle, Washington.

Introduction

Surface Design for Fabric is both an introduction and an invitation to a varied and fascinating field of applied design. It is also a technical resource book, an idea book, and an instructional methods book. Explained here are virtually all of the hand processes used to embellish or alter fabric surfaces. Many of these processes can be used on leather, paper, and other nontextiles and methods for their adaptation are covered here as well.

The presentation is primarily visual, with techniques illustrated in easy-to-follow steps. Every effort has been made to provide material that is inspirational, informative, accurate, and exemplary of good design.

Part One offers fundamental material on design, color, and the classification and characteristics of fibers, fabrics, and dyestuffs. Six major chapters form Part Two, the body of the book: Direct Dyeing, Liquid Resists, Bound Resists, Direct Printing, Stencil Printing, and Needlework. Each of these chapters typically consists of three sections:

1. *Equipment.* Usually a photograph with all items explained. A list including acceptable substitutes accompanies the illustration.
2. *Techniques.* Close-up detail photographs of visual and/or textural effects and how to achieve them, including design-oriented studies exploring each technique. In many cases the entire design process is shown from concept sketch to finished product.
3. *Examples.* A selective survey of historical and contemporary examples, including folk and ethnic works. This is not a history or chronology in the usual sense, but a visual frame of reference for the student and designer.

Following the text are the appendices. The first, entitled "Finishing," suggests methods of presenting, mounting, hanging, and caring for completed work. The second appendix lists supply sources. A topical bibliography is also provided.

Surface Design for Fabric is chiefly oriented toward students, educators, and beginners learning independently. It should also be of interest to professional textile designers, wall-covering designers, fashion designers, interior designers, architects, bookbinders, textile craftsmen, industrial designers, graphic designers, occupational therapists, recreational departments, libraries, and educational resource centers.

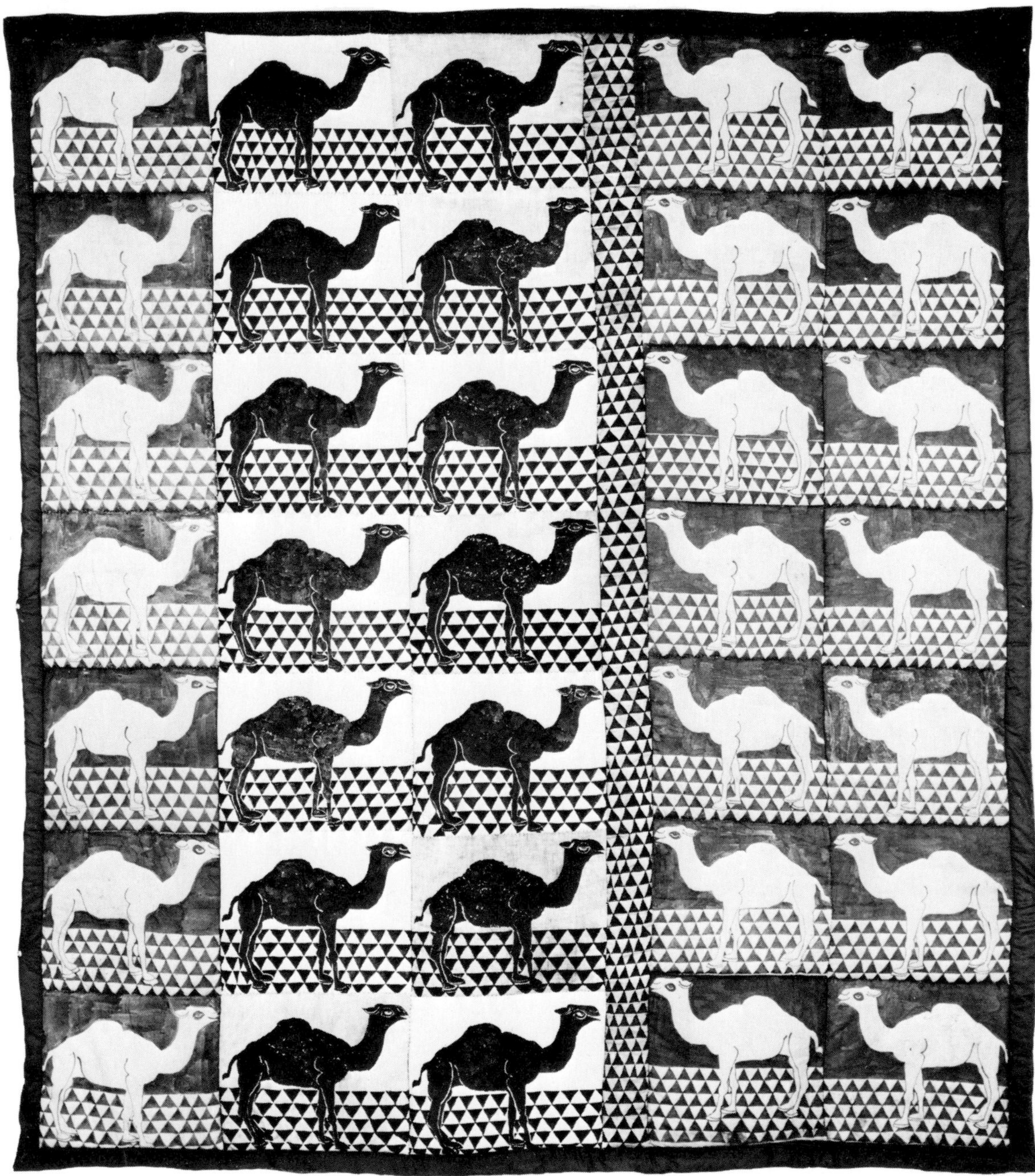

Jennifer F. Lew. Walk a Mile Quilt. Cotton fabric wax resisted, discharged with chlorine bleach, and overdyed with fiber-reactive dyes, ca. 60"x 72"(152 x 183 cm).

Left: *Ragnhild Langlet.* Cumulus Nimbus, *1972. Stretched wall piece, resist vat-dyed linen ground richly embroidered with gold lurex thread in the couching technique, 54″ x 56″ (137 x 142 cm).*

Right: *Fragment of an embroidered border. Human figure wearing ceremonial zoomorphic mask. Peruvian, Paracas culture (Necropolis style) from south coast, ca. 850 B.C.–A.D. 200. Alpaca wool gauze ground solidly embroidered in stem stitch technique, 8″ x 2¾″ (20 x 7 cm). Courtesy of Seattle Art Museum, Eugene Fuller Memorial Collection.*

PART ONE

Fundamentals of Surface Design

Contemporary Fon appliqué cloth, Abomey, Dahomey, Africa. Brilliantly colored pieces such as this are worked only by men or boys and represent insignias for all the kings of the Aladaxanou Dynasty, ca. 1629-1892, cotton, blind stitch and stem stitch, 34"x 62"(86 x 157.5 cm). Collection of Richard M. Proctor.

1. Design and Color

The Scope of Fabric Design

Fabric design includes any of the many concepts and activities that may be used for the enrichment of the fabric medium. For example, the designer may produce color by dyeing, remove color by discharging, increase contrast by printing, decrease contrast by overdyeing, suggest texture with a liquid resist, develop actual texture by quilting, juxtapose textures by applique, or create volume by stuffing. In every case the action or technique is the result of a design need and an expression of a design principle or element. Also at work is a seemingly universal human need related more to instinct than to intellect—that is, the need to embellish an otherwise plain surface.

As fabric designers, we strive to create objects that reflect an awareness of good design, a proficiency of technique, and our need for self-expression. The design component suggests the ordering of such formalistic elements as balance, unity, dominance, and rhythm. Proficiency of technique depends on skill, quality of hand, attention to detail, craftsmanship, and the sensitive adjustment of appropriate physical materials. The self-expressive component will communicate our attitudes toward such matters as style, taste, sophistication, whimsy, tension, repose, or mood. These three essential components may be likened respectively to the mind, the body and the soul of a creative fiber work.

A Starting Point

The more specific the requirements are for a surface-designed fabric in terms of function, color range, lighting, texture, technique, and style, the fewer variables there will be in its design. The reverse is equally true, as is the case with the fiber artist who creates thematic works for nonspecific spaces. Some designers view such factors as function and site as stifling, while others see them as constructive sources of focus and challenge.

Let us assume that the designer has come to terms with these concerns and the time for design and selection has arrived. (The term *design* technically refers to the planning of all aspects of a project, but in this paragraph it refers specifically to composition or arrangement of the motif or subject.) The next problem to be solved is not unlike the familiar "chicken or egg" conundrum except that three variables must be dealt with instead of two. A decision must be reached as to whether the fabric itself will suggest the choice of technique and design, whether the technique will control the fabric selection and design, or whether a design or compositional idea will determine the fabric and technique. The answer, of course, is that any of the three is valid.

At some point a commitment must be made to the visual ordering or composing of one or more of the so-called elements of design: line, form, texture, space, pattern, and color. One working method is to depend on intuition and begin dyeing, resisting, cutting, stitching, or painting, as the case may be, solving problems as they occur. The opposite approach is to work everything out to scale on paper in advance, including color placement and even the location of the artists' signature. Certain risks are involved in either case. In the former, there is little room for hindsight and a potential for unmanageable chaos. In the latter case, overdesigning may kill the spirit of the piece and it may become a dreary reenactment of a once inspired concept. The best plan is to work from known to unknown factors, possibly establishing major color areas or guidelines, then returning to the drawing board and determining the next series of known factors. These processes are repeated, and by working in this manner interest is sustained and a vital balance is struck between impulse and intellect. Granted, there are some cases where this method simply will not work. A regulated stripe print in one color, for instance, must be designed, measured, and printed without variation.

Regardless of the working method, the technique, or the fabric selected, the designer creates visual or textural forms that the viewer perceives as content—as a subject, theme, or design motif. The three fundamental sources of design motifs are organic, geometric, and classical (see Diagrams A, B, and C). Organic designs evolve from nature, geometric designs depend on the rectilinear or curvilinear figures used in geometry, and classical designs are based on traditional styles. Although most motifs fit one of these categories, dovetailing often occurs. The well-known Greek key motif, for example, is both classical and geometric. Abstract compositions may defy categorization, but tend to be geometric or organic in derivation

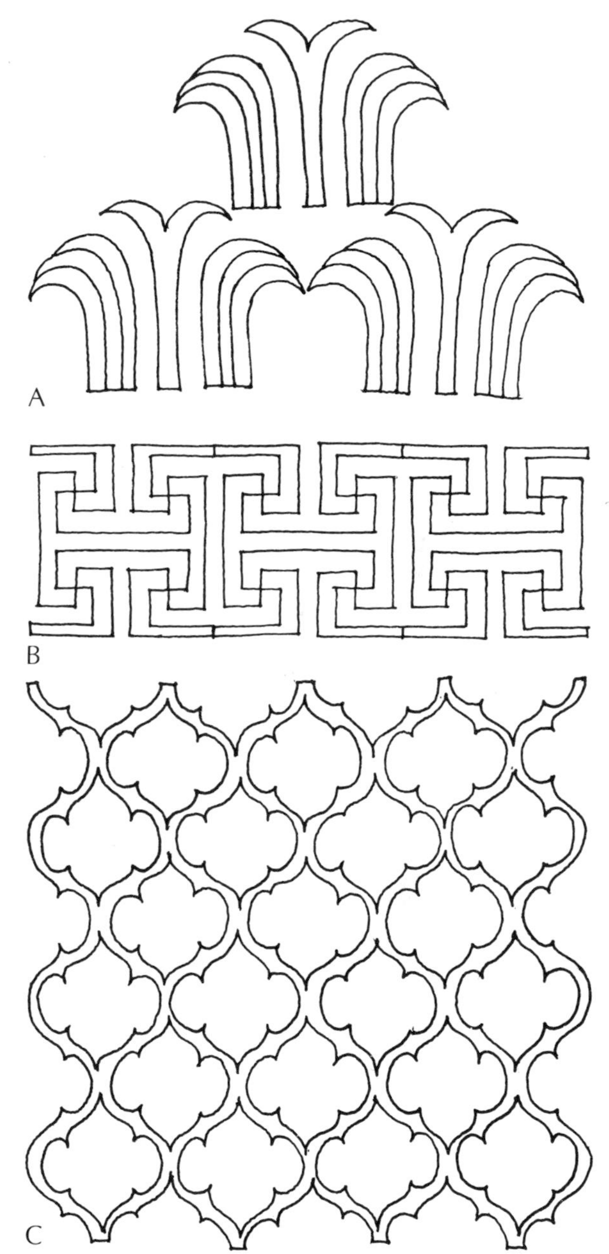

Top to bottom: *A. Organic motif; B. Geometric motif; C. Classical motif.*

Developing a Design

Eventually, the question arises as to how a particular motif or fabric design idea was arrived at. It may have come directly from the source and be quite representational of that source, be it a fern frond, a pre–Columbian textile, or an Egyptian frieze. More than likely, however, the motif that we see has gone through a transposition or stylization in which the designer has taken liberties with the source by altering its shape, contour, color, texture, or complexity.

In adapting a motif to a specific project, the designer may decide to change the basic compositional relationship from closed to open or the reverse. A closed composition is self-contained and tends to be static, either by itself (Diagram D) or when repeated (Diagram E). In an open composition, on the other hand, forms touch the edges, and the whole may appear to be cropped or to be seen through a viewfinder (Diagram F). Open forms used by themselves often seem compositionally incomplete. When they are repeated, however, they become more interdependent than closed forms because their lines and shapes move to the borders as in Diagram G.

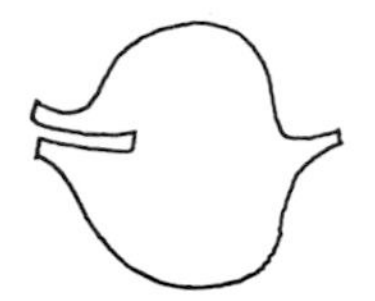

D. Closed motif.

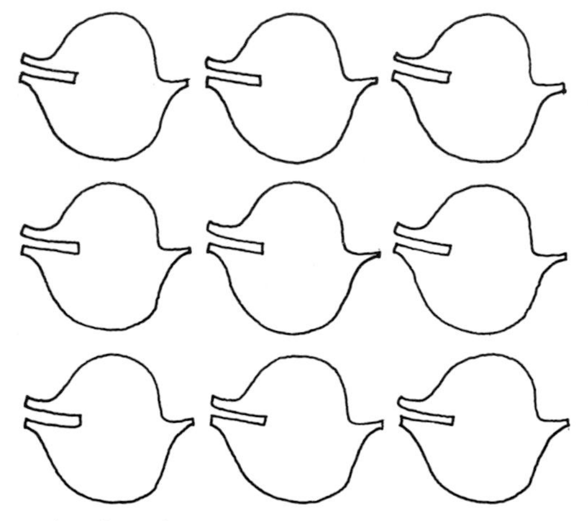

E. Closed motif in repeat.

PATTERN: REPEATING A MOTIF

All pattern depends upon the repetition of an element or a motif. Broadly speaking, all patterns or repetitions may be divided into two groups: those that have ordered placement, and those that are arranged in random fashion. The first and largest group is referred to as formal pattern, and the second as informal or random pattern. Formal, all-over pattern requires even distribution and generally follows one of the basic networks illustrated in Diagram H. Most often these networks form invisible guidelines for the placement of repeat units. Occasionally, networks are not only visible but actually become the pattern. Checks, lattice patterns, stripes and plaids are examples of this type. The spaces between the net lines are in fact shapes that will interlock or connect endlessly in any direction. This feature is characteristic of the basic networks.

F. Open motif.

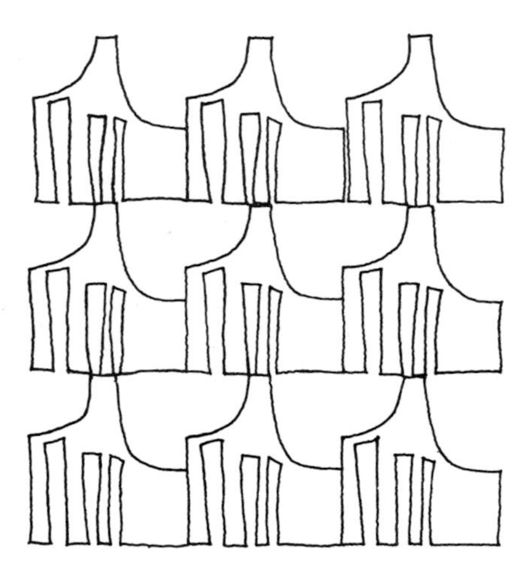

G. Open motif in repeat.

Units may also be designed to connect with each other in such a way that it is impossible to determine where one ends and the next one begins. The example in Diagram J is based on a square unit (Diagram I), but the same principle of measured line-up can be applied to most networks if it is desirable to do so. Units of this type tend to produce a unified, all-over surface with nearly equal figure–ground emphasis and little, if any, reference to network structure. Additional information on special repeat systems may be found in the screen process printing section in Chapter 8.

H. Eight basic pattern networks:

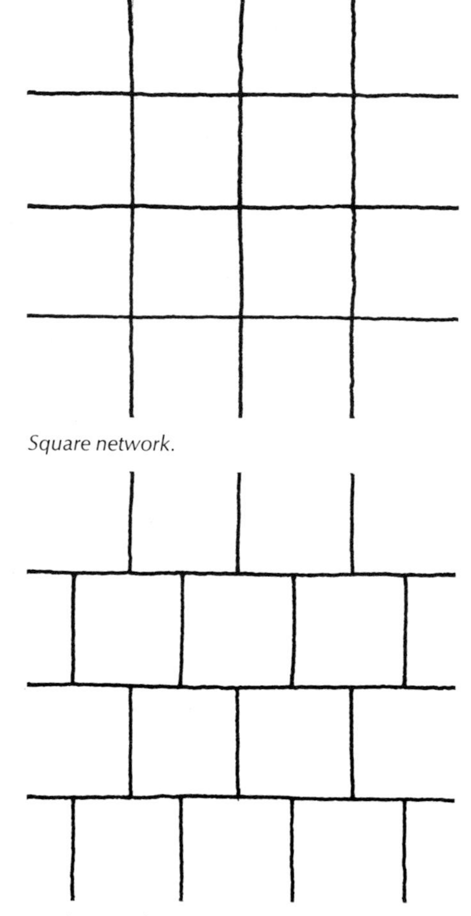

Square network.

Brick network.

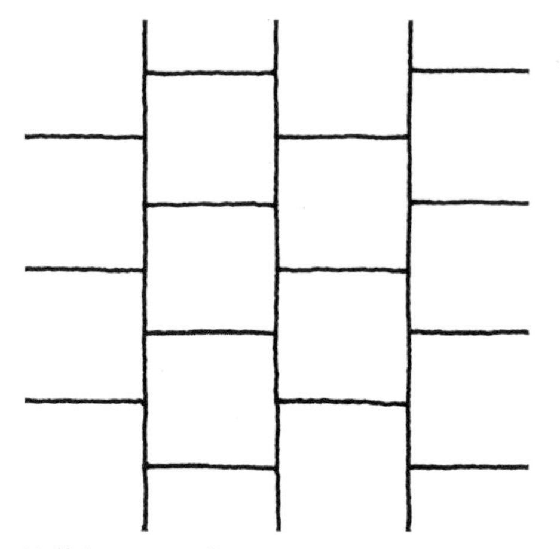
Half-drop network.

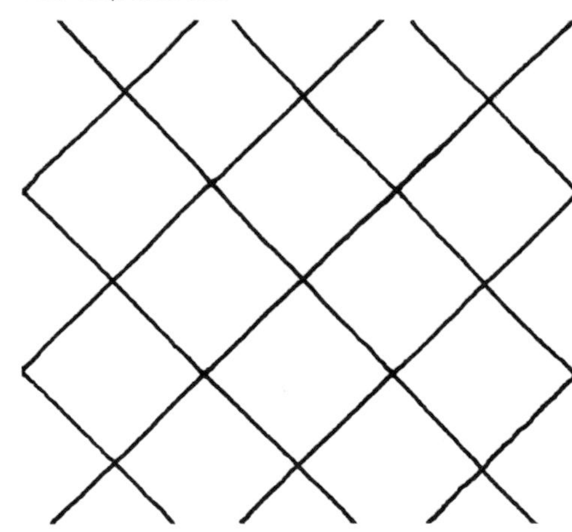
Diamond network.

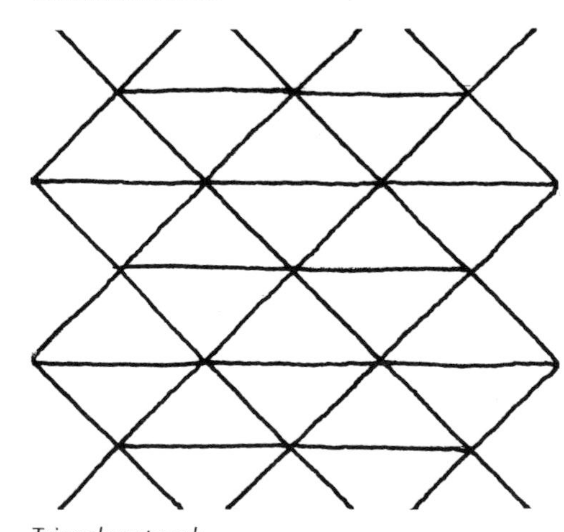
Triangle network.

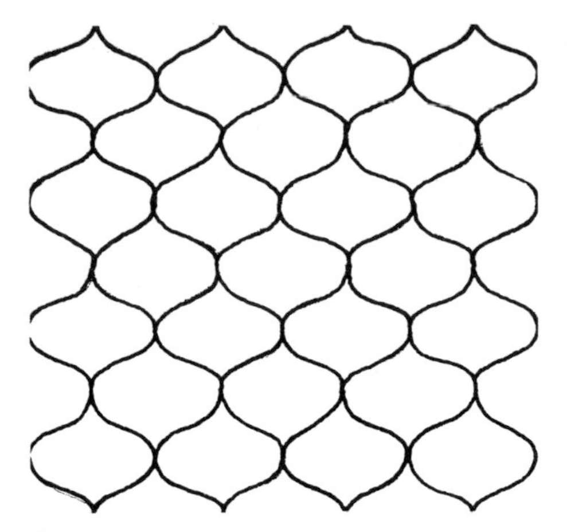
Ogee network.

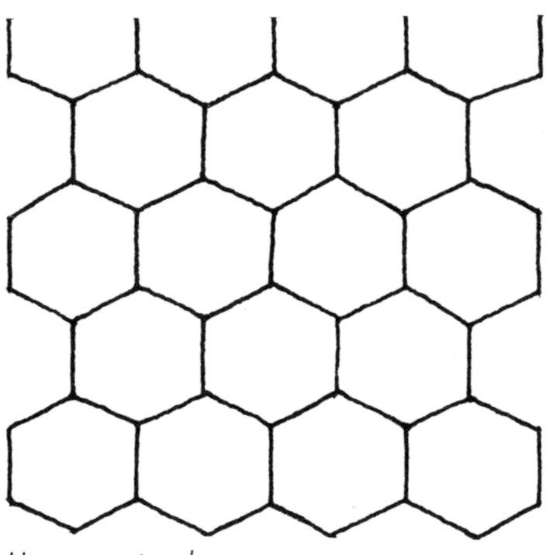
Hexagon network.

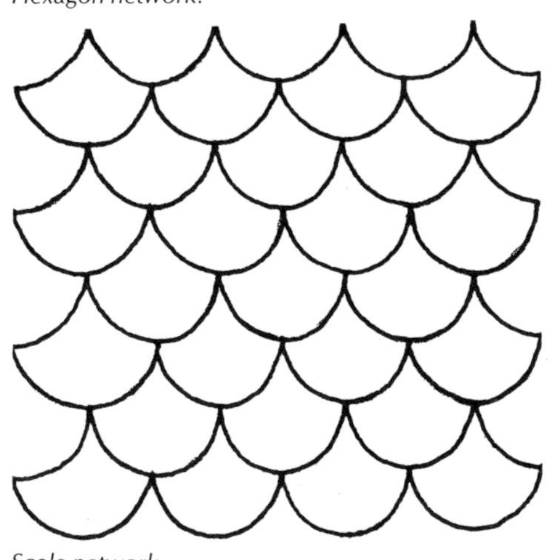
Scale network.

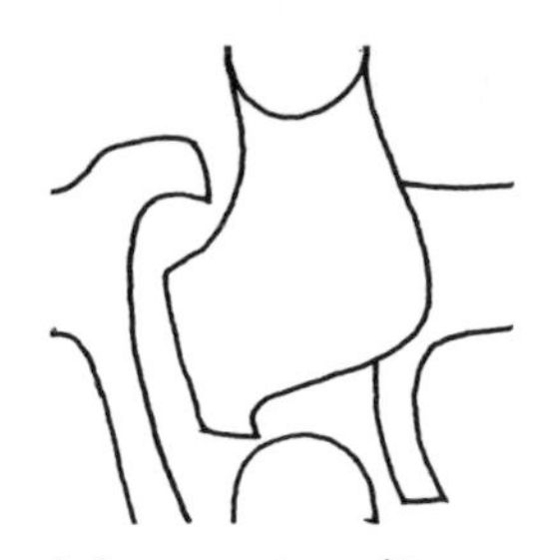
I. Square unit used in repeat design below.

J. Repeat design based on measured alignment.

SPACE AND DISTRIBUTION

Regardless of the style, complexity, or arrangement of a motif, many options are at the designer's disposal concerning emphasis, movement, and space distribution. The diagrams in K demonstrate relative changes in space allocation to the figure or motif and to the ground. Diagram L illustrates the comparative effects of pattern in the figure and the ground, and Diagram M suggests possibilities for altering arrangement for direction and movement. Please remember that these observations and diagrams are not intended as rules but rather as alternate suggestions.

K. Space relationships between figure and ground:

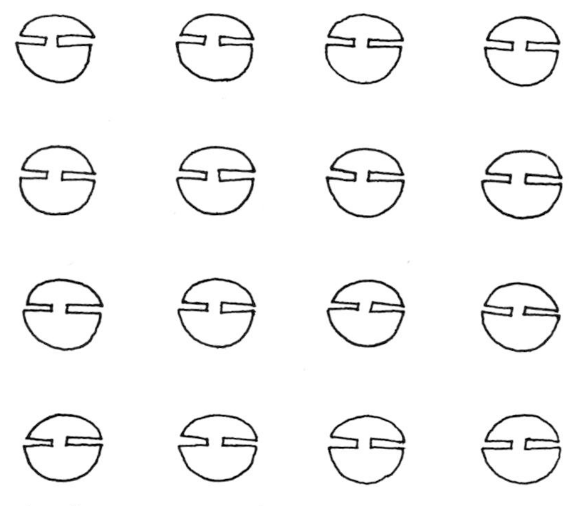

Less figure, more ground.

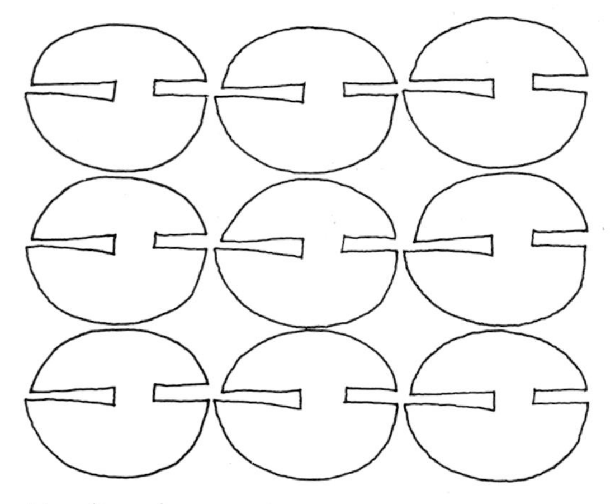

More figure, less ground.

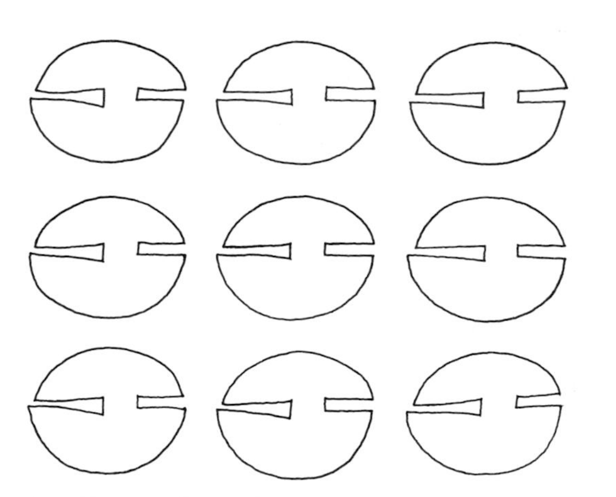

Equal figure and ground.

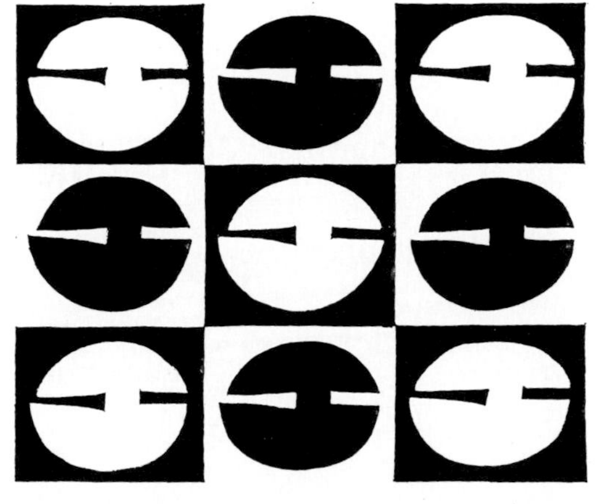

Counter-change.

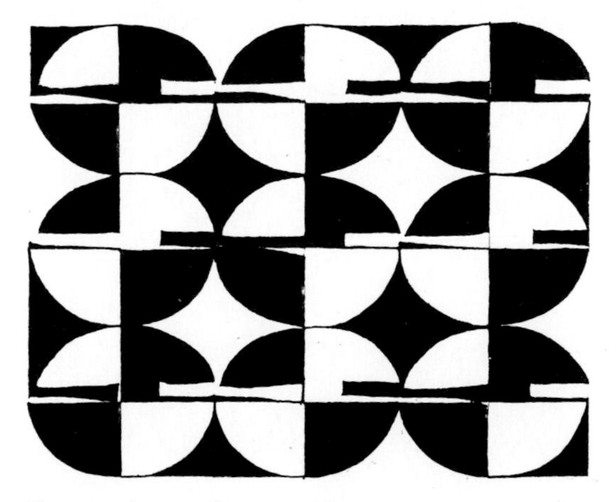

Counter-change, alternate grid.

L. Pattern in the figure and ground:

Patterned figure, solid ground.

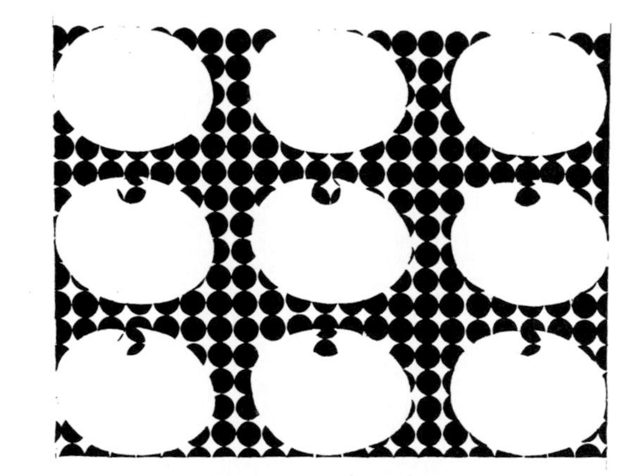

Patterned ground, solid figure.

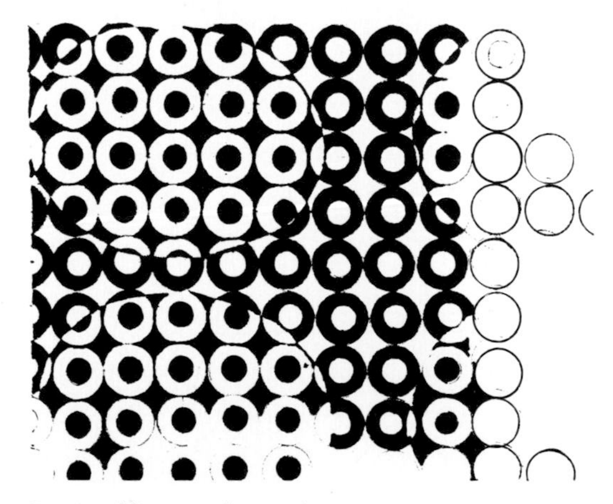

Patterned figure and ground.

M. Direction and movement in figure and ground:

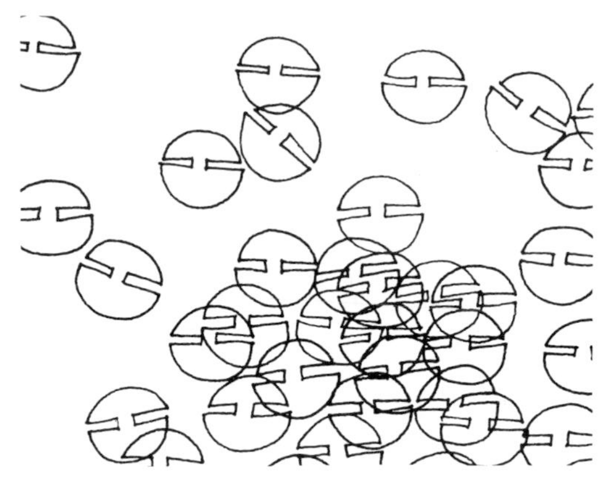

Radial diffusion.

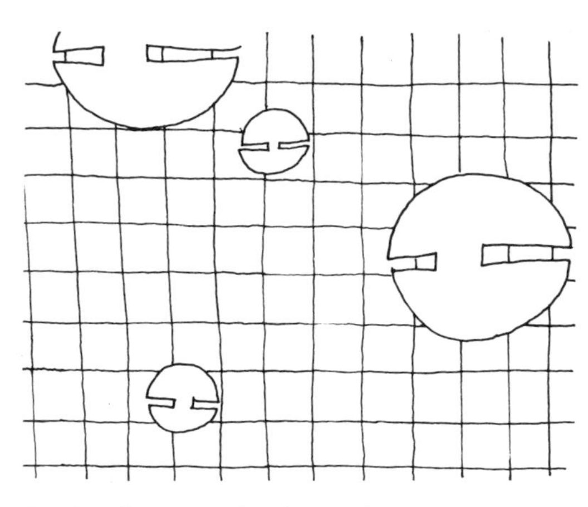

Random figures, regulated ground.

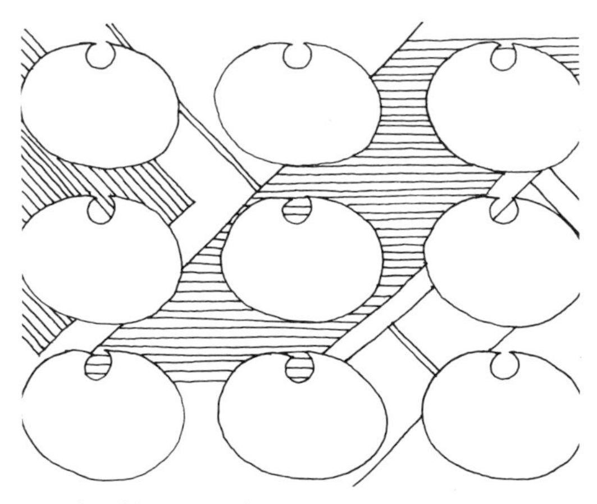

Regulated figure, random ground.

Introduction to Color

Books, films, and research libraries have been devoted to color and its theories, psychology, symbolism, nomenclature, and application. Color can be evocative, emotional, natural, associative, neutral, or deceptive. For our fabric design purposes, we will omit most of the theory and focus on the practical matters of color behavior and color mixing.

COLOR PROPERTIES

What we most frequently call "color" is actually an eye–mind translation of light waves being selectively absorbed or reflected by an object. This complex series of events results in our recognition of hue, that is, an identifiable color name such as red or violet. The term *hue* then refers to nomenclature and is one of three measurable color properties, the others being value and intensity. *Value* refers to the amount of dark or light existing in a hue, while *intensity* refers to the amount of brightness or dullness existing in a hue. Chroma is generally synonomous with intensity. The terms value and intensity may be clarified by referring to the chart on color effects given later in this chapter. Warmth or coolness is seldom listed as a measurable property of color, due possibly to its variable associative nature. However, the relative warmth or coolness of a hue can vastly alter its visual effect, as we shall see shortly.

THE COLOR WHEEL

The most convenient and frequently used means of visualizing the interrelated nature of color is a circular arrangement called the color wheel or color circle. It is created by bending a color spectrum until the ends touch and traditionally consists of twelve hues, sometimes called the twelve chromatic hues. Three of these are the primary hues, three are secondary hues, and six are tertiary hues. The primary hues—red, yellow and blue—are placed equidistant from each other in triadic formation. The mixing of any two primary hues produces a secondary hue, and these secondaries—green, violet, and orange—are placed equidistant between their primary parents. When neighboring primary and secondary hues are mixed, they result in the six tertiary hues, each of which occurs between its primary and secondary parents. Thus blue-green appears between its primary, blue and the secondary, green. The other tertiaries—blue-violet, red-violet, red-orange, yellow-orange, and yellow-green—are formed and located by the same principle.

Perhaps the most helpful observations to be made from the color wheel is what hues appear opposite each other. These opposing paired hues are referred to as complements or as complementary colors. In color mixing, the addition of one complement to the other will neutralize or gray the original hue. For example if a bright red is to be made less bright but not appreciably darker, then a small amount of its complement, green, should be added. Such changes are referred to as changes of intensity.

Alterations in the darkness or lightness of a color are referred to as changes in value. These are achieved by adding black or white to opaque colorants such as inks or paste paints. In the case of dyes, which of course are transparent, black is added to darken the value, and some form of clear extender is added to lighten the value. These additive mixtures primarily control value but will alter the intensity as well. Black will dull a color, while white or clear may tend to brighten it slightly.

To change the visual temperature of a color add a warm or cool color to the basic hue. Changes such as these are particularly useful in making subtle alterations to relatively neutral hues like grays and browns when several will be used in combination. In general, warm colors are associated with fire, and cool colors are associated with water.

Color Schemes

A number of traditional color schemes exist, most of which border on being cliches. Nonetheless, they provide assurance of color unity and are useful points of departure, especially for the novice. The traditional schemes are monochromatic, analogous, triadic, complementary, and split complementary. Each is described in the vocabulary of design and color terms.

Hints on Mixing Opaque Colors

For our purposes opaque colors will include the inks and paste paints which, when applied to the fabric surface, will not be appreciably affected by the original color of the fabric.

For tints, begin with white or the light value, placing the estimated volume in an appropriate container, and then add the dark paint to it in small quantities until the proper color is achieved. Test swatches will be necessary since light paints and inks tend to dry somewhat darker.

For tones, begin with the required volume of gray and add the stronger color in small quantities until the desired color is achieved. If the strong color is dark in value, begin with a gray of a slightly lighter value, but if the color is of a light or middle value, begin with a gray of the value desired in the final mixture. Make test swatches and adjust as necessary.

For shades, begin with about three-quarters of the predicted volume of the shading hue and slowly add black or a dark value to it in small batches until the proper shade is reached. Such mixtures tend to dry lighter than they look while wet. Test and make corrections as suggested above.

Hints on Mixing Transparent Colors

In fabric design, transparent colors refer to dyes in both their liquid and paste forms. They differ from opaque colors in that there is no such thing as a white dye. For white, we must depend upon the reflective surface of white or near-white fabric in the same way that the watercolorist depends upon white paper. The same hints listed above for opaque colors can be applied to transparent colors if we substitute a clear extending agent such as water, chemical water, or clear thickener for the opaque white. It is very important to test dyes on fabric of the exact color, fiber content, and structure for which they are being formulated. Bear in mind that transparent colors dry lighter than they appear while wet.

With dyes there are two basic approaches to color mixing: one is to pre-mix color which is applied to a white ground, and the other is to arrive at color by overdyeing. For example, green dye might be used in the first approach, and in the second, yellow might be overdyed with blue to produce the same green. More information on overdyeing may be found in Chapter 3 on "Dyes and Colorants."

Color Effects

It is one thing to be able to create any desired color but quite another to use it skillfully in combination for a desired effect. The chart below is not infallible, and some of the effects may be altered or even reversed by factors of scale, proportion, texture, light quality, or surface movement.

COLOR EFFECTS

	Hue *(temperature)*	**Value**	**Intensity**
Size	Warm colors tend to increase the size of objects; cool colors usually decrease size	Dark values tend to decrease the size of objects; light values tend to increase size, but strong contrast with backgrounds can have a similar effect	Bright colors increase the size of objects; dull colors reduce the size of objects
Distance	Warm colors advance; cool colors recede	Light values usually advance, as do heavily patterned elements; dark values tend to recede	Bright colors advance; dull colors recede
Emphasis	Warm colors command more attention than cool colors; strong warm–cool contrasts are also arresting	Both dark and light values attract equally when they appear on a contrasting ground	Bright colors are the most attention-getting especially when juxtaposed with their complements or with neutrals
Mood	Warm colors tend to stimulate; cool colors tend to relax	Light values tend to be cheerful; dark colors tend to be restful and sometimes suggest depression. Dark–light contrasts are stimulating	Bright colors suggest power and excitement; dull or neutral colors tend to be relaxing
Contour	Contours or outlines are emphasized by contrast rather than by any inherent characteristics of color		

Jennifer F. Lew. Parrots. *Waterproof marker ink on cotton upholstery velvet, 14″ × 21″(ca. 35.5 cm × 53.3 cm).*

Dona Anderson. Partly Cloudy/Rainbow. *Stitched and reconstructed fabric surface, 52″ × 44″ × 4″(ca. 132 cm × 111.6 cm × 10.2 cm).*

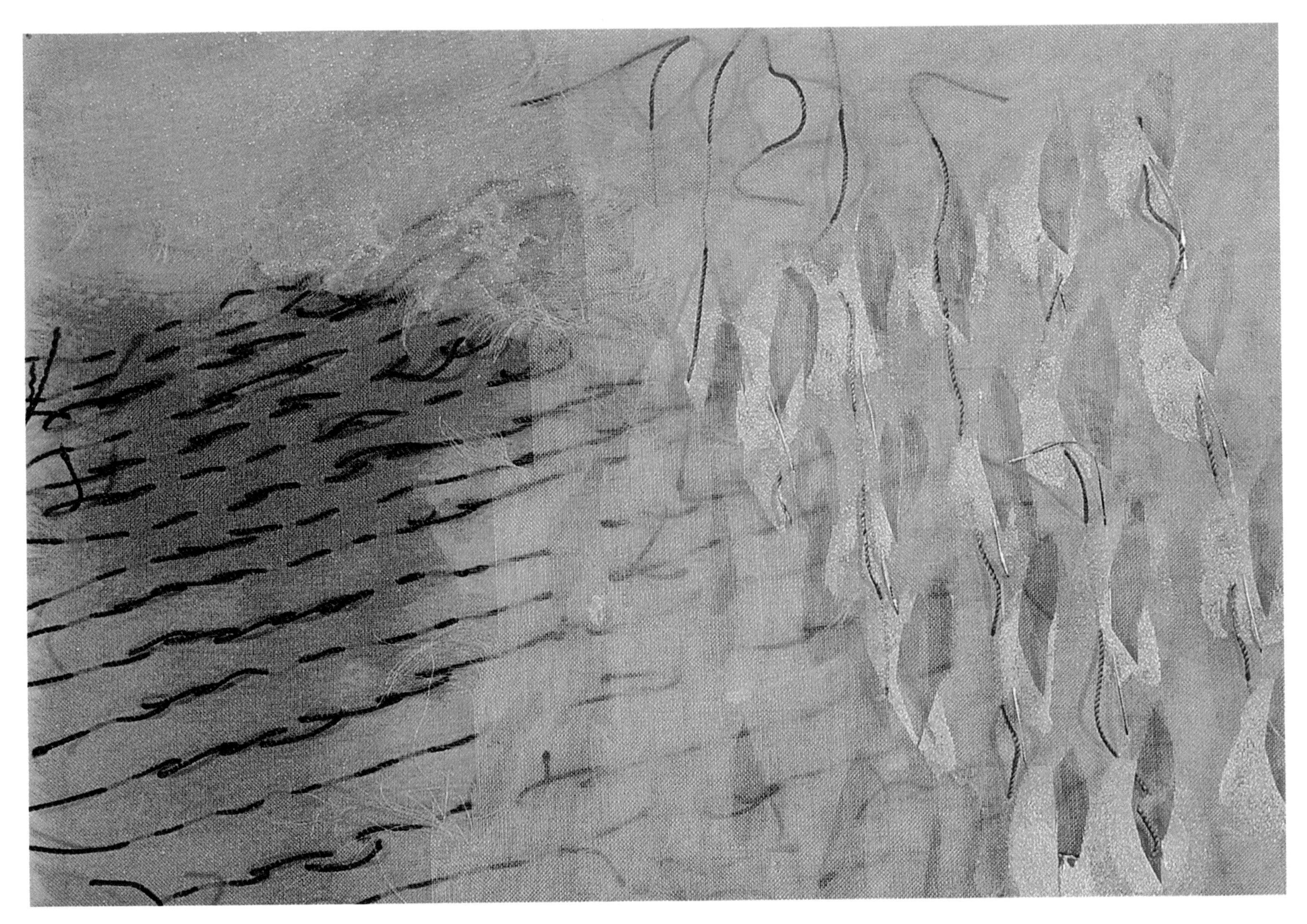

Caroline Cooley Browne. Murmuring 5, *1981. Mixed media on silk, 4¾″ × 9″(ca. 12 cm × 22.9 cm).*

Richard M. Proctor. Cruciform, *1983. Stamp printed wax resist with reactive dye on cotton, 42″ × 42″(ca. 106.7 cm × 106.7 cm). Collection of Dennis and Katherine Holzknecht, Woodinville, Washington.*

Vocabulary of Design and Color Terms

Accent: The emphasis or dominance of an attention-getting element in a composition.
Advancing colors: Hues that appear to move forward. These usually include colors of high intensity, colors of light value, and warm colors.
Analogous colors: Adjacent or neighboring hues on the color wheel. Closely related hues.
Asymmetric: Not identical on both sides of a central line. Informal arrangement of elements in a composition.
Axis: An imaginary line around which the components of a composition are organized.
Balance: The quality of equilibrium in a design. Formal balance is symmetric, while informal balance is asymmetric.
Bilateral: Two-sided.
Bisymmetric: Alike or similar on two sides of an axis (i.e., the Parthenon).
Cartoon: A full-size preliminary drawing, usually a "map" to guide the progress of an artwork.
Chroma: The intensity, or degree of brightness in a color.
Color: Depends on the reflection or absorption of light by a given surface and may be described by three distinct characteristics: hue, value, and intensity.
Color scheme: A specific arrangement of hues. Appropriate amounts may be noted, as well as placement.
Colorway: A trade term for any of several color schemes in which a single design is produced.
Color wheel: A circular arrangement of the twelve spectral colors.
Complementary colors: Opposite hues on the color wheel (for example: red-green, orange-blue, yellow-violet).
Composition: An arrangement of visual elements. Frequently the tangible result of the design process.
Contrast: The basic means of perception. The difference between things compared, i.e., light-dark, bright-dull, rough-smooth.
Cool colors: Generally, hues related to blue such as blue-green and blue-violet. Often associated with water, ice, and sky.
Counter-change: Reversing values or hues on both sides of a line. The checkerboard is a simple form of counter-change.
Delineation: To represent by outline.
Design elements: The basic formal elements the designer works with in creating a composition: color, form, line, pattern, and texture.
Design principles: The fundamental means by which the designer relates the elements of design: accent, balance, rhythm, unity, and variety.
Dominance: The prevailing or accented element in a composition.
Figure: A form or shape determined by outlines or exterior surfaces. Often the dominant element in a composition.
Figure-ground: The relationship of positive to negative shapes in a composition. In a figure-ground reversal, any shape may be perceived as either figure or background.
Focal point: The center of interest in a composition.
Form: The shape of volume or mass.
Gradient: Gradual progression by degrees.
Graphic: Represented or designed with clarity. Refers to an orderly diagrammatic approach.
Ground: The foundation surface or background in a composition.
High-key: Colors of increased value and/or intensity.
Hue: The name of a color. One of the three measurable properties of color, the others being value and intensity.
Intensity: The degree of brightness or dullness existing in a color. One of the three measurable properties of color, the others being hue and value. The chroma.
Interval: A measured area or span between recurring elements.
Line: The trace of a moving point. A mark defining the contour or edge of a shape.
Low-key: Colors of reduced value and/or intensity.
Mass: Having weight, bulk, or density.
Module: A measured unit or shape used in planning a design.
Monochromatic: One hue. A monochromatic color scheme consists of different values and/or intensities of a single hue.
Motif: The theme or dominant recurring visual element, form, or subject in a composition.
Negative space: Spaces or shapes between or around positive forms in a composition.
Network: Repeating combination of curved or straight lines. The basic understructure of all repeat patterns.
Neutral: Usually a dulled or "grayed" hue resulting from mixing any two complementary colors.
Neutralize: To dull or "gray" a hue by adding its complement.
Opaque: Non-translucent, absorbing rather than transmitting light.
Pattern: Regular repetition of an element or motif.
Pigment: The color-producing component of paints and inks.
Plane: A fixed two-dimensional surface.
Polychrome: Multi color.
Positive space: Dominant spaces or shapes in a composition.
Primary colors: The three basic colors from which all others are theoretically derived: red, yellow, and blue.
Proportion: See *Scale*.
Radial: Generally pertaining to symmetric forms that radiate from a central point, (i.e., a dandelion).
Receding colors: Hues that appear to move back. These usually include colors of low intensity, colors of dark value, and cool colors.
Relief: The raised portions of a sculptural surface.
Rhythm: Repetition of a motif or element.
Saturation: The degree of intensity existing in a hue.
Scale: The size of an object in relationship to another. Synonymous with proportion.
Secondary colors: The results of mixing equal parts of two primary colors, (i.e., red + yellow = orange; blue + yellow = green; blue + red = violet).
Shade: A hue plus black.
Shape: Definable form or figure.
Space: Distance, interval, or area between or within shapes.
Spectrum: The continuous visible band of colors produced by the dispersion of a beam of sunlight or white light passing through a prism.
Split complement: A hue and the two hues adjacent to its complement on the color wheel (i.e., red, blue-green, and yellow-green).
Stylize: To treat decoratively rather than according to nature.
Subordination: Diminishing certain elements in a composition, thereby making them secondary or dependent.
Symmetry: Formal arrangement of parts. Most often bilateral or radial.
Tertiary colors: The results of mixing equal parts of a primary color with an adjacent secondary color (i.e, red + violet = red-violet).
Texture: The surface quality of materials. May refer to physical or tactile texture as distinct from visual or implied texture.

Three-dimensional: Having the dimension of depth as well as width and height.

Tint: A hue plus white.

Tone: A hue plus gray.

Transparent: Capable of being seen through. Transmitting rather than absorbing light.

Triadic colors: Any three equidistant hues on the color wheel.

Two-dimensional: Having its elements organized on a single plane.

Unity: A harmony of related parts, oneness or consistency.

Value: The degree of lightness or darkness existing in a color. One of the three measurable properties of color, the others being hue and intensity.

Variety: Difference or multiplicity. The absence of monotony.

Volume: The amount of space occupied by a shape or mass.

Warm colors: Generally, hues related to red and orange. Often associated with heat or fire.

Jennifer F. Lew. Cotton fabric resisted with rice paste and brush dyed with prepared vat dye, 24″ x 30″ (61 x 77 cm).

2. Fibers and Fabrics

An Overview

A familiarity with fibers and textile structure is necessary for the practical and aesthetic union of media and fabric. In general, natural fibers and fabrics are best suited to the needs of the textile craftsman. It is preferable that these fibers be untreated, although mercerization, which assists in the absorption of dye in cellulosic fibers, is an exception to this rule. Such fabrics are often difficult to locate, but the list of suppliers provided at the end of this book should prove helpful.

There are two basic categories of textile fibers: natural and manmade. Natural fibers may be vegetable (cotton, linen, jute, hemp, sisal, and ramie) or animal (silk, wool, and hair). Technically, the natural fibers also include the less common mineral fiber, asbestos, and metallic filaments of gold, silver, and copper. Rubber is a synthetic, organic-based product.

Manmade fibers may be categorized in various ways, but three useful groupings are: (1) modified cellulosic fibers (the rayons, acetate, and triacetate); (2) synthetic long-chain polymer fibers (nylon, aramed, polyester, acrylic, modacrylic, poly-propylene, spandex, and saran); and (3) the mineral fiber, glass.

The chart below lists some basic fiber characteristics as an aid in selecting the most appropriate fiber for its intended function or means of decoration. Bear in mind that variations exist within any category, and that fiber properties may be altered in the transformation of fiber into fabric. A change in yarn twist, ply, weave, or knit structure, finish, or aftertreatment will modify the stated behavior of any given fiber.

FIBER CHARACTERISTICS

Natural Fibers	Absorbency	Bleach reaction	Drapability	Dye affinity	Elasticity	Light reaction
Cotton	mod.-high	chlorine ok	fair	good	poor	weakens and yellows
Linen	high	chlorine ok	good	poor	poor	light resistant
Silk	high	hydrogen peroxide only	excellent	excellent	good	weakens rapidly
Wool	very high	hydrogen peroxide only	excellent	excellent	excellent	weakens in time, improves dye affinity
Manmade Fibers						
Viscose Rayon	high	chlorine or hydrogen peroxide	fair	good	fair	weakens in time
Cuparammonium Rayon	high	chlorine or hydrogen peroxide	fair	good	poor	weakens in time
High Wet-Modulus Rayon	high	variable	fair	good	poor	weakens in time
Acetate	low	mild solutions only	good	fair	fair	good resistance, weakens in time
Arnel Triacetate	low	mild solutions only	good	fair	fair	good resistance, weakens in time
Nylon	very low	mild solutions only	good-excellent	fair	excellent	good resistance, weakens in time
Aramed	low	chlorine ok	good	poor		good resistance, weakens in time
Polyester	very low	mild solutions only	fair to good	fair	poor	good resistance, weakens in time
Acrylic	very low	chlorine ok (except creslan)	fair to good	fair	poor	good resistance, weakens in time
Modacrylic	very low	variable	fair to good	fair	poor	good resistance, weakens in time
Poly-propylene	none	chlorine ok	fair	poor	good	weakens rapidly
Spandex	very low	variable	good when combined	excellent	excellent	weakens in time
Saran	none	mild solutions only	poor	poor	good	darkens but does not deteriorate
Glass	none	mild solutions only	good	surface only	none	light resistant

Natural Fibers	Heat reaction	Luster	Mildew resistance	Shrinkage	Strength	Washability	Wrinkle resistance
Cotton	scorches at 300°F. burns at 475°F.	very little	poor	medium	good	excellent (soils easily)	poor-fair
Linen	scorches at 300°F. burns at 475°	moderate-	poor	medium	excellent	excellent (soil resistant)	poor
Silk	decomposes at 330°	moderate-high	good	low	excellent	excellent (soil resistant)	excellent
Wool	decomposes at 260° burns at 572°	dull-moderate	good	high	good-fair	dryclean or special care	good-excellent
Manmade Fibers							
Viscose Rayon	decomposes 325° burns 475°	high, but varies with manufacturer	poor	medium	good	fair-dryclean, or special care	poor
Cuparammonium Rayon	decomposes at 325° burns at 475°	high, but varies with manufacturer	poor	medium	good	fair	poor
High Wet-Modulus Rayon	decomposes at 325° burns at 475°	high, but varies with manufacturer	poor	medium	good	good	fair
Acetate	decomposes at 350° burns/melts at 500°	high, but varies with manufacturer	good	low	poor	fair-dryclean or gentle wash	good
Arnel Triacetate	melts at 572°	high, but varies with manufacturer	good-excellent	none	fair-poor	fair-dryclean or gentle wash	good-excellent
Nylon	yellows at 300° melts at 420°–480°	high, but varies with manufacturer	excellent	none	good	excellent (soil resistant)	good-excellent
Aramed	chars at 700°	high, but varies with manufacturer	excellent	low (boiling water) none (cold water)	good	good-excellent	good-excellent
Polyester	melts at 450-500°	high, but varies with manufacturer	excellent	none	good	excellent (soil resistant	good-excellent
Acrylic	deteriorates at 487°	high, but varies with manufacturer	excellent	none	good-fair	excellent (soils easily)	good-excellent
Modacrylic	variable, won't flame deteriorates at 260°-390°	high, but varies with manufacturer	excellent	none	good	excellent (soils easily)	good-excellent
Poly-propylene	decomposes at 212° melts at 325°	high, but varies with manufacturer	excellent	low (warm water) none (cold water)	good	excellent (avoid high temp.)	good-excellent
Spandex	variable melts at 466°-511°	dull	good-excellent	none	good	excellent (avoid high temp.)	excellent
Saran	decomposes at 210° melts at 340°	lustrous	excellent	none	excellent	good (avoid high temp.)	good
Glass	weakens at 600° melts at 1350°	lustrous	excellent	none	excellent	excellent (soil resistant)	good (fiber will crack)

Textile Structure

Weaving is the primary process by which threads are interlaced to form cloth. The parallel lengthwise threads in woven construction are called "warp." The parallel threads interlaced at right angles to the warp are called "weft" or "filler." For our purposes, woven structures may be divided into four general classes:

Plain weave depends on the simple over and under passage of weft through adjacent warp. The sequence reverses in alternate rows. A balanced plain weave exposes equal amounts of warp and weft. A warp-faced fabric conceals the weft, and a weft-faced fabric conceals the warp.

Twill weaves produce a characteristic diagonal pattern by the passage of the weft over one or more warp yarns and under two or more others. In each succeeding row this progression moves one or more spaces to the right or left. Herringbone, satin, sateen, damask, and reverse twill are a few derivatives in this class.

Compound weaves employ supplementary yarns in either or both the warp and weft to create pattern or texture. A few examples of compound structures are brocade, double weave, inlay, velvet, velveteen, and knotted pile fabrics.

Open weaves with lacelike appearance comprise the last major class of structures. In gauze and leno weaves the warp yarns are twisted at the juncture of the weft. In either of these "finger techniques" the weaver controls weft placement. Other open weaves result from irregular spacing of warp and/or weft for contrasting negative and positive effects.

There is also a rapidly expanding family of nonwoven textiles important to the craftsman. These include felt, pellon, vinyl, and a myriad of knit fabrics.

Like the previous chart, the chart below is offered as a guide in selecting the best fiber class for the project at hand, but in addition it lists weave structure, texture, weight, color availability, and predictable shrinkage.

FABRIC CHARACTERISTICS

Cotton Fabrics	Weave Structure	Texture	Weight	Colors			Approximate Shrinkage
				Nat.	White	Colors	
Batiste	plain	soft sheer	med.-light		x	x	
Broadcloth	plain	smooth, fine rib	medium		x	x	none
Canvas	plain	coarse	heavy	x	x		
Corduroy	compound	napped ribs	med. to heavy		x	x	slight
Denim	twill	med. smooth	med.-heavy			x	
Duck	plain	coarse	med.-heavy	x	x	x	variable
Flannel	plain or twill	soft with nap	lt.-med.		x	x	
Hopsacking	plain	med. smooth	medium	x			slight
Indianhead	plain	med. to coarse	medium		x	x	slight
Jersey	knit	soft and stretchy	lt.-med		x	x	
Monk's Cloth	plain (basket weave)	med. pronounced basket weave	med.-heavy	x			3″ per yd.
Muslin (unbleached)	plain	soft	full range	x			3″ per yd.
Organdy	plain	sheer and crisp	light		x	x	
Osnaburg (linen)	plain	rough	med. to heavy	x			3″ per yd.
Percale	plain	smooth	medium		x	x	slight
Poplin	plain	rib effect	medium		x	x	slight
Print Cloth	plain	smooth	lt.-med.		x	x	slight
Sateen	satin	very smooth	med.-heavy	x	x	x	none
Sheeting	plain	smooth	lt.-med.		x	x	variable
Terrycloth	compound	rough	lt.-heavy		x	x	slight
Velveteen	compound	soft pile	med.-heavy		x	x	variable

Wool and Hair Fibers	Weave Structure	Texture	Weight	Colors			Approximate Shrinkage
				Nat.	White	Colors	
Batiste	plain	Smooth	light		x	x	
Bedford Cord.	plain	Warp rib	med-heavy		x	x	
Broadcloth	plain	fine-smooth	lt.-med.		x	x	
Camels Hair	var.	soft	var.	x			
Cashmere	twill or var.	ultra soft	light	x	x	x	
Challis	plain	soft pliable	light		x	x	6%
Crepe	plain	crinkly	light		x	x	8–9%
Flannel	twill	soft	medium		x	x	
Gabardine	twill	hard finish	medium		x	x	
Homespun	plain	coarse and uneven	med. to heavy	x	x	x	
Hopsacking	plain (basket)	rough	med. to heavy		x	x	
Jersey	knit	elastic with slight rib	medium		x	x	
Melton	plain	smooth	very heavy			x	
Mohair	var.	lustrous smooth	var.				
Serge	twill	smooth	medium			x	
Sharkskin	twill	sleek	medium			x	
Shetland	twill or plain	soft	var.	x	x	x	
Tweed	var.	med. to coarse	medium			x	
Velour	compound pile	ultra smooth	medium		x	x	
Whipcord	twill	hard, diagonal wale	med. to heavy			x	

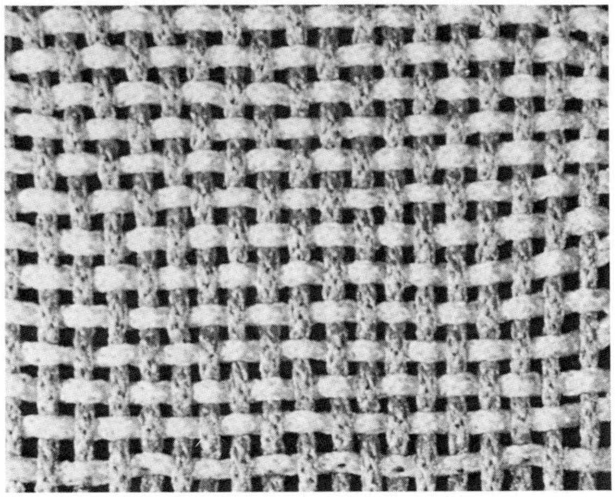

Plain weave.

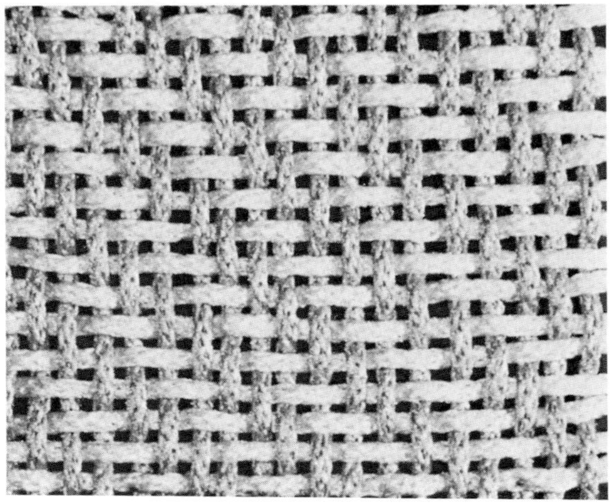

Twill weave.

Linen Fabrics	**Weave Structure**	**Texture**	**Weight**	**Colors**			**Approximate Shrinkage**
				Nat.	White	Colors	
Alter linen	plain	sheer, fine, crisp	light		x		slight
Art linen	plain	smooth	lt.-med.	x	x	x	slight
Cambric	plain	fine, smooth	light		x	x	slight
Canvas	plain	coarse	med. to heavy	x	x		slight
Crash	plain	medium	med.-heavy	x			1″ per yd.
Damask	twill	smooth	medium		x	x	slight
Drapery Linen	plain	med.-rough	heavy	x	x	x	slight
Handkerchief Linen	plain	fine, smooth	light		x	x	slight
Irish Linen	plain	smooth	medium		x	x	slight
Silk Fabrics							
Broadcloth	plain	fine, smooth	med.-lt.	x	x	x	3–4%
Chiffon	plain	sheer	lt.		x	x	8%
China Silk	plain	soft	lt.		x	x	3–4%
Crepe		crinkled	med.-lt.		x	x	8%
Georgette		crinkled/ sheer	light		x	x	8–10% 8–10%
Noile	plain	medium	med.-heavy	x	x	x	3%
Pongee	plain	medium	medium	x	x	x	4%
Radium	plain	supple but crisp	med.-lt.		x	x	
Satin	satin	lustrous	variable		x	x	5%
Shantung	plain	med.-rough	medium		x	x	3%
Surah	twill	lustrous	medium		x	x	4%
Taffeta	plain	smooth/crisp	med.-heavy		x	x	6%
Tussah	plain	rough	heavy	x	x	x	
Velvet	pile	nappy	variable		x	x	

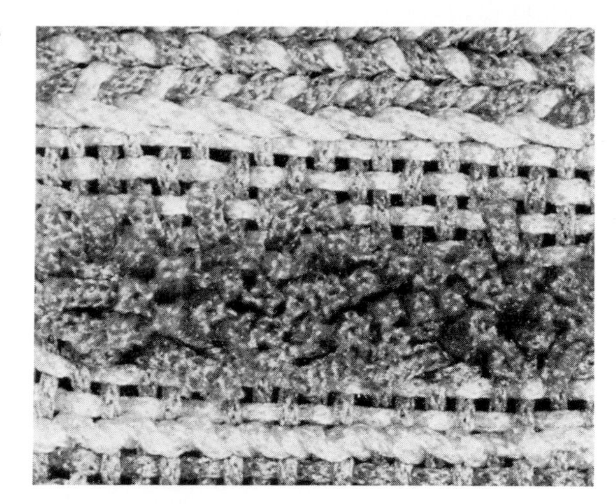

Compound weaves.

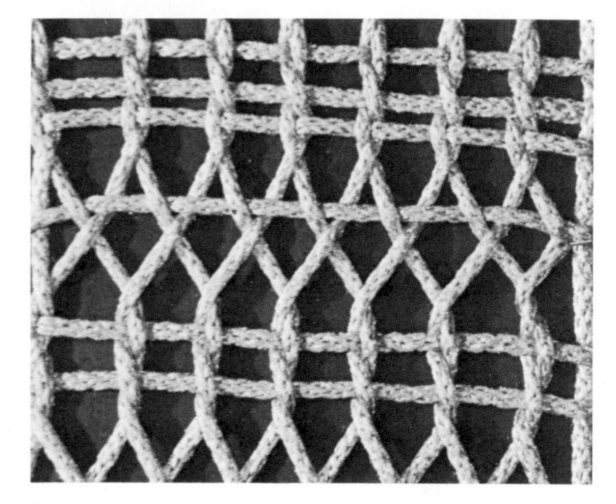

Open weaves.

Carol Clarkson Wood. Wall piece. Stuffed, plaited fabric elements most of which were dye printed prior to manipulation, rayon challis, ca. 36" x 48" (91 x 122 cm).

3. Dyes and Colorants

Introduction

Dye technology would be blissfully simple if any single dye worked equally well on all fibers, but such is not the case. Every dye or colorant has special advantages. The selection of a colorant will depend upon fiber content, desired color scheme, intended function, and durability and maintenance required of the finished object. Because accurate dye information is a requisite for most textile processes, we have placed it in the front of the book for easy reference. We hope the beginner will not be intimidated by the seeming complexity of the subject. Several dyes are in fact very easy to use. By gaining experience with these, the novice will develop confidence for working with the others. Before we begin, a vocabulary of dye terms, an equipment list, and some procedural hints will prove helpful.

Vocabulary of Dye Terms

Affinity: The technical suitability of a specific dye for a specific fabric, or vice-versa.
Aftertreatment: Post-dye fixation or finish.
Assistant: A chemical substance that helps to join fiber to dye.
Binder: The adhesive component of a dye paste.
Bleeding: The running of dye during washing. See *Migration*.
Crocking: The rubbing-off of dye, either wet or dry.
Discharge: Subtraction of color from a fabric.
Discharge paste: A bleaching substance printed or directly applied for color removal.
Dye affinity: Compatability of dye to fiber.
Dyebath: Liquid mixture of dyestuff, water, and assistant and exhausting agent.
Dye paste: An admixture of dyestuff, thickener, and assistant for printing and/or direct application.
Dyestuff: An organic or synthesized material producing color by chemically bonding with fiber.
Exhausting agent: A chemical catalyst causing the absorption of dye by fiber.
Extender: Inert ingredient in an ink or a dye paste resulting in a diluted hue.
Fastness: Relative durability of a dye or coloring agent: specifically, to light, boiling, abrasion, washing, etc.
Finishing: (1) Simple washing, dry-cleaning, and pressing of dyed or printed fabric; (2) special finishes such as flame-retardants, mothproofing, soil release, permanent press, etc.
Fixation: Permanent attachment of dye or colorant to fiber.
Free dye: Excess dye particles not absorbed by a fiber or fabric.
Fugitive dye: Not colorfast.
Hand: The feel or tactile quality of a fabric.
Ink: A surface coating substance composed of a pigment, a binder, and often an extender. A paste paint.
Level dying: Consistent all-over color of a dyed fabric.
Immersion: Dyeing. Conventional means of dyeing by submersion in a dyebath.
Mercerizing: The processing of cotton or linen yarn or fabric with caustic soda for improved strength, luster, and affinity to dye.
Migration: The halolike spread of a dye color outside the original boundaries.
Mordant: A chemical link between the dye molecule and fiber molecule, usually a metallic salt.
Overdyeing: Superimposing one or more dyes over a previously dyed fiber or fabric.
Overprinting: Superimposing one or more prints over a previously printed area.
Paste paint: A surface coating ink or inklike substance. See *Ink*.
Pattern book: A dyer's notebook containing sample swatches, technical notes, and formulas.
Pigment: The insoluble, powdered coloring component in an ink or paste paint.
Pretreatment: One or more predye fabric processes such as soaking, scouring, shrinking, mercerizing, etc.
Resist: Means or material for preventing the penetration of dye in prescribed areas of a fabric or yarn.
Size: A starchlike substance for improving the weight and body of a fabric. Usually an aftertreatment or finish.
Stripping: Discharging or bleaching from a colored fabric.
Thickener: An inert, viscous substance that regulates the consistency of a dye paste.

General Materials for Dyeing

Stainless steel or enamel kettle—A canning kettle is good and will hold at least a pound of yarn or fabric. Enameled containers must be unchipped, since contact with aluminum or ferrous metals can cause chemical problems. The same is true of enameled spoons, tongs, etc.
Glass, plastic, or stainless steel turning rods—The grain tends to raise on wooden dowels or spoons in liquids so that they absorb dyes and chemicals. Plastic is suitable only for cold dye solutions.
Stainless steel or plastic spoons—A set of stainless steel measuring spoons can do double duty.
Pyrex measuring cups—Several sizes will be helpful.
Funnel for transferring liquids
Glass or plastic covered jars—Essential for storing dyes, thickening agents, etc.
Kitchen scale or balance—Accurate measurement is essential.
Thermometer—The type used for candy or hot fat will be handy when working with hot dyebaths.
Plastic dishpans, buckets, or tubs—Important for rinsing, washing, and cold dyeing. A large rectangular plastic pan designed for mixing small batches of concrete, available from building-material dealers under the trade name Crete Mixer, is ideal.

PROCEDURE FOR DYEING

Safety factor. Most dyes and dyebath components are toxic to some degree, and a few are truly poisonous. Common sense dictates that one wear rubber gloves, avoid breathing dye powder, and protect children from contact with dye chemicals. Home dyers usually work in the kitchen—which is convenient, but can be dangerous. For example, an unlabeled jar of blue-violet dye paste in the refrigerator looks for all the world like grape jelly. Label everything! Never prepare food with dye equipment.

Soft water. Soft water should be used throughout the dyeing process. The alkalinity of hard water attacks fiber and produces dull hues and uneven dyeings. Rain water is excellent for dyeing purposes, although city rain water is not suitable since there is often soot and harmful acids dissolved in the water because of smog and industrial pollution. When in doubt, it is advisable to use a commercial water softener, such as Calgon, according to the instructions given for the degree of hardness in your area.

Recordkeeping. Samples of every dyeing should be kept with all information necessary to repeat them. Write down what you do and note quantities of dye, assistants, water duration, and date. Ultimately, this becomes one of the most important items of a dyer's equipment. In the textile trade, such a collection of dye samples is called a pattern book.

Removing fabric finishes. Unless specifically untreated fabric is purchased, one or more finishes may need to be removed before dyeing begins.

Sizing: Added to most yard goods to make them appealing on the bolt and easier to cut. Remove by standard washing or drycleaning procedure relative to fiber content. Rinse thoroughly.

Wash and wear: Simple resin finishes may be removed by soaking the fabric for 30 minutes in a solution of 2 gallons of water and 1 tablespoon of hydrochloric acid at 190°F. Add the acid to the water, *not* the reverse. Wash and rinse thoroughly. Modern wash-and-wear finishes will not respond to this procedure.

Water repellents: Try a hot washing with strong detergent and repeat if necessary. Test fabric for dye absorption.

Stain-release treatments: Treatments such as Scotch Guard, Zepel, etc. are difficult or impossible to remove and are best avoided.

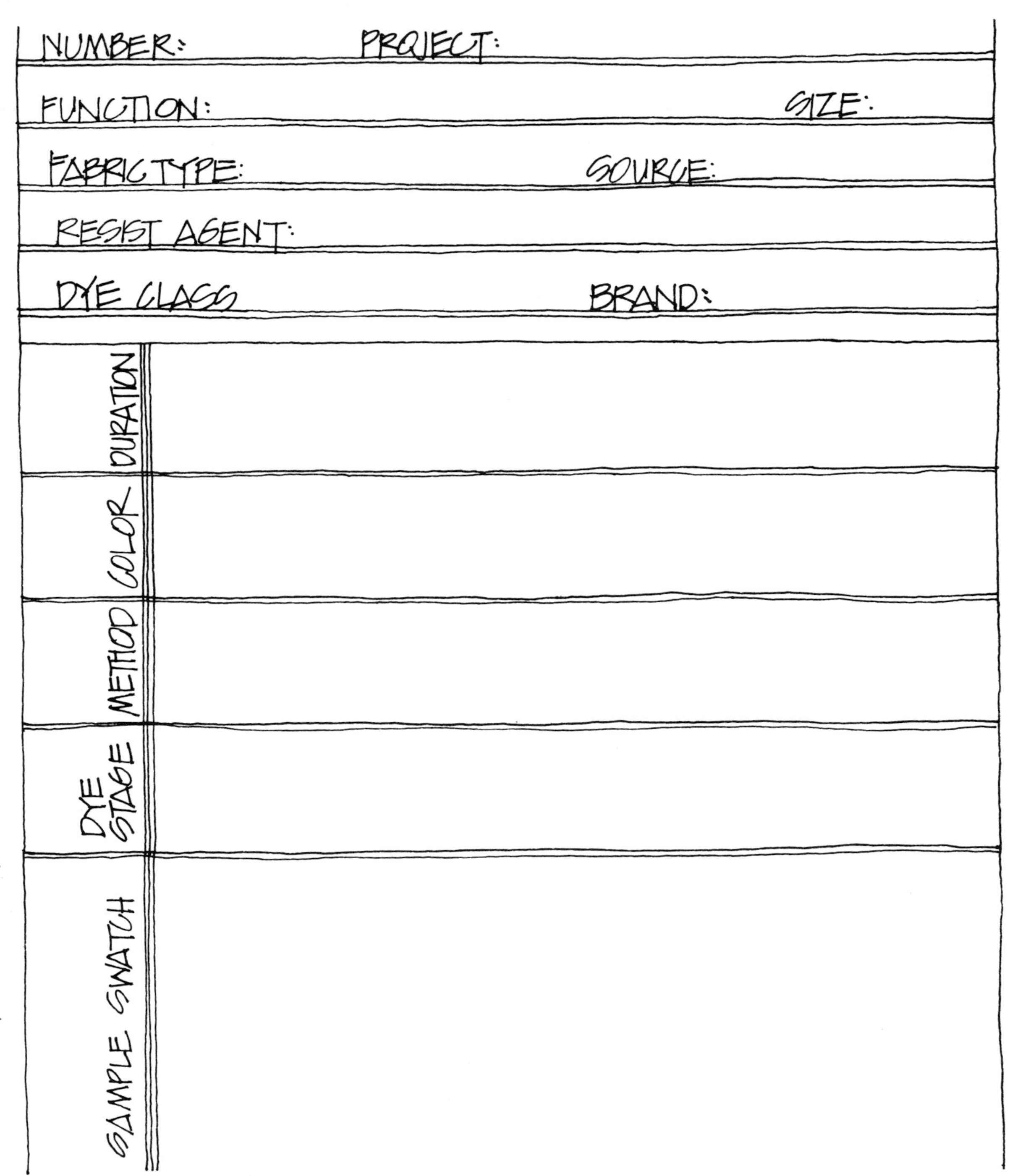
NUMBER:
PROJECT:
FUNCTION:
SIZE:
FABRIC TYPE:
SOURCE:
RESIST AGENT:
DYE CLASS
BRAND:
DURATION
COLOR
METHOD
DYE STAGE
SAMPLE SWATCH

A sample page from a dyer's notebook.

Dyeing Wool

Special care is necessary when dyeing wool, regardless of whether it is fleece, yarn, or fabric. Abrupt temperature changes or severe agitation causes the scaly surface of the fibers to cling to each other, producing tangles, stiffness, or even a form of felt. To avoid these problems, the wool dyer must change temperatures gradually and stir very gently.

Wool must be scoured before dyeing. Fleece and handspun yarn or fabric must have as much lanolin as possible removed to insure even penetration of the dye. Commercial yarns often are treated with sizing, which must also be removed. Scouring is best accomplished by gently simmering about 8 ounces of wool in 1½ gallons of water and 3 tablespoons of Nahptha soap for approximately 45 minutes, followed by a thorough rinse in hot tap water.

Fleece should be teased thoroughly to remove all lumps and then tied up loosely in a square of cheesecloth or porous muslin. About 4 ounces of fleece can be safely handled in this way.

Skeins should be tied loosely but securely in four places. Ties that are too tight will not allow the dye to penetrate evenly, and light spots will result in a tie dye effect. A good choice for ties is a length of cotton carpet warp. With long skeins of 8 ounces or more, it is advisable to use interlaced ties. Divide the skein into several strands, and interweave the ties loosely around these to hold them in position.

Color changes. Remember that colors lighten when they dry so it is usually necessary for a fabric to look darker in the rinse stage than you intend it to be.

Pre-soaking. All fibers have a certain natural resistance to water when dry. Some yarns put up a strong resistance and appear to be thoroughly wet on the outside when the water is actually just lying on the surface. Soak in soft, warm water prior to dyeing. Just before dyeing, gently squeeze the excess water out evenly.

Weights and Measures

The following conversion tables should prove especially useful as different dye manufacturers and distributors specify quantities by dissimilar systems of measurement.

Standard volumes to cubic centimeters:

	1 tsp.	⅙ fl. oz.	5 c.c.
3 tsp.	1 Tbsp.	½ fl. oz.	15 c.c.
	2 Tbsp.	1 fl. oz.	30 c.c.
16 Tbsp.	1 cup (½ pint)	8 fl. oz.	240 c.c.
2 cups	1 pint	16 fl. oz.	480 c.c.
2 pints	1 quart	32 fl. oz.	960 c.c.
8 pints	1 gallon	128 fl. oz.	3,840 c.c.

Standard weights to grams:

1 oz.	= 28.35 grams	
16 oz./1 lb.	= 453.60 grams	= 0.4536 kilogram
0.03527 oz.	= 1 gram	
2.2046 lb.	= 1 kilogram	

NATURAL DYES

All dyes belong to one of two major categories: natural and synthetic. Natural dyes derived from animal, vegetable, and mineral sources produce an extensive range of colors. With a few exceptions, hues tend to be richly muted and "earthy" in character. In combination, natural dyes have a remarkable compatibility and tend to result in harmonious schemes. Because simmering is required for optimum color, the contemporary craftsman uses natural dyes primarily for yarn or for piece dyeing. Natural dyes have their greatest affinity for protein fibers (wool especially), which tends to restrict their use.

The discussion of natural dyeing given here is only an overview of the process. Elaborations and variations can be found in the books and pamphlets on natural dyes listed in the Bibliography.

The general procedure for natural dyeing consists of five basic steps, the last two being optional: scouring, mordanting, dyeing, aftertreatment, and overdyeing. It is important to use gradual temperature changes throughout the following steps.

Scouring. Scouring removes foreign substances and can be achieved by gently simmering 8 ounces of material in 1½ gallons of water and 3 tablespoons of Naphtha soap for approximately 45 minutes, followed by a thorough rinse in hot tap water.

Mordanting. Mordanting increases absorption and fastness of the dye. Alum, tin, chrome, iron, copper, and tannic acid are commonly used. A simple alum mordant consists of 1½ tablespoons sodium *or* potassium alum dissolved in 1 gallon heated water. Approximately 4 ounces material is then simmered for one hour.

Dyeing. The dyestuff (animal, vegetable, mineral, berries, fruits, roots, etc.) is covered with water and boiled for approximately one hour. Next, the liquid is strained and the bath is ready to receive enough material to be submerged and simmered. Duration may vary depending on depth of shade desired. Gentle agitation is advised for uniform dyeing and a thorough rinse in hot tap water should follow.

Aftertreatment. Aftertreatment produces variations from the basic dye color. One tablespoon of ammonia, baking soda, cream of tartar, *or* vinegar to approximately ½ gallon dyebath will instantly modify the hue.

Overdyeing. If a previously dyed material is dyed a second time to produce a third color, the process is called overdyeing.

SYNTHETIC DYES

William Henry Perkin, an Englishman, developed the first of the synthetic dyes in 1856. These dyes quickly revolutionized the dye industry and have been developed and diversified until nearly 2,000 exist today. Of this staggering total, the majority have been designed for industrial use and require specialized equipment and/or highly toxic ingredients. Fortunately for the home or studio fiber artist, there is a good range of dyes that may be used with relative ease, permanence, and safety. Synthetic dyes are ordinarily categorized by function-related family names known as "dye classes." These classes are acid, azoic (naphthol), basic, direct, disperse, fiber-reactive, household, mordant, mineral, oxidation, premetallized, and vat dyes.

The following dye chart gives attributes of the selected dye classes. As you use this chart, please bear in mind that it deals in general conclusions based on experience with one or more brands within each class. There are in fact many different types, brands, and subgroups within each dye class that will yield varying results.

ATTRIBUTES OF SYNTHETIC DYE CLASSES

Dye Class	Affinity to Fiber	Brilliance of Color	Dyebath (Room Temperature)	Dyebath (Simmering)	A Dye Paste	Resistance to Light
Acid	Wool, silk, nylon, some types dye acrylics	Excellent	Yes	Yes	Yes	Good
Basic	Wool, silk, acrylic, modacrylic	Excellent	Yes	Yes	Yes	Poor
Direct	Cotton, linen, viscose rayon, silk, wool	Good	Dubious	Yes	Yes	Good to poor
Vat	Cotton, linen, viscose rayon, wool, silk acetate	Excellent to good	Yes	Variable according to type	Yes	Excellent
Fiber-reactive	Cotton, linen, viscose rayon, silk, wool	Excellent	Yes	Yes	Yes	Excellent
Disperse	Polyester, acetate, acrylic, nylon	Excellent	No	Yes	Yes	Excellent
Azoic (Naphthol)	Cotton, linen, viscose rayon, nylon, acrylics	Good	Yes	No		Excellent
Household	Cotton, linen, viscose rayon, wool, silk, acetate, some blends	Good to fair	Dubious	Yes	Yes	Good to fair
Pigment Pastes and Inks	No natural affinity but may be applied to nearly all fibers	Excellent	No	No	Pigment paste	Excellent to good

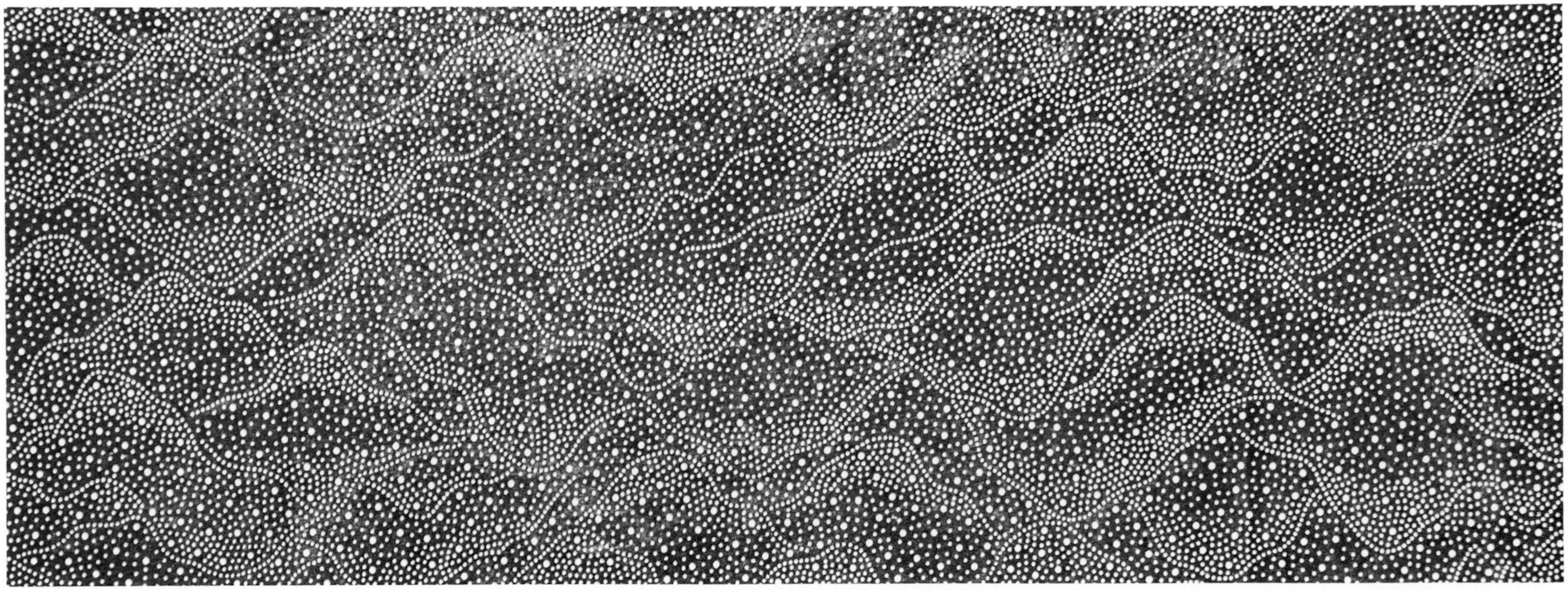

Resistance to Washing	Resistance to Boiling	Resistance to Bleach	Resistance to Crocking (Friction)	Marketed as
Poor	Fair		Excellent	Powder
Fair	Poor		Good	Powder
Poor to fair			Good	Powder
Excellent	Excellent	Excellent	Good	Powder, liquid or paste
Excellent	Excellent	Excellent	Excellent	Powder
Excellent			Fair to good	Powder, paste, or heat transfer paper
Excellent		Excellent to good	Fair	Powder (two components)
Poor to fair	Fair	Poor		Powder or liquid
Good	Good	Good	Good, but some darks crock	Paste

Katazome stencil. Japan, late 19th or early 20th century. Collection of Warren T. Hill, Seattle, Washington.

Because of variations in the manufacture and intended purpose of different brands within any class of dye, it is impossible to give a comprehensive method or recipe applicable to any single class. To do so would require excessive generalization and result in misinformation. The only alternative is to select one or two established brands within each class and deal with them directly.

Acid Dyes

Acid dyes are designed for protein fibers and substances (silk, wool, and leather) and come in a wide variety of brilliant intermixable colors. They will also dye nylon at elevated temperatures. They are versatile, easy to use, keep well, and may be used as hot or cold liquid baths or thickened as dye pastes. On the other hand, some acid dyes tend to fade in strong natural light and others bleed and/or waterspot. They will, however, hold up well if dry-cleaned and if kept away from sunlight and moisture. An application of fabric protector scarcely alters the color and provides considerable stain and moisture protection.

FEZAN BATIK DYE FOR SILK

Fezan "batik dyes" are especially well suited for dyeing silk at room temperature, making them ideal for batik but also for all other processes. Wool seems to accept this dye best at a simmering temperature. Two colors—French Blue and Pink—are actually of the "basic" dye class, but for all practical purposes they behave like the acid dyes and use the same recipe. Fezan batik dyes work very well on leather when applied with a brush or sponge. The following colors are presently available: French Blue, Azure Blue, Royal Purple, Jade Green, Pink, Poppy Red, Vermillion Red, Canary Yellow, Tan, Chestnut Brown, Black, Bright Orange, and Turquoise.

Standard Fezan dyebath recipe:

2 oz. dye powder
1 c. white vinegar
1 Tbsp. plain salt
1 gal. water

Cold Bath Method for Fezan Batik Dye

The following method works for all colors except Pink, French Blue, Jade Green and Royal Purple.

Make a paste of the dye powder and a small amount of warm water. Add the remaining ingredients and stir until thoroughly dissolved. Most powdered colors dissolve easily, but Pink, French Blue, Jade Green, and especially Royal Purple should be added slowly while stirring to one gallon of hot water. Vinegar and salt should then be added and the mixture allowed to cool to room temperature. Two colors (Bright Orange and Tan) produce floating clouds of fine, white particles which have no adverse effects and rinse off when the time comes. The dye should not come in contact with any metal except stainless steel. Plastic pails make convenient dye containers. Fezan dyes may be diluted with water, and except for Pink and French Blue they are fully intermixable.

Immerse the washed and presoaked fabric into the room-temperature dyebath and occasionally agitate. Optimum color is reached in approximately twenty minutes but, when a tint is required, duration may be reduced to a quick dip in the dyebath solution. Very dark shades may be achieved by dyeing for extended periods or increasing the dye-to-water ratio.

Rinse the dyed fabric in running room temperature tapwater until it runs clear.

It is best to dry the dyed fabric flat because if line dried any free dye that remains after the final rinse will be pulled downward by gravity resulting in unevenness. A simple alternative is to spread the rinsed, dyed fabric on newspaper and blot it thoroughly with paper towels. This will speed the drying time for lightweight fabrics sufficiently to allow safe line drying. No special aftertreatment is necessary.

Dye powder should be stored in a cool, dry place. Mixed dyes may be easily kept in covered, nonmetallic containers. If a blue-green floating mold develops during extended storage, simply skim it off, stir well, and proceed as before.

Hot Bath Method for Fezan Batik Dye

Dye is mixed as described above for cold bath method. The washed and presoaked fabric is added to the dyebath at room temperature. The temperature is slowly raised to about 190°F. (below simmer). Maintain this temperature for about 20–30 minutes. Allow bath to cool to room temperature, then remove, rinse, and dry the dyed material as described for the cold bath method. This method is particularly useful for dyeing skeins of wool yarn or scoured fleece. A hot bath is not necessary for silk as it accepts this brand of dye exceptionally well at room temperature. Colors will, however, have much greater fastness on silk if applied hot.

When prepared at full strength directly from the package, Fezan batik dyes are very intense but somewhat limited in color range. Fortunately, they may be easily overdyed to produce virtually any hue imaginable. Since it is difficult to rinse out every bit of free dye, we advise dyeing the lighter or brighter colors before overdyeing with darker or duller colors. This practice will insure the continuing brilliance and purity of the dyebaths. The chart below is offered as a starting point for your experimentation.

Occasionally a fabric dyed with either the cold or hot bath method will go too dark too fast, when a lighter shade is actually desired. A moderate amount of dye may be removed by soaking the fabric in a tepid detergent solution (i.e., Spic and Span, Mr. Clean, etc.). Experiment with a scrap to determine the strength of the solution and duration in the bath. Some surprisingly beautiful, although unpredictable, colors may be achieved by this process. Rinse well before proceeding.

Dye Paste

Fezan dyes are primarily intended for dyebath use, but they may be thickened for printing and direct application by the following simple method.

Standard dye paste recipe:

1 c. standard dyebath recipe
1 tsp. Keltex (sodium alginate)

Sprinkle Keltex slowly into dye solution while stirring constantly. Allow the mixture to stand at least 10 minutes, stir again, and thin slightly if necessary. The very small lumps that form will have no adverse effect on the evenness of the result.

Allow the dyed fabric to dry thoroughly. Dry-clean to remove thickener for best results. The thickener can be removed by a thorough rinse in running water, but some colors tend to migrate before the fabric is dry.

OVERDYE CHART FOR FEZAN BATIK DYE

First Color	no. of min.	Second Color	no. of min.	Results
Azure Blue	1–3	Black	Dip	Light silver gray
Azure Blue	3–5	Black	1–2	Steel blue gray
Azure Blue	20	Pink	2–3	Bright cobalt blue
Chestnut Brown	10–20	French Blue	5–10	Cool brown range
French Blue	30	Black	30	Nearly black
Bright Orange	10	Pink	Dip	Bright coral
Pink	5	Violet	10–15	Bright purple
Tan	10–20	Azure Blue or Jade Green	5–10	Olive range
Canary Yellow	20	Black	1–2	Bone-ochre
Canary Yellow	20	Azure Blue	1	Chartreuse
Canary Yellow	20	Azure Blue	3–5	Kelly green

Jennifer F. Lew and Richard M. Proctor. Quilt. Constructed of seven-inch black cotton squares discharged with chlorine bleach. Techniques include wrapping, clamping, sewing, folding, and pleating. Created for Fabric Vibrations Exhibition, Museum of Contemporary Crafts, New York.

INKO SILK DYE

Inko Silk Dyes come from the manufacturer as ready-to-use liquids formulated from acid and direct dyestuffs for raw or untreated silk. Their consistency is ideal for screen printing or direct methods of application, but they may be thinned with water for techniques requiring dipping or submersion. A clear extender is available for producing tints and pastels without watering down the original consistency. In addition to the extender, there are eight basic colors: Red, Yellow, Blue, Green, Violet, Orange, Black, Brown. The intermixing of Inko Silk Dyes follows the same rules as does the blending of pigments; e.g., blue plus yellow produces green; orange plus blue produces gray, etc. In addition, these colors are transparent and, like watercolor, produce secondary colors when one color is applied over another; e.g., blue over yellow produces green.

Nearly any chromatic color can be made from a mixture of a color, brown, and clear. To lower the saturation (vividness), add increasing amounts of brown. To produce colors of light value (pastels and tints), add increasing amounts of clear. To produce a color of low saturation and light value, proportions of 10 parts clear to 1 part color would not be uncommon. Water may be used in place of the clear when it is desirable to reduce or thin the consistency for dipping or tie dyeing.

Color fixation is best accomplished by steaming:

1. Prepare a pressure cooker or autoclave by supporting a wire rack about 2 inches from the bottom. A piece of wadded up chicken wire is ideal. Put in ½ inch water, put on the lid and cap, place over heat, and bring up to 3 pounds pressure.
2. Allow dye to dry thoroughly on fabric. Place fabric between sheets of newsprint, four below and four on top. Fold and roll into a loose bundle, and tie with a string.
3. Take pressure cooker from heat, release pressure, remove lid, pop bundle in, replace lid and cap, and bring steam up to 3 pounds pressure as quickly as possible. Dry steam (steam under pres-

sure) will fix the dye properly. Wet steam, or condensation, will cause the dye to run, hence the precaution to fix the dye in dry steam only. Maintain pressure for 20 minutes. Three pounds pressure is ideal; higher pressure may cause a yellowing of the fabric.

4. Remove bundle from pressure cooker, rinse fabric in warm water, wash in soapy water, and rinse again.

CIBA KITON SERIES DYES

Ciba Kiton Series Dyes are manufactured by Crompton and Knowles Corp. as Intracid. This highly efficient series of hot bath acid dyes is especially suited for wool in any form: fleece, yarn, or fabric. For this reason it will be of interest to spinners and weavers as well as to fabric artists. Each color requires a different amount of dyestuff to achieve full intensity, and the dyes take differently on different yarns and fleece. The available colors are: Red, Yellow, Blue, Orange, Turquoise, Magenta, Black, Scarlet, Green, Golden Brown, Dark Brown, Lemon Yellow, Purple, and Royal Blue.

Method for Dyeing Wool

1. Prepare wool as directed on page 27.
2. Assemble equipment and supplies. You will need a stainless steel or enamel kettle, turning rods, measuring spoons and containers, covered quart jars, rinsing buckets and, if possible, a thermometer.
   The recipe requires Glauber's Salt (anhydrous sodium sulfate) and 56 percent glacial Acetic Acid, for which distilled white vinegar may be substituted.
3. Prepare the dye concentrate by placing 1 oz. of dye powder in a quart jar that has been heated first with hot water. Add a small amount of cold water and work into a smooth paste with a stainless steel or plastic spoon. Add 1 quart of hot or boiling soft water to the paste and stir until all dye is completely dissolved. This solution is called the dye concentrate. Label the jar and the lid plainly. Store dye concentrate in a cool, dark place, covering tightly to prevent evaporation. Should sediment show at the bottom of the jar after storage, or should the solution look cloudy, place the jar in a hot water bath and heat to redissolve before use.
4. Prepare the dyebath by filling the pot ⅔ full of warm tapwater (100–120°F.). Add water softener if necessary and the required amount of the dye concentrate, measuring carefully and recording the amount used. The average amount of concentrate required to obtain deep colors on one-half pound of wool is four tablespoons. Colors that by their nature are light in value (yellow, orange, etc.) may require one or two additional tablespoons of concentrate. When attempting to achieve very dark shades, such as brown, navy, and especially black, the concentrate should be increased as well. Mix colors in separate containers or in the dyepot, as desired. Add 2 Tbsp. Glauber's Salt per ½ lb. of wool to the dyepot and stir until dissolved. Add the acetic acid, 1 tsp. per ½ lb. of wool (or white vinegar, ¼ cup per ½ lb. of wool), and stir.
5. Enter the wetted-out yarn or fleece to the dyebath, stirring or agitating gently until the wool is uniformly saturated with dye. Use glass or stainless steel rods, and turn skeins instead of stirring to avoid tangled skeins. Note the level of the dyebath liquor in the pot and try to maintain this same level during the entire dyeing process by adding hot water when the level has gone down noticeably.
6. Raise the temperature of the dyebath slowly, allowing about 30 minutes to reach 180-90°F. or just below simmer. Since most of the dye is absorbed during this time, it is very important that the wool be frequently agitated or stirred gently to avoid streaking or splotching. Keep the wool in the dyebath for another 30–45 minutes, stirring occasionally and making sure the dyebath remains below a simmer. Homewashed fleece and handspun may take longer to develop deep colors. If the wool is a lighter shade than desired, it is best to complete the dyeing process and then repeat the dyeing. If the wool is coming out darker than desired, transfer the wool to a pot of clear water at the same temperature, with the same concentration of Glauber's Salt and acetic acid, and continue to the end of the dying cycle. Remember that wool always appears darker wet than dry. If your colors are too deep, you have used too much concentrate.
7. Rinse the dyed wool thoroughly in hot water, gradually lowering the temperature of the water to room temperature. Wash with a neutral detergent and rinse again. This removes excess dye on the surface which might otherwise run to the bottom of the skein or fleece as it dries and cause uneven color. Gently squeeze excess water from the wool and allow to drip dry. Never dry wool in the sun or wind.

"Exhaustion" describes the transfer, in the dyebath, of the dyestuff in solution to the material being dyed. Acid dyes can be nearly exhausted by leaving the wool in the unheated dyepot overnight. The next day the water should be nearly clear. This can be done with previously dyed wool or with white wool. However, it is not the best way to get even colors, and the fastness properties of the dye suffer somewhat as well.

A nearly exhausted dyebath can be used to dye pale colors which will be later overdyed during your next session. If there is not enough dyestuff left in the pot to get the pale color you desire, add dye concentrate sparingly until the desire color is reached. Experience will help make your determinations and measurements more accurate. Leftover dye solutions can be mixed together to get unusual browns, greens, grays, etc.

Strong dye solutions can be saved in the dyepot for another day if you have the space. Or, you can simmer the dye for a few hours to reduce the amount of liquid you need to save. The liquid may be bottled in gallon jugs and stored in a cool, dark place for up to six months or so. Occasionally, mold will form on the top; simply strain it off when you pour the liquid into the pot to dye again. Although the mold may affect the color, it does not weaken the intensity. Bring the dyebath to a boil before using.

Direct Application by Printing or Painting

1. Mix the stock thickener by dissolving 1 teaspoon Calgon (sodium hexametaphosphate) in 2 cups water. Sprinkle 4 teaspoons of sodium alginate a little at a time into this mixture and stir constantly for 10 minutes or use an electric blender or mixer. There may be some lumps after mixing, but they should disappear while the formula is left overnight to bulk up. This is an organic solution and it

will mold or go sour if left at room temperature. It can, however, be stored indefinitely if refrigerated. Be sure to label properly.

2. To mix ½ cup dye paste, consult the table below, and place the required amount of dye for the shade desired into a Pyrex measuring cup, add the required amount of glycerin and work into a smoothly, lump-free paste with a stainless steel spoon. Add ⅛ cup boiling water and stir to dissolve completely. Allow to cool to room temperature.

	Dye	*Glycerin*
Pale	⅛ tsp.	1 tsp.
Medium	½ tsp.	2 tsp.
Deep	1-3 tsp.	1-2 Tbsp.

3. Dissolve 1 teaspoon ammonium oxalate in 1 tablespoon hot water and stir into ¼ cup stock thickener. Stir in dye/glycerin mixture and add water to make ½ cup or until desired consistency is reached. Larger quantities can be prepared by multiplying the above measurements.
4. After printing or painting, allow the fabric to dry and then steam fix for 1 hour under moist steam conditions such as in a pressure cooker, steam cabinet, or autoclave. Note that dry heat such as ironing (even with a steam iron) will not be sufficient to fix these dyes.
5. After steam fixing, rinse thoroughly in cold running water. Then wash carefully in warm water (105°F) containing a small amount of Synthrapol or other mild detergent such as Joy or Ivory liquid. Rinse off again in cold running water.

Basic Dyes

We have little experience with dyes in the basic dye class, and their tendency to fade and wash out does not generally recommend them. However, they will dye acrylic fibers with remarkable brilliance and good light-fastness.

Direct Dyes

The direct dyes, also known as the substantive dyes, differ from acid and basic dyes in that cellulosic fibers have a strong affinity for them. Direct dyes are generally inexpensive and easy to apply, although their washfastness can only be rated as fair.

Vat Dyes

Vat dyes are among the oldest on record, with indigo and the famous Mediterranean shellfish dye, Tyrian Purple, both predating the time of Moses. They are among the most durable dyes known, and most possess wash and lightfastness. All vat dyes can be applied to cellulosic fibers and some may be applied to wool, silk, nylon, and acetate fibers as well.

The dye procedure for vat dyes is more time-consuming and complex than most and, in addition, requires sodium hydroxide or lye, which is an extremely caustic substance. Nevertheless, vat dyes produce deep, intense colors that are difficult, or in the case of indigo, impossible to duplicate with other dyes.

Vat dyes are all insoluble in water and cannot be used for dyeing without some change in form. When treated with reducing agents, such as lye, they are converted into leuco compounds, all of which are soluble in water in an alkaline environment. These leuco compounds have an affinity for cellulose and reoxidize to the insoluble pigment from within the fiber when exposed to oxygen in the air. The leuco forms are often colorless or quite a different color from the oxidized form.

DYEING WITH INDIGO

Until the beginning of this century, indigo could only be obtained from plants, the most important of which was *Indigofera tinctoria*, but many varieties of plants have been, and still are, cultivated for the production of indigo in India, China, Japan, the West Indies, Central America, Brazil, South and Central Africa, Java, and Madagascar. For instance, woad, which is extracted from the plant, *Isatis tinctoria*, contains small amounts of indigo pigment.

In 1897, Badische Anilin and Soda Fabrik, A.G. developed the first commercially successful operation for manufacturing synthetic indigo. With the introduction of this chemically identical product, cultivation of natural indigo declined rapidly until at the present time, it is grown primarily for local consumption in very small amounts.

Vat dyes, including indigo, are insoluble in water and cannot be used directly for dyeing. They must first be converted to a form which has some affinity for the fiber being dyed. Chemically, this is accomplished by "reducing" the vat dye to a "leuco compound," which then becomes soluble in water in the presence of an alkaline substance. A solution of this leuco compound can be applied by dyeing or printing and, upon exposure to the oxygen in the air, the original insoluble pigment is reformed within the structure of the fiber. Chemically, this is called "oxidation" and is the complement of "reduction."

What all this means is that two things are required to make indigo work: a "reducing agent" to reduce the indigo to its leuco compound, and an "alkali" to make this leuco compound soluble in water. The reducing agent for indigo and all other vat dyes is free hydrogen generated by a variety of chemical reactions or by the fermentation of organic matter by certain bacteria (originally done in a wooden vessel called a "vat," hence the name "vat dyes"). Until modern reducing chemicals such as sodium hydrosulfite became available, fermentation was the only method of reducing the indigo. It is still extensively used in several cultures.

Alkaline substances used in the indigo dye process consist chemically of carbonate or hydroxide compounds. These were originally obtained by leaching wood ash or from the decomposition of urine by the same fermentation that produced the reducing agent. Sodium hydroxide (caustic soda or lye) or sodium carbonate (soda ash or washing soda) are the alkalis most commonly used in modern recipes.

Indigo is available in a variety of forms, and it can be confusing and difficult at times to know exactly what one is getting. Below is a short description of the forms most likely to be encountered.

Indigo powder, grains, and cake are the forms most commonly available. The strength can vary a great deal depending primarily on whether the indigo is natural or synthetic in origin. Because of the much higher

percentage of indigo pigment in the synthetic form, it is generally much stronger. Cake indigo should be thoroughly ground with a mortar and pestle before using.

Indigo paste is the most common form of synthesized indigo. Actually, it is not a "paste," but rather consists of indigo powder mixed with water and a small amount of emulsifying agent to keep the powder from settling. Indigo powder must be very finely dispersed to yield consistent results and if used by itself would become a nuisance. This "paste" form permits ease of handling and is used primarily by the denim industry for blue jeans, etc.

Indigo plant consists primarily of the chopped leaves and can be used and vatted according to any of the standard recipes. Although it lends itself well to fermentation methods because of the ready-made supply of organic matter, it can become messy when dyeing yarn because of the extraneous vegetable matter.

Indigo root is often found in Chinese herbal medicine stores. Since little or no indigo pigment is contained in the root, trying to dye with this part of the plant is an exercise in frustration.

Indigo crystals are not actually indigo but rather a water soluble acid or direct dyestuff which yields a blue similar to indigo blue. Genuine indigo is not water soluble and can only be applied by a reduction-oxidation process.

There are almost as many recipes for indigo as there are forms. A brief survey the various vatting methods follows, with the reducing agent and alkali for each.

Fermentation vat:
Reducing agent: free hydrogen from micro-organisms feeding on organic matter
Alkali: a variety of available sources including ammonium carbonate or ammonium hydroxide from decomposition of urine, potassium hydroxide from leaching of wood ash, and calcium hydroxide (slaked lime)

Copperas-Lime vat:
Reducing agent: free hydrogen from reaction of copperas (ferrous sulfate) and lime-water (calcium hydroxide in water)
Alkali: excess of calcium hydroxide in vat

Zinc-Lime vat:
Reducing agent: free hydrogen from reaction of powdered zinc and lime-water
Alkali: excess of calcium hydroxide in vat

Hydrosulfite vat:
Reducing agent: free hydrogen from reaction of sodium hydrosulfite (sodium dithionite) and water
Alkali: sodium hydroxide (caustic soda or lye), potassium hydroxide (caustic potash) or sodium carbonate (washing soda or soda ash)

The Hydrosulfite Vat Method

Of all the vatting methods, the most simple, reliable and safe is the "hydrosulfite vat" using sodium hydrosulfite as the reducing agent and sodium carbonate as the alkali. In other recipies it is much more difficult to control the degree of reduction of the indigo and/or a rather large amount of sediment collects which, if disturbed, can greatly interfere with the even absorption of the indigo leuco compound in the vat.

EQUIPMENT

Stainless steel or unchipped enamel kettle—An eight-to-nine quart canning kettle is good, although a tall, small diameter vessel works best.
Glass, stainless steel or wood turning rods—A good length is two feet, wood rods tend to absorb dye and chemicals so don't use them for anything else.
Stainless steel or plastic spoons for mixing dye powder and chemicals—A set of stainless steel measuring spoons can do double duty.
Mixing cups—One-or-two cup Pyrex types are the best.
Thermometer—Convenient, but not essential.
Plastic dishpans—Or buckets, for rinsing, washing, etc.
Rubber gloves

SUPPLIES

Indigo (not indigo crystals)
Sodium carbonate—Also known as washing soda, sal soda or soda ash; available in most large supermarkets.
Sodium hydrosulfite—Also known as sodium dithionite.
Distilled white vinegar
Soap flakes or mild detergent—Ivory flakes or liquid work well.

PREPARATION

1. Wear old clothes and rubber gloves. Note that sodium carbonate (washing soda, etc.) is a mildly caustic substance and can cause skin irritation. Also note that indigo can stain porcelain or enamel, so be careful if you are dyeing near such surfaces.
2. Fleece should be teased thoroughly to remove all lumps and then tied up loosely in a one-yard square of cheesecloth or porous muslin. About 4 ounces of fleece can be safely handled this way. Yarn skeins should be tied loosely but securely in four places. Ties that are too tight will not allow the dye to penetrate evenly and light spots will result (a tie-dye effect). A good choice for ties is a length of acrylic knitting yarn. Acrylic does not dye well with indigo and this will make the ties easy to see. With larger skeins—8 ounces (250 grams) or more—it is advisable to use interlaced ties. Divide the skein into several strands, and interweave the ties loosely around these to hold them in position. Note, however, that larger skeins are more difficult to dye evenly.
3. All fibers should be scoured before dyeing. Wool fleece and handspun must have as much lanolin as possible removed to insure even penetration of the dye. Commercial yarns often are treated with sizing which must also be removed. Scouring is best accomplished by soaking with gentle agitation in warm water (100°–120°F) with a mild detergent (use 1 Tbsp. Ivory liquid per gallon of water). Two such soakings followed by rinses in water the same temperature should be sufficient. Be sure to use soft water for scouring. All fabric should be washed in hot water and detergent before dyeing to remove all sizing and starch. The fabric should be rinsed well, but need not be dry.
4. All fibers or fabric should be thoroughly wetted out before being placed in the dyebath. All fibers have a certain natural resistance to water when dry. Some yarns put up a strong resistance and appear to be throughly wet on the outside when the water is actually just lying on the surface. Soak

wool or silk for at least 20 minutes in soft, warm water prior to dyeing. Just before dyeing, gently squeeze the excess water out evenly. Of course, the easiest way is to leave the fiber in the final rinse water after scouring. Cellulose fibers (cotton, linen, rayon, hemp, etc.) tend to absorb water much more easily and can simply be soaked briefly in warm water prior to dyeing.

DYEING

1. Place 3 teaspoons (10 g.) indigo powder or grains in a mixing cup. Gradually add small amounts of warm water and work into a smooth, lump-free paste with a stainless steel or plastic spoon.
2. Into another mixing cup, put ½ cup (125 ml.) warm water, add 1½ teaspoon (30 g.) sodium hydrosulfite and stir to dissolve. Carefully add 2 Tablespoons (25 g.) sodium carbonate and let it sit. The solution should have a milky appearance.
3. Into the dyepot, put 2 gallons (8 l.) warm water (105°–120°F.) Try to maintain this temperature throughout the dyeing process by heating very gently on the stove if necessary. The indigo vat is easily destroyed by excessive temperature. To this add the sodium hydrosulfite/sodium carbonate mixture and stir.
4. Submerge the mixing cup with the indigo paste into the dyebath (be sure to wear rubber gloves), and gently work it into solution stirring very gently to disperse the indigo and dissolve the paste. Try to avoid making air bubbles (this introduces oxygen, the enemy of indigo vats). A dark-blue, metallic-looking scum will form on the surface of the vat. This is indigo that has oxidized because of contact with the air at the surface. Allow the vat to rest undisturbed for 15-20 minutes. The solution in the vat should be yellow with a slight greenish cast (the color of indigo's leuco compound). You are now ready to dye.
5. Carefully enter the wetted-out fleece, yarn, or fabric (wetting-out helps avoid streaking and introducing oxygen into the vat). Try to avoid the dark-blue scum by gently pushing it aside or by quickly passing a paper towel over the surface of the vat. Where it clings to the goods, it will look dark blue, but would later wash off. Also try as much as possible to avoid carrying down into the vat pockets of air that may be trapped in the folds of fabric pieces. Use the stirring rods to work the goods gently for 10-15 minutes, making sure that they are completely submerged at all times.
6. Gently lift the goods from the vat and hold just clear of the surface while excess dye solution runs back into the dyepot. Try to avoid excessive dripping or splashing, as this also introduces oxygen into the vat. This process can be speeded up a bit by gently squeezing out the excess dye solution by hand.
7. Allow the goods to oxidize by spreading out on a flat surface (a layer of newspapers spread on a floor or a shaded area of a lawn works well for this purpose; avoid direct sunlight, however). As oxidation takes place, the goods will go from the yellow color of the vat through various shades of green to the blue of indigo as the unstable leuco compounds revert back to stable oxidized indigo blue. Although this process may take several hours to complete, most workers allow about 30 minutes. Be sure to turn fabric often and open out skeins and fleece to allow air to penetrate completely.
8. Deeper shades are built up by successive immersions and exposures to the air and may be continued until the desired depth of shade is reached. In Java, goods may be dipped and oxidized as many as forty times over a period of a month or more.
9. When the desired depth of shade is reached, allow the goods to oxidize a little longer than usual, say 1 or 2 hours. Silk or wool goods must then be immersed in a "scouring" bath of 2 gallons of warm water to which ½ cup white vinegar has been added. This neutralizes any alkali remaining on the goods which might cause damage to the fiber.
10. As a final step, "soaping" is recommended to prevent crocking (rubbing off) of any insoluble indigo blue deposited on the surface of the fibers and also to promote "aggregation" so that the pigment particles group together and become firmly fixed within the fiber. Wash thoroughly in hot (simmering is best), soapy water for about 15–20 minutes, rinse well, and dry.

TROUBLESHOOTING

Below are suggestions for coping with a few troublesome conditions that may arise when working with indigo:

1. If the vat begins to turn blue, this means that specks of precipitated indigo blue are in the vat. Usually this is the result of oxygen being introduced into the vat during the course of dyeing. Correct by small additions (1¼-1½ t.) of sodium hydrosulfite accompanied by gentle stirring. Wait 3 5 minutes between additions. The vat should become clear yellow again. This process is called "sharpening" the vat.
2. If the vat appears "milky" instead of a clear yellow, there is an imbalance in the amount of alkali in the vat, resulting in reduced but undissolved indigo clouding the vat. Correct by making very small additions of sodium carbonate accompanied by gentle stirring. The vat should become clear yellow again.
3. If successive immersions do not build up deep shades, there is an excess of alkali and/or reducing agent in the vat. The indigo blue already deposited within the fibers is being re-reduced as the goods are entered for another dip. An excess of alkali will strip some of this re-reduced indigo blue from the fiber and carry it back into solution in the vat, thus making any build-up of color impossible. Since reduced indigo is much more readily dissolved by the alkali, an excess of reducing agent (sodium hydrosulfite) will also contribute to this problem. Correct by adding very small amounts of white vinegar to neutralize some of the alkali and try it again. Remember, the goal is to have just enough sodium hydrosulfite to reduce the indigo in the vat (plus a little bit more to drive the oxygen out of the vat initially) and just enough alkali to dissolve the indigo reduced by the sodium hydrosulfite.
4. If the finished dyeing is not fast to rubbing, i.e., the blue rubs off on you or on other material, it could be caused by: indigo oxidizing on the goods during dyeing, which occurs because the goods were allowed to float on or above the surface of the dyebath; too short an oxidizing time between dips or after final dip; or an imbalance during dyeing in the amount of sodium hydrosulfite. See 1. above.

REUSING AND REVIVING

A properly cared for indigo vat can be made to last through many dye sessions over a period of many months. Carefully transfer the vat to narrow-mouth plastic or glass jugs, making sure to pour slowly to avoid creating air bubbles and to fill all the way to the top to expose as little surface area as possible to the air. Cover and store at room temperature until the next dye session. For longer vats, a layer of household plastic wrap can be carefully floated onto the surface of the vat and run a few inches up the sides of the vat vessel. Try to make as complete a seal as possible to the outside air. In either case, however, atmospheric oxygen can gradually seep back into the vat and change the reduced indigo back to indigo blue.

When the time comes for the next dye session, uncover the vat or carefully pour the saved liquid into a dye vessel. If the vat has turned blue, correct by the addition of small amounts of sodium hydrosulfite—try 1-2 tsp. (20-40 g.) to start—followed by heating to 105°–120°F. with gentle stirring. Let the vat stand for 15–20 minutes before using.

Eventually of course, most of the indigo in the vat will be exhausted onto the goods that have been dyed. Additional indigo powder or grains can be added at any time. Just remember to add the corresponding amount of sodium hydrosulfite and sodium carbonate at the same time and then allow the vat to rest 15–20 minutes before using (see steps 1 through 4 under "Dyeing" above.) One additional point to consider: it is generally much better to dye deep shades by repeated dips in a weak or moderately concentrated vat than it is to try doing it all at one time in a very concentrated vat.

Inkodye Prepared Vat Dyes

We are aware of only one brand of solubilized vat dye in its ready-to-use leuco-base form for cellulosic fibers or fabric: namely, Inkodye, manufactured by the Screen Process Supplies Manufacturing Co. of Oakland, California. In this leuco-base form, the dyes do not exhibit their final color. Only when the dyes are developed through proper heat or light treatment and are regenerated on the fabric will the final colors appear.

Inkodye is exceptionally permanent and will withstand strong soaps, boiling water, rubbing, dry-cleaning, common bleaches, and sunlight for moderate periods. In addition it does not stiffen the fabric and is ideally suited for use by the fabric artist who desires a simple, easy-to-use dye that is extremely permanent. The technique is not difficult, and clean-up is achieved simply with water. Since the procedure is specialized, however, it is important that beginners follow the directions carefully.

As it comes from the bottle, this product is a thin paste of an ideal consistency for screen printing or direct application to fabric with brush, sponge or squeeze bottle. For screen printing, a somewhat finer screen fabric mesh than usual is recommended. For most purposes a 12XX is best, but for unusually fine lines a 14XX is required, and for fabric of dense pile or coarse texture a 10XX will give the best results.

To thin Inkodye, simply add water, but do so in subdued light, preferably in an opaque nonmetallic vessel. To thicken Inkodye, add a small quantity of sodium alginate, stir well, allow to rest for 10 minutes or so then stir again or blend in a blender or with a hand mixer also in subdued light. Dye paste not used immediately must be kept cool and away from light. Age, light, and heat have a deleterious effect on the dye solutions. For best results store Inkodye in opaque plastic or plastic or glass bottles, store in a cool place, keep covers tight, and purchase dyes in quantities that will be used within 2 years.

A full range of spectral hues plus brown, black, and a clear extender are available. They include: Red, Red orange, Orange, Orange yellow, Yellow, Yellow green, Green, Blue green, Blue, Blue violet, Violet, and Red violet.

The intermixing of Inkodye colors follows the same rules as does the blending of pigments: e.g., blue plus yellow produces green, and orange plus blue produces gray. Inkodye colors are transparent and, like watercolor, produce secondary colors when one color is applied over another: e.g., blue over yellow produces green.

Because the final color cannot be seen until development, it is customary to test color blends during the mixing process by developing a small sample with a hot iron.

Nearly any chromatic color can be made from a mixture of an Inkodye color, brown, and clear. To lower the intensity, add increasing amounts of the complement or brown. To produce colors of light value (pastels and tints), add increasing amounts of clear. To produce a color of low saturation and light value, add both brown and clear. For colors of very light value, proportions of 10 parts clear to 1 part color would not be uncommon. Water may be used in place of Inkodye clear when it is desirable to reduce the consistency, as in application techniques such as dipping or tie dyeing.

Inkodye colors develop best on untreated cotton, linen, rayon, and raw silk. Some synthetic, drip dry, permanent-finish, and crease-resistant fabrics accept Inkodye quite well; on others the dyes will produce colors of light to medium value. Do not purchase or dye fabric without first testing, on a piece of the fabric, the Inkodye colors you expect to use.

Methods of Developing Inkodye

1. Sunlight affords the best means of the three alternate methods for developing Inkodye colors. Expose the dyed fabric to warm direct sunlight; the colors will develop in one half-hour or less. Sunlight through a window is also effective, but development will be somewhat slower on cloudy or overcast days. Development is better if the fabric is exposed while the dye is still damp.
2. Development by ironing may be accomplished while the dye is still slightly damp on the fabric or after it has dried. If the dye has dried, the use of a steam iron will hasten the development process. Adjust the iron to a "cotton" setting and iron the fabric very, very slowly. Do not rush. As long as fuming continues, development is taking place. If the fabric you are using is subject to scorching, iron on the back side of the fabric or use a steam iron.
3. Baking in an oven at 280° F. will also develop the colors. Do not let the temperature go over 280°. A higher temperature will cause darkening of the yellow and orange-yellow colors. A flat piece of fabric placed on a cookie sheet will develop in 5 minutes. A piece of fabric that is tie dyed will take from 15 minutes to 1 hour. Progress of the color development is easily followed by observing the color change. Because of the hazard of fire, development by baking is not recommended if a wax-type resist has been used.

4. Household pressure cookers of 3-quart capacity are adequate for small pieces of fabric up to 5 square feet. However, for medium to large size pieces of fabric a 22-quart canning pressure cooker or an autoclave is recommended. Allow the printed fabric to dry before setting. If desired the fabric can be left for a day or two before setting.
   a. Fit the pressure cooker with a wire rack raised 2 inches from the bottom. A wad of chicken wire is convenient for this purpose. Put ½ inch water into the cooker, place the lid and cap in place, turn on the heat, and bring up to pressure. Minimum pressure required is 3 pounds, but the full 15 pound pressure of standard pressure cookers will cause no harm.
   b. Sandwich the fabric between sheets of newsprint, 4 below and 4 on top. Fold and roll into a loose bundle and tie loosely with a string.
   c. With the bundle of fabric ready, remove the cap and lid from the cooker, pop the bundle in, replace the lid and cap, and bring up the pressure as quickly as possible. Dry steam will develop the dye properly; wet steam or condensation will cause the colors to run. Therefore, it is important to take precautions to subject the fabric to dry steam only. Continue steaming at least 20 minutes.

After the dyes are set, remove the residual chemicals by rinsing the fabric in warm water, washing in soapy water, and then rinsing again. When the fabric is dry it will return to its original hand and draping characteristics.

Fiber-Reactive Dyes

Dyes in the fiber-reactive class are probably the most important to the fabric artist. The dye colors are exceptionally clear and have excellent fastness to light, washing, and mild solutions of chlorine bleach. They are readily available and may be adapted for bath dyeing and direct application.

During the dye process, the dyes react chemically with the fiber molecules, becoming integral with them. Fiber-reactive dyes are used primarily for cellulosic fibers, but some types are suitable for silk, wool, nylon, acrylics, and blends.

The word "Procion" has become almost synonymous with fiber-reactive dye. Procion fiber-reactive dyes were introduced by Imperial Chemical Industries, Ltd. in England in 1956. Other fiber-reactive dyes are also produced by Ciba-Geigy, Crompton-Knowles, Verona, and other dye houses.

Procion M-Series dyes are "cold water" type dyes for batik and tie-dye as well as for printing and painting when added to the proper chemical solutions. They are recommended for all immersion techniques.

Procion H-Series dyes are formulated for fabric printing and painting only and cannot be used for immersion techniques. They have much better wash-off characteristics, that is, they are less prone to bleeding or migrating. They remain usable up to four weeks when added to thickner or chemical water, and deeper colors may be achieved especially on silk and wool.

PROCION DYE: M-SERIES

Procion fiber-reactive dyes are cold-water bath type dyes for batik and tie-dye and for textile printing and painting when used with a thickener. These dyes will dye mercerized and unmercerized cotton, rayon, linen, silk, jute, wool, leather, wood, paper, and other natural fibers. They will not dye acetate, nylon, polyesters, acrylics, poly-propylene, or other synthetics. Nor will they dye any fabric with a permanent wash-and-wear, crease-resistant, drip-dry, permanent press, or soil-release finish.

Procion dyes are highly concentrated in dry powder form: two ounces will dye between ten and thirty yards of fabric, depending on the color, the intensty desired, and the weight of the fabric. You need only use a few teaspoons at a time, and the dyes can be stored dry until needed.

Marketed under a variety of brand names, fiber-reactive dyes are often elaborately packaged and are occasionally cut with extending agents. If packaged as the pure hue in bulk form, Procion is one of the most economical dyes available.

Procion M-Series dyes come in the following colors:

Brilliant Blue—light, bright, sky blue
Blue-Green—medium teal blue, almost aqua
Fuchsia—ranges from pink to hot fuchsia
Red—cardinal red
Scarlet—rose-coral to bright orange-red
Brilliant Orange—bright, clear orange
Lemon Yellow—bright lemon
Gold Yellow—warm, almost apricot color
Red Brown—deep burgundy
Black—a difficult color to get. This one works, however. Requires more dye than other colors.
Turquoise—aquamarine turquoise
Brown—auburn brown
Navy Blue—light to dark cobalt blue
Fire Engine Red—bright, vermillion red
Rust—earthy rust brown
Brilliant Yellow—bright, almost flourescent yellow
Cerulean Blue—bright blue, concentrated color
Hunter Green—deep forest green
Prussian Blue—deepest blue, almost black

All fabric should be washed in hot water and detergent before dyeing to remove sizing and starch. The fabric should be rinsed well, but need not be dry. Dense, tightly woven fabrics yield more intense color than thin, filmy fabrics. Also note that cellulose fibers, particularly viscose rayon and mercerized cotton dye significantly better than other types of fibers. For instance, it is very difficult to build up full, deep shades on silk, especially lightweight silks, using bath-dyeing techniques. Unmercerized cottons such as muslin can also yield disappointing results.

Dye vessels or containers should be chosen according to the amount of fabric to be dyed. The fabric should be completely immersed in the dyebath and must be uncrowded and able to move freely. Generally, large shallow containers work better than tall, narrow ones. The best vessels to use are those of plastic, glass, stainless steel, or enamel. Do not use tin, iron, copper, aluminum, or galvanized containers. A washing machine can be used to dye large quantities of material a single color. The older-style wringer models are ideal, but automatic machines whose cycle timing may be controlled are equally suitable.

Except for the dye itself other recipe ingredients are readily available grocery store items. Plain salt is clearly labeled, but washing soda may be called Sal Soda or soda ash and should not be confused with baking soda, also known as bicarbonate of soda. The recipe for wool also calls for white vinegar. If the water in your area is very hard, use a water softener such as Calgon in the proportion of about 1 tablespoon (15–20 g.) to each gallon (4 l.) of dyebath water. Temperatures are not terribly critical. For example, 60°C (140°F) is about what the average hot-water tap produces and 40°C (105°F) is slightly warmer than body temperature. Exact quantities are not critical either. There is plenty of room to experiment. Essentially, the salt causes the fiber and the dye molecules to combine and the washing soda sets the color. These two ingredients are important; the rest is open to experimentation.

DYEBATH PROCEDURES FOR PROCION M-SERIES DYES

Long Dyebath Method

The long dyebath method requires smaller amounts of dye to produce a given shade than the short method. It also produces a more level dyeing. The table below is a guide to the amount of dye and salt to be used for the desired depth of shade for each pound (450 g.) of dry fabric (approximately 2 to 4 yards, 36 inches wide).

	Dye	*Salt*
Pale	¼ tsp. (0.75 g.)	3 Tbsp. (90 g.)
Medium	½ tsp. (1.5 g.)	6 Tbsp. (180 g.)
Deep	1-3 tsp. (3-9 g.)	9-27 Tbsp. (270-810 g.)

1. Place the required amount of dye for the shade desired into a 1 quart (1 l.) Pyrex measuring cup. Add a small amount of cold water and work into a smooth paste free of lumps with a stainless steel or plastic spoon.
2. Add enough water at a temperature of 60°C (140°F) to dissolve the dye completely. This will require at least 1 cup (250 ml.) of water for each teaspoon (3 g.) of dye.
3. For each pound (450 g.) of fabric, use 2½ gallons (9 l.) of water at 40°C (105°F). Add the dissolved dye and stir. Add the cleaned fabric and stir frequently for 10 minutes.
4. Add the required amount of plain salt to the dyebath in 3 equal parts with 5 minutes between additions. Continue to stir frequently for 15 minutes after all the salt is in. You should notice the fabric becoming darker with each addition as the salt forces the fabric to absorb the dye.
5. For each pound (450 g.) of fabric, dissolve 3 Tablespoons (40 g.) of washing soda in a small amount of warm water and add to the dyebath. Dye the fabric for 1 hour more, stirring continuously for the first 10 minutes and every 5 minutes or so for the rest of the time.
6. Rinse the dyed cloth well in cold running water. Allow the fabric to dry naturally without forced air or sunlight.
7. As a final step, fabric should be thoroughly washed in hot water to remove excess dye. Use a mild detergent or soap and avoid enzyme-based detergents or fabric brighteners.

Short Dyebath Method

The short dyebath method, although much shorter than the long method in terms of time, is less economical since more dye is required to produce the same depth of shade. There is a greater tendency for the dyed color to be uneven (not level) with the short method than with the longer method. A flat nonreactive pan or sink must be used for this method since the amount of water is relatively small. Since the dyeing time is so short, the small quantity of water will, of course, affect the color. Use only enough water to cover the material completely and allow freedom of movement. Blotching and streaking may result if the fabric cannot be easily moved in the dyebath.

1. Place 1 to 5 teaspoons (3–15 g.) of dye, depending on the shade desired, into a one-quart (1 l.) Pyrex measuring cup, add a small amount of cold water, and work into a smooth paste with a stainless steel or plastic spoon. Add 1 cup (250 ml.) of water at 60° C (140°F) to this dye paste and stir well to dissolve all the dye.
2. Add 6 to 9 tablespoons (180–270 g.) of salt dissolved in 2 cups (500 ml.) of cold water to the dyebath container. Add the dissolved dye and stir well.
3. Add the material with just enough warm water to cover, and turn continuously for 6 to 10 minutes or more.
4. Dissolve 2 tablespoons (14 g.) of washing soda dissolved in 1 cup (250 ml.) of warm water and add to the dyebath. Dye the fabric for 15 minutes more, turning frequently.
5. Rinse the dyed fabric well in cold running water. Allow the fabric to dry naturally without forced air or sunlight.
6. As a final step, fabric should be thoroughly washed in hot water to remove excess dye. Use a mild detergent or soap, and avoid enzyme-based products or fabric brighteners.

Procion Dye with Wax Resist

The washing soda present in the dyebath for the long and short methods described below combined with strong agitation can cause wax resists to separate from the fabric. This problem can be reduced to some extent by using a significantly higher ratio of beeswax to paraffin in the wax mixture, say two to three parts beeswax to one part paraffin. Gentle and careful handling without crushing, and dyeing in larger, more shallow vessels rather than small, narrow ones will also help. Be sure to check batiks after all dyeings for areas of wax resist which may need reinforcing.

Dyebath Method for Wool

The best results with Procion dyes on wool are obtained with high-quality, white, pure virgin wool; reused wool and other fibers or impurities present in the yarn or fabric interfere with the dye reaction. The following recipe is per pound (450 g.) of dry weight of wool.

1. Place 1 to 5 teaspoons (3-5 g.) of dye (depending on the shade desired) into a one-quart (1 l.) Pyrex measuring cup, add a small amount of cold water and work into a smooth paste with a stainless steel or plastic spoon. Add 1 cup (250 ml.) of water at 60°C (140°F) to this dye paste. Stir well to dissolve all the dye and pour into the dyebath container (should be stainless steel or enamel).
2. Dissolve 3 to 9 tablespoons (180–270 g.) of plain salt (depending on the intensity desired) in 2 cups (500 ml.) of warm water and add to the dyebath. Add enough water to cover the material plus a little extra to allow the yarn or fabric to move freely in the dyebath.

3. Place the dyebath container on the stove and heat gradually to a simmer (just below boiling) and hold there for 10 minutes, stirring frequently. Add ⅔ cup (85 ml.) white vinegar and continue to simmer for another 10 minutes, stirring occasionally.
4. Remove from heat, rinse in hot tapwater, and wash with a mild detergent. Rinse until free of dye, gradually lowering the temperature of the rinse water to that of the room. Remember that sudden changes in temperature can damage wool and cause it to felt up. Heat and cool slowly!

General Notes on Procion Dyebath Methods

It should be noted that in all of the dyebath recipes, after a dyebath has been prepared and used once, it is considered spent and cannot be used again. Although the dye would rather react with the fiber, it will also react with the water at a much slower rate. This is called "hydrolysis" and after about four hours, a large percentage of the available dye molecules will have reacted with the water instead of the fiber. The addition of the washing soda accelerates this reaction. These compounds of the dye and water are responsible for the "bleeding" and staining occasionally experienced with the use of these dyes, since they still have a low degree of attraction for the fibers even though no reaction has taken place. Thus, it is very important that the fabric be thoroughly washed after dyeing to prevent staining by these unreacted compounds.

Also note that each color varies slightly in its nature. For instance, turquoise will yield deeper shades by maintaining the 40°C (105°F) dyebath temperature for the entire dyeing process. To obtain a really deep shade of Navy Blue and all the darker colors including Black, it is necessary to double the amount of dye and quadruple the amount of salt. Up to a certain point, the more salt you add, the deeper the shade you are going to get. Salt is relatively cheap, so don't skimp if you want dark shades.

Alternate Application Methods

There are certain situations in which neither the dyebath nor the direct application methods are ideal. Teachers may find that these methods do not lend themselves well to the classroom situation. Resist dyers may also find that the sequence of ingredients prevents the best use of the dyes. Two alternative methods are provided below. They can be adapted for easy and effective use in the classroom or for a variety of resist techniques.

METHOD A

1. Soak the fabric in a solution of 3 tablespoons (40 g.) washing soda to each gallon (3.6 l.) of water for 15 minutes before dyeing.
2. In plastic or stainless steel tubs, mix a concentrated solution of dye (5-10 teaspoons [15-30 g.] in 1 quart [1 l.] of water) and plain salt (1 tablespoon [30 g.] uniodized salt to 1 teaspoon [3 g.] dye).
3. Dip or soak the fabric in the dye until the desired depth of color is achieved.
4. The fabric must be allowed to cure naturally for at last two hours before drying or rinsing. This period gives the dyes time to react. This is best achieved by placing the damp fabric in a plastic bag.
5. The fabric should then be allowed to dry naturally. When dry it should be rinsed in cold running water then washed in hot water and a mild detergent.

This method allows containers of many colors to be available without having to go through the recipe each time. Be sure to replenish the salt and dye periodically.

METHOD B

1. Soak the fabric in a solution of chemical water for 5-10 minutes. Wring out well.
2. Apply the dye by dipping or soaking the fabric in a concentrated solution of dye, baking soda, and washing soda (see recipe for "thin applications" for proper proportions). Alternatively, the dye may be applied with spoons or from a squeeze bottle to selected areas.
3. Fixing and wash-off procedures are the same as for other direct application methods. This method will produce colored areas with soft edges. For sharper edges, add about ⅛ teaspoon (0.5 g.) sodium alginate per cup of concentrated dye solution.

Direct Application

Procion dyes may be directly applied onto the fabric by screen printing, block printing, painting, sprinkling, spraying, sponging, etc. These methods require the addition of other, often difficult-to-obtain, ingredients.

For applications such as spraying that require a thin dye solution, the dyestuff is added to a mixture that has been dubbed "chemical water." For thicker applications, sodium alginate, a seaweed-derived thickening agent, and the sodium salt of nitrobenezene sulfonic acid, are added. This last chemical prevents the dye from decomposing during the fixation process and thus insures maximum color yield. It is sold under a variety of names, including Resist Salt L, Atexal PA-L, Sitol, Nacan, and Ludigol.

Standard chemical water recipe:

1 tsp. Calgon (4–5 g.)
10 tbsp. Urea (140 g.)
2 c. hot water (500 ml.)
2 c. cold water (500 ml.)

Use a 1-quart (1 l.) jar and stir the Calgon and Urea into 2 cups (500 ml.) of hot water. When dissolved, add the cold water and shake well. This solution may be stored indefinitely.

Thin Applications:

For thin applications, the recipe for Procion dyes must be completely watery and suitable for spraying or brushing as one would with watercolor or colored drawing ink. To 1 quart (1 l.) of chemical water add:

1 tsp. (3 g.) dye for pastel shade *or*
4 tsp. (12 g.) dye for medium shade *or*
8 tsp. (25 g.) dye or more for deep shades, *plus*
4 tsp. (20 g.) baking soda *and*
1 tsp. (5 g.) washing soda dissolved in a small amount of hot water

Measure the required amount of dye powder into a small container and add a small amount of chemical water to dissolve thoroughly and make a paste. Add this paste to the total amount of chemical water. Add the required amount of baking and washing soda *just before using*. Once the sodas have been added, the dye starts reacting and cannot be stored. After the fabric has dried, it must be fixed by one of the methods described on the following page. Smaller amounts of dye solution can be prepared by adjusting the proportions of dye and soda.

Thick Applications:

The thickened Procion dye paste is ideal for screen printing, painting, or applying with a squeeze bottle.

1. Prepare stock paste as follows—To 1 quart (1 l.) of chemical water, add 4 tsp. (18 g.) sodium alginate, and 2 tsp. (10 g.) Ludigol.

Sprinkle the sodium alginate a little at a time over the chemical water and stir constantly for 10 minutes or use an electric mixer or blender. Add the Ludigol and stir until dissolved. This thickened solution is called the "stock paste" and can be used immediately or allowed to stand overnight and become smoother. If the stock paste does not have the proper consistency at this point, it can be thinned by adding more chemical water or thickened by adding slightly more sodium alginate and stirring. This is an organic solution and will mold if left at room temperature. It can, however, be stored indefinitely if refrigerated. Be sure to mark: "Do Not Eat!"

2. Activate the dye paste as follows—Pour off as much of the prepared stock paste as is required for the specific application you are doing, sprinkle the dye powder into it and stir until dissolved. This will require 3 to 4 minutes. The amount of dye will vary depending on the dye and shade desired, but will probably fall between ½ and 5 teaspoons (1–15 g.) per cup (250 ml.) of stock paste. The color can be judged visually. More than one color can be added to produce different hues and shades. This combination of stock paste and dye is called the "dye paste."

Baking soda must also be added to the dye paste, in the proportion of 1 teaspoon (5 g.) per cup (250 ml.) of dye paste. This is best added dissolved in as little water as possible. Once the soda has been added, the dye paste has a usable life of only 1 to 2 days if refrigerated between uses. Beyond that point the dyes will not fix properly.

The dye paste described above should be of proper body for screen printing as prepared. For painting, a thinner consistency is generally desired. Chemical water must be used to dilute the paste. For painting, brushes with nylon or synthetic bristles tend to work best. Natural bristles absorb water and soon become unmanageable and useless for anything but the broadest of areas.

Fixing Procion Dye Applied Directly

After the dye paste or solution is applied, the fabric must be allowed to dry thoroughly and then must be fixed by one of the following methods. The first three methods below require that the fabric be loosely rolled or wrapped in blank newsprint, paper towels, or muslin cover cloth in such a way that dyed surfaces do not come in contact with each other.

Atmospheric steaming. Place in a steam cabinet or canning kettle being certain that neither water nor condensation will contact the wrapped fabric. Use a rack and aluminum foil "tent" for this purpose. Steam for 15 minutes. This is the safest method for heat-sensitive fabrics such as silk and viscose rayon.

Pressure steaming. Prepare an autoclave or pressure cooker as above and hold pressure for about three minutes. Not recommended for silk.

Steam baking in an oven. Place a flat pan of boiling water underneath the oven rack, holding the wrapped fabric. Keep refilling the pan with boiling water as necessary to maintain a steady flow of steam. Bake at 285°F for 30 minutes. For fabric larger than a square yard, reroll in the opposite direction and bake an additional 30 minutes. Not recommended for silk or viscose rayon.

Steam ironing. Iron for 5 minutes at proper temperature for the fabric being used.

Final Wash-off

After fixing, rinse the fabric in cold running water, preferably in open width, until the rinse water runs clear. Gradually increase the temperature of the rinse water, making sure the rinse water runs clear after each increase. Work quickly to avoid staining by unfixed dye. Finally, boil the fabric for 5 minutes using ⅛ cup (30 ml.) of Synthrapol detergent in 3 gallons (12 l.) of water. Other mild synthetic detergents may be substituted for Synthrapol. A hot washing-machine setting can be used instead of boiling. Dry the fabric as quickly as possible. A clothes dryer works well for this purpose.

Color Mixing

The color possibilities obtainable with the Procion dyes are almost unlimited. The following chart should give you a basis from which to begin experimenting. Similar but not identical colors may be achieved by overdyeing.

COLOR MIXING CHART FOR PROCION M-SERIES DYES

First color	Added to Second Color	Results
1 part Red	4 parts Lemon Yellow	Salmon
1 part Scarlet	4 parts Lemon Yellow	Coral orange
1 part Brilliant Blue +	½ part Fuchsia	Red-violet
2 parts Prussian Blue	½ part Fuchsia	Deep purple
1 part Brilliant Blue	1 part Red Brown	Violet
1 part Hunter Green	½ part Fuchsia	Mauve
1 part Navy Blue	1 part Scarlet	Light burgundy
3 parts Turquoise	1 part Lemon Yellow	Apple green
1 part Turquoise	1 part Brilliant Yellow	Brilliant green
Pinch Hunter Green	1 part Lemon Yellow	Lime green
1 part Hunter Green	1 part Lemon Yellow	Avocado green
1 part Hunter Green	1 part Gold Yellow	Bronze green
2 parts Navy Blue	1 part Lemon Yellow	Dark green
1 part Hunter Green	1 part Brilliant Orange	Rust brown
1 part Brilliant Blue	1 part Brilliant Orange	Copper brown
2 parts Navy Blue	1 part Brilliant Orange	Chocolate Brown

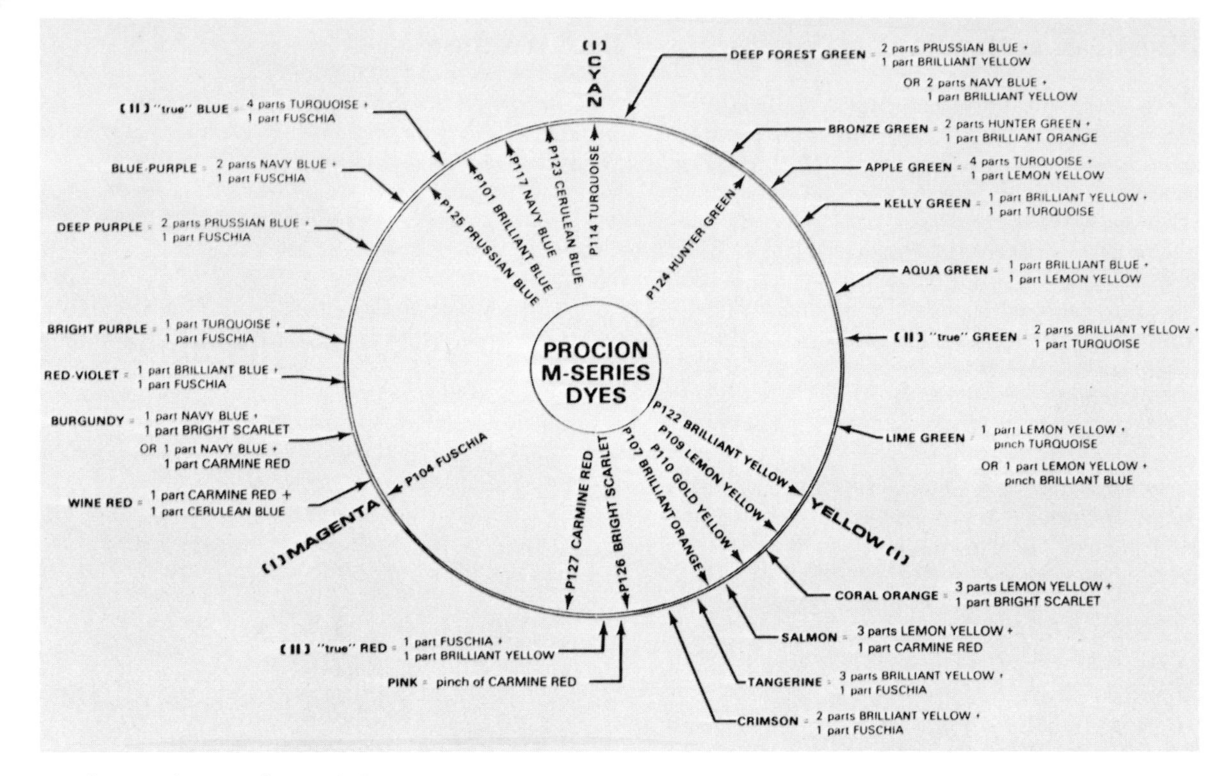

Subtractive Color Mixing System

Textile artist Ann Marie Patterson and Ronald Granich of Cerulean Blue Ltd. of Seattle have worked out a most effective color mixing system for the Procion M-Series dyes. Only three dyes are required, and they are far more effective than the conventional red, yellow, and blue trio.

In the diagram above, the Procion M-Series dyes listed inside the circle are roughly arranged in relation to the primary colors of the "subtractive" color wheel (the same one used by photographers). Dyes affect light in a "subtractive" manner, that is, they absorb or "subtract" certain portions of white light and allow the fabric to reflect the remainder back to our eyes. As more dyes are applied, a smaller and smaller portion of the spectrum is reflected back to our eyes until, when the fabric is dyed black, most of the light is absorbed and we see essentially no reflected light.

The primaries of the subtractive color wheel are different from the ones we all learned in school: they are Magenta, Cyan, and Yellow. The Procion M-Series Dyes that most closely correspond to these primaries are an amazingly wide range of the color spectrum and can be easily mixed from combinations of these three colors.

Primaries (I):
Magenta = Procion Fuchsia (MX-8B)
Cyan = Procion Turquoise (MX-G)
Yellow = Procion Brilliant Yellow (MX-8G)

In the subtractive color wheel, the three secondary hues which result from combining two primaries are listed below along with the combinations of Procion M-Series dyes which approximate them. Because individual Procion dyes all differ in terms of strength of color (saturation), the amounts of each Procion dye needed to make "true" secondaries unfortunately may not be equal. This is evident from the proportions indicated in the mixes listed blow.

Secondaries (II):
Cyan + Magenta = Blue
Magenta + Yellow = Red
Yellow + Cyan = Green

Blue = 4 parts Turquoise + 1 part Fuchsia
Red = 1 part Fuchsia + 1 part Brilliant Yellow
Green = 1 part Brilliant Yellow + 2 parts Turquoise

This inconsistency of unequal strengths of color is also reflected in the color wheel above by showing the "true" secondaries at a position between, and in proportion to, the amounts of the Procion dyes required to mix the color. For example, the secondary hue, blue, results from mixing Cyan and Magenta together, but requires 4 parts Procion Turquoise and only 1 part Procion Fuchsia to produce the approximation of "true" blue. For this reason, the color, "true" blue, is positioned much closer to Procion Turquoise than it is to Procion Fuchsia. (Note the similar positioning for "true" Green.) Other suggested color mixes using the remaining Procion dyes are listed around the color wheel in the same manner. Neutrals or Browns result from mixing some proportion of all three primary hues together, either as individual hues or by mixing any hue with the hue lying opposite it on the color wheel. Because we cannot show three-color combinations on the diagram above, suggested mixes for Neutrals and Browns are listed separately below. There are also several Neutrals or Browns available as individual Procion M-Series dyes: Rust, Red-Brown, Brown, and Black.

1 part Brilliant Orange + 1 part Brilliant Blue = Copper brown
2 parts Navy Blue + 1 part Brilliant Orange = Dark brown
1 part Brilliant Blue or pinch Brown + 1 part Brilliant Orange = Ecru
2 parts Hunter Green + 1 part Scarlet = Mahogany brown
1 part Turquoise + 1 part Brilliant Orange = Khaki
Pinch Rust = Rust
1 part Brilliant Orange + pinch Brilliant Blue = Burnt orange
Pinch Black = Gray
4 parts Prussian Blue + 1 part Brilliant Orange + pinch Brilliant Yellow = Black

This theory of color mixing can be easily extended to the Procion H-Series dyes by choosing the dyes listed below as primaries:

Cyan = Turquoise (H-AS)
Magenta = Fuchsia (H-8B)
Yellow = Yellow (H-4G)

PROCION DYES: H-SERIES

Procion H-Series dyes are high-temperature dyes useful for textile printing and painting only. They may not be intermixed with the Procion M-Series dyes. They have a much longer stability when mixed into chemical water for thick or thin application, and complete wash-off is much easier. Procion H-Series dyes come in the following colors:

Black—blackest of blacks; also pleasant blue-grays
Turquoise—bright, rich turquoise
Yellow—bright, lemon yellow
Blue—bright, electric blue
Red—fire engine red
Scarlet—bright, orange red
Orange—bright, clear orange
Fuchsia—pink to bluish red
Violet—lilac to deep purple
Green—muted olive to deep forest
Brown—tan to deep chocolate
Rust—muted peach to earthy rust
Navy—light blue-violet to deep navy

Procion H-Series dyes must be applied with chemical water or with sodium alginate thickened chemical water as previously described for the M-Series Procions (see p. 39). They should be treated in the same way, except for Procion H-Series Black (Sp-L), which is a glaring exception to these instructions. This dye requires that washing soda be substituted for baking soda. This particular color also benefits from a reduction in the amounts of Urea in the chemical water solution to 3½ Tbsp. (50 g.) per quart.

A second exception is the heat required for fixation. The following changes should be made in previous instructions:

1. Atmospheric steaming: 30 min.
2. Pressure steaming: 5 min.
3. Steam baking in an oven: 45 min. at 300°F, rerolling if necessary.
4. Steam ironing: 10 min.

Disperse Dyes

Disperse dye is an industrial dyestuff originally developed for use on acetate fibers, but now used to produce brilliant shades with excellent light- and washfastness on Triacetate (arnel) and polyester fibers such as dacron, kodel, fortrel, mylar, etc. Disperse dye attaches itself to the fiber surface and then dissolves into the thermoplastic fiber at elevated temperatures. It is suitable for bath dyeing, direct application and heat transfer printing.

Bath dyeing and disperse dye requires boiling water and the addition of a chemical "carrier" to aid the penetration of the dye into the fiber. "Carrier" comes in kit form from any dye seller. Direct application by screen or block printing, hand painting, spraying, etc. is also possible by using an available printing base kit and then fixing the colors by ironing, steaming, or baking. Disperse dye is very concentrated: a one-ounce package will dye as much as twenty-five yards of medium-weight fabric. The following colors are available:

Yellow—bright lemon
Orange—bright, clear orange
Plum—red-violet to purple
Red—bright, warm red
Royal Blue—bright, clear blue
Navy Blue—darker, midnight blue
Black—charcoal gray to black
Turquoise—aquamarine turquoise
Fuchsia—light to deep hot pink

All fabric should be washed in hot water and detergent before dyeing to remove sizing, starch, and/or processing oil. The fabric should be rinsed well, but need not be dry. Dense, tightly woven fabrics yield more intense color than thin, filmy fabrics. Dye vessels must be able to withstand boiling on the stove and consequently should be glass, stainless steel, or enamel. Do not use tin, iron, copper, aluminum, or galvanized containers. Dye vessels should also be chosen according to the amount of fabric to be dyed. The fabric should be completely immersed in the dyebath and must be uncrowded and able to move freely.

Bath Dyeing Method

The following is a basic recipe for dyeing about one pound of fabric (from two to four yards of medium-weight fabric). The proportions given may be multiplied or divided according to individual requirements.

1. To 2 gal. of boiling water add:
   2 Tbsp. carrier
   1 Tbsp. white vinegar
   1 tsp. disperse dye and stir well
   (Add more for deeper color; for dark Navy or Black, double the amount of carrier and quadruple the amount of dye.)
2. Add the fabric to the dyebath and continue boiling for 1 hour, stirring occasionally.
3. Remove the fabric and rinse well in hot water. Thoroughly wash in hot, soapy water.

Direct Application

Disperse dyes may be directly applied to the fabric by screen printing, block printing, painting, sprinkling, sponging, etc. These methods require the addition of other ingredients. For applications such as spraying requiring a thin dye solution, the dyestuff is added to a mixture known as "chemical water." For thicker applications, sodium alginate is added. The chemicals required are available either separately or premeasured in kit form to make up quart and gallon amounts.

Standard chemical water recipe:

1 tsp. Calgon (4–5 g.)
10 Tbsp. Urea (140 g.)
2 tsp. Ludigol (10 g.)
2 c. hot water (500 ml.)
2 c. cold water (500 ml.)

Use a 1-quart (1 l.) jar and stir the Calgon, Urea, and Ludigol into 2 cups (500 ml.) of hot water. When dissolved, add the cold water and shake well. This solution may be stored indefinitely.

For thin applications, this stock solution of chemical water is used by itself.

For thick applications, to 1 quart (1 l.) of chemical water, add up to 4 tsp. (18 g.) sodium alginate to make whatever consistency desired. To obtain a thickened solution of silk-screen consistency, use the entire recommended amount of sodium alginate; use less for painting applications. Sprinkle the sodium alginate a little at a time over the chemical water and stir constantly for 10 minutes or use an electric mixer or blender. This thickened solution can be used immediately or allowed to stand overnight and become smoother. This is now an organic solution and will mold if left at room temperature. It can, however, be stored indefinitely if refrigerated. Be sure to label carefully.

To apply the disperse dyes directly, pour off as much plain or thickened chemical water as is required for the specific application you are doing, sprinkle the dye powder into it, and stir until dissolved. This will require 1 to 2 minutes. The amount of dye will vary depending on the dye and shade desired, but will probably fall between ½ and 5 teaspoons per cup of chemical water solution. For each teaspoon of disperse dye used, add 1 tablespoon white vinegar and apply in any desired manner.

The fabric must then be fixed by one of the following methods:

1. Use a steam-iron for several minutes set at the steam setting (be sure the entire printed image gets heat).
2. Bake 45–90 seconds at 375°F. in a home oven. (Be sure to try a small test piece first as some fabrics tend to melt or scorch easily.)
3. Pressure steam 30 minutes at 260°F. (=20 lbs./in^2) in an autoclave or pressure cooker. (This method works much better if the Urea is replaced by water in the chemical water recipe.)

After fixing, rinse the fabric in cold running water until the rinse water runs clear. Gradually increase the temperature of the rinse water until the rinse water runs clear. A final wash in Synthrapol detergent followed by a thorough hot-water rinse could prove helpful in eliminating possible "bleeding" by dyes into white or light-colored areas.

Heat Transfer Method

The heat transfer method is based on the principle that disperse dyes "sublime," i.e., they pass from a dry, solid state directly into a gaseous state when subjected to heat. Thermoplastic fibers, such as polyester and acetate can absorb these dyes in the gaseous state. So, when applied to newsprint or special heat-transfer paper by painting or screen printing, disperse dyes can be "transferred" to any fabric that is at least 50 to 100 percent polyester or other suitable synthetic. This "transfer print" is just as fade-resistant and washable as applications by the dyebath or direct method. The intensity of the color can be increased, of course, by adding more dye than called for in the recipe below. Be sure to add a proportionate amount of denatured alcohol, however.

1. Mix 1 Tbsp. disperse dye with 1 Tbsp. water and work into a smooth paste.
2. To this paste, add 1 cup of water (which may be thickened to any desired consistency with sodium alginate).
3. Add 1 Tbsp. denatured alcohol (available from any hardware store).
4. Paint, screen, or blockprint onto blank newsprint or onto special heat-transfer Thermo-master paper and let dry. This paper is readily available at dye suppliers and screen process supply houses.
5. Place paper on the fabric, printed side down and iron for 45–60 seconds. The image will transfer from the paper to the fabric. (Remember, the image will be reversed after transferring.)

Naphthol or Azoic Dyes

Naphthol dyes are cold-water type dyes for batik and tie-dye and are intended for use with cellulose fibers such as mercerized and unmercerized cotton, linen, rayon, jute, etc. They will work on some synthetic fibers as well, but are not recommended for protein fibers such as silk and wool because of the detrimental effect of the lye on these fibers. As with all dyes, they will not dye any fabric with a permanent wash-and-wear, crease-resistant, drip-dry, permanent press, or soil-release finish.

Naphthol or azoic dyes produce color as a result of a reaction within the fiber between a naphthol compound (called a "base" or azoic coupling component) and a stabilized diaonium salt (called a "fast color salt" or diazo component). These dyes produce deep, brilliant shades with extremely high fastness, particularly to washing.

At the present time, most dealers stock five naphthol compounds or "bases" designated "A" through "E" and five fast color salts referred to simply as "salts" and designated "1" through "5". Each of the bases will combine with each of the five salts to produce different

COLOR MIXING CHART FOR NAPHTHOL COMPOUNDS

	Base A *(Naphthol AS)*	**Base B** *(Naphthol AS. G)*	**Base C** *(Naphthol AS. GR)*	**Base D** *(Naphthol AS. LB)*	**Base E** *(Naphthol AS. BO)*
Salt "1" (Fast yellow GC)	Red-orange	Lemon	Magenta	Tan	Bright red
Salt "2" (Fast Scarlet R)	Pink	Bright yellow	Red-violet	Chocolate	Deep red
Salt "3" (Fast Red B)	Red	Saffron	Purple	Red-brown	Maroon
Salt "4" (Fast Blue BB)	Bright blue	Gold	Blue-green	Purple	Blue
Salt "5" (Fast Blue B)	Blue-violet	Ochre	Green	Deep violet	Blue-black

hues and vice versa, thus yielding a total of twenty-five different hues. They are listed in the chart below, e.g., Base "D" and Salt "3" yield Red-Brown. The industrial names of the naphthol bases and fast color salts are also listed in the chart.

MATERIALS

Nonreactive dye vessels—You will need two of these, and they should be made of plastic, glass, stainless steel, or enamel. Since the amount of water called for in the dye recipe is small in relation to the fabric, shallow, flat containers tend to work much better than tall, narrow ones for immersion methods of application. Good choices would be dishtubs, baby bathtubs, or children's wading pools for larger pieces.
Pyrex measuring cup—The one-quart size is best.
Stainless steel or plastic measuring spoons—For mixing dye powder and chemicals.
Rubber gloves—Wear these when mixing and using the dyes.
Naphthol bases—"A", "B", "C", "D", "E".
Fast color salts—"1", "2", "3", "4", "5".
Lye—Also known as caustic soda or sodium hydroxide, available in most large supermarkets or hardware stores.

PREPARATION

All fabric should be washed thoroughly in hot water and detergent before dyeing to remove all sizing, starch, or processing oils, which might interfere with the absorption of the dye. The fabric should be rinsed well, but need not be dry. Wear old clothes and rubber gloves. Please note that lye is an extremely caustic substance. It can cause severe skin burns on contact and can do the same to the inside of your lungs if you should inhale lye particles or dust. Be extremely careful when handling or using this product. Always wear rubber gloves and obey all package instructions. When dissolving lye, always use cold water and always add the lye to the water, never the reverse.

To prepare the lye solution, dissolve one 13-ounce can (371 g.) lye (equal to approximately 24 Tbsp.) in 28.5 fluid ounces (840 ml.) of cold water. This is a stock solution and will keep indefinitely. Be sure to mark: "Corrosive and Dangerous. Do Not Take Internally. Keep away from Children." This is the only chemical assistant required for these dyes. Even though the concentrated lye solution prepared above is dangerous, the amount used in the dye baths is very small and can be considered harmless.

To prepare the dye baths, two separate solutions must be mixed according to the instructions below.

1. *Base Solution.* In a 1 quart (1 liter) Pyrex measuring cup, place 1 teaspoon (2 g.) naphthol base and work into a smooth paste with a little boiling water. Add 1 cup (250 ml.) boiling water and stir well. Carefully add lye solution drop by drop until the mixture clears (should be about ½ Tbsp. or 5–10 ml.). Add cold water to bring the mixture up to 1 quart (1 l.). Pour this mixture into the first dye container.

2. *Salt Solution.* In a 1 quart (1 l.) Pyrex measuring cup, place 1 teaspoon (4 g.) fast color salt in a small amount of cold water. Add 1 quart (1 l.) of cold water and stir until completely dissolved. (This may require 5–10 min.). Pour this mixture into the second dye container.

DYEING PROCEDURE

Dyeing with Naphthol dyes is a two-stage process: the fabric must be impregnated with the naphthol base solution, and the fast color salt must be coupled with the base to form the insoluble (and hence, washfast) pigment within the fiber.

1. Wet out the fabric thoroughly in plain, cold water.
2. Enter the fabric into the first dye container (base solution) and agitate gently for 3–5 minutes.
3. In order to achieve maximum rub-fastness after the developing stage, the excess naphthol base must now be eliminated. This can be accomplished in a number of ways:
   a. Remove the fabric and allow the excess naphthol base solution to drip out (away from the sunlight). This is the most economical method in that it conserves base solution. Unfortunately, it is also the slowest method, taking 15 minutes for a lightweight fabric to drain. A heavyweight fabric may require 1–3 hours. If a piece of fabric becomes dried out, dampen it with cold water before proceeding.
   b. Remove the fabric from the naphthol base solution and give it a quick rinse in a container of cold water containing common table salt in the ratio of ½–2 tablespoons per quart (15–60 grams/liter). This will draw off excess naphthol base from the goods and extend the life of the fast color salt bath. Don't use this method for highly absorbent fabrics such as velveteen, etc. Use Method a. instead.
   c. Remove the fabric from the base solution and gently squeeze between paper towels. Change layers once or twice. Again, this method is not for highly absorbent fabrics.
   d. At the risk of streaky or blotchy results, waiting for excess naphthol base to disappear can be eliminated by simply painting the naphthol base directly onto the fabric. Brushes with synthetic bristles are best since they resist the corrosive qualities of the lye best. Use the largest brush you can easily handle and apply the base as evenly as possible with broad, sweeping strokes. Allow to dry slightly before proceeding.
4. Carefully immerse the fabric in the second dye container (fast color salt solution) and agitate gently for at least 5–10 minutes. The color will begin to develop immediately on contact. Allow the fabric to develop completely or a loss of rub-fastness will result. As with the naphthol bases, the fast color salt solutions can also be applied directly by brushing, spraying, etc. In fact, more than one salt can be applied over the same base to achieve a variety of color effects. To avoid streaky or blotchy results, try to apply as evenly as possible with a large brush.
5. Rinse the fabric thoroughly in cold water to remove excess dye particles that may be clinging to the outside of the fiber. For deeper shades, the fabric may be dyed again by starting at step 2 and repeating the process. Make sure the fabric is rinsed thoroughly before redyeing to prevent contamination of the base solution. Batik workers may stop at this point and allow the fabric to dry, reinforce wax, add wax to areas, and redye. Dyes are boilfast at this point, and wax can be removed by ironing and subsequent boiling. Do not dry-clean to remove the wax. Certain base/salt combinations are partially soluble in dry-cleaning fluids.

Mixing Colors

Combine two or more naphthol bases in the same solution or combine two or more fast color salts in the same solution. Never mix bases and salts together in the same container. For instance

To mix:	Immerse in:	Then immerse in:
Gold-brown	3 parts base "B" + 1 part base "D"	salt "1"
Red-violet	base "A"	4 parts salt "3" + 1 part salt "5"

1. Test color produced by above solutions with a small swatch of fabric or yarn before committing the entire batch. It will only take a few minutes.
2. For darker colors, increase the concentration of the naphthol base solution by repeating the steps for mixing base solutions except do not add any extra cold water to the initial 1 cup (250 ml.) of base/lye solution. Add that solution to the first dye container. Add the proportionate amount of salt and water to the second dye container.
3. For lighter colors, use less base, lye, and salt to begin with, or add equal amounts of water to both dyepots.
4. Any concentration will produce a color.

Naphthol base and fast color salt powders may be stored in airtight, nonmetallic containers. Base solutions can be stored in airtight bottles and used repeatedly, while salt solutions cannot be kept more then 6–8 hours. If the goods are carefully rinsed before immersion in the salt solution, it should be good for other dyeings on the same day only.

The optimum proportion for the base/salt solution is 1 part naphthol base to 2 parts fast color salt by weight in equal volumes of water. Since one teaspoon of fast color salt weighs roughly twice as much as one teaspoon of naphthol base because of the greater density of the salt, for large-scale economy or for very precise shade-matching work, we recommend measuring by weight rather than volume and using the 2:1 proportion. For everyday use, the volume measure will be accurate enough.

Household Dyes

Household dyes are sometimes listed as a separate dye class but are actually compounded from several classes of dye to produce a multipurpose dye product, their disadvantages result from generalization and when dyeing cotton, for example, only the chemical components for cellulose are absorbed and all of the dye components for protein and synthetics go down the drain with the rinse water. Nevertheless they are inexpensive, readily available, easy to use, and supplied in a good range of colors. They are particularly useful for tinting or dyeing fabrics to be overprinted or decorated by other techniques.

COLOR CHART FOR OVERDYEING WITH PUTNAM DYE

Dye Color	Over Red Produces	Over Blue Produces	Over Yellow Produces	Over Brown Produces	Over Orange Produces	Over Green Produces	Over Purple Produces
Red	Darker Red	Purple	Scarlet	Reddish Brown	Light Red	Dull Brown	Reddish Purple
Blue	Purple	Deep Blue	Green	Very Dark Brown	Dull Dark Gray	Bottle Green	Bluish Purple
Yellow	Scarlet	Green	Deep Yellow	Golden Brown	Yellow Orange	Light Green	Greenish Brown
Brown	Brownish Red	Almost Black	Yellowish Brown	Darker Brown	Yellowish Dark Brown	Greenish Brown	Chocolate
Orange	Red	Dull Dark Gray	Light Orange	Tobacco Brown	Deep Orange	Yellowish Green	Reddish Brown
Green	Almost Black	Greenish Blue	Light Green	Olive Drab	Myrtle Green	Darker Green	Dull Dark Gray
Purple	Reddish Purple	Plum	Almost Black	Very Dark Reddish Brown	Light Dull Purple	Dull Dark Purple	Darker Purple

EXAMPLE:
Pink over Light Blue produces Lavender
Pink over Light Yellow produces Shell Pink
Pink over Light Orange produces Coral Pink

The original color (unless white or off-white) will always affect the color you are dyeing.
Dark dye shades of Red, Blue, Green, etc. will usually cover light shades of other colors.

To dye fabric Black:

Over Green, Brown, or Yellow, use one package Putnam's Navy Blue for each two or three packages Putnam's Black.

Over Red or Purple, use one package Putnam's Forest Green or Olive Green for each two or three packages Putnam's Black.

Over Blue, use one package Putnam's Orange for each package Putnam's Black.

If too much Black is used, material will have a brownish cast.

PUTNAM FADELESS DYE AND TINT

Putnam dyes were one of the first household dyes available in the United States. They are capable of producing rich shades as well as soft pastel tints on cotton, linen, wool, silk viscose rayon, and numerous blends.

Putnam dyes come in convenient half-ounce packets that dissolve in hot water to release the dye. In addition to the colors listed below, there is a very efficient stripping agent (not bleach) called "No-Kolor":

Black	Orange	Light Blue
Sky Blue	Olive Green	Mahogany Brown
Old Rose	Cardinal Red	French Blue
Bronze Green	Golden Brown	Brandy Brown
Purple	Pink	Turquoise Blue
Bright Green	Garnet	Dusty Rose
Turkey Red	Henna	Jade Green
Lemon Yellow	Navy Blue	Mulberry
Scarlet	Royal Blue	Gold
Gray	Forest Green	Nile Green
Tan	Chartreuse	Silver Gray-Green
Dark Brown	Lavender	

Simmer Dyeing

Optimum color is achieved by the simmer bath method. Allow at least one package of dye per pound of dry fabric. Be certain the fabric is clean and presoaked.

1. Put enough lukewarm water in an enamel or stainless steel pan to cover the fabric yet allow it to move freely.
2. Add the appropriate number of dye packets and stir. The packets will dissolve within 90 seconds.
3. Shake folds and wrinkles from wet, clean fabric and place it in the dyebath.
4. Raise temperature to a simmer while stirring. Maintain this temperature until the fabric is a few shades darker than desired, approximately 30 minutes.
5. After dyeing, rinse fabric in lukewarm water until it runs clear.
6. Allow dyed fabric to dry naturally on a flat, clean surface. Do not speed dry with sunshine or heat.
7. Press fabric while still damp for final heat-setting treatment.

Special Instructions for Wool

In order to avoid pilling, stiffening, or felting of wool special handling is advisable. Start with lukewarm dyebath, add clean, wet material, and bring to a gentle boil while stirring. Turn off heat and allow bath to cool to lukewarm. Allow material to dry on a flat surface, and finally press, if required, with a dry iron on lowest setting with a pressing cloth. Light pressure should be used.

Putnam's produces an inexpensive pamphlet, *The How to Dye Book*, giving detailed instructions for washing machine dyeing, tie-dye, batik, and low-temperature dyeing, as well as numerous helpful hints. See Appendix 2 for the address.

Discharge Substances

To discharge color from fabric is to strip, subtract, or bleach it out. Not all dyes may be discharged, nor may all fibers withstand the discharging agent, especially when that agent is chlorine bleach. Therefore it is necessary to purchase fabric colored with a not colorfast dye or, alternatively, to produce such fabric in the studio. Typically the colored areas would be protected with a resist and the unprotected areas subjected to the discharging agent. An attempt would then be made to stabilize or set the fugitive dye. Commercial color removers sold with household dyes, Inko Discharge Paste, thiourea dioxide, and chlorine bleach are the four most common discharging agents.

The discharge process contains so many variables that it is impossible to give reliable rules or recipes. The information provided here should serve as a guide for individual experimentation.

COLOR REMOVER

Commercial color remover sold with many brands of household dye is available as a discharging agent. Putnam's No-Kolor is one such brand. All of them require a hot bath, making them unsuitable for wax or paste-resist work, but they are very useful for the various bound-resist techniques. Instructions for this very simple procedure are provided by the manufacturer. Caution should be exercised since some of these products produce toxic fumes.

INKO DISCHARGE PASTE

Inko Discharge Paste will strip the color from fabrics that have been dyed with fugitive dye or normally stable dye that has not been set. The prepared paste may be screen-printed through 8XX mesh screen fabric or applied directly. When fabric is dry, apply heat with an iron, or steam in a pressure cooker for 7 minutes. Slight stiffness in the fabric is easily washed out with warm soapy water. A warm rinse should follow.

DISCHARGE PRINTING WITH THIOUREA DIOXIDE

Thiourea dioxide can be used to strip colors from most cotton, rayon, linen, and blends which have been dyed with either fiber-reactive dyes or direct dyes. Not all color will bleach out 100 percent, but most can be made light enough to overdye deep colors. Yarn, fabric, or already made-up garments can all be stripped successfully. The following recipe is for one pound dry weight of fiber and should be cut down or increased according to the amount of fiber.

Ingredients include thiourea dioxide, washing soda (soda ash), and liquid detergent, preferably Synthrapol. For each pound of fabric fill an enamel or stainless steel pot with 2 to 2½ gallons of water.

Add: 1 Tbsp. washing soda
½ tsp. liquid detergent (Synthrapol)
1 pound of fabric to be stripped

Bring to a boil and, while boiling, add 1 teaspoon thiourea dioxide total, divided into 3 equal parts, waiting 5 minutes before each addition, that is, adding ⅓ teaspoon thiourea dioxide every 5 minutes. Do not add all at once. Stir gently and simmer for an additional 20 minutes or so. Rinse well. If you intend to overdye with a fiber-reactive dye like Procion, it is a good idea to add a little vinegar to the final rinse water to neutralize any remaining washing soda which might cause premature fixation.

Wool can also be stripped with thiourea dioxide, but because protein materials are especially sensitive to alkalis, reduce the amount of washing soda to ¼ the above amount. Also reduce the simmering time to only 5-10 minutes and rinse with vinegar immediately after stripping. Not all acid dyes are strippable so be sure to do a small experiment first.

Fiber artists are experimenting with the use of thiourea dioxide in a discharge paste for screen printing or direct application. Thiourea dioxide powder is dissolved in sodium alginate thickener (page 40). The ratio of thiourea dioxide to thickener should be determined by testing samples of the fabric to be stripped. If heat can be applied while the discharge paste is still slightly damp, lighter values may be achieved.

CHLORINE BLEACH

Liquid household bleach, containing from 5.25 to 6 percent sodium hypochlorite and 94 to 94.75 percent water, is the standard discharge product for stripping color from dyed fabric. Chlorine bleach may be used with the cellulosic fibers cotton, linen, and rayon as well as some synthetics but never on the protein fibers silk and wool. The latter will in fact completely deteriorate when exposed to household bleach. Some fiber deterioration occurs even with the cellulose group, making the process a bit risky. Bleach discharging enjoys several distinct advantages: it is very easy, quick, inexpensive, and it can be done anywhere, even out of doors, without special equipment.

MATERIALS

Dark colored fabric—Usually cotton that is known to lighten in chlorine bleach. When shopping for dischargeable fabrics, carry a small tightly sealed container of strong discharge solution (half water and half bleach) for on-the-spot testing of a swatch. If the fabric does not lighten in one to two minutes it will not be suitable.

Plastic dishpans or similar receptacles—Three plus a sink is ideal.

Water source—Sink, hose, or even a lake or stream.

Rubber gloves—And/or plastic or stainless steel kitchen tongs.

Resist materials—The usual objective of discharging is to retain some of the original fabric color with melted wax or one of the tie-dye binding techniques described later in the text. Discharge and redye procedure is explained in chapter 5.

Household bleach—The discharging agent

Kitchen vinegar—The neutralizer

Measuring cup

METHOD

1. Apply resist to the fabric.
2. Determine the bleach to water ratio necessary for the desired shade. In a measuring cup place ¼ cup chlorine bleach and ¾ cup warm water. Immerse a small swatch of your fabric and agitate until it lightens. Remember that the fabric will be considerably lighter when dry. Experiment until the proper ratio is achieved, but the proportions should not exceed half bleach and half water. Some dyes discharge more readily if the fabric is exposed to the air several times during the process. Use plastic or stainless steel tongs or a rubber-gloved hand to retrieve the swatch.
3. Prepare the work area. It is best to work out of doors or in a very well-ventilated area as the fumes created by bleaching even a yard of fabric are annoying at best and may be toxic at worst. Observe all cautions printed on the bleach container. Have ready all items on the equipment list.
4. Prepare discharge solution. Use the ratio determined in step 2, and pour enough solution to cover the fabric in one of the dishpans.
5. Prepare the neutralizer. In a second dishpan place enough water and vinegar (3 parts water : 1 part vinegar) to cover the fabric.
6. Prepare a rinse pail of clean water.
7. Prepare a pan of warm, soapy water.
8. Discharge the fabric.
9. Rinse fabric in water.
10. Soak fabric in neutralizer for 1 to 2 minutes, agitating frequently.
11. Rinse fabric again in clean water.
12. Wash thoroughly in warm soapy water.
13. Rinse again.
14. Allow to dry.
15. Remove the resist material. Bound resists may be removed between steps 13 and 14.

Here are several hints to keep in mind:

Try to use the least possible amount of bleach to achieve the desired shade.

If the bleaching solution is warm, the action will be accelerated.

Wash and rinse discharged fabric very thoroughly. Never force dry or iron discharged fabric that may contain residual bleach or vinegar because of possible fiber deteriorating. Proceed with extended rinsing.

Pigment Pastes or Paste Paints

The dyes and dye pastes we have encountered thus far put color *in* the fabric, but the pigment pastes and inks put color *on* the fabric. Each has its advantages and disadvantages. Dyes must be specific and consideration of their affinity to fiber content is crucial. In addition, dyes often require elaborate fixation and washout procedures. Pigment pastes, on the other hand, can be applied to virtually any fabric surface because of their remarkably adhesive nature. Fixation of pigment pastes is very simple, and washout is usually unnecessary. Still, there is an unpleasant tendency of many pigment pastes and inks to alter the hand of a fabric, whereas dyes or dye pastes properly applied hardly ever do so.

In evaluating whether to use a dye or a paste paint the following generalized chart may be helpful:

Characteristic	*Dye*	*Paste Paint*
Light fastness	−	+
Wash fastness	+	−
Quality of hand	+	−
Relative complexity	−	+

The composition of the various inks and pigmented products varies a great deal, but most contain a thickener, a solvent, a binder or resin, and, of course, finely ground pigment.

VERSATEX FABRIC PAINT

Versatex is a pigmented, water-base ink that can be applied to all natural fibers and a variety of synthetics. Unlike other pigmented products, Versatex will not affect the texture, softness, hand, or drape of the fabric, whether it be heavy canvas or filmy organdy. Also, unlike most pigmented products, Versatex can be easily cleaned from screens, brushes, and other equipment with warm or cold water, thus eliminating the use of dangerous, flammable solvents. The advantages of using a pigmented product as opposed to a dye product are brilliant shades, especially in the green-blue range, and excellent lightfastness and permanence on a wide range of synthetic fibers.

Since Versatex colors are semitransparent, best results are obtained on white or light-colored grounds. The colors are concentrated and an extender is available to obtain translucent pastel shades. White may be added for opaque pastels. When printing on synthetic fibers or using large amounts of water to thin, Versatex binder should be added to improve adhesiveness.

Although designed primarily as screen printing inks, Versatex colors can also be used for block printing, stenciling, painting, or air-brushing. For silk-screen applications, only waterproof screen fillers and stencils such as lacquerproof maskout and knife-cut lacquer film or direct photo emulsion can be used.

On fabric, Versatex colors become permanent and washable only with heat-setting after the colors have dried thoroughly. Heat-setting is accomplished by ironing on the back side for three to five minutes with a hot iron, using a system of infrared heat lamps or by tumble-drying for twenty minutes at the highest temperature setting.

Versatex is packaged in 3¾ oz., pint, quart, and gallon plastic jars. The colors mix easily and almost any chromatic color can be obtained. The following colors are available:

Red	Yellow-Green	Violet
Scarlet	Green	Magenta
Orange	Turquoise	Black
Golden Yellow	Blue	Brown
Yellow	Royal Blue	Binder
White	Sky Blue	Extender

OIL-BASE BLOCK PRINTING INKS

Several suitable brands of oil-base block printing inks are available and they behave in a similar fashion. The product is in many respects like artists' oil paint, with which it may be intermixed to produce nearly any color imaginable. Mineral spirits or paint thinner is used for thinning and cleaning up. To thin a color or make it transparent without altering its consistency or viscosity, add the required amount of transparent extender. To speed the drying time add dryer in roughly a 1:10 ratio. The dryer is essential if black ink is used, since it is abnormally slow-drying. Allow printed fabric to dry thoroughly, then press on the back side for a final heat setting. Press for 3 to 5 min. per sq. yd at setting that is correct for the fabric being printed. Very heat sensitive fabrics may be tumbled at maximum safe heat in an electric clothes dryer, but only when ink is bone dry.

Because dry-cleaning solvents are designed to remove oil base materials, fabric should be laundered with a mild soap.

Blueprinting on Fabric

The cyanotype or blueprint process used to copy architectural or mechanical drawings is also applicable to untreated natural fiber content fabrics. This includes 100 percent rag papers. Fabric that has been sensitized with ferric salt is exposed to ultraviolet light, causing reduction of the ferric salt to ferrous and producing Turnbull's Blue. This color is insoluble in water thus an image can be formed by simply washing away with water areas not exposed to light.

MATERIALS

Ferric ammonium citrate—Yellow-green powder or flakes.
Potassium ferricyanide—Orange-red crystals, caution: poisonous!
Two bottles—For storage of each solution; brown, green, or clear wrapped with aluminum foil.
Sunlamp—Quartz lamp, carbon arc, or direct outdoor sunlight.
Filter paper or muslin
Sheet of nonglare glass or Plexiglas
Flat, plastic or glass dish or pan
Hairdryer—Darkroom dryer set up or fan (optional).
Distilled water
Fabric—Natural fiber, no permanent finish, prewashed, dried, ironed flat.

Prepare the following stock solutions:

1. Weigh out 50 grams of ferric ammonium citrate (yellow-green powder) and dilute with 1 cup (250 ml.) distilled water.
2. Weigh out 35 grams of potassium ferricyanide (orange-red crystals) and dilute with 1 cup (250 ml.) distilled water. (8 fluid oz. or 1 cup)

Make these two solutions up separately, being sure to wash mixing vessel and stirring rod thoroughly between solutions. Filter each solution into an amber bottle. These solutions should stay active for about four months. Once mixed together, they will remain potent for only six hours. Mix together just prior to sensitizing the fabric. Instructions for this process are given under "Brownprinting on Fabric" which follows.

Brownprinting on Fabric

Renewed interest in producing photograph or photogram images on fabric or paper has resulted in the revival of a number of sensitizing formulas, including the Van Dyke sensitizing process described here. This is a contact formula, i.e., no enlargement is possible. When the print is dry, the image will be brown-black on a white background if a negative is used, and the reverse if a positive is used. This is also one of the most reliable methods of sensitizing fabric and is easy to prepare and use. Major dye sellers also carry premeasured kits that are convenient and contain all the chemicals.

MATERIALS

Ferric ammonium citrate—Yellow-green crystals.
Tartaric acid
Silver nitrate

Sodium thiosulfate—Photographic fixer of "hypo".
Opaque bottle—1 qt. (about 1 liter) capacity for storage of sensitizing solution; glass or plastic, amber, green, or clear wrapped with aluminum foil.
Sunlamp—Or reflector photolamp, quartz lamp, or bright sunlight out-of-doors.
Sheet of nonglare glass or Plexiglas
Flat, plastic or glass dish or pan
Distilled water
Fabric—Natural-fiber, no permanent finish, prewashed, dried, ironed flat.
Hairdryer—Darkroom dryer set-up or fan (optional).
Rubber gloves

Prepare the following stock solution:

1. Weigh out 90 grams of ferric ammonium citrate, 15 grams of tartaric acid, and 37.5 grams of silver nitrate. *Caution:* Silver nitrate in either the dry chemical or solution form can cause burns both to skin and to eyes! When handling silver nitrate, always wear rubber gloves and be careful not to inhale dust or powder. Silver nitrate will also form brown stains, which are virtually impossible to remove, on clothing and countertops, as well as on skin and nails.
2. Dissolve each of the chemicals in a separate container, using 8 fluid ounces (1 cup) (250 ml) of distilled water at 65 to 75°F (18.5 to 21°C) for each. Use stainless steel, glass or plastic for containers and stirring. The container for the ferric ammonium citrate should hold 32 ounces (approximately 1 liter or 1 quart).
3. Mix the ferric ammonium citrate and tartaric acid solutions together. Then add the silver nitrate solution slowly while stirring. Add enough distilled water to make a total of 32 fluid ounces (approximately 1 liter). This solution should remain good for several months if stored in a brown container away from direct sunlight.

Sensitizing Process:

1. Under dim incandescent room light or yellow safelight (such as Kodak Safelight Filter, or Wratten Series OA or OO), pour stock solution into a flat tray.
2. Sensitize the fabric by soaking thoroughly for 3 to 5 minutes. It is possible to spray or brush the solution onto large areas rather than immerse them. This is less wasteful and works especially well with heavier fabrics. Using rubber gloves, carefully squeeze out excess solution and hang fabric by clothespins to dry. During the drying time, reverse the ends so that the fabric dries evenly (a clothesline strung across a bathtub in a darkened bathroom is a satisfactory and fairly neat set-up). Drying time depends on the fabric thickness and size (10–15 minutes for cotton about 12 in. square).
3. Under light-safe conditions as above, place a high-contrast negative or positive (Gevalith, Kodalith), or an actual object on the fabric. This latter method produces what is called a photogram. The sheet of glass or Plexiglas should be placed over a negative or positive to insure good contact with the fabric. Exposing when the fabric is just slightly damp produces the best results: however, the negative or positive must be protected with clear plastic wrap. Totally dry fabric produces nearly equal results.
4. Expose by placing the above-assembled package outside in direct sunlight or use any of the suggested high ultraviolet-light sources. When details are visible in the highlight areas of the image, the print is properly exposed. This will happen very rapidly in summer sunlight (45–60 seconds) but could take up to 15 minutes under one of the suggested lamps. A test strip can be used to determine the best exposure time; the longer the exposure, the deeper the resulting browns. However, be careful not to overexpose as this results in severe loss of detail. Remember, also, that you are working actual size and no enlargement is possible.
5. Wash the exposed print in running water at 65–75°F (8–21°C) for about 1 minute or until all unexposed areas are clear of the brownprint chemicals. The image will be light tan-yellow, but will change to dark brown when the print is immersed in the "hypo" solution. To make "hypo" solution, dissolve 1 part sodium thiosulfate in 20 parts water at room temperature. (We have achieved better results by using pure sodium thiosulfate rather than a prepared product. Immerse print until it turns from tan-yellow to gray-brown (30–60 seconds). Don't overfix or the image will disappear!
6. Rinse fabric for 30 minutes in cool running water. Heavier fabrics will require longer rinse time (2–4 hours) to remove all unexposed sensitizer and chemicals. Hang finished fabric to dry out of direct sunlight. The fabric may be washed and laundered, but don't use bleach.

Jennifer F. Lew. Batik wall hanging. Silk with acid and basic dyes, ca. 42″ x 90″ (107 x 229 cm). Collection of Anne Hauberg, Seattle, Washington. Detail on facing page.

PART TWO

Techniques and Examples of Surface Design

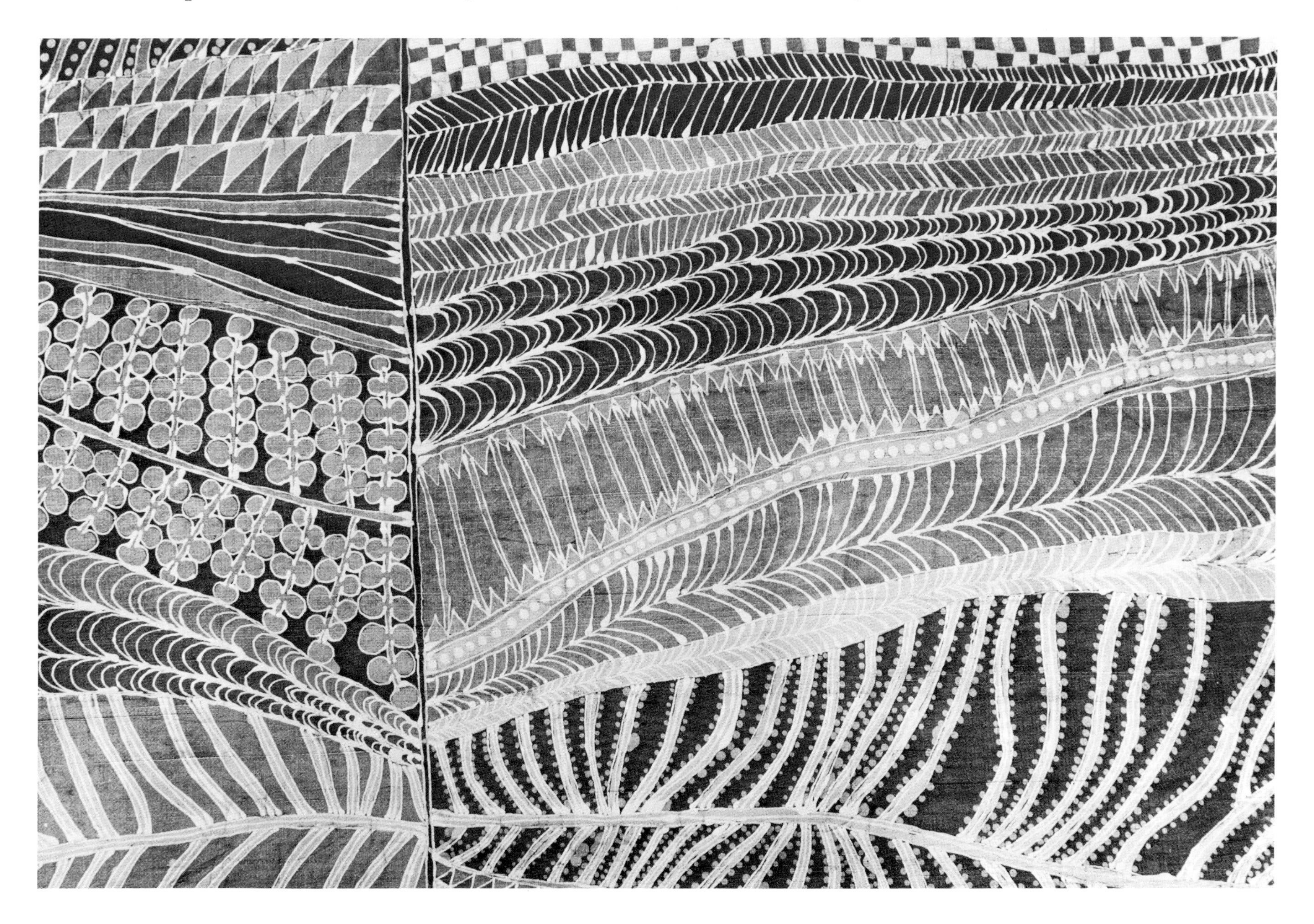

Jennifer F. Lew and Richard M. Proctor. Rondo Capriccioso. *1973. Fold dyed paper mural for the Seattle-Tacoma International Airport, 8½′ x 11′ (777 x 1006 cm).*

4. Direct Dyeing

Direct dyeing, as the title implies, refers to a process group in which dye, or more correctly, color, is applied to fabric, paper, or leather without intermediate steps. As in painting and drawing the application may be spontaneous or studied, but in either case it is achieved without stencils, resists, elaborate equipment, or restrictions such as repetition of the image. It is primarily this last characteristic, the potential for asymmetric or nonrepeating compositions, that sets the direct dyeing techniques apart from other means of surface embellishment.

Equipment for Direct Dye Application

Only a few of the tools or pieces of equipment mentioned in this chapter are specialty items; a majority of them are common household objects.

Polyfoam sponge paint-"brushes"—These are ideal for dye application and will be found in most paint stores in a variety of sizes.

Housepainting rollers—These are also well suited for applying dye and are stocked in many sizes. Additional painting appliances are shown on page 59.

Plastic squeeze bottles—These multipurpose containers may serve as storage containers, as decanters for liquids or pastes, or as tools for squeezing colorants directly on fabric, paper, or leather.

Japanese wash brush—Suitable for application of thin dye or stain solutions. Several sizes are available at art supply stores or specialty import shops.

Japanese bamboo brush, round—These are generally of ox hair. The best ones have the hairs set in plastic rather than directly into the bamboo handle. Size range and sources are the same as above.

Round red sable brush—These afford excellent control and come in many sizes. Squirrel or so-called camel hair is a suitable substitute.

Square-ended or "bright" red sable brush—Suitable for paste paint, dye paste, or liquids. Nylon or synthetic bristles rather than natural hair may be substituted and are in fact recommended if used with a dye paste containing soda.

Cotton swabs—Disposable applicators for dyes and stains.

Dye applicators—Primarily used for leather dye but suitable for other liquids. Available at craft suppliers and shoe repair shops.

Dye crayons—Coloring agents for a wide range of fabrics. See details and example on page 60. Available at art supply stores.

Permanent felt-tip markers—A wide selection is readily available. Avoid water-soluble products for fabrics requiring washing. See details and example on page 61.

Airbrush outfit—Should include double action airbrush, color jar, airhose, air pressure regulator, and air source. The latter may be a compressor or a carbon dioxide tank. Cans of pressurized air are also available.

Other useful equipment for direct color application not shown in the illustration includes: *water containers, mixing pans, rubber gloves, paper towels, rags, sponges, pencils, masking tape, a fan or hairdryer to speed drying time, clothesline or drying rack, and newspaper or dropcloth to keep work table clean.*

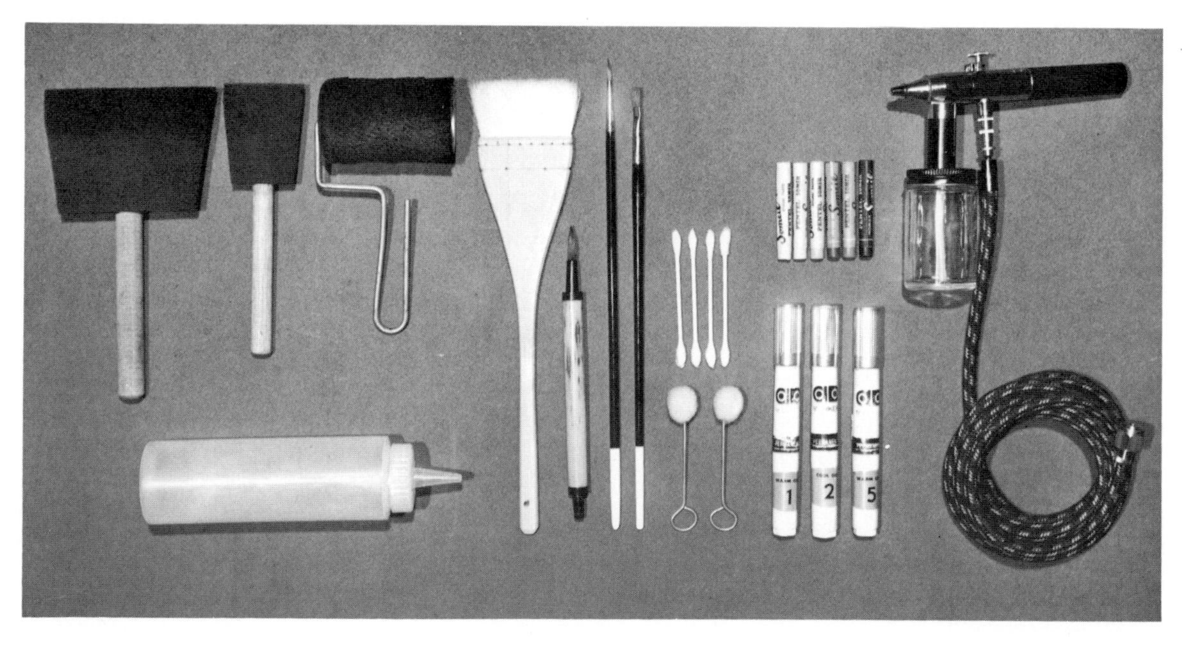

Tools for direct dye application.

Techniques for Direct Dye Application

Dip Dyeing Folded Paper

The fold dye process is applicable to both fabric and paper and results in kaleidoscopic or symmetric pattern effects. Regardless of medium, the pattern will be largely governed by the type and configuration of the folds. Great complexity is unnecessary: most of our examples are based on the same folds children use to cut snowflakes or paper dolls.

MATERIALS

Paper—Medium-weight silkspan paper sold for model airplanes is especially well suited for this process, but any light- to medium-weight, thin porous paper may be used.
Dye—Food coloring is recommended, as well as liquid household or acid dye. May be mixed or diluted.
Shallow pans or jars for dye
Paper towels—In abundant supply for blotting.
Working surface—Clean, dry, and paper-covered.
Drying area—Clean, dry, and paper-covered.

METHOD

1. Fold paper to desired shape.
2. Moisten paper in water until all layers have been penetrated. Gently squeeze out excess water.
3. Blot well with toweling until paper is just damp. This will take some experimentation.
4. Dip a corner or edge in the dye solution. The dye will be quickly absorbed by the damp paper and bleed inward. You may wish to blot the paper lightly after dipping in the dye to stop the action of the dye. This is particularly true if the paper is too moist. Repeat this process as desired in other edges or corners. Use several colors for varied effects.

Moist folded paper is being dipped in a jar of dye. The rectangular paper has been pleated regularly then folded into triangles as shown.

A finished damp piece is being carefully unfolded.

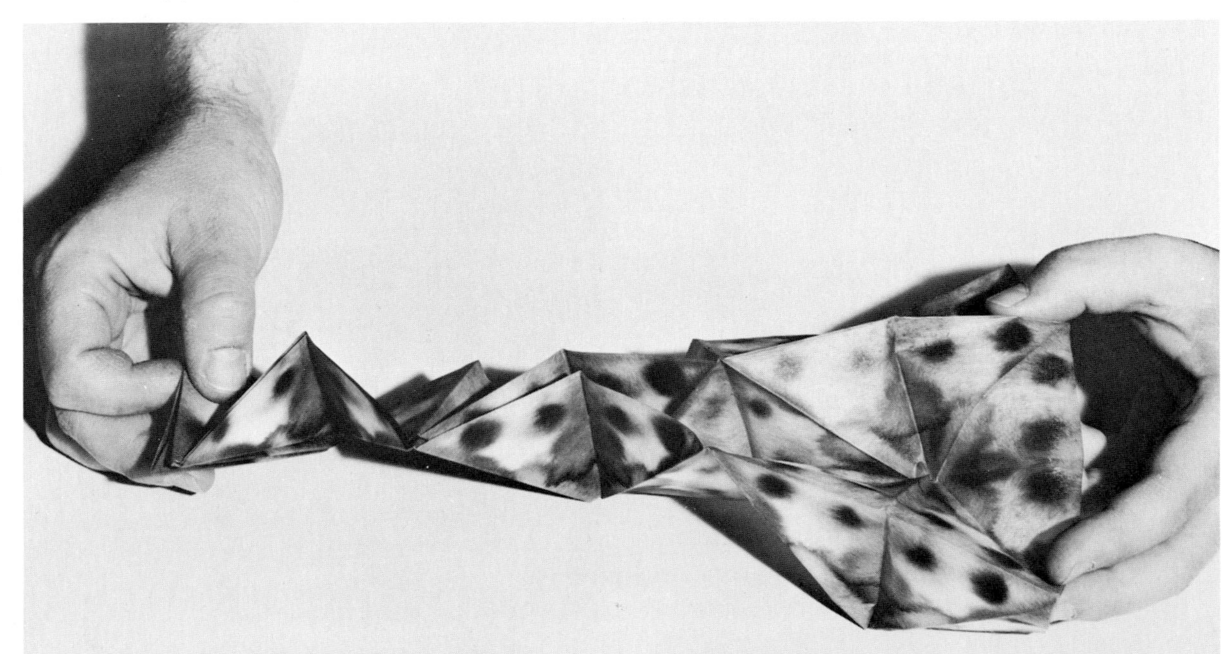

5. Carefully unfold the paper about halfway and lay it on a flat, paper-covered surface to dry. If dye bleeds or runs into unwanted areas while paper is being unfolded, the paper should have been blotted more thoroughly.
6. When nearly dry, the paper may be unfolded completely for final drying.
7. Press with a "cool" iron to remove creases.

SPECIAL EFFECTS

1. Try combining dip dyeing with brush or squeeze bottle dyeing. This could be done while the paper is still damp or after it has been allowed to dry.
2. A finished piece may be refolded on an entirely new network and redipped for greater complexity or color movement.
3. Experiment with unusual folding techniques described in books on origami and paper design.
4. Unusual halolike or waterspot effects may be achieved by a simple color subtraction technique. First dip dye a paper as described in Steps 1 through 6 above. Then refold on its original creases and dip one or two corners only in clear water. Next, wrap the water-dipped corners in several layers of paper toweling and press out as much water as possible (foot pressure is best). This action will remove some but not all of the color. When the water-dipped portions are dry, they will reveal a delicate "high water line" obtainable by no other means.

Dip Dyeing Folded Fabric

MATERIALS

Sheer or lightweight fabric
Dye—A liquid, room-temperature dye with affinity for selected fabric.
Needle and thread
Iron
Shallow pans or jars for dye
Paper towels—In abundant supply for blotting.
Working surface—Clean, dry, and paper-covered.
Drying area—Clean, dry, and paper-covered.

METHOD

1. Fold the fabric with the aid of an iron to the desired shape. It is best to keep the number of folds to a minimum. If the layers of fabric seem to shift it is a good idea to baste them together with a few long running stitches. Instructions for running stitches are given in the chaper on Needlework.
2. Moisten fabric in water until all layers have been penetrated. Gently squeeze out excess water. Try a sample piece first. You may find that you have too many layers, that the fabric is too wet, too dry, or that a particular dye works best on dry fabric.
3. Blot well with toweling until fabric is just damp. This will take some experimentation.
4. Dip a corner or edge in the dye solution. The dye will be quickly absorbed by the damp fabric and bleed inward. Repeat this process as desired in other edges or corners. Use several colors for varied effects.
5. Carefully unfold the fabric about halfway and lay it on a flat, paper-covered surface to dry.
6. When nearly dry, the fabric may be unfolded completely for final drying.
7. Set or fix the dye by appropriate method.

SPECIAL EFFECTS

Most of the special effects explained under "Dip Dyeing Folded Paper" will apply to fabric as well. You may wish to try refolding and redyeing the fabric on the same or a different grid for greater complexity or variety.

Dip dyed folded fabric. In this case acid dyes have been used on a sheer silk crepe shown both flat and gathered.

Brush Dyeing Folded Paper

MATERIALS

Brushes—Small round watercolor or oil painting brushes are best. A # 5 or 6 round sable oil painting brush works well.
Paper—Medium-weight silkspan paper sold for model airplanes is especially well suited for this process, but any light- to medium-weight, thin porous paper may be used.
Dye—Food coloring is recommended as well as liquid household or acid dye. May be mixed or diluted.
Shallow pans or jars for dye
Paper towels—In abundant supply for blotting.
Working surface—Clean, dry, and paper-covered.
Drying area—Clean, dry, and paper-covered.

METHOD

1. Fold paper to desired shape.
2. Very involved designs may be easier to execute if a few light pencil guidelines are applied to both outer surfaces of the folded paper. Remember to make the lines mirror images of each other for exact registration.
3. Moisten paper in water until all layers have been penetrated. Gently squeeze out the excess water.
4. Blot well with toweling until paper is just damp. This will take some experimentation.
5. Apply the first color to the top surface of the damp folded paper in the desired composition of lines, dots, or areas. Two coats may be advisable, depending on the number of paper layers.
6. Flip your work over and you should be able to see the composition penetrating lightly through the back, upturned surface. Pressing downward with a clean finger on the exposed surface will usually force the dye to become more visible.
7. Apply the color to corresponding areas on the back of the folded paper. This process assures even penetration of dye to the inside folds.
8. As you work you may wish to use a combination of thin and thick lines, mix some of your colors for greater variety and interest, retain some white lines or spaces for more sparkle, or dye the entire piece for rich muted effects.

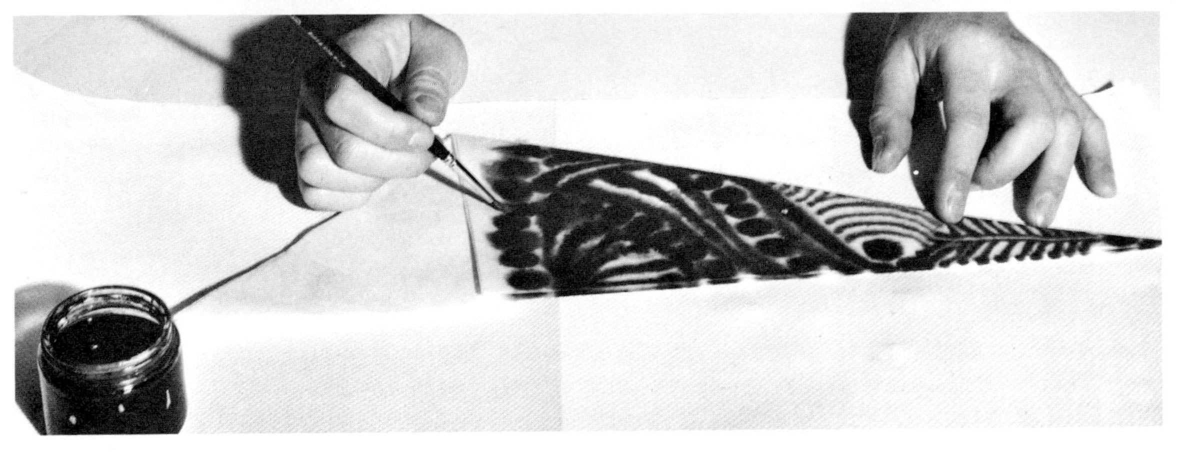

Food color is being applied with a #5 round paintbrush to the top surface of folded and moistened medium-weight silkspan paper.

When color is applied to only one surface, penetration is incomplete. Be sure to follow method Step 5.

9. Repeat Steps 5, 6, and 7 for the desired number of colors.
10. Carefully unfold the paper about halfway and lay it on a flat, paper-covered surface to dry. If dye bleeds or runs into unwanted areas while paper is being unfolded, it probably should have been blotted more thoroughly.
11. When nearly dry, the paper may be unfolded completely for final drying.
12. Press with a "cool" iron to remove creases.

SPECIAL EFFECTS

1. Dots or lines may be made by squeezing the dye from a syringe, squeeze bottle, or eye dropper. Some brands of food color may be purchased in plastic squeeze bottles. When the food color is used up, these little bottles may be refilled with mixed colors.
2. Felt-tip pens may be used to embellish or correct dyed papers once they are dry.

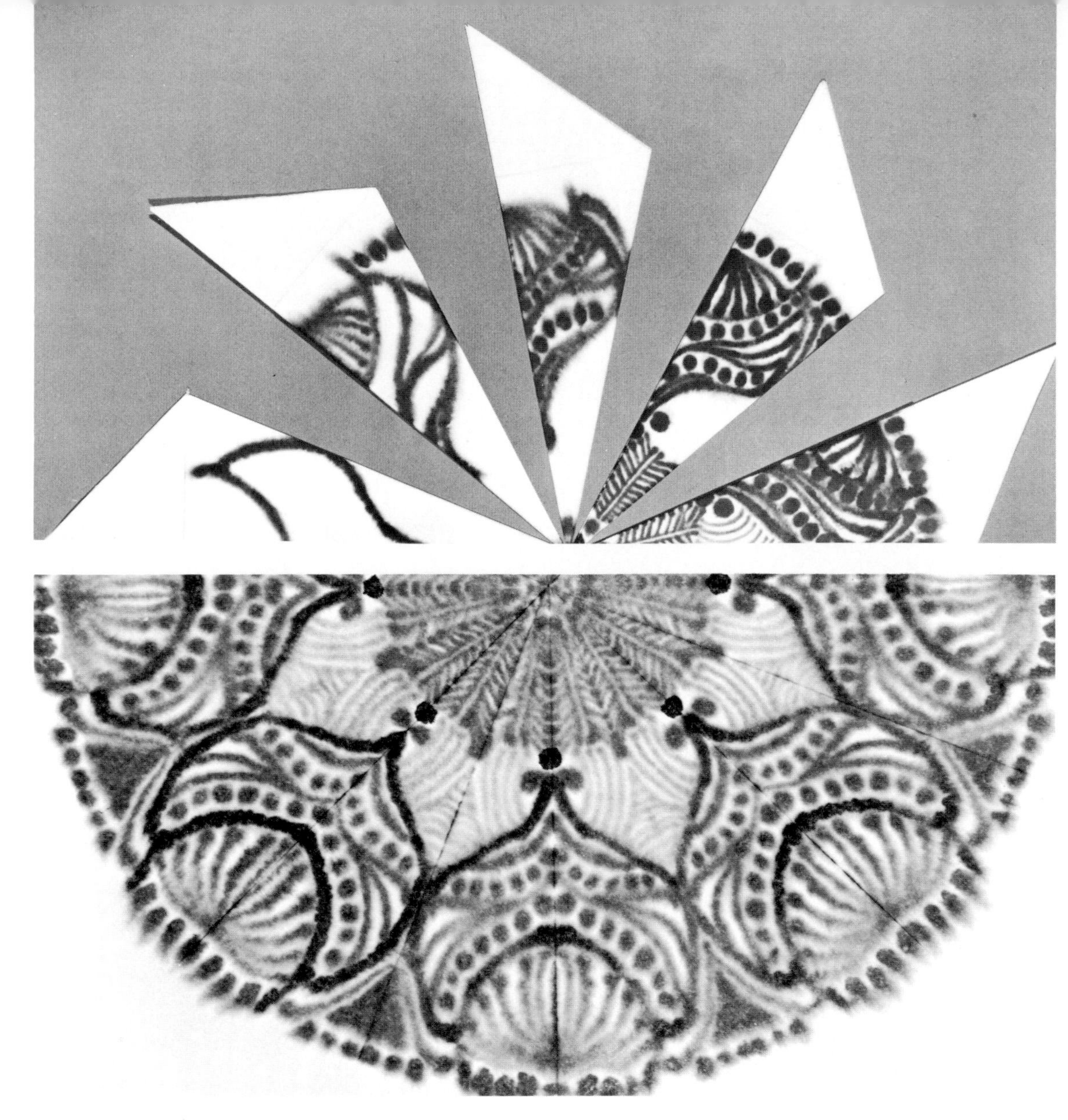

Top: *Five color stages required for the circular composition. Note the variety of line weight, the grouping of dots, and the retention of the narrow white lines.*

Bottom: *Finished and mounted fold and brush dyed paper. Note the manner in which each segment is a mirror-image of its neighbor.*

Brush Dyeing Folded Fabric

MATERIALS

Brushes—Round or flat watercolor-type brushes as required.
Sheer or lightweight fabric
Dye—A liquid, room-temperature dye with affinity for selected fabric.
Needle and thread
Iron
Shallow pans or jars for dye
Paper towels—In abundant supply for blotting.
Working surface—Clean, dry, and paper-covered.
Drying area—Clean, dry, and paper-covered.

METHOD

1. Fold the fabric with the aid of an iron to the desired shape. It is best to keep the number of folds to a minimum. If the layers of fabric seem to shift it is a good idea to baste them together with a few long running stitches.
2. Very involved designs may be easier to execute if a few light pencil guidelines are applied to both outer surfaces of the folded fabric. Remember to make the lines mirror images of each other for exact registration.
3. Moisten fabric in water until all layers have been penetrated. Gently squeeze out excess water.
4. Blot well with toweling until fabric is just damp. This will take some experimentation.
5. Apply the first color to the top surface of the damp folded fabric in the desired composition of lines, dots, or areas. Two coats may be advisable depending on the number of layers.
6. Flip your work over and you should be able to see the composition penetrating lightly through to the back, upturned surface. Pressing downward with a clean finger on the exposed surface will usually force the dye to become more visible. If fabric resists the penetration of dye, it may be necessary to release some or all of the basting stitches, peel back a few layers, and apply dye to one or more layers inside.
7. Apply the color to corresponding areas on the back of the folded fabric. This process assures even penetration of dye to the inside folds.
8. Repeat Steps 5, 6, and 7 for the desired number of colors.
9. Carefully unfold fabric about halfway and lay it on a flat, paper-covered surface to dry. If dye seems to bleed or run as unfolding begins, try allowing the piece to dry overnight in its folded position.
10. When nearly dry, the fabric may be unfolded completely for a final drying.
11. Set or fix dye by the appropriate method.

Brush Dyeing Fabrics

Brush dyeing is simply a more accurate term for hand painting as it relates to surface design on fabric. It is indeed a form of painting and can produce any painterly effect, from the soft flowing quality of a transparent watercolor to the most precise hard-edge detail. Even thick impasto effects are possible with inks or paste paints, though seldom practical.

MATERIALS

Fabric—Any type of fabric may be used providing it has high affinity for the selected dye or paste paint. Should be washed and pressed.
Dye paste, paste paint, ink, or stain—Should have an affinity with the selected fabric.
Brushes with moderately short stiff bristles—Those designed for acrylic paints are ideal since their synthetic bristles are less affected by dye chemicals than natural bristle.
Dye or paint containers—And extras for mixing colors.
Frame and pushpins—For stretching the fabric (optional).
Pencil, HB or softer (optional)
Appropriate solvents, if any, and clean-up supplies

METHOD

1. Apply drawing or guidelines directly to the fabric with a soft lead pencil or a soluble marker. Omit this step if desired.
2. Stretch fabric evenly on a wooden frame. This is especially important for light unwieldy fabrics. Heavy fabrics tend to stay put and may be worked on unstretched.
3. Check carefully the affinity of dye to fabric using the chart, page 19. Thickened Procion fiber-reactive dye on cotton velvet or velveteen is a lush and highly effective combination. Paste paints such as oil-base block printing ink or Versatex thinned to brushing consistency work well on a wide variety of fabrics.
4. Prepare dye paste or paste paint. Experiment for best consistency.
5. Apply colors one at a time to prescribed areas or lines, allowing each to dry before applying the next unless a bleeding or "wet on wet" appearance is desired.
6. Allow the fabric to dry thoroughly.
7. Set or fix by appropriate means where required.

Fiber-reactive dye thickened with sodium alginate is being brushed on stretched cotton fabric. Note the short stiff bristle brush and the pencil guidelines, which have been slightly over-emphasized for the photograph.

SPECIAL EFFECTS

1. Soft and crisp edges may be combined in the same composition by applying dilute dye on slightly damp fabric, allowing it to dry thoroughly, and applying a thicker more stable dye paste.
2. A slightly blurred effect will occur if a wash or dilute dye is laid over a thicker dye paste applied previously.
3. Brush dyeing works well in combination with other processes such as spraying, printing, or even resist dyeing.

Direct Dyeing with Plastic Squeeze Bottle

Direct dyeing with a plastic squeeze bottle is a simple, efficient, and expressive method of drawing on fabric akin to the ceramic decorating process of slip trailing. Fabric artists with a strong interest in drawing and painting will find this technique especially appealing and expressive.

METHOD

Simply fill a squeeze bottle or ear syringe with thickened dye paste, draw directly on the fabric, allow it to dry, fix the dye, and finally wash and press the fabric. For variety of line quality, try changing the pressure on the bottle or the speed at which it is moved.

Direct Dyeing with House Painting Appliances

A trip to your local hardware or paint store will reveal a varied range of painters' brushlike appliances and rollers. Because the viscosity of dye pastes and paste paints is similar to that of house paint, most of these tools can be used without modification. In general they are simple to use, flexible in application, easy to clean, and modest in price. Materials and methods are very similar to those for brush-dyed fabrics, above.

Above left: *Thickened dye is being applied to fabric from a plastic squeeze bottle. This series of small studies combines some brush dyed areas and demonstrates a range of textures and linear qualities.*

Left: *House painters' brushlike appliances and rollers are shown with their characteristic lines, in this case Inko prepared vat dye on cotton muslin. Note that the polyfoam "brush," second from left, has been altered with sharp utility scissors to produce multiple lines.*

Applying Color with Dye Crayons

Very efficient dye crayons are now available for the direct application of color to fabric. They are inexpensive, portable, surprisingly colorfast, and easy to use. They are of course ideal for children, but artists of any age can achieve striking results.

MATERIALS

Fabric—Any fabric without a heavy nap that will withstand ironing at about a "cotton" setting is satisfactory. Knits are suitable, but fabrics with soil-release finishes are not. White or light colors allow maximum color flexibility.

Dye crayons—We recommend Somiel Dye Pastels by Pentel which come in a good color range and include black, white, and gray.

Iron—For setting the color.

METHOD

1. Guidelines may be applied to the fabric if desired with a soft pencil or one of the crayons themselves.
2. Apply color where desired in the same way that crayons are applied to paper. The full range of coloring effects is possible.
3. When the piece is complete, iron it slowly and carefully with a hot iron set on a "cotton" setting. Colors will wash out in hot, soapy water unless they are heat set, so mistakes may be corrected if they occur before ironing.
4. Finished heat-set fabrics may be hand- or machine-laundered but should not be dry-cleaned.

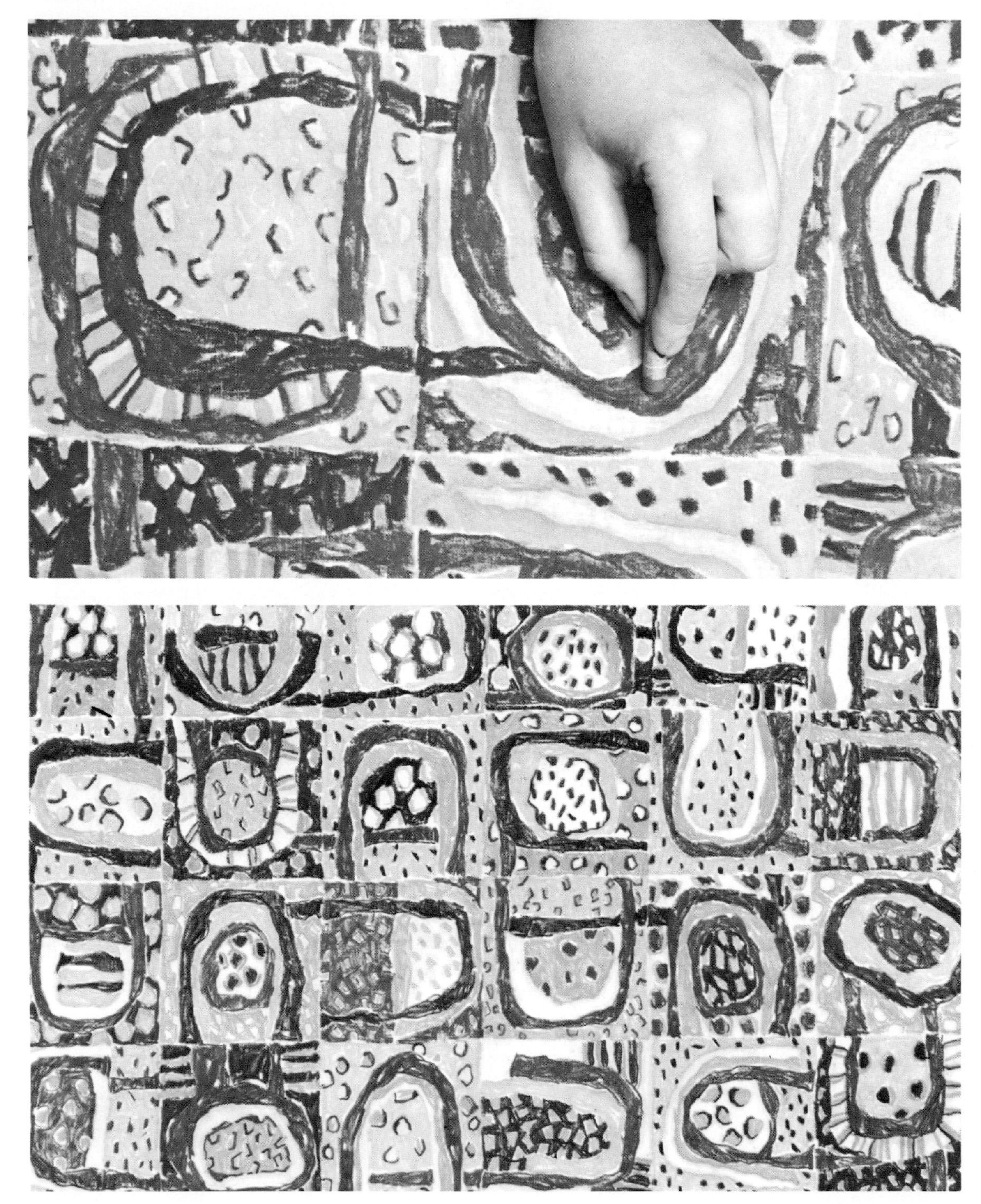

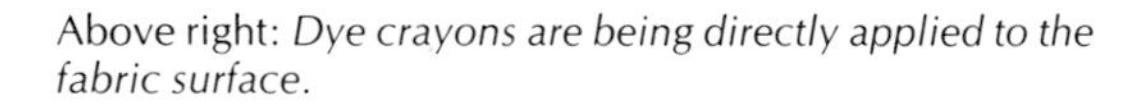

Above right: *Dye crayons are being directly applied to the fabric surface.*

Right: *Finished dye crayon composition on cotton, ca. 24″ x 36″(61 x 91.5 cm).*

Jennifer F. Lew. Black laundry marking pen on white cotton size, ca. 18"x 20"(46 x 51 cm).

Applying Color with Waterproof Markers

Colored waterproof felt-tip pens, currently available in hundreds of colors including neutrals and black, have long been in use for paper. Some are being produced especially for fabric decoration. They are at their best on pile surfaces such as velvet and waleless corduroy but exhibit excellent color quality on cotton and linen flat weave fabric as well. They seem to be prone to sun fading and poor washfastness in strong detergent solutions. However, excellent results have been achieved by warm water washing in a detergent-free soap solution.

Direct Dyeing with an Airbrush

For many years the airbrush has been considered the exclusive property of the commercial illustrator, who uses it for special rendering effects including highlights, reflections, and volume illusions. Actually it is a very versatile tool with a wide range of capabilities recently adapted to the crafts, notably ceramics and fabric design. The fabric designer uses the airbrush principally for applying dyes or paints where soft or graded effects are desired and occasionally for producing lines or textures. In this chapter we are concerned with the direct use of the tool for drawing and painting on fabric but you may wish to refer to page 133 where the airbrush is used with various combinations of masks and stencils. In both chapters, however, we are only introducing the tool on a basic level, and those with specialized interests should seek first-hand instruction or refer to the bibliography for additional sources of information.

MATERIALS

Fabric—Preferably with some nap for improved dye absorption, or better still, a pile fabric. The fiber content as always must have an affinity for the dye to be sprayed.

Dye—Should be of a relatively thin or watery consistency, intended for application at room temperature, and compatible with the selected fabric. Thorough mixing is very important.

Airbrush outfit—Consisting of the following:

1. Air supply, which may be an air compressor, carbon-dioxide tanks with appropriate valves, or canned propellant. The latter is suitable only for small jobs.
2. Air hose, approximately 6 to 8 feet in length with appropriate connecting devices at both ends.
3. Airbrush, preferably a top-quality, double-action brush with which it is possible to control both the volume of color and the force of air. The second choice is a single-action brush in which only the volume of color can be regulated. In either case be certain that it is fitted with a color jar rather than a small color "cone" used by illustrators.
4. Extra color jars.
5. Appropriate solvent for immediate clean up of the airbrush.

METHOD

1. Attach fabric to be sprayed to a frame or convenient backing surface such as cardboard or particle board with pins, tacks, or tape. Guidelines may be indicated if desired.
2. Attach air hose to the airbrush and to the air source. This may require gentle pressure from a small wrench after determining that the threads are properly aligned.
3. Fill color jar about two-thirds full with dye or pigment. Be certain that the product you are using has been ground ultra fine, is thoroughly dissolved, and is a "watery" liquid.
4. Attach color intake tube and color jar to the airbrush.
5. Adjust brush for size of line and density of spray. The procedure may vary according to the manufacturer's instructions. Clockwise or right turns however generally increase the size and coarseness of a line. Counterclockwise or left turns usually result in thinner diameter and more finely textured lines.
6. Regulate air pressure to a setting between 25 and 30 pounds.
7. Hold airbrush as you might hold a pen but with your index finger resting gently on the front double-action lever and the hose as much out of the way as possible.
8. Airbrushing is accomplished by the coordinated pressure of the index finger and movement of the hand. Pushing down on the lever increases the flow of air, and pulling back on the lever increases the flow of color. Movement of the hand and of course the airbrush determines the configuration and diameter of the line. At the end of the stroke try to release the double-action lever as evenly as possible, but *never* allow it to snap forward.
9. Clean airbrush immediately after use. Most airbrush problems result from delayed or inept cleaning. First, clean color jar by filling it with clean water or solvent that is room temperature or lukewarm but *not* hot. Spray liquid through brush until clean, then alternately spray and force bubbles back into clean color jar. This is accomplished by pulling back on the lever while holding a finger over the opening of the air regulator. Dry inside by allowing air only to pass through the airbrush.

Correct hand position for airbrush painting.

Various effects that may be achieved by airbrushing dye directly on fabric.

Canning

Canning involves moving a bottomless cylinder or vessel of dye paste over the surface of the fabric and may perhaps best be described as "dye drawing." The process is just that simple, but practice and a degree of dexterity are the best assurances of success. Like most of the direct dye techniques, canning may be made simple or elaborate depending on the designer's wish. There is probably no more efficient way of dyeing vertically striped fabric in the classroom or limited production studio.

MATERIALS

Assorted tin cans with both ends removed and no sharp edges—They may be round cylinders, carefully bent ovals, or triangles. Sardine, paté, and ham cans will also work well. The entire process may be scaled down by using very small cans such as plastic 35 mm film cans with the solid end removed. Any small tube may be adapted so long as the bottom edge is level and smooth.
Dye paste—Must be mixed to the consistency of pancake batter, so it spreads easily but does not run. A smooth or lightweight fabric requires a slightly thicker dye paste, while a nappy or pile surface will best accept a somewhat thinner or more liquid dye mixture.
Larger measuring cup with spouted lip—Or batter bowl with spout; a two-cup capacity Pyrex or plastic measuring cup works well.
Stirring spoons
A good supply of tagboard
Scissors
Lightly padded printing surface—A screen printing table is ideal.
Masking tape
Appropriate solvents and clean-up supplies

METHOD

1. Prepare the working surface. A large smooth table covered first with a blanket and then with vinyl fabric or oilcloth will serve the purpose.
2. Smooth the fabric out on the work table and tape it in place as tautly as possible.
3. Place the can on a square of tagboard cut about an inch larger than the can. Hold it down firmly with one hand, while pouring the required quantity of dye paste into the can from the spouted vessel with the other hand.
4. Slip one hand gently under the tagboard while the other hand maintains enough pressure to avoid dye leaking around the lower edges of the can. This step will take a bit of practice.
5. Place the tagboard, can, and dye combination at the desired starting point on the stretched fabric or slightly overlapping its taped edge.
6. Slowly, and with gentle pressure, move the can on the fabric surface, literally "drawing" with the can. If the fabric puckers slightly as the can is drawn over its surface, the can pressure is too great or the fabric is not stretched evenly. If the dye paste is too liquid, the can must be moved quickly. Move it more slowly if it is too thick.
7. When a stopping point is reached, the can must be removed. If the can happens to be empty simply pick it up, taking care not to drip dye. If dye still remains in the can, hold a square of tagboard at the stopping point with one hand and "ride" the can onto it with the other hand. Now lift the paper and can as in Step 4. Return excess dye to its container by slowly sliding the can over the edge of the tagboard, allowing it to flow downward.
8. Allow the dye to dry or at least set up a bit and repeat Steps 3 through 7 with additional colors and/or cans of different diameters until the composition is complete.
9. Allow fabric to dry, set the dye, wash out, and press.

SPECIAL EFFECTS

1. Lines of irregular width result from rotating oval or rectangular cans.
2. Securely applied lines or shapes of masking tape, press-apply paper, or contact paper may be used to resist dye canned gently over them. Isolated shapes are challenging but easy to make. Simply move the can of dye over a well-masked edge onto the fabric and return it to the same spot before sliding tagboard square under it.

Top: *Three different sizes of cylindrical cans were used for this composition. The curved endings of the horizontal lines and the vertical center wedge shape were protected with masking tape.*

Bottom: *The three dark lines were made with an oval can and the triangles were made with a three-cornered can.*

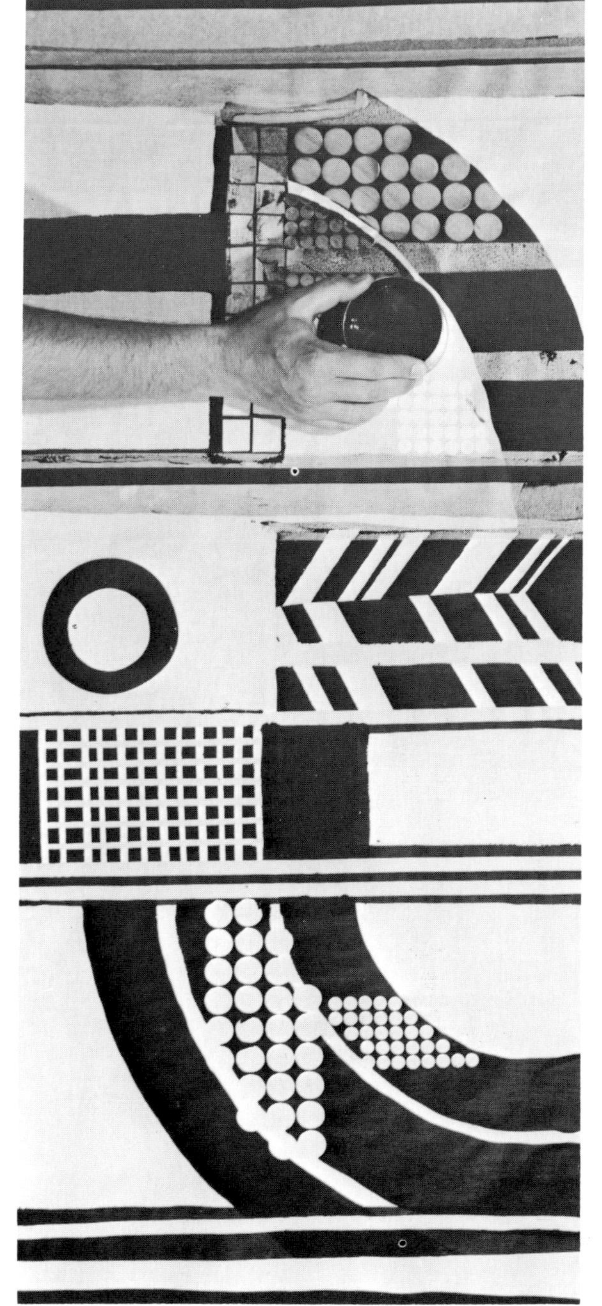

Masking tape, press-apply pricetag dots, and contact paper are being used to preserve the original fabric from the canned dye. Resist materials have been removed from the bottom section to show their respective effects.

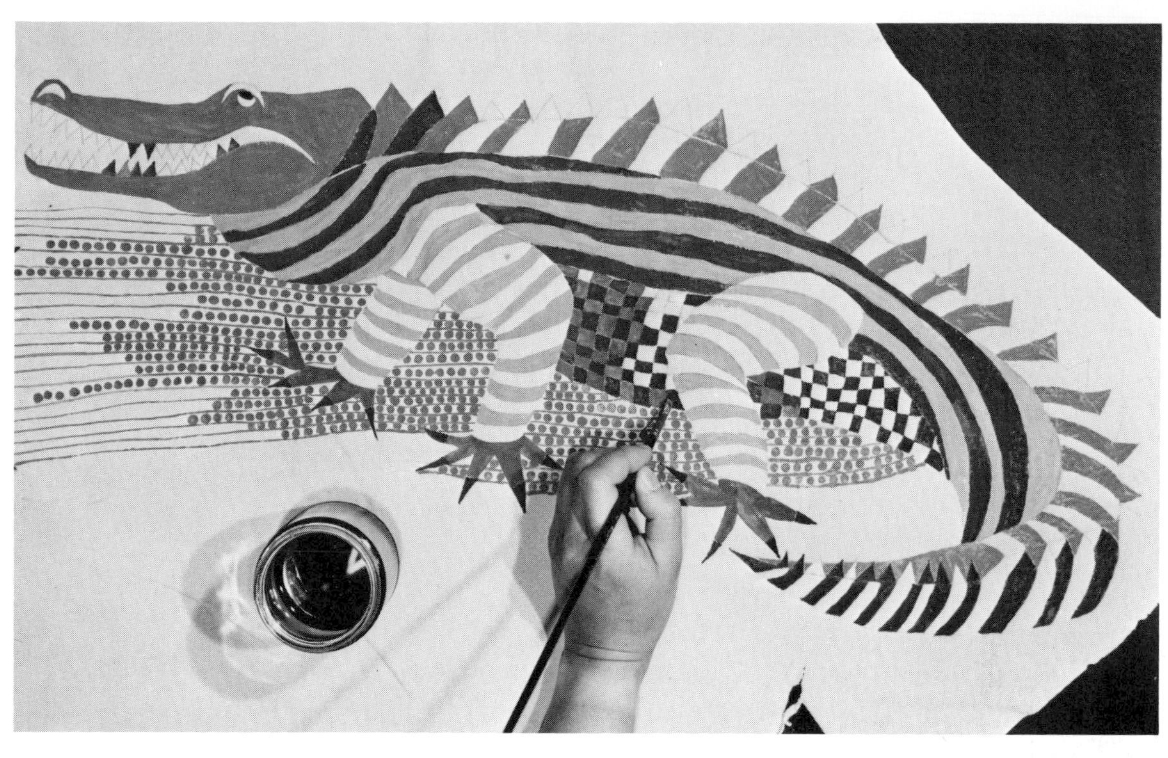

Semi-opaque leather dye is being applied with brush to pigskin.

Direct Color Application on Leather

There are two basic types of coloring products for leather: transparent stains or dyes and opaque paints. Both are readily available from leather shops, shoe repair shops, and large crafts materials supply houses. The transparent products tend to spread very rapidly and are generally used with a resist to keep them in controlled areas as described on page 79. Opaque products are best suited to freehand brush painting. They behave very much like acrylic artists' paint in that they are fully intermixable and they tend to remain where they are applied, appearing very much the same dry as when they are wet.

METHOD

1. If the leather has a finish coat of wax this should be removed with commercial leather cleaner or one teaspoon of oxalic acid dissolved in one pint of water.
2. Remember that the base color of a leather will affect the transparent dye color in the same way colored paper will affect transparent watercolor.
3. Keep in mind that transparent leather dyes will dry lighter than they appear when applied except for black.
4. Experiment with combinations of transparent dyes and opaque pigments. First apply the transparent dyes with their felt applicators for bold fluid lines and areas, and later apply opaque leather paints for crisp outlines or detail treatments.
5. Consult a book on leather techniques for assistance with embossing, forming, sewing, or texturing leather that may then be hand-colored.
6. Pay careful attention to labels, especially on the transparent products, since many are toxic and/or flammable.
7. Transparent-finish coating products such as clear shoe polish or a commercial leather conditioner may be applied to protect your work.

Examples of Direct Dyeing

Painted fabric, Senufo, Ivory Coast, Africa. Handspun and handwoven cotton, 24″ x 39″ (61 x 99 cm). Private collection, Seattle, Washington.

Painted fabric, Senufo, Ivory Coast, Africa. Handspun and handwoven cotton, 12″ x 18″ (30.5 x 46 cm). Collection of Ronald Childers, Langley, Washington.

Tapa, painted palm bark. Uyaku or Waningela, Tufi Subdistrict, Papua, New Guinea. Collection of Richard M. Proctor, Langley, Washington.

Man's shirt, shown flat, Mali. Bokolanfini (mud cloth), 28″ x 59″ (71 x 150 cm). Courtesy of Leslie Grace Hart, Folk Art Gallery, Seattle, Washington.

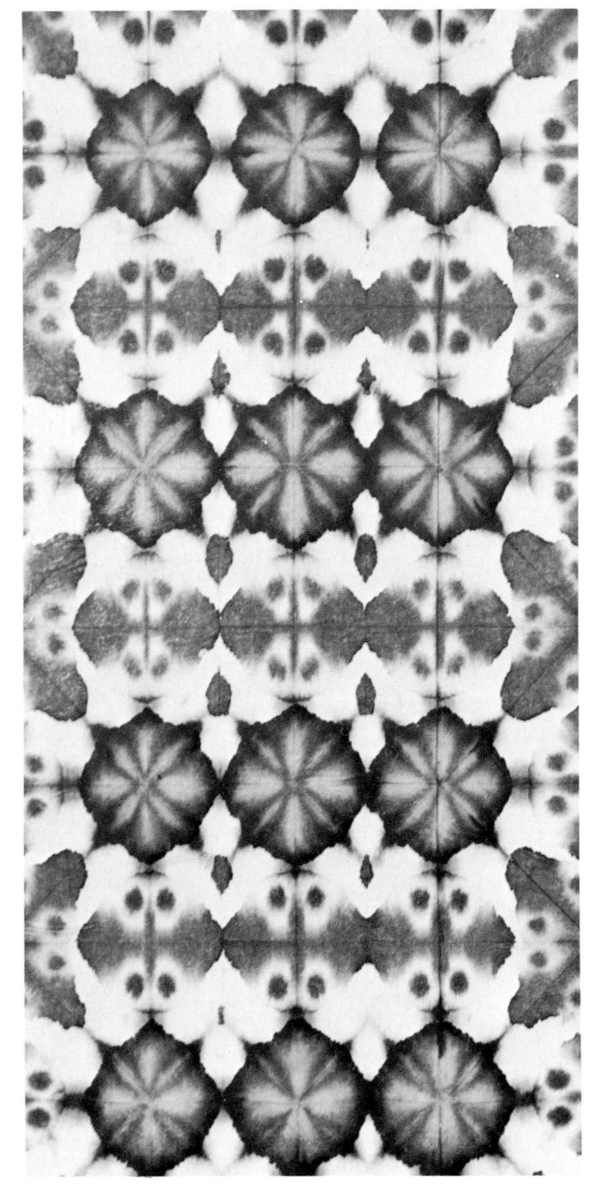

Richard M. Proctor. Fold dyed papers produced by the dipping process. Dye, ink, and food color on silkspan paper, H. ca. 30"(77 cm).

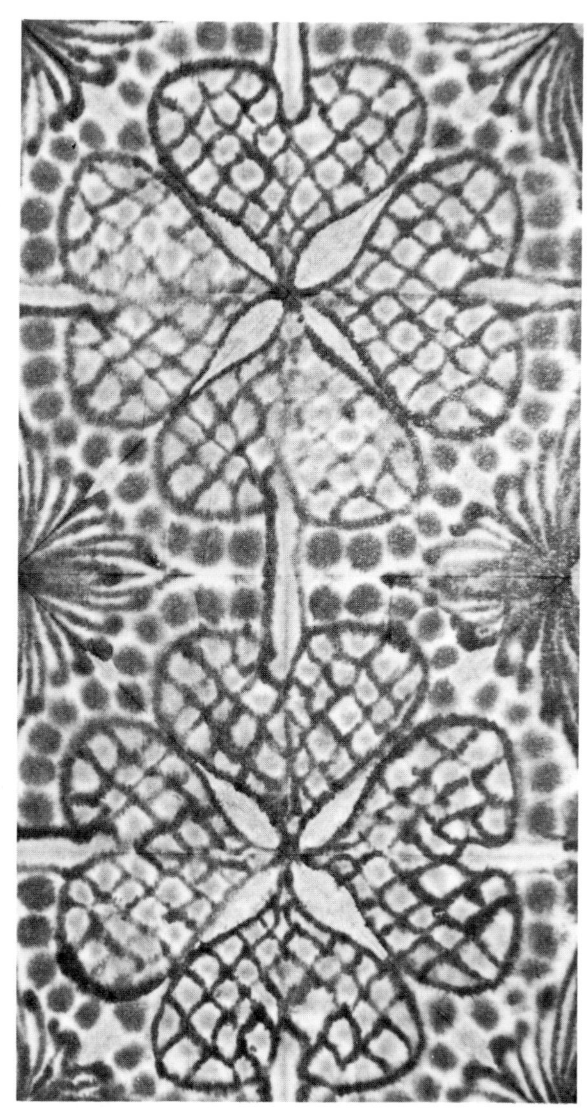

Jennifer F. Lew. Fold dyed papers produced by the brushing process. Dye, ink, and food color on silkspan paper, H. ca. 30"(77 cm).

Left: *Jennifer F. Lew.* Crests. *Hand-painted Versatex textile paint on cotton, ca. 48" x 60" (91 x 152 cm). Detail shown above.*

Tapa, decorative ending (detail). Walls or Fortuna Island. Courtesy of the Lowie Museum of Anthropology, University of California, Berkeley.

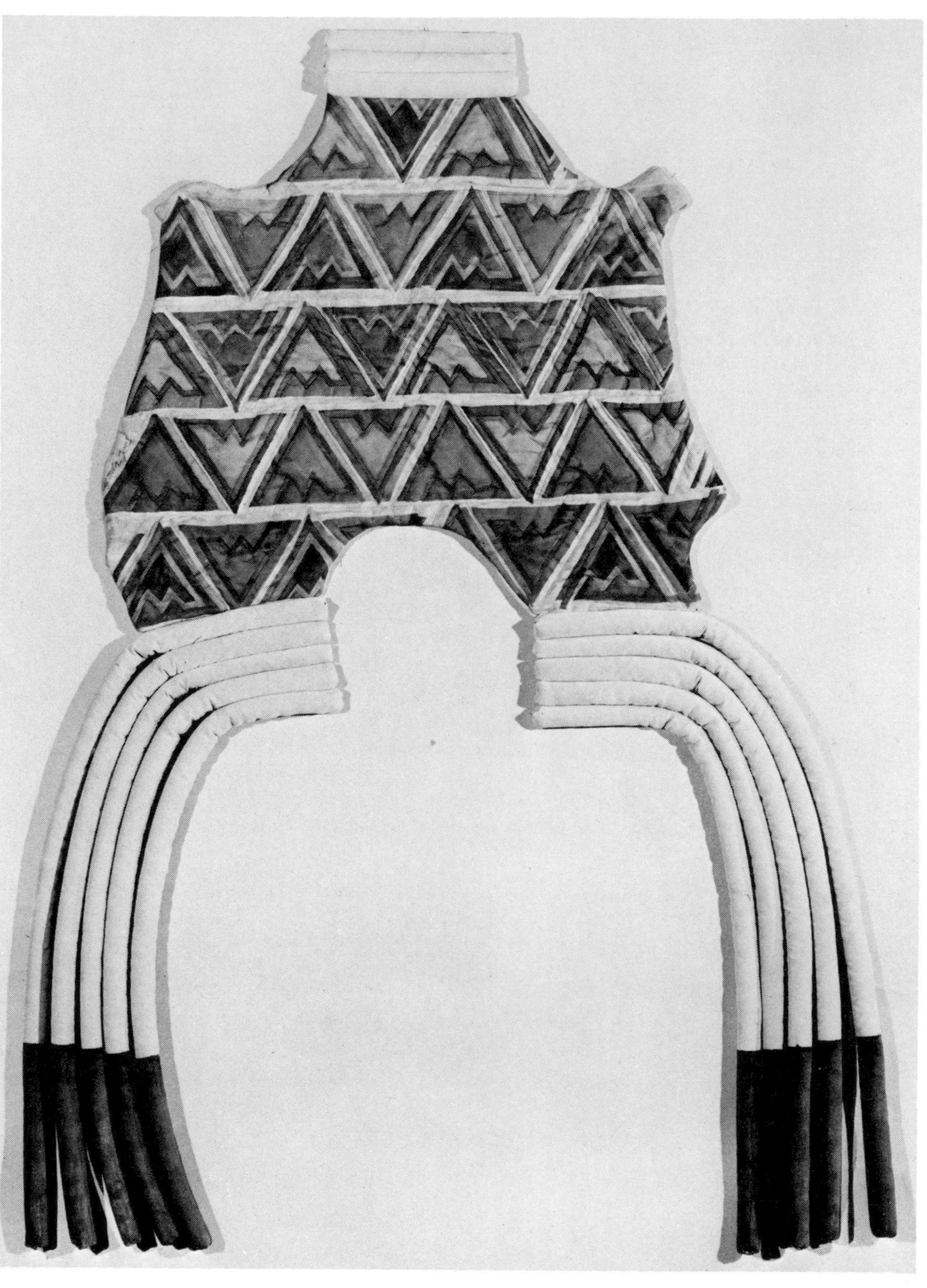

Pamela Pearce. Four Mile Ruin, *1976. Dye painted lambskin suede with machine quilting, 36" x 72" (91.5 x 183 cm).*

5. Liquid Resists

If a substance is to be used as a liquid resist, it must be able to be applied in liquid or paste form, yet must dry to a stable, nonabsorbent solid that will resist dye. It should also be easy to remove from the fabric once its function as a resist is complete. Liquid resists are several, the best known being melted wax and starch paste. Both are Asian in presumed origin, with the melted wax being used for batik and its variants and the paste for stencil printing and direct application. In West Africa the Yoruba of Nigeria have for years compounded a semiliquid resist from cassava for use with indigo dye on cotton.

Batik is probably the best known and most frequently practiced of the liquid resist processes. The work *batik* originated in Java (Indonesia) and roughly translates to "wax writing." This term describes the process admirably, since it depends upon the successive applications of wax lines or masses and liquid dye. In Europe, the United Kingdom, and North America, there has been since the early 1960s an acceleration of interest in batik as a contemporary craft medium. This is due in large measure to the inherent flexibility of the process and the unique characteristics of the wax-resisted fabric. There is a highly appealing quality in the crackle effects and flowing waxed edges produced by batik.

Sarong (detail of Kain pandjang type). Batik with moth and leaf motif, 19th century, Java, Indonesia, ca. 99" x 42" (251 x 107 cm). Eugene Fuller Memorial Collection. Courtesy of Seattle Art Museum.

Tools for Liquid Resist Application

Adjustable frame—Primarily used for batik but applicable to starch paste resist work and direct dye application. All four parts are of clear fir 1 by 2 inch stock with 1 by 1 inch notches removed at regular intervals to allow for snug interlocking. Such a frame could vary considerably in size but must be of relatively soft wood for easy insertion and removal of pushpins or tacks. Acceptable substitutes are artists' stretcher bars, picture frames, or even a sturdy box-top.

Tools for liquid resist application.

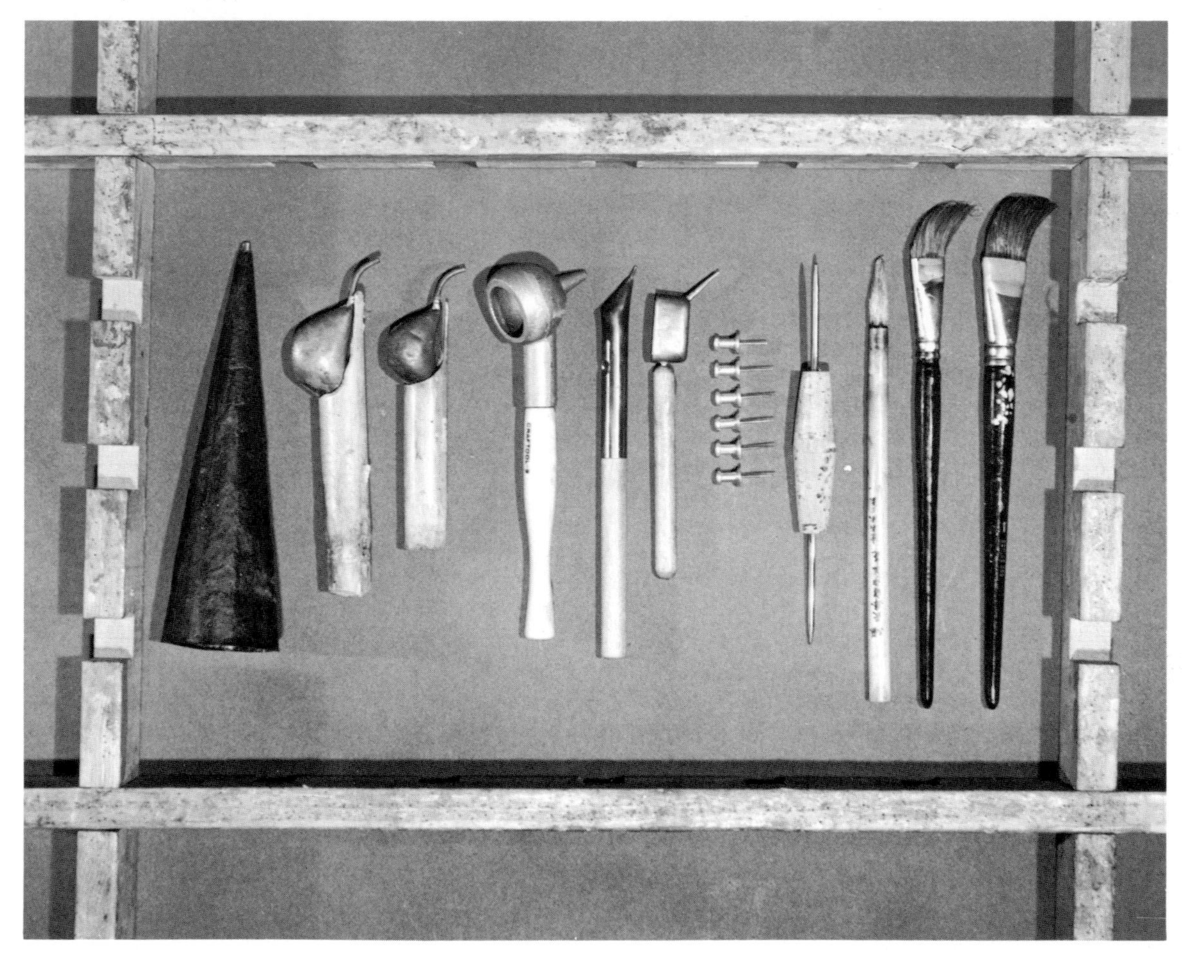

Japanese paste tube with metal tips—Used to apply starch resist paste. Sources are listed in Appendix 2. A plastic squeeze bottle or a pastry decorating tube or cone would be logical substitutes.

Tjantings—These tools are designed to produce lines of melted wax on fabric paper or leather. In all cases the vessel and spout are of metal and the handles are of wood. They include Indonesian, American-made cast aluminum available in several sizes, and excellent Japanese tjantings available in three sizes and imported by Aiko's.

Pushpins—Ideal for attaching fabric to the frame. Size #4 has a long point and is most useful but #3 is more readily available and will suffice. Thumbtacks may be substituted but are difficult to remove and are more likely to cause runs in lightweight fabrics such as China silk.

Engraving tool—Convenient for sgraffito or scratching into waxed fabric. A blunt needle, sharp stick, fine crochet hook or even a spent ballpoint pen may be substituted.

Brushes for applying melted wax—They should be of hair as most synthetic bristles melt or contort at high temperatures. Wax may be removed from brushes with mineral spirits, however, it would be unwise to subject large or costly brushes to hot wax if they are to later be used for painting. The Japanese ox hair brush with bamboo handle is an excellent choice. The tip will make fine lines while the body of the brush will make broad lines or areas. The best quality Japanese brushes have the hairs set in heat- and chemical-resistant plastic rather than directly into the bamboo. Any similar round brush may be substituted. Watercolor brushes of hair that are designed for laying in washes or for lettering may also be used. Narrow wax lines may be made with the edges, and large areas may be filled in efficiently with the broad side.

Other useful equipment not shown in the illustration are listed below. Some of these items are necessary, while others are optional.

Appliance for melting wax—A small electric deep fat fryer or electric fry pan with accurate temperature control is ideal. A double boiler will suffice. For safety reasons, wax must not be heated over an uncontrolled heat source.

Double boiler—Used to cook starch resist paste and sometimes to melt wax.

Vegetable steamer—For preparing starch resist paste. May be commercial or improvised.

Heat source for double boiler or steamer

Rubber gloves for protection

Measuring cups and spoons—Stainless steel is preferred.

Kitchen timer—(Optional).

Iron

Newspaper and clean newsprint for removing wax

Plastic dyebath containers—A large flat pan sold by building material dealers as a "crete mixer" is best, but a large dishpan or plastic wastebasket may be substituted.

Clothesline or drying racks

Electric fan or hairdryer—(Optional) to speed drying of heavy fabrics.

Techniques for Liquid Resist Dyeing

SGRAFFITO

In the sgraffito process, wax-covered fabric is scratched with a sharp tool to expose fine lines of the base fabric. When this scratched fabric is placed in a dye solution, a small amount of color penetrates the exposed areas. This may happen within an hour or may take several days. The effect of the finished work is very similar to an etching. Sgraffito works well in combination with other dye processes, especially batik.

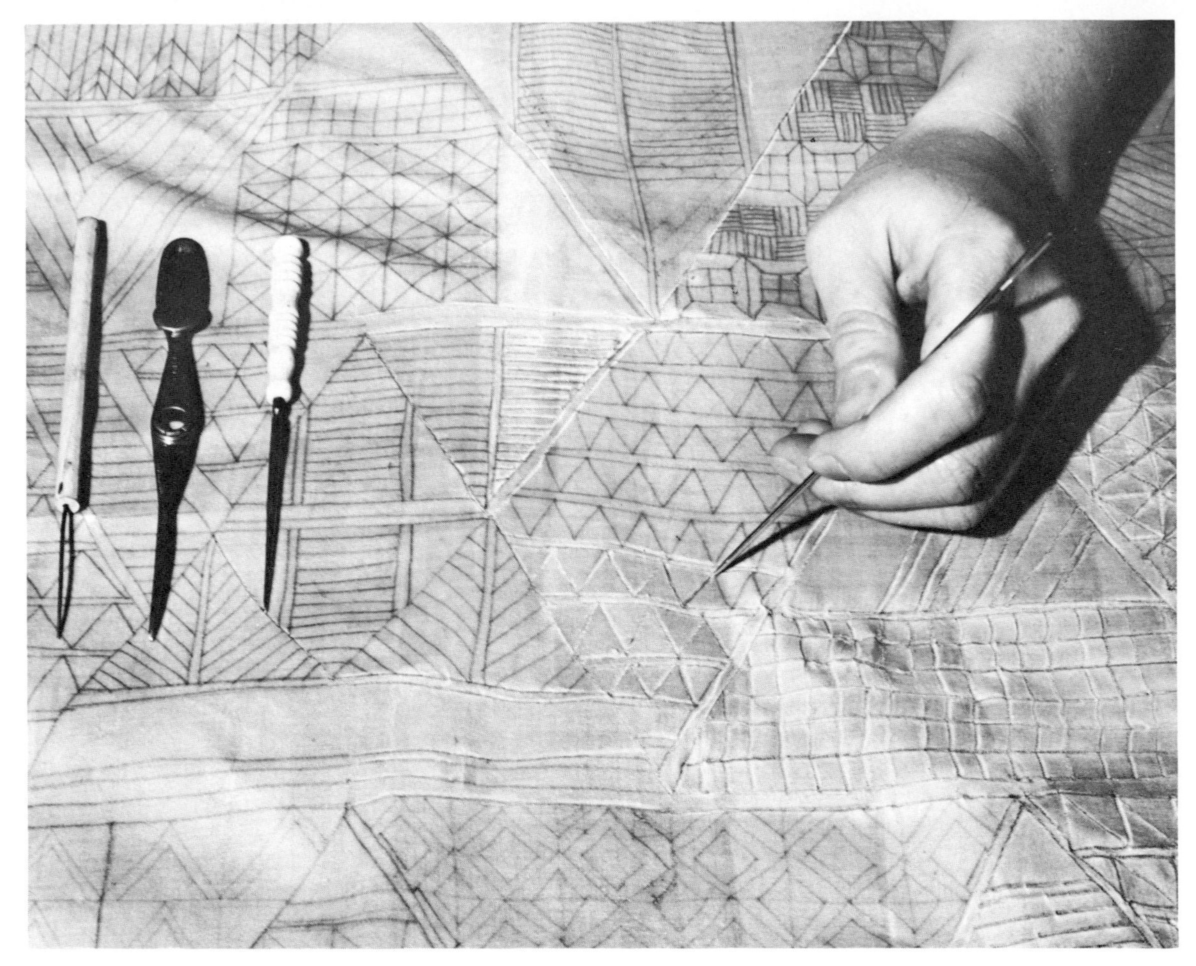

Waxed fabric is being scratched with a semi-blunt needle in preparation for dyeing in the sgraffito process.

MATERIALS

Fabric—Best results are to be had with even-grained, finely woven fabric in white or a light value.
Assorted scratching tools—They should be well pointed but not cutting sharp. Tapestry needles, dissecting needles, a scissor point, a compass tip, or similar tool will do.
Dye—Must be a cold water type that is compatible with the fabric selected. Consult the dye chart on pp. 28–29 if you are in doubt.
Pan of melted wax—Equal parts of beeswax and paraffin make an excellent mixture.
Brush for wax—Should be of natural hair, nylon brushes melt in hot wax.
Wooden frame
Pencil, HB or softer
Absorbent paper—Newsprint is ideal.
Iron

METHOD

1. Wash and press the fabric.
2. Trace the design or a few guidelines on the fabric with a soft pencil.
3. Apply the wax to the fabric by either of the following methods:
   a. If fabric is small enough it may be dipped in the pan of wax. Sew a piece of string or strong thread in two adjacent corners of the fabric, hold onto them, dip the fabric in wax, and lift it out. A light tension on the strings will keep the fabric in shape while extra wax drips back into the pan.
   b. Attach the fabric to a frame so that surface tension is relatively even. Dip a brush in the melted wax and apply it to the fabric. Be certain that the wax penetrates well. It should appear translucent when backlit and have a distinct "grease spot" effect. If wax on the fabric seems milky and opaque, the chances are that it is not really penetrating so check the back of the fabric from time to time. Let the strokes overlap slightly and brush in directions that relate to the design. The latter is suggested because if or when the wax breaks down it is best to have the resulting subtle tone of dye related to the composition rather than be arbitrary.
4. Remove the waxed fabric from the frame and place it on a clean, paper-covered work surface.
5. Scratch the top surface of the waxed fabric. Experiment with pressure and perhaps make a small trial sampler of lines and textures. Be careful not to press hard enough to cut into the fabric.
6. Prepare dye solution according to instructions and pour into large flat pan.
7. Enter fabric into dye and weight it down with two or more small stones or other convenient nonporous weights.

Jennifer F. Lew. A finished sample of sgraffito, acid dye on silk, ca. 18″x 24″(46 x 61 cm). Private collection, Seattle, Washington.

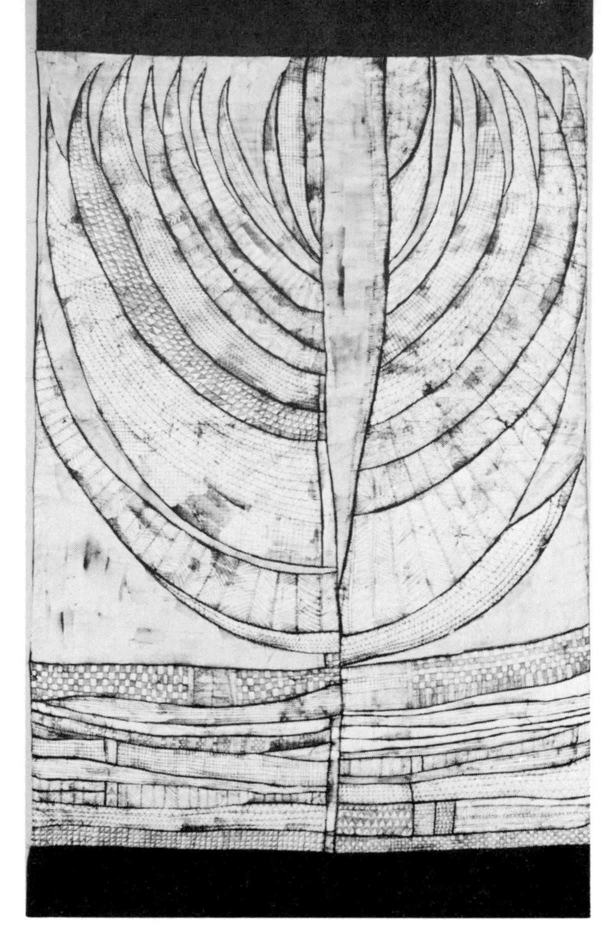

Jennifer F. Lew. Untitled composition. Sgraffito technique with acid and basic dyes on silk shantung, 46″x 84″(117 x 213 cm). Collection of Stock Exchange, Seattle, Washington.

8. After an hour or two in the dye, the piece may be removed and rinsed. Some color should appear in the scratched lines but it probably won't be too dark yet. Return it to the dye for as long as desired. Some tones as well as lines will probably appear if the waxed fabric is dyed overnight or for several days.
9. When the desired result is achieved, rinse well, allow to dry, and place between sheets of absorbent paper such as newsprint and press with a hot iron. Beware of newspapers since printers' ink may be transferred to the fabric.
10. Dry clean the fabric to removed any remaining wax.

SPECIAL EFFECTS

Combine sgraffito with conventional batik, or first dye the cloth with any of the direct dye processes from the previous chapter. The same processes can be used after the sgraffito piece is dry-cleaned. For a multicolor line effect, do the following series of steps: (1) wax fabric; (2) scratch; (3) dye color A; (4) wax over color A lines; (5) scratch again; (6) dye color B; (7) wax over color B lines; (8) scratch once more; (9) dye color C; (10) wax over color C lines; (11) scratch again; (12) dye and continue the process as desired.

BATIK

Applying Melted Wax Resists

Melted wax is certainly the most important liquid resist, with the possible exception of the various so-called pastes. The chart below gives the attributes of each of the three basic types of wax in common use.

Wax Mixtures. During the dye segment of the batik process, waxed fabric is moved about in cool or room-temperature liquid. At this point the wax has a natural tendency to crack, producing a characteristic appearance closely associated with batik. Some cracking is bound to occur, but too much can be distracting and seem contrived. To a large extent the amount of crackle can be controlled by the composition of the resist mixture. The more beeswax or microcrystalline

	Melting pt.	*Flash pt.*	*Characteristic*	*Relative cost*	*Availability*
Beeswax	120°F	400°F	soft, pliable, tenacious, not likely to crack	medium to high	good
Paraffin	90°F	450°F	hárd brittle, very likely to crack	low	good
Microcrystalline	176°F	540°F	soft, similar to beeswax	low	fair

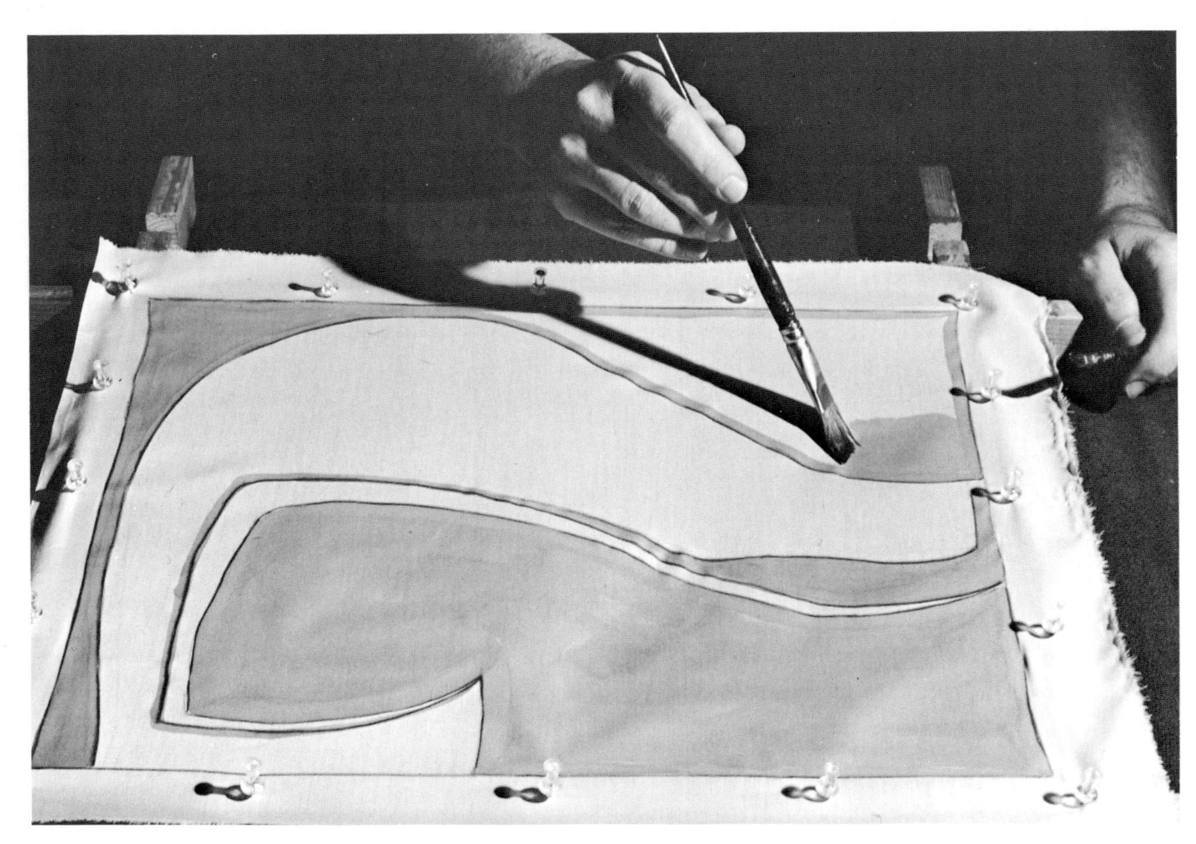

Wax outlines are made with a small brush but large areas are brushed in with a large flat brush.

mobilwax #2305 there is in the recipe, the fewer cracks and the more pliable the work will be. The more paraffin, the more crackling will occur and the more brittle the work will be. A good all-purpose mixture is one-half beeswax and one-half paraffin. Products labeled batik wax are premixed, but we favor the "from scratch" approach.

Occasionally the wax may become fouled with dust, dirt, or a few fugitive brush hairs. If this happens melt the contaminated wax and strain it through two or three layers of cheesecloth into a clean, dry milk carton. When it has solidified, peel the paper carton away.

Melting Wax. From a safety standpoint, melting wax in a double boiler is best. Unfortunately, however, it never gets quite hot enough to penetrate medium or heavyweight fabric. By far the best solution is an electric deep fat fryer or electric fry pan with an accurate temperature control unit. With such an appliance it is possible to retain an even level of heat at any desired temperature. Specifically not recommended are constant heat sources without thermostatic controls such as hot plates, corn poppers, or hot pots having only off-on options. Open flame is also a very poor choice. All of these are dangerous because as wax approaches its flash point it may ignite, and in addition smoke from overheated wax presents a potential health hazard.

Penetration. Regardless of how it is applied, you must be certain that the wax penetrates well. It should appear translucent when backlit and have a distinct grease spot effect. If wax on the fabric seems milky and opaque it probably isn't penetrating. Check this often if unsure by turning work over and adjusting the wax temperature if needed.

Brush Application. The brush is an excellent tool for applying wax. It should be a natural hair rather than bristle or a synthetic material. Bristle is generally too stiff, and synthetics such as nylon are susceptible to melting in hot wax. For small lines and detail work a round, red sable oil or watercolor brush is best.

In the later case, however, the hairs should not be too long or limp. The technique is quite simple and not unlike painting in that large brushes fill large spaces, and small brushes outline or fill small spaces. A good brush can be used on edge to make outlines or fine lines or it may be brushed flat for broad line work. A common procedure is to outline all areas to be waxed with a small brush then fill them in with a large one. When hot wax touches the fabric it has a tendency to

Tjanting position 1 for large bold movements.

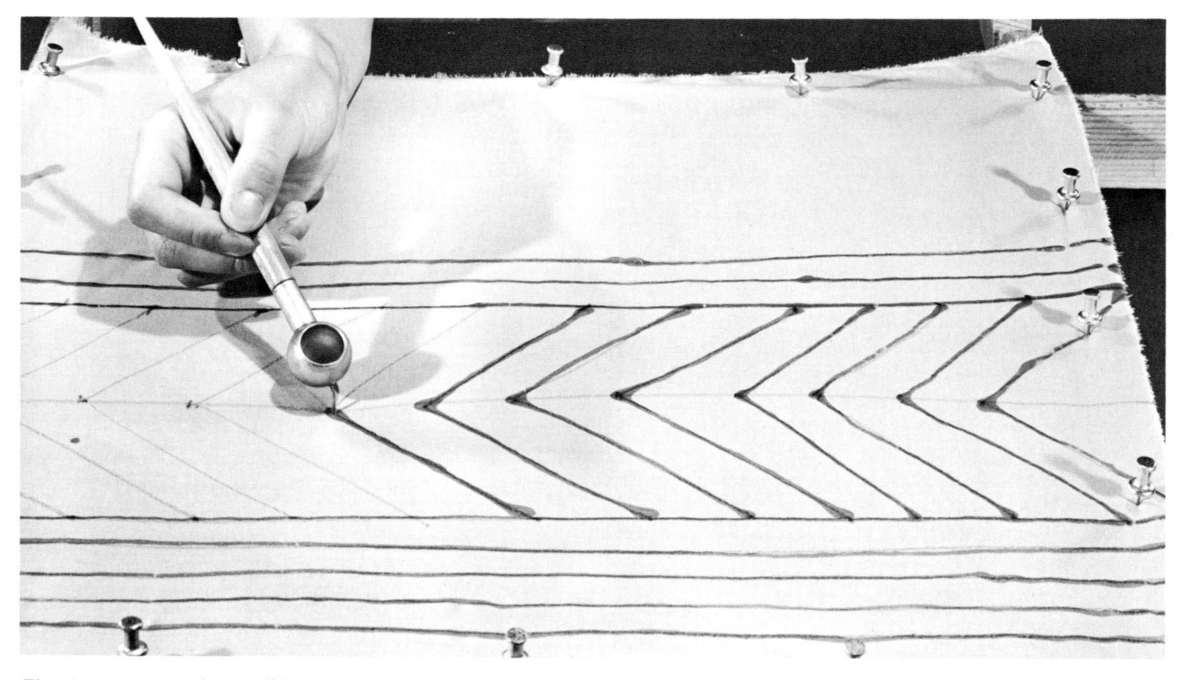

Tjanting position 2 for small fingertip movements.

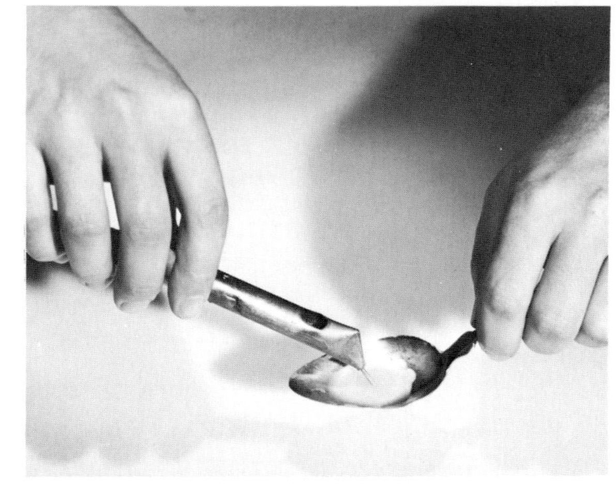

A spoon is used here to catch drips of wax from the tjanting tool until it is in the desired position.

spread as well as penetrate. This means that the brush must be set in motion or a sizable blob or dot will result. Do not leave a brush in melted wax too long or it may become misshapen. Wax may ultimately be cleaned from a brush with mineral spirits.

The Tjanting. The tjanting consists of a reservoir for melted wax and a spout through which it pours onto the fabric. Both are of metal, usually copper or brass due to their superior heat conduction qualities. The handle is most often made of wood. Individual design and spout diameter may vary greatly, and there are even multi-spouted models in use. After a little practice you will find the tjanting a versatile and exciting tool for wax drawing. First, dip the metal parts of the tjanting in melted wax and allow them to remain for a few minutes to heat them up. Next, submerge the reservoir to fill it and lift it from the wax. After the tjanting has been filled with melted wax, it will drip unless a spoon, small cup, or similar receptacle is used to catch the surplus. The spoon is also used as one moves from one section of the fabric to another. It is advisable to practice on scrap fabric until the operation becomes smooth and comfortable. When you are ready to draw on the fabric, use one of the following hand positions:

1. With tjanting held lightly in the fingers opposed by the thumb, it is possible to move quickly and smoothly over the working surface with movement from the shoulder. The tjanting tip barely touches the surface. This position is particularly useful for tjantings with larger diameter tips or with higher wax temperatures.

2. The tjanting is held exactly as one holds a pencil and movements are finger-controlled as in drawing or writing. It is best to use a tjanting with a small-diameter tip or a slightly cooler wax mixture. This method is especially useful where fine detail is desired. If lines become extremely fine, it is a good idea to double-check penetration.

Applying Dye Directly. By far the most common method of applying color to wax-resisted fabric is by submersion or dipping in a dye solution. There are, however, times when it is desirable to apply zones or areas of color more directly. This is especially true of accent colors, although it is possible to complete a wax-resist dyed piece without submersion. A sponge or brush is generally used for applying dye.

Top: *An outline batik in progress.*

Bottom: *A synthetic sponge dipped in acid dye with a rubber-gloved hand is being applied to wax-resisted fabric. Most of the painting appliances shown on p. 59 would be equally suitable.*

INSTRUCTIONS FOR OUTLINE BATIK

In outline batik, wax is applied to fabric or other materials so that there are many areas outlined with continuous borders of wax. Dye is carefully applied with a brush and not allowed to cross over the outline. The general effect is that of a leaded glass window except that the lines are light rather than dark. The finished piece is ironed between absorbent paper for wax removal and dry-cleaned if desired to extract the last traces of wax.

On Paper. For outline batik on paper, follow the general instructions above, substituting transparent watercolor or drawing ink for dye and eliminating the dry-cleaning process. Examples of paper batiks appear at the end of this chapter.

On Leather. Most leather dyes are intended for direct application rather than submersion, and outline batik is a perfect but seldom seen method for decorating this material. The wax is applied with a brush or tjanting tool to tanned but unglazed leather. The leather will darken temporarily but ultimately will return to its original color. Transparent leather dye is next applied with a cotton swab or dye applicator. When the dyeing is complete, the wax is gently scraped off with a plastic scraper. Care should be taken not to scratch the leather surface. Finally, a clean rag saturated in mineral spirits is rubbed over the surface to dissolve any remaining wax. Do not be alarmed when the mineral spirits darkens everything as it will soon evaporate leaving the original hue. The leather batik is now complete and may be given a transparent protective finish if desired.

Modulating Tone

An often misunderstood but fascinating way to achieve soft tonal change and gradation is to apply wax that is on the verge of being too cool in combination with very hot wax. Where the wax is hot its penetration and tenacity are excellent and when dyed, the fabric will retain its original color. Where the wax is cooler or the strokes are longer, penetration and adhesion are less pronounced. When fabric so treated is left in a dark value dye for many hours or even overnight, the cooler wax-coated areas tend to break down and commence absorbing small amounts of dye. This would ordinarily be considered a flaw or mistake, but when done purposefully the effect can be striking.

In the panel showing the eagle carrying a fish, it is relatively easy to pick out the areas that received wax of various temperatures. This is a detail of the batik cross shown in its entirety on page 190. It was waxed with a 3/8 inch watercolor wash brush and is of silk shantung dyed approximately six hours in Fezan batik (acid) dye.

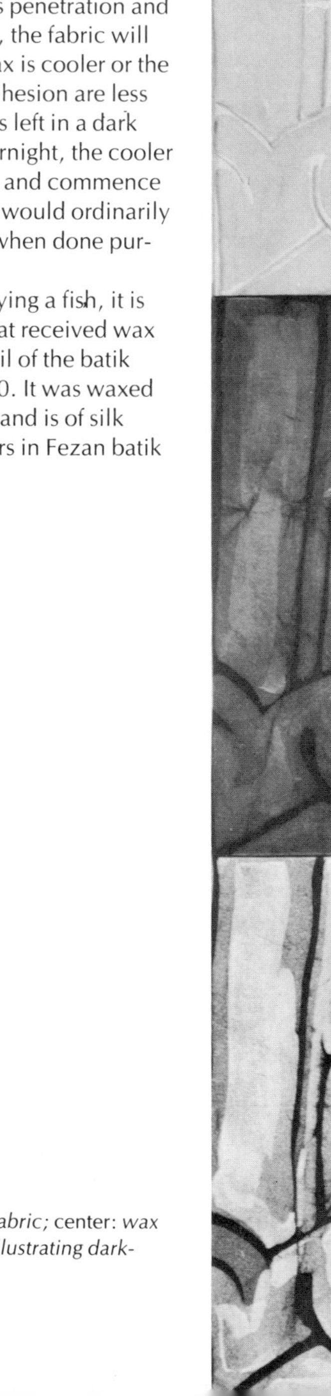

Sample set for a batik panel. Top: *wax on fabric;* center: *wax and dye on fabric;* bottom: *wax removed illustrating dark-light modulation.*

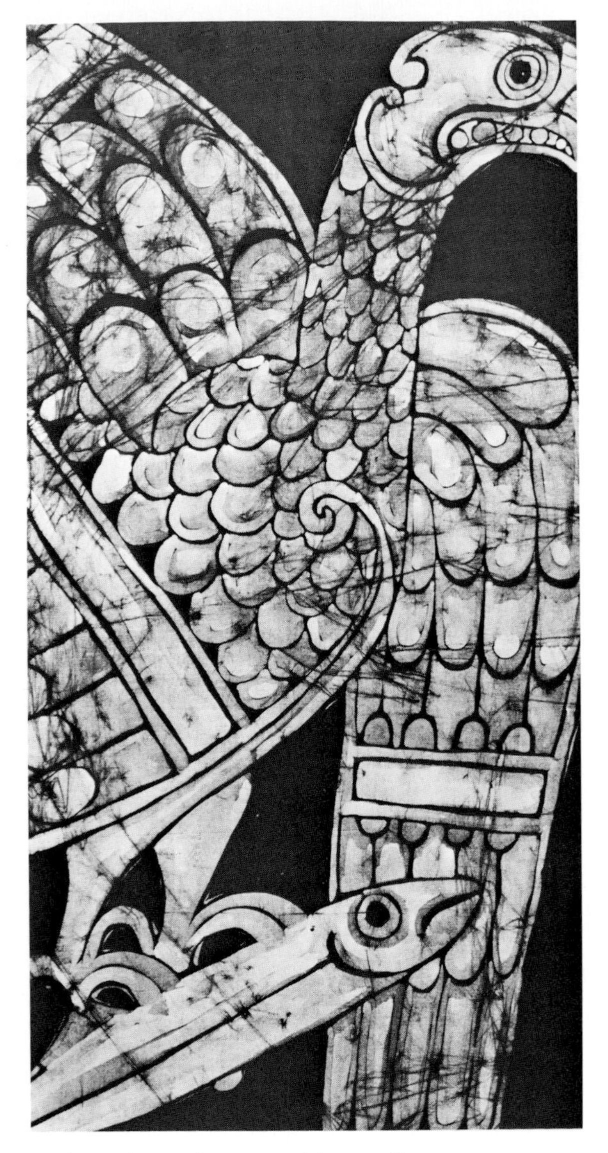

Batik panel, one of seven, acid dye on silk. See entire piece on p. 190.

METHOD

1. Set the wax temperature at a normal setting of about 275° F.
2. Allow the brush to heat up well in the wax.
3. Working quickly, make only short deft strokes in areas or on lines you wish to be the lightest. Return the brush to the wax often to assure that it never cools off very much. Fill areas with short strokes that overlap slightly.
4. For lines that gradate in tone, begin with hot wax and simply allow it to cool on the brush slightly as it is drawn slowly over the fabric.
5. Darker tonal areas can be had by allowing the wax to cool on the brush for a few seconds before applying it to the fabric. The darker tone will occur more readily if the strokes do not overlap each other as they did in Step 3.
6. When the piece is complete, wet it with cool water and enter it in the dye solution which is generally of a dark hue.
7. Allow the fabric to remain in the dye for several hours. The duration will depend on the effect desired, the composition of the wax, the temperature of the wax, the strength of the dye, the class of dye, and the composition of the fabric. To accurately check the effect of the dye, retrieve the batik with a rubber-gloved hand, rinse it in cool water for a few minutes, and blot gently. Now hold the waxed fabric to the light and you can accurately see how much dye has penetrated. Return the batik to the dyebath if necessary.
8. When results are satisfactory, rinse the batik well, blot it dry, iron it between absorbent paper and dry-clean it to remove the last traces of wax. See steps 13 and 14 on page 81.

General Instructions for Batik

This method is for conventional wax-resist batik in which the dye colors move in orderly progression from light to dark or bright to dull.

MATERIALS

Fabric to be dyed—A light color or white fabric of light to medium weight and even grain is best. If the dye is a known factor then be certain that you select a fabric that will accept it. Consult the dye chart on pp. 28–29 if in doubt.

Pencil—Soft lead, HB, or softer.

Frame—The purpose of the frame is to keep the fabric suspended with even tension above the working surface while wax is being applied. Four pieces of 1 by 2 inch wood nailed, screwed, or clamped together will serve the purpose admirably, but there are many alternatives. The top of a sturdy cardboard box or an old picture frame would work. Artists' stretcher bars for stretching canvas come in many interchangeable sizes and disassemble for storage or easy transportation. Special interlocking batik frames are also available. In any case the frame need not be the size of the fabric since the fabric may be shifted and restretched without any problem.

Pushpins—Tacks will do, but pushpins are much easier to use. Have about a dozen on hand.

A container of melted wax—An electric deep fat fryer with half beeswax and half paraffin at approximately 270°F. is suggested, but alternates are listed at the beginning of this chapter.

Brushes, assorted as required—They are described at the beginning of this chapter.

Tjanting tool—(Optional).

Dye and dye equipment—Be certain that the dye has an affinity for the fabric being used. Refer to the dye chart on pp. 28–29 and the dye methods beginning in chapter 3.

Water source

Drying rack or clothesline

Newspaper—For blotting, catching drips, and protecting table surfaces.

Rubber gloves

Absorbent paper such as newsprint—Endrolls from a newspaper publisher are ideal and are usually either free or inexpensive.

Iron

Mineral spirits (paint thinner)—This is an alternative to commercial dry-cleaning for final wax removal, although the latter is recommended.

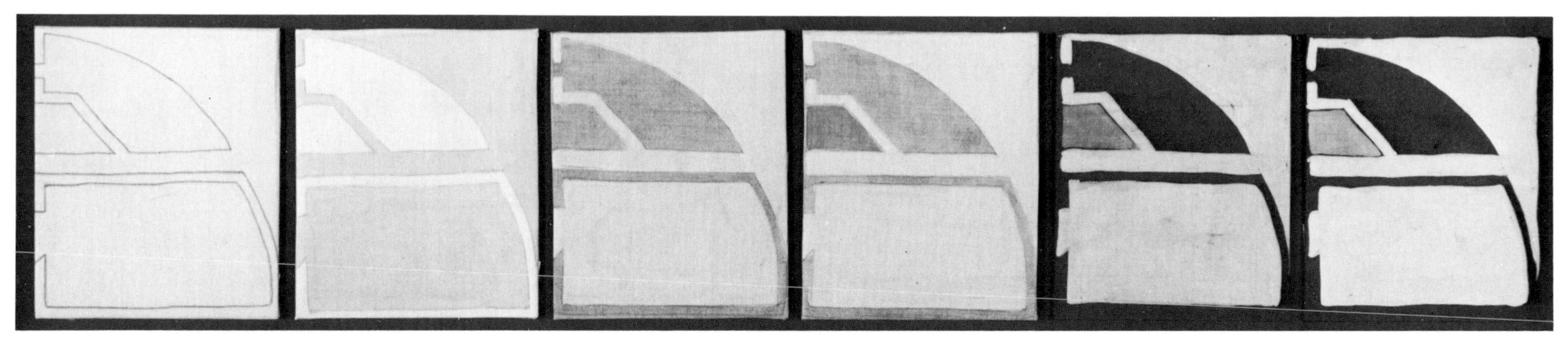

Six steps in the development of the finished batik hanging shown on p. 82. The steps are described in the text.

METHOD

1. Wash and press fabric.
2. Apply the design or cartoon to the fabric with a soft pencil. The lines will eventually disappear. If you have prepared a full-scale cartoon that can be seen through the fabric, simply tape everything in place and trace the lines. If the full-scale cartoon is not easily visible it may be backlit with a light table or with daylight through a convenient window, again securing everything with tape. If you have access to an opaque projector, a small drawing may be enlarged many times its size for tracing in a darkened room. Most opaque projectors accommodate drawings up to nine inches square.
3. Stretch the fabric on the frame by securing it with pushpins. Try for an even tension and keep the weave structure as parallel to the frame as possible. Tacks or pushpins may distort the structure of very light fabrics such as China silk and for this reason you may wish to wrap the frame with scrap fabric and attach the batik fabric to it with very small diameter pins such as silk pins. Fortunately most fabrics recover very well from piercing with regular pushpins.
4. Assuming that the fabric is light in value, wax is now applied to all lines and spaces that are to remain lightest in the final piece. Note that the waxed areas now appear darker than the unwaxed areas.
5. Remove the fabric from the frame and dye it the first color according to instructions for the specific dye. Be certain to wear rubber gloves.
6. Rinse well in running water.
7. When water runs clear, blot with newspaper or towels and allow to dry. Notice that the dyed unwaxed fabric is now darker than the waxed area.
8. Stretch the fabric on the frame.
9. Apply wax to the lines or areas that are to remain the first dye color. Notice that wax has slightly darkened the pointed central shape which is to remain. When wax is applied to fabric it always darkens and distorts the actual color. For this reason it is wise to hold the batik to the light occasionally to ascertain the true color and judge the successive dye wisely.
10. Remove the fabric from the frame and dye it the second color according to instructions for the specific dye.
11. Rinse and dry as before, which completes the dyeing for the sample piece. The darkest line around the central pointed shape exists because in Step 9 wax was stopped just short of filling the space. In batik, dark lines are the result of waxing out everything but the lines before dyeing.
12. Repeat steps 8 through 11 for the desired number of colors.
13. Sandwich the finished batik between absorbent paper, preferably clean newsprint and press with a hot iron. Replace the paper as it absorbs the wax. Work out of doors if possible or in a well-ventilated space. Make every effort not to press wrinkles in the hot waxy fabric as they are very difficult to remove later.
14. The best and safest way to remove the residual wax and restore the batik to its original hand is to entrust it to a good dry-cleaner. A satisfactory, though less thorough, job can be accomplished by agitating the batik for a few minutes in mineral spirits. The odor dissipates in a few days. Notice in the finished sample that the darkest value remains the same, and that the middle and lightest values have returned precisely to their original condition.

Batik hanging with gray and black dye on off-white fabric. Wax was brush-applied.

Batik: Discharge and Redye

For those who prefer to start with dark lines before adding color, discharge batik is the answer. Wax is applied to dark fabric, usually black cotton, and the fabric is then bleached to lighten untreated areas. If simple darks and lights are the objective, the process ends here, but waxed dark lines that resisted the bleaching action form perfect, ready-made boundaries for direct dye application.

MATERIALS

Dark bleachable cotton or viscose rayon, preferably black—Take a small jar of discharge solution (one-half warm water and one-half bleach) to the fabric store and test a swatch before purchasing in quantity. The fabric should lighten in one or two minutes.
Light-colored chalk
Frame
Brushes and/or tjanting tool
Melted wax
Discharge materials and equipment—See the section on "Discharge Substances," chapter 3.
Inko brand prepared dye for cotton, or substitute dye paste
Small containers for mixing dye
Natural or synthetic brushes
Iron
Absorbent paper
Mineral spirits (paint thinner)

METHOD

1. Wash and press the dark fabric.
2. Sketch the composition or a few guidelines on the fabric with light-colored chalk.
3. Stretch the fabric on the frame.
4. Apply melted wax as desired with a brush or a tjanting tool. Refer to the first part of this chapter for suggestions if necessary.
5. Discharge the waxed fabric to a light hue in a solution of one-half household chlorine bleach and one-half warm water. Remember that the bleached areas will be still lighter when the fabric is dry. Complete instructions for discharge appear in chapter 3.

Completed composition. Waxed and discharged black cotton with additional wax and directly applied vat dye. Collection of Dr. Robert Wilkus, Seattle, Washington.

6. Rinse the fabric well in running water for about three minutes, blot well, and allow to dry.
7. Restretch the fabric on a frame.
8. Additional wax may be applied if some of the light discharged fabric is to be retained.
9. Inko brand prepared vat dye is now brushed or sponged into the desired ares. Detailed instructions for using this dye are given in Chapter 3. If the sun happens to be shining when you are finished dyeing, expose the dyed fabric to it for three to five minutes or until the colors develop. If not, simply proceed to Step 10.
10. Carefully place the fabric between absorbent paper and press with a hot iron. This will serve two purposes: first, it will remove most of the wax, and second, it will develop the Inko dye if sunlight is not available.
11. Residual wax may be left in the fabric or may be removed by dry-cleaning.

Interim Wax Removal

In most conventional batik examples an orderly dye progression occurs from light to dark or bright to dull or both. There are times however when it is desirable or necessary to have this progression in two or more totally unrelated color groups. For example, let us say that a piece needs an orange to red range (range A) and a blue to violet range (range B). If we begin with orange and complete the dyeing of the warm colors it will be impossible to achieve the cool range because transparent dye will produce only neutrals when near opposites are superimposed. The best way to solve the dilemma is to first preserve the spaces for color range B with wax, dye color range A, remove all the wax, wax the dyed colors of range A, and dye color range B.

This method for batik with an interim wax removal is a bit indirect but permits unusual color ranges and juxtapositioning of opposing hues impossible to achieve by any other means.

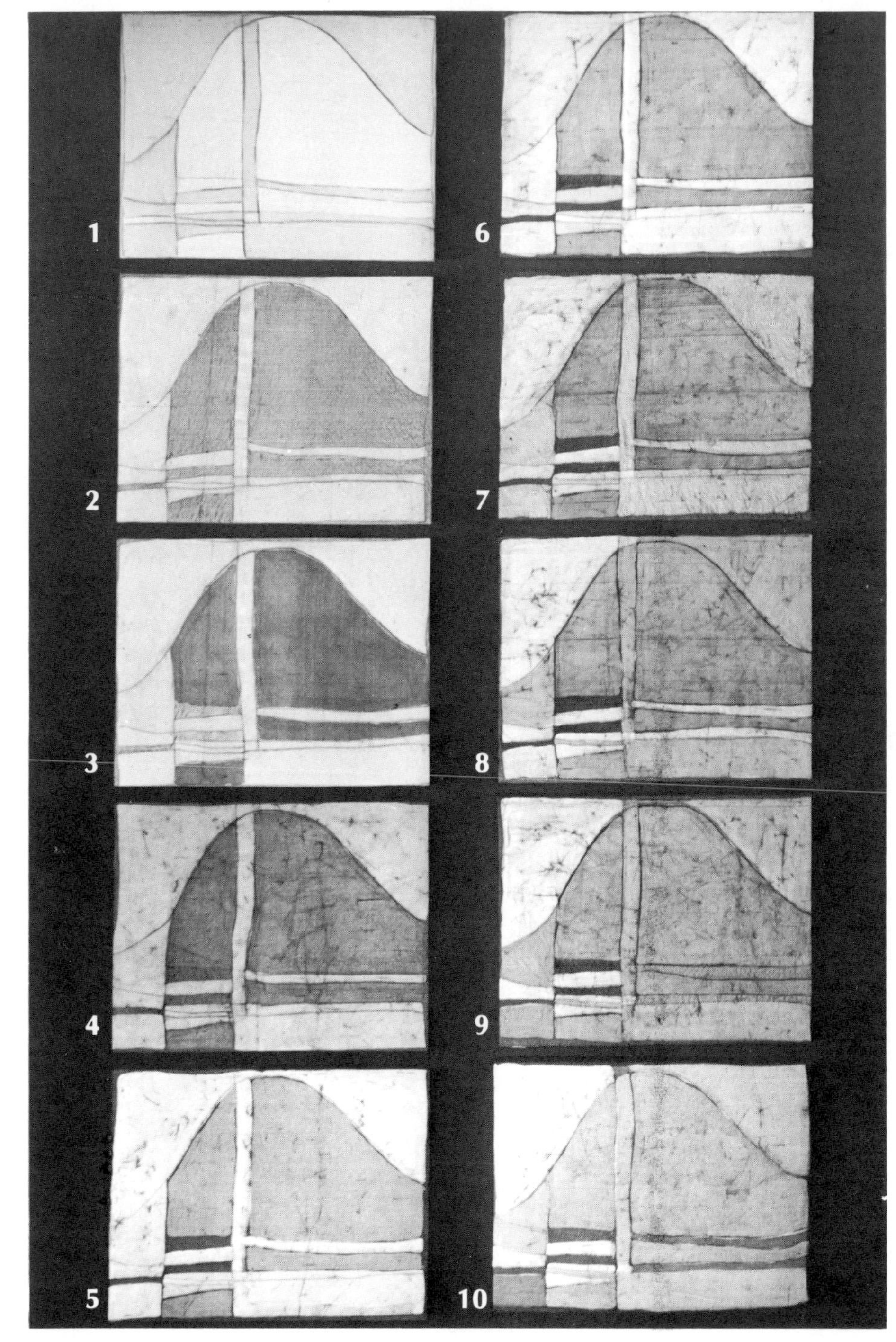

Sample set demonstrating batik with interim wax removal:

1. Beginning with white fabric, wax has been applied to all areas except those to be dyed with blue dyes.
2. Dyed light blue.
3. Wax has been applied to all areas that are to remain light blue.
4. Dyed dark blue.
5. All wax has been removed.
6. Wax has been applied to all areas that are to remain light blue, dark blue, or white.
7. Dyed orange.
8. Wax has been applied to all areas that are to remain orange (in addition to Step 6).
9. Dyed a bright cool pink which changes exposed orange to red.
10. All wax has been removed and the piece is finished. It contains white, light blue, dark blue, orange, and red.

PRINTING WAX RESISTS

Pipe-Cleaner Stamps

An extremely effective and generally overlooked stamping tool for wax is the chenille wire more commonly known as a pipe cleaner. Actually it is available in several sizes from hobby craft shops where it is stocked for fabricating artificial flowers and such novelties. The wax absorption quality is excellent, and it is easily bent into a variety of linear single plane designs. Several lengths may be joined, with some portion of one or more serving as a short handle. Very elaborate stamps, however, tend to flop around and be unruly to print.

METHOD

Follow the general instructions for batik given previously. In this method the wax is stamped rather than brushed or applied with a tjanting tool.

The actual stamping requires that the fabric be evenly stretched and that any excess wax on the stamp be made to run back into the wax container before stamping. The stamp can be scraped gently over the lip of the wax melting appliance to accomplish this. The flow of wax will be determined by its temperature, its volume, and the texture of the fabric, as it was with the brush or tjanting tool.

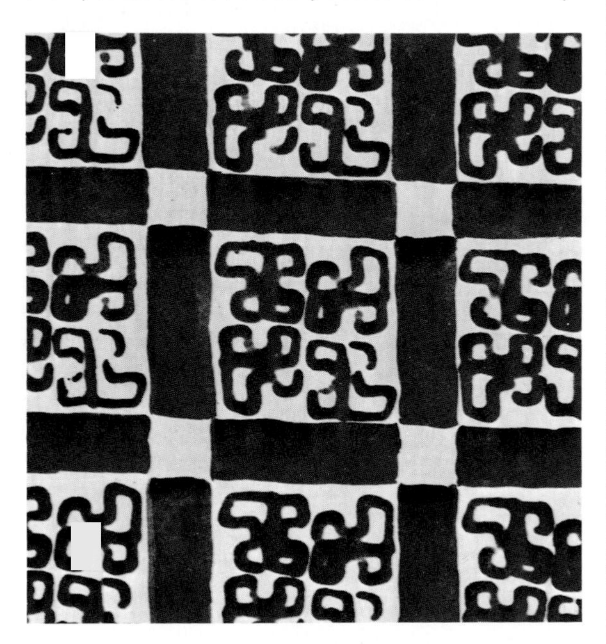

Each unit consists of four prints of the same stamp in rotation. The fabric was black to begin with and was discharged. Black areas resisted with brushed wax.

A chenille wire or pipe cleaner stamp is being printed with hot wax to resist dye.

Cord-Covered Blocks

When absorbent cotton cord is glued to a plywood block, the result is a device that very efficiently prints waxed lines on fabric. It is similar in some ways to the Indonesian tjap or copper wax stamp shown on page 96. The block may be of any size or shape so long as it clears the edges of the wax melting pan. This versatile and fast moving process was developed by Edward Lambert at the University of Georgia.

MATERIALS

Plywood—3/8", 1/2", or 5/8". The thickness is not critical.
White casein base glue
Pencil
Razor blade or sharp knife
Cotton cord—For blocks approximately 8 by 8 inches size 72 cotton cable cord is ideal. Sash cord and clothesline are acceptable. The cord should be of cotton or at least a natural fiber as synthetics may melt in the hot wax.
Pushpins—(Optional).
Scissors
Melted wax—In a low flat container such as an electric fry pan.
Fabric to be stamped—Must be washed, pressed, and compatible with the intended dye.
Dye and dye materials—Review dye information in chapter 3 if necessary.
Large flat working surface
Wax paper—(Optional).
Absorbent paper
Iron
Mineral spirits

Size 72 cotton cord is being applied to plywood. Raw ends will be cut and sealed with white glue before printing.

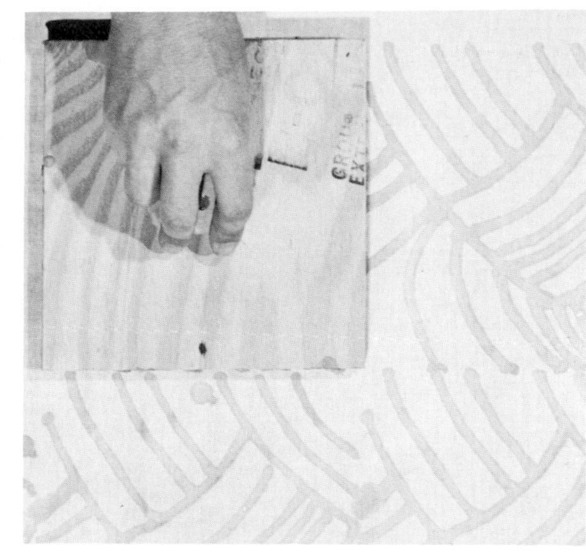

Block printing in progress.

Finished textile with a single dye. Procion fiber-reactive dye on cotton, 32″ x 40″ (81 x 101 cm).

METHOD

1. Trace or draw the design on the plywood with a pencil. Remember that when the design is printed, it will mirror image itself. Also make sure that the block will fit the wax container.
2. Squeeze glue on several of the lines and apply cord to them. Gentle curves and straight lines present no problems, but if sharp angles are involved pushpins at corners will be helpful. Allow cord ends to extend slightly beyond the block. Allow the glue to dry thoroughly.
3. With a razor blade or sharp knife, cut overhanging cord ends flush with the block and seal them with a drop of glue. If the cord is badly unraveled it may be necessary to pinch the ends with glue-covered fingers to reshape them. This is also true of ends occurring inside the design. If the cord ends are left unsealed, they will act like miniature brushes and print wax dots and the end of the lines which will be emphasized as a special effect. Allow all the glue to dry thoroughly.
4. Attach a handle to the other side of the block. A wooden drawer pull held in place with a wood screw works well.
5. A dot or an arrow should be applied to the block so it can't be accidentally printed sideways or upside down. This is especially true of square blocks.
6. Heat the wax to about 275°F.
7. Lay the fabric out on a smooth flat surface either with or without a protective covering of wax paper or butcher paper.
8. Apply guidelines or registration marks if desired.
9. Dip the block in hot wax and allow it to float there for a few minutes. At first it will sizzle and perhaps foam a bit, but this will subside shortly and will not reoccur.
10. Lift the block from the wax, give it a shake or two, and print on the fabric. If wax paper is under the fabric, simply redip the block and proceed as before. Later, the wax paper may be peeled off. If the fabric is stamped directly on the work surface, it must be lifted immediately so the wax cools in mid-air and does not attach the fabric to the table. Later the work surface may be scraped and sponged off with mineral spirits.
11. Continue stamping until the piece is complete.
12. Dye fabric according to plan following manufacturers' instructions or consult the instructions in chapter 3 for the dye you have chosen.
13. Rinse well, blot, and dry thoroughly. When fabric is dry a number of alternatives are available. If a single dye color is required, the process may stop here and the wax may be removed. As an alternative, the block may be rewaxed and the fabric be overprinted with the block reversed, sideways, or on a new grid system such as brick or half-drop. Or the block could be dropped and moved to the right or left about one-half inch for a shadow effect. Use of the block could also be discontinued at this point and the stamped fabric treated as for conventional brush batik. Dye paste could also now be brushed or sponged directly onto the fabric, possibly using the wax-stamped lines as color boundaries.
14. Overdye as required, rinse, dry, and repeat the process until the composition is complete.
15. Remove the wax by ironing the fabric between absorbent paper and dry-clean if required.

RESIST PASTES

Resist pastes, which are rapidly gaining acceptance in the West, offer the fabric dyer many advantages. They are economical, they may be applied at room temperature, and each type produces unique, characteristic effects. All of the pastes produce effects that are unlike batik. Their chief drawback is that they are all water soluble and are not suited for lengthy submersion dyeing. In other words, the dye must be applied with a brush, sponge, or similar means. For the novice, vat dye submersion, such as for the indigo process is workable only for small, manageable-sized fabrics. Only after considerable experiences should one attempt submersion dyeing of large fabrics. If the paste dissolves in the dye solution, the resist effect will disappear or be muted at best. We have experimented at length with three resist pastes: one is a premixed, ready-to-use commercial product (Inkodye resist), and two can be formulated in the studio.

Inkodye resist being applied with plastic squeeze bottle.

Inkodye Resist

Inkodye resist is a commercially prepared, water-soluble resist paste made by the Screen Process Supplies Manufacturing Co. of Oakland, Calif. It has excellent adhesion properties and is capable of producing very crisp fine lines.

METHOD

1. Prepare fabric by stretching it securely to a frame.
2. Apply design guidelines if desired. This is best accomplished with a "wash out tint" as decribed on page 89.
3. Pour or squeeze the paste from its original container into a plastic squeeze bottle. Attach conical plastic bottle top.
4. Squeeze paste onto fabric where desired. Work from top to bottom, side to side, or center to edges in order to prevent possible smudges. If the hole in the squeeze bottle is too fine, cut part of it off with a sharp knife. If the hole is too large, use a different cap or squeeze the paste into another size bottle. Clear, graceful lines are more easily made if the squeeze bottle is small enough to be held easily and if it will yield its contents with gentle pressure.
5. Allow paste to dry thoroughly.
6. Apply dye with a brush or perhaps a sponge to the top surface of the fabric only. If the color appears uneven, apply a second coat after the first is dry. When the dye is dry, it is possible to repeat steps 4 through 6 by overdyeing all or parts of the piece with additional colors. However, if one color plus the resisted fabric color is sufficient, proceed with step 7.
7. Fix dye as recommended by manufacturer.
8. Soak the fabric in cool or lukewarm water for about 20 minutes. Most of the paste should be dissolved, but some agitation may be necessary.
9. Rinse in clear water and allow fabric to dry.

Quick Paste Formulas

This quick paste formula is a very simple recipe that takes only a short time to make. The resulting paste is less adhesive and more difficult to control than either of the others. Nevertheless it has a very appealing soft-edge effect that is well worth experimenting with.

1. To make 2¼ cups of paste, in the top unit of a double boiler, stir to a thick smooth paste:

½ cup white flour	¼ cup instant laundry starch
½ cup rice flour	¾ cup cold water

2. Then stir in ½ cup of hot water.
3. Cook this mixture over boiling water for approximately 15 minutes, stirring often and slowly adding another 1-½ to 2 cups of hot water. The finished paste should be semitranslucent, and the consistency of thin mashed potatoes. It should be applied while warm to a thickness of about one-eighth inch. This may be achieved with a soft brush, squeeze bottle, or a small spatula such as a palette knife. Follow steps 4 through 9 for Inko dye resist.

Dye is applied to the fabric when the paste is thoroughly dry.

The finished piece. Inko prepared vat dye on cotton.

JAPANESE RICE PASTE OR "NORI"

Japanese dyers perfected the use of rice paste as a resist sometime near the beginning of the Edo period (roughly 1700). Since then they have adapted this process, called "norizome" to the many technological and social changes that have transpired. Today, norizome is used chiefly for apparel and display purposes.

Norizome is a general term for two distinctly different methods of paste, or "nori," applications. One method, "tsutsugaki," provides for the freehand application of paste through a pliable paper cone, or "tsutsu." The other method, called "katazome," involves spreading the paste over a stencil-covered fabric. The two processes have much in common, but the recipes and techniques are sufficiently different that they will be covered in separate chapters—tsutsugaki here, and katazome in chapter 8 on stencil printing.

Our first experiences with tsutsugaki, or "cone writing" as the term is literally translated, were based on the 1976-77 graduate research of Ms. Shigeko Spear, at the University of Kansas. In 1978 we had the good fortune to study with the master dyer Shizuo Okawahara, of Takamatsu City, Japan, while he was visiting professor of art at the University of Washington. The following instructions are based on a composite of these experiences. Please bear in mind that a major ingredient for success with any norizome process is perseverance. Some immediate results are possible, but before the process can become second nature a few awkward attempts and one or two lumpy batches of paste will probably find their way to the refuse can. However, when all goes well, tsutsugaki can produce very beautiful results with absolutely razor-sharp edges and extraordinary detail.

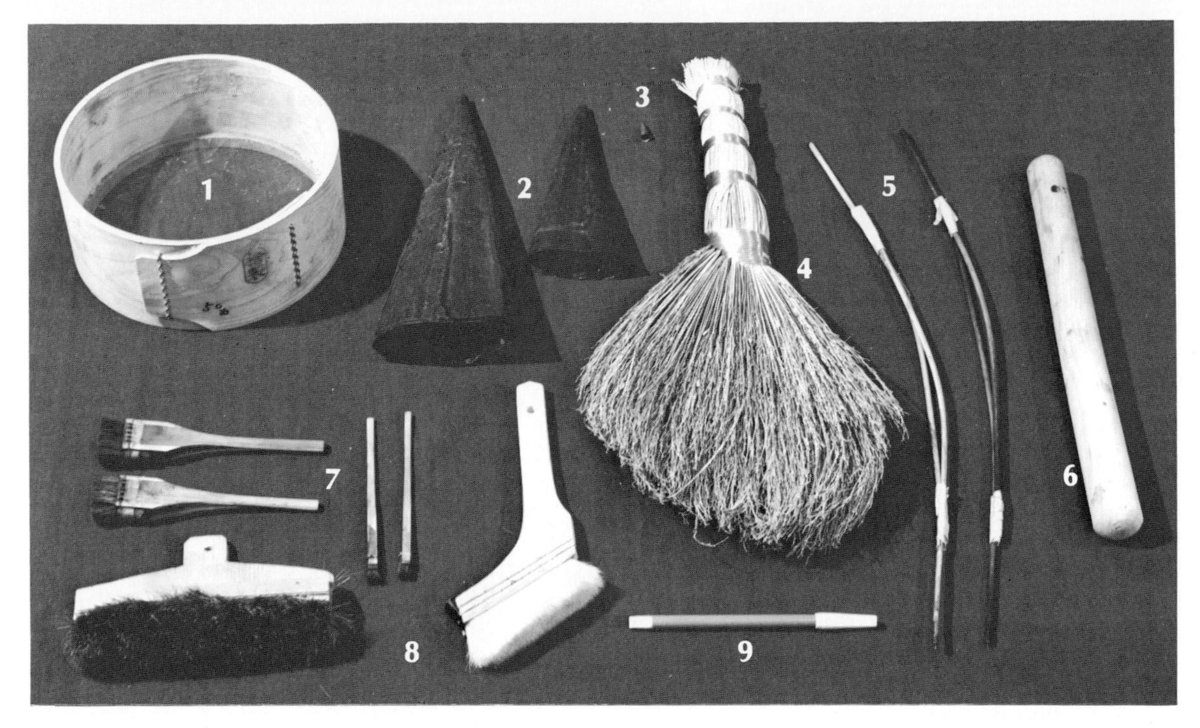

Materials and tools for tsutsugaki: (1) sifter for ogakuzu or sawdust; (2) tsutsu or paper cone; (3) tsutsugane or brass tip for cone; (4) hoki or straw broom; (5) shinshi or fabric stretchers; (6) pestle for mixing nori or rice paste; (7) small Japanese dye brushes; (8) large Japanese dye brushes; and (9) water soluble pigment marker.

Preparing the Tsutsugaki Paste or Tsutsu-nori

There are probably as many ways to prepare the paste for tsutsugaki as there are practitioners of the craft, but we will offer two versions or methods: one involving steaming, and another involving boiling or poaching.

Recipe for Steamed Tsutsu-Nori. The following recipe will yield about 2½ cups of paste. We do not recommend attempting a larger batch the first time. The procedure is rather complicated but well worth the effort and time expended. The paste is wonderfully adhesive, easy to handle and apply, and it may be stored in the refrigerator for a month or so.

1¾ cups mochiko (also called sweet rice flour or glutinous rice flour)
¾ cup komon nuka (a very finely ground rice bran devoid of fat and oil)
4–7 Tbsp. salt
2–3 Tbsp. Calx (calcium hydroxide or slaked lime)
¾ cup water

METHOD

1. Sift together mochiko and komon nuka. Mix well.
2. Add water gradually to make batter come together in a ball. Add more water if necessary. Knead well. Shape into 3 or 4 donut-shaped cakes.
3. Wrap cakes with a thin damp piece of cotton cloth and place them in a steamer. Steam for 50 to 60 minutes.
4. Remove the cakes from steamer and immediately mash them in a bowl while steaming hot. A wooden pestle or 18-inch length of broom handle works best for mashing and mixing.
5. When the paste has been thoroughly mashed, gradually add the appropriate amount of salt. The amount will differ depending on the season and weather conditions. In humid weather, 4 or 5

tablespoons of salt dissolved in ½ cup water works well. In dry weather about 7 tablespoons may be necessary. The proper consistency should be that of taffy.

6. Beat the paste, which initially is thick and hard to stir, until it becomes smooth and very sticky. This is a difficult task but it is essential that the paste be smooth before proceeding.
7. Add about ½ cup of water to 2 or 3 tablespoons of Calx. Dissolve thoroughly and let settle for a few minutes. Gradually pour a small amount of liquid from the top of the settled lime into the paste mixture.
8. Gradually add most of the Calx solution and continue beating the paste until the color changes from a light tan to a light yellowish straw color. The lime sediment should not be used.
9. Add small amounts of warm water to bring paste to a smooth, elastic thickness. The paste will stir more easily at this stage. At this point the paste is ready to be used. Never add lime in its powdered form or it will make the paste lumpy like tapioca. Always add lime water gradually to the paste. If too much lime water is added, the paste will lose its adhesiveness and become lumpy. If the paste does become lumpy, it can sometimes be saved by adding a few drops of vinegar. If the paste becomes too thin, it can be thickened by heating the paste slowly, sprinkling small amounts of komon nuka over the paste, and stirring well.

With experience it is possible to change the ratio of the mochiko and komon nuka or to eliminate the latter altogether and to estimate the amount of Calx required by the color of the paste. In Japan, the larger dye works use commercial bread dough mixers for quantity yields. It is probably possible to entrust the hardest part of the hand operation to an electric food processor.

Recipe for Poached Tsutsu-nori. This is a version of Professor Okawahara's less time-consuming tsutsu-nori technique. It yields about 2½ cups of paste.

2½ cup mochiko
¾ cup water
2–3 Tbsp. Calx
9 Tbsp. salt

METHOD

1. Slowly add water to the mochiko while stirring until a doughlike ball is formed. Use less or more water as required to make a kneadable ball that is stiff enough not to stick to the hands yet soft enough not to crumble or crack.
2. Knead well and shape into three or four donut-shaped cakes.
3. Drop the donuts one at a time into boiling water "two times as salty as sea water" (allow approximately 9 Tbsp. of salt per gallon of water).
4. After about 15-20 minutes, watch the surface of the water, and as the donuts begin to float they should be removed and thoroughly mashed with a wooden pestle or dowel. Reserve the salt water.
5. Stir and mash while slowly adding small amounts of the hot salt water until you have a sticky, glutinous paste.
6. Proceed as in steps 5 through 9 for steamed tsutsu-nori.

Mochiko or glutinous rice powder, unlike wheat flour or ordinary rice powder, has a strong adhesive quality even when ground to a fine powder. The grains do not lose their adhesive quality in water or during the cooking process. This makes it possible for the paste to adhere to the threads of fabric as a perfect resist medium. Mochiko is available at large grocery stores or from Asian food specialty shops.

Komon nuka, a finely ground fat-free rice bran powder, mitigates the extreme adhesiveness of glutinous rice paste and makes it easier to handle. It also gives the paste the correct thickness when it is applied to the fabric and further helps to make the paste easier to wash off during the final stage. This product occasionally appears at health food stores but is best purchased from a dye specialty shop to assure that it is ground sufficiently.

Salt draws moisture from the air and keeps the paste properly soft. This is why it is necessary to change the amount of salt according to the weather conditions. The drier the air, the more salt is required. Salt also helps the paste to adhere tightly to the fabric and prevents it from cracking after it has been applied.

Calx (calcium hydroxide or slaked lime) gives the paste body. It also functions as a preservative. With lime added, the paste may be kept in the refrigerator for a month or more. The exact amount of lime required will vary according to its age and length of time it has been in contact with the air. Aging weakens its effectiveness.

MATERIALS FOR TSUTSUGAKI

Fabric—White or light-colored fabric with little or no nap is best. Fabric must have an affinity to the dye that is being used.

Tsutsu-nori—Or resist paste described previously.

Tsutsu or paper cone—These come in several sizes and are made from shibugami, a form of mulberry paper treated for pliability with persimmon juice and smoke. When softened in warm water these paper cones house the paste for "pastry tube like" application to the fabric.

Tsutsugane—These are the brass tips for the paper cone of tsutsu. They come in assorted sizes. Some come in pairs: one shorter one for the inside, and one longer one for the outside while some have inside fittings only. Some are uncut so that openings may be filed to the desired diameter, and some are prefinished. In addition to the rounded ones, there are various sized tips with oval configurations for filling in broad areas.

Water-soluble pigment powder—For applying guidelines that will be followed with the nori or paste. Two are available: red, or akabana, and blue, or aobana. These are very useful since they wash out completely and are easy to apply with a long, pointed brush.

Stretching device for fabric—This may be a stretcher bar frame or traditional Japanese stretchers called shinshi. Shinshi are flexible bamboo rods with metal needlelike ends. They are available in several lengths and generally are used for selvage to selvage tension while cut ends are wrapped around dowels and secured the required distance apart.

Hoki—A Japanese straw broom not unlike a large whisk broom or hearth sweeping broom excepting that its broad face is triangulated. It is used to burst air bubbles trapped in the freshly applied tsutsu-nori.

Ogakuzu—Finely ground sawdust which is sifted atop still wet nori to prevent cracks and assist in even drying. Ground walnut shells from a paint store may be substituted.

Large flat brushes for water and dye products—The best ones are made of badger and deer hair, have wooden handles and are called shime naoshi hake. A very broad wash brush might be substituted or perhaps a polyfoam "brush."

Small flat dye brushes—The best are beautiful bamboo-handled tools called iro sashi hake. Any number of Western brushes could be trimmed to simulate these.

Dye—Preferably one that is applicable with a brush or polyfoam applicator. We recommend Inkodye prepared vat dye or a fiber-reactive dye dissolved in chemical water (see chapter 3).

A flat, dry, clean, nonabsorbent working surface

A large sink or soaking pan for removing the nori

METHOD

1. Trace or draw your design on the fabric with a small amount of water-soluble pigment powder dissolved in water. Strength of color should be similar to transparent watercolor. Use the tip only of a Japanese lettering brush or any long, pointed brush. Don't be too concerned if a blob or drip of pigment should occur: it will wash out when the paste is removed. Akabana is red pigment, and aobana is the blue pigment.
2. Tape, pin, or otherwise attach the fabric to a flat surface. Fabric must be smooth and wrinkle-free but need not be stretched excessively.
3. Soak the paper cone or tsutsu in a pan of warm water for about 30 minutes. If there are large areas to be filled with paste, a second cone should be soaked as well. When they are pliable, blot with paper and fit one with its small- or medium-sized round or elliptical ended brass tip(s) or tsutsugane. It may be necessary to file the tip for the desired size of opening. Use a fine metal file, emery paper, or carborundum. Some norizome experts prefer that the cone tip be elliptical rather than flat. Fit the second cone with a medium or large oval tip. The tip of the cone may need to be trimmed to accommodate the tip.
4. Half fill (or one-third fill) both cones with paste. Traditionally, it is lifted on a rounded bamboo splint and twirled like honey or taffy and neatly placed in the bottom of the cone. Gently fold over the top of the cone, expelling as much air as possible.
5. To produce a line, take the middle of the cone in your right hand and apply pressure as evenly as possible with a left-to-right rolling motion of the thumb. The cone rests on the *palm,* not on the fingertips. Reverse instructions for left hand operation. Hold the cone at a 45 degree angle and apply pressure evenly making certain that the elliptical tip is relatively firm in its pressure to the cloth. As you complete a stroke, release pressure and lift the tip abruptly to stop the flow of paste neatly.
6. Work from left to right, right to left, top to bottom, or center to edge to avoid the problem of having to lean over fresh paste. Outline areas not much larger than one foot square at a time. When you have done so, fill in the broad areas with the oval-tipped cone first, working next to the outlines and being sure that the new paste adheres to the still wet outlines. The oval cone is moved in a tight circular direction. Fill in all of the open areas in this fashion, working from the outline to the middle of each section.
7. Repeat steps 5 and 6 until work is complete. Refill the cones as necessary as in step 4.
8. Dip the hōki or a similar straw broom in water and shake it several times so that it is just damp. Now fan the fresh paste with short vigorous strokes allowing the broom tips to barely touch the paste. Surprisingly, this will not smear the paste but will release any trapped bubbles of air in your work. These little bubble "craters" should now be filled with fresh paste. Check for thin spots and be sure that all of the required fabric is covered evenly.
9. Now sift ogakuzu over all of the fresh paste. This may be accomplished with a sieve or piece of stretched wire screen.
10. With great care, stretch the fabric on a frame or attach shinshi so that it floats horizontally with the under surface free and touching nothing. With this accomplished, shake off loose sawdust and brush the underside of the fabric with water. This allows the paste to penetrate the fibers and assures a crisp edge resist.
11. Make sure the design is not distorted and allow the piece to dry in a horizontally suspended position.
12. When thoroughly dry, apply liquid dye with a wide flat brush or shime naoshi hake. Application is made on the paste side of the fabric only. If small color areas are to be dyed this should be done with a small brush or iro sashi hake. Apply dye as evenly as possible with short, even, rapid strokes.
13. Allow to dry thoroughly and apply a second coat for greater evenness and depth of shade.
14. Allow to dry thoroughly and fix dye as recommended by manufacturer.
15. Soak fabric in clean cool water for about an hour. Change water if dye appears to run. Soft paste that does not fall off may be scraped off with a dull blade such as a plastic knife or a credit card. Do not scrub the dyed fabric or unnecessarily rub it against itself. Rinse well, blot excess moisture, and dry.

Shizuo Okawahara. Rice paste resist banner, 1979. Cotton, ca. 18"x 63" (46 x 160 cm). Photograph courtesy of Greenwood Galleries, Seattle, Washington.

Examples of Liquid Resist Dyeing

Shawl or slendang (detail). Batik on silk; late 19th or early 20th century, Java, Indonesia. Collection of Mr. and Mrs. Russell Day, Everett, Washington.

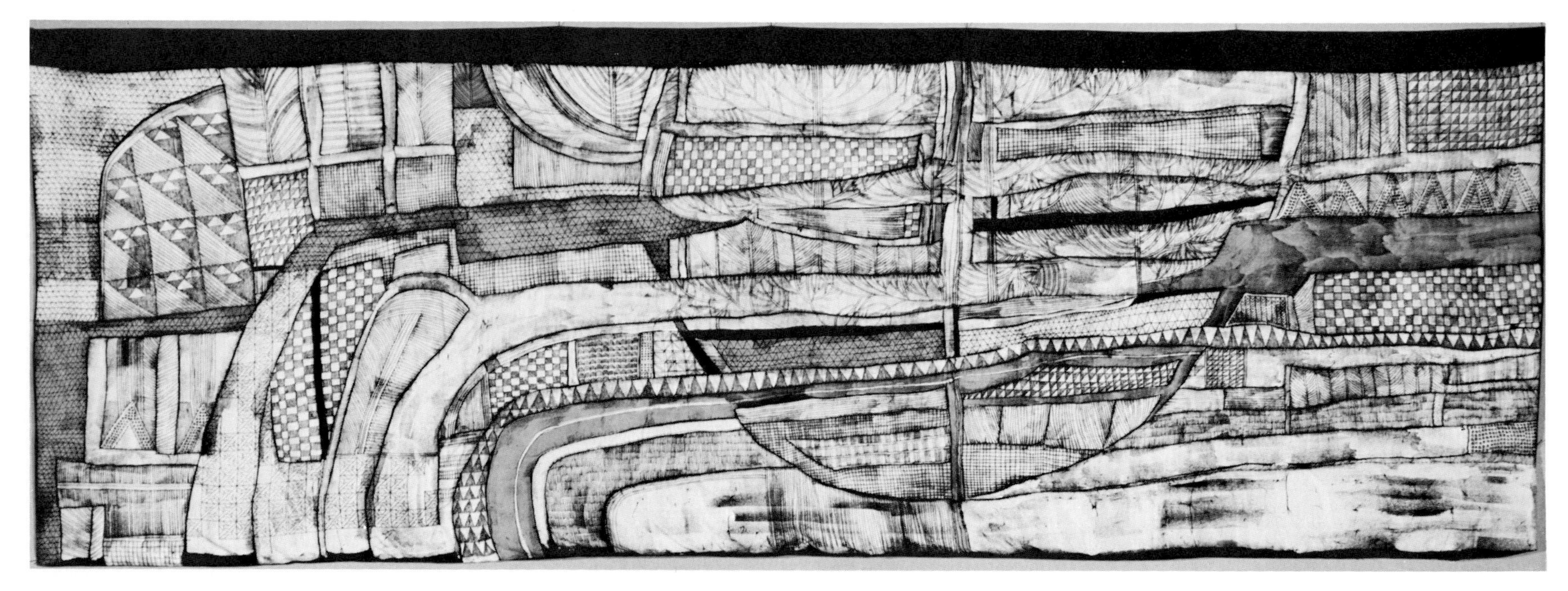

Jennifer F. Lew. Untitled composition. Sgraffito technique with acid and basic dyes on silk broadcloth, 44"x 72"(112 x 183 cm). Collection of Chemical Corporation, Seattle, Washington.

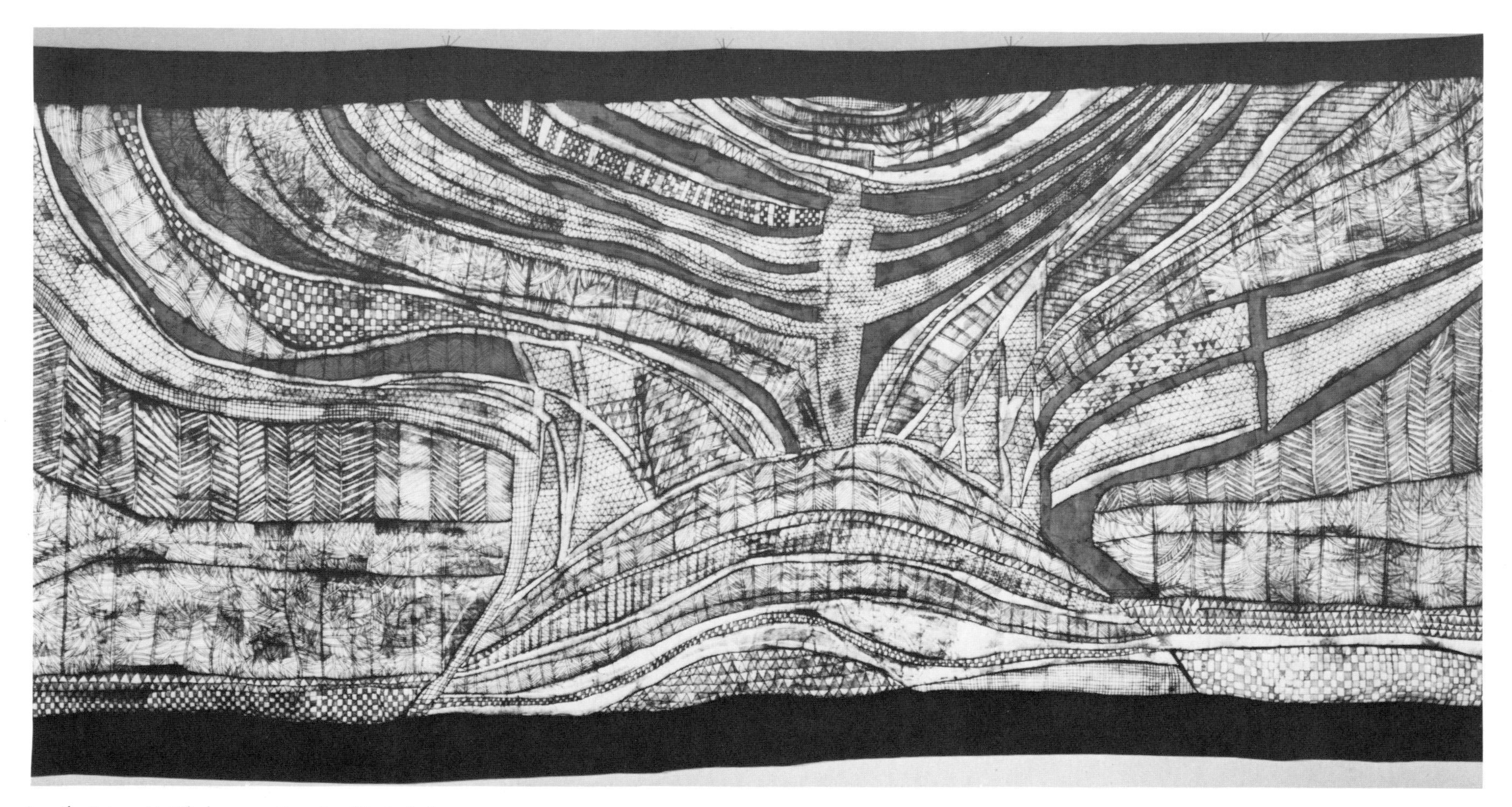

Jennifer F. Lew. Untitled composition. Sgraffito technique with acid and basic dyes on silk pongee, 42" x 72" (107 x 183 cm).

Left and right: *Contemporary batik on cotton. Begong Kussudiardja, Jogjakarta, Java, Indonesia. Dyes unknown but probably naphthol, ca. 36″ x 45″ (91 x 114 cm).*

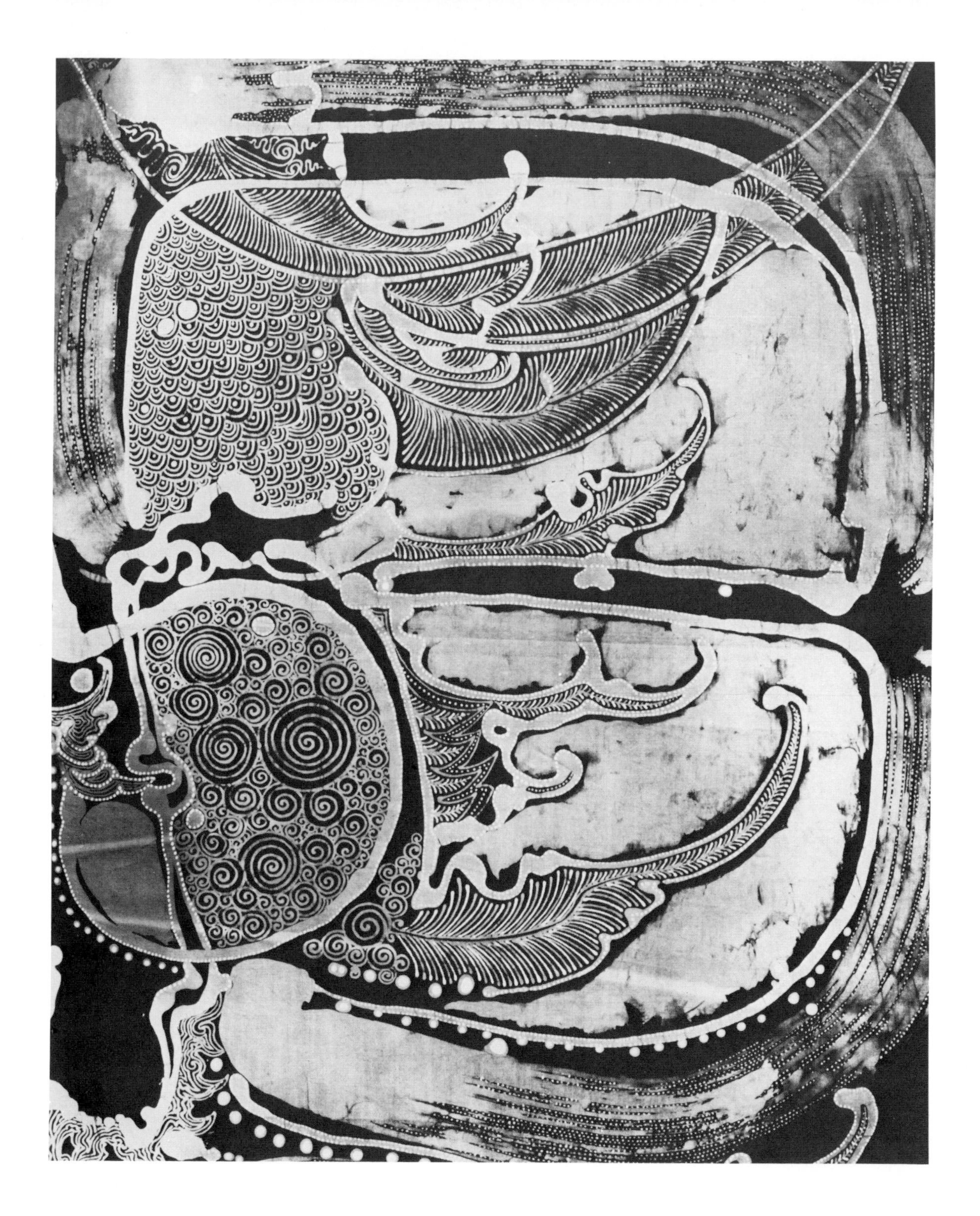

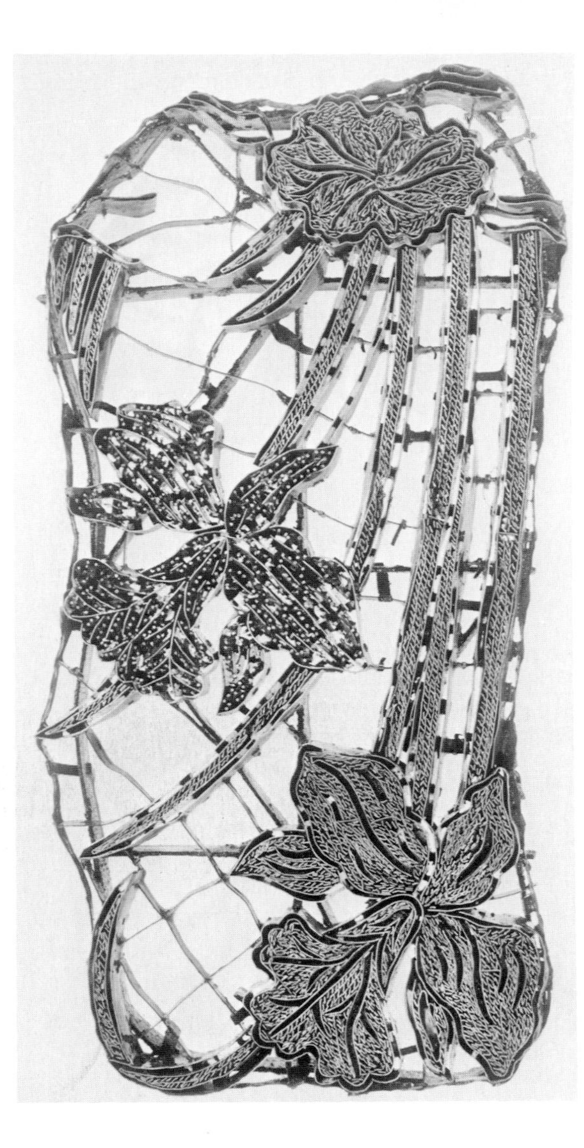

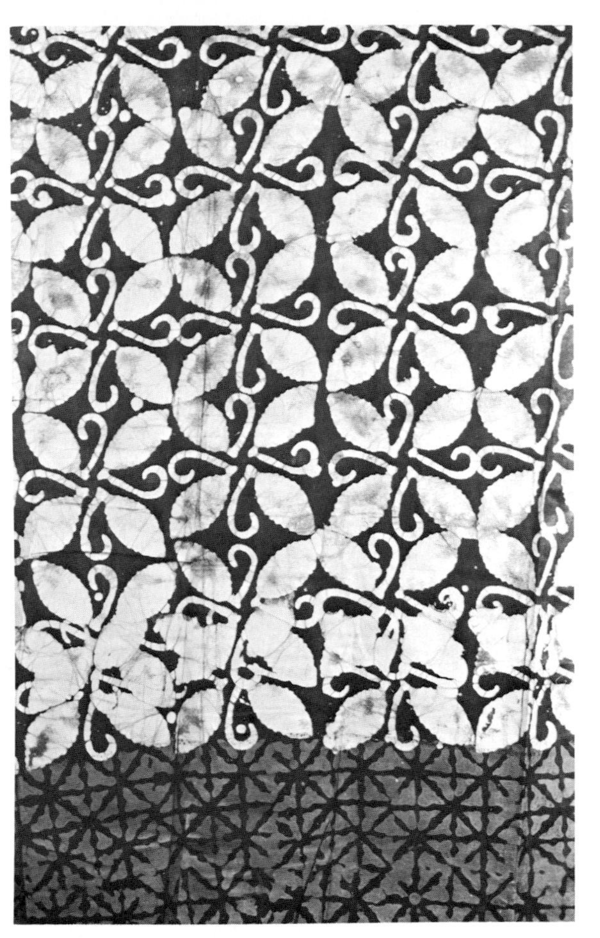

Left: *Indonesian tjap. A linear metal stamp which is dipped in hot wax and pressed onto fabric, Jogjakarta, Java. Private collection, Bellevue, Washington.*

Center: *African resist dyed cloth. Yoruba, Nigeria. Starch paste and indigo dye on cotton. The process is called "adire eleko," and this particular pattern is known as "Ibadan Dun" for its city of origin. Collection of Mr. and Mrs. Russell Day, Everett, Washington.*

Above: *Contemporary African wax stamped cloth, Sierra Leone. Designed and printed by Mrs. Kadiato Kamara, Freetown, Sierra Leone. Stamp is carved from wood by local men. Courtesy of the Field Museum of Natural History, Chicago, Illinois.*

Detail of batik with design showing Chinese influence. Pekalongan, Java, Indonesia. Collected by Hadidjah Fielding and Irwan Holmes. Courtesy of the Anneberg Gallery, San Francisco, California.

6. Bound Resists

Bound resists depend on constriction as a means of disallowing dye to penetrate selected lines, spots, or zones of fabric. Just as *batik* is the common blanket term for the liquid resists, *tiedye, tie and dye,* or *plangi* are frequent catch phrases for the bound resists, which actually include sewing and clamping in addition to the better known tieing and wrapping. *Tri-tik* refers to the stitched resists.

The bound-resist processes are practiced in many parts of the world, where they seem to have emerged independently. Asia is sometimes attributed with the origin of this process group, but tie dye has long been practiced in West Africa and was well known to the textile artists of pre-Columbian Peru.

Much of the appeal of fabric that has been bound before dyeing is the soft edge that develops between dyed and undyed areas or spots. This softness of edge is uncommon to other methods of dyeing woven fabric and tends to produce a feeling of fluidity and movement. Even when taut, dyed fabric resisted by binding may appear to undulate gracefully. Occasionally, weavers using a technique known as ikat tie dye or spot dye their warp and or weft elements before they are interwoven.

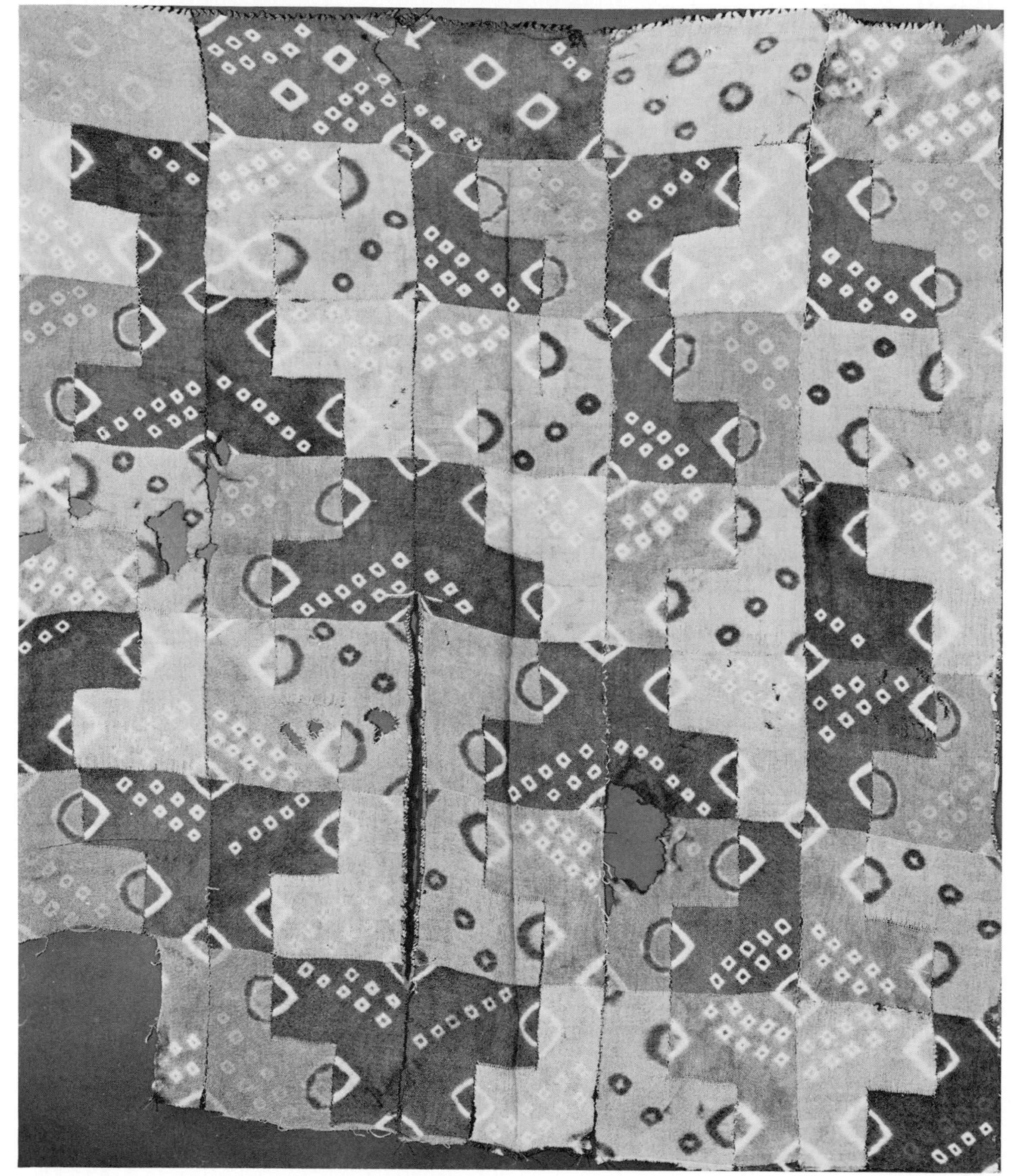

Peruvian poncho (fragment), late Nazca or Coastal Tiahuanaco culture. A very complex textile with discontinuous warp and weft elements, conventional tie dye and dye painting. Harriet Tidball Collection, Costume and Textile Study Center, University of Washington.

Tools for Bound Resist Dyeing

These following tools for bound resist dyeing are for the most part common household items readily available in most parts of the world.

Four-ply mercerized crochet cotton—Very strong, inexpensive and excellent for detail work.
Jute twine for medium detail—Strong and tends to produce a fuzzy edge.
Rayon and cotton rug yarn—Suitable for wrapping broad areas or where fine detail is not desired.
Strong plastic package tie wrap—Used to preserve broad areas.
C-clamps—For compressing folded fabric between shaped templates. One or more as needed.
Rubber bands—For simple alternative means of wrapping fabric.
Sharp, pointed scissors
Seam ripper—A quick convenient means of releasing binding material, especially on intricate projects.
Needle and thread—For sewn resist work or tritik.
Appropriate dyes and dye equipment
Rubber gloves

Tools for bound resist dyeing.

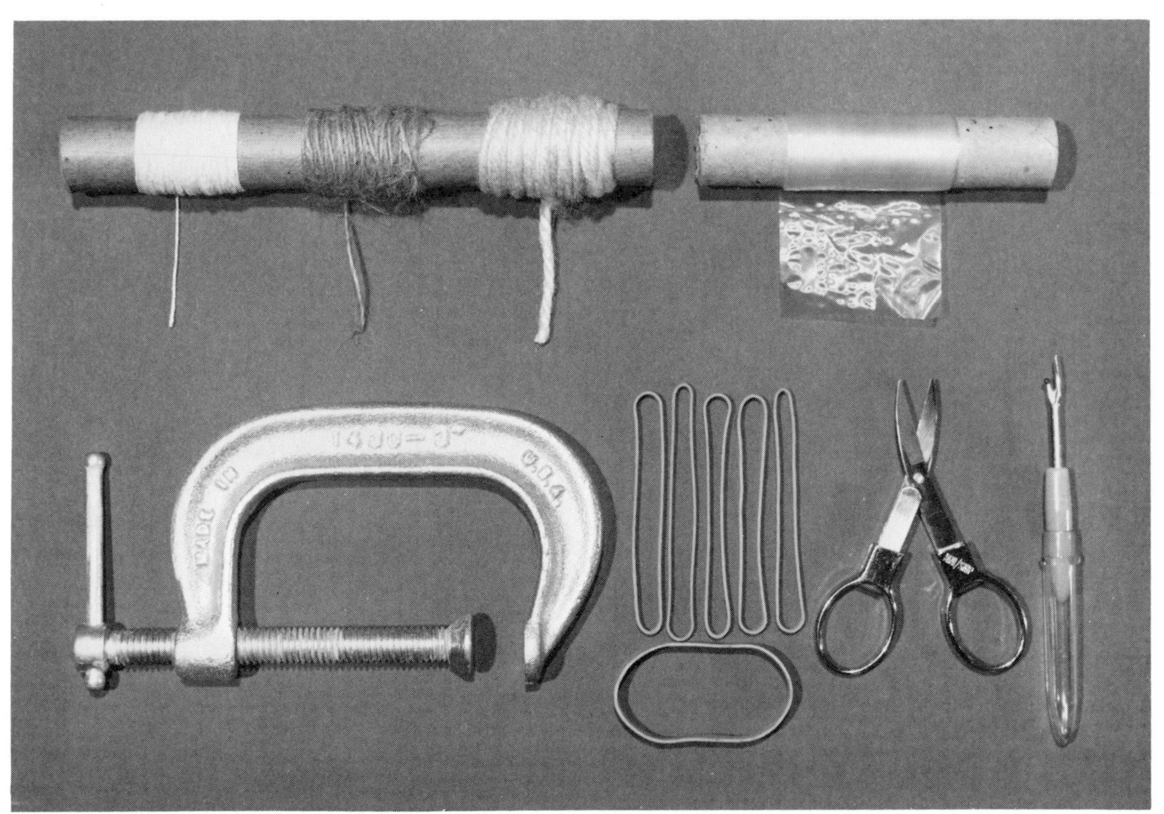

Techniques for Bound Resist Dyeing

INSTRUCTIONS FOR TIE DYE

MATERIALS

Fabric to be tie dyed—Lightweight, finely woven fabric such as crepe, China silk, percale, or batiste are best when great detail is important. Medium- to heavyweight fabrics are best for bold strong effects. Refer to the fabric chart in chapter 2.
Binding material—One of the best, all-purpose binders is mercerized, four-ply crochet cotton as it is relatively fine but extremely strong. Other materials include pearl cotton, button and carpet thread, rubber bands, raffia, wire, yarn, and plastic package wrap.
Dye and equipment required for the specific dye selected—Detailed dye instructions are given in chapter 3.
Needle and thread
Sharp scissors or a seam ripper
Chalk and/or artists' charcoal (optional)
Ruler or straight edge (optional)

METHOD

1. Wash and press the fabric to be dyed.
2. Guidelines are recommended, especially for complex designs and should now be applied with chalk of contrasting value. Use a straight edge if necessary.
3. Following the guidelines, the fabric is folded or gathered to the desired shape, and then tied, stitched, clamped, or bound. As binding proceeds the fabric will change its shape radically and special care is needed to keep from missing portions of the pattern.
4. Select a dye that is appropriate for the fiber content of the fabric. See dye chart on pp. 28–29.
5. Soak the bound fabric in warm water so that it is evenly moist and allow it to drain.
6. Dye the fabric.
7. Rinse well in running water. The fabric may be allowed to dry in its bound state or may be released and rinsed a second time before drying flat. Some dye manufacturers will specify a preference.
8. At this point in the process there are a number of options. Each has its own special advantage depending on design and function: stop here if a single dye process is sufficient; leave binding in place and bind additional sections, then overdye a second color; release binding and rebind or clamp different areas of the fabric using the existing folds and overdye a second color; release binding and refold the fabric before binding or clamping the desired areas prior to overdyeing.

TIE DYEING CIRCLES

Circles are among the easiest shapes to make with the tie dye process. One method is to form a ring with the thumb and forefinger of one hand, pull a point of fabric up through this circle with the other hand, and then bind it firmly where desired. This will yield a somewhat irregular circle. The following method will produce a more precise circle:

1. Draw a circle of the desired size on the fabric with a water-soluble marker or vine charcoal.
2. Fold the fabric over in such a way that exactly one half of the circle guideline is on each side.
3. Make even running stitches on the semicircular guideline with a needle and strong thread through both layers.
4. Hold the thread taut and gather the fabric on it. This will produce a flat, slightly pointed fanlike form.
5. Bind as desired.

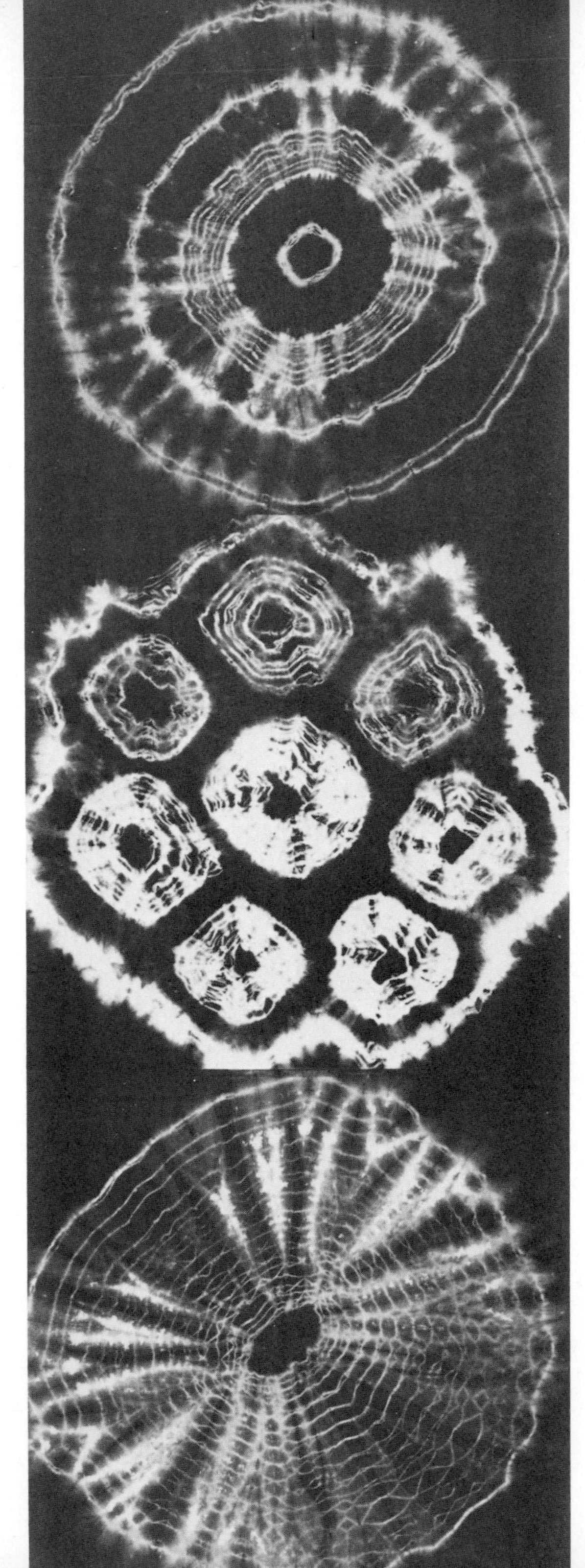

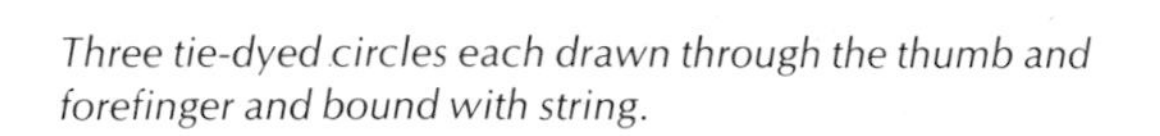

Three tie-dyed circles each drawn through the thumb and forefinger and bound with string.

SIX BASIC TIE DYE TECHNIQUES

In addition to circles, there are many other processes for producing pattern and texture with tie dye. All examples are of lightweight cotton bound with pearl cotton and dyed with household dye.

Wrinkling. The fabric strip was simply wrinkled up in random fashion and casually bound.
Clips. The fabric strip was accordion-pleated and constricted with six small and one large clip.
Knotting. The fabric strip was folded in half (end to end) and the center was knotted once in a simple overhand knot. The ends were then each knotted twice.
Pleating. The fabric was accordion-pleated with very narrow pleats and bound. An iron helps when sharp creases are important.
Twisting. The fabric strip was twisted for some time until it doubled back on itself. The doubling back was coaxed to the center while the ends were held tight. The entire length was then bound at even intervals.
Folding. The fabric was alternately folded vertically and diagonally. Two ends of the resulting triangle were then bound.

Right, from top to bottom: *Methods 1, 2, 3, 4, 5, and 6.*

TIE DYEING WITH GATHERED RUNNING STITCHES

Gathered running stitches on evenly pleated fabric are the basis for the two beautifully regulated repeat patterns shown. The process is similar to the method for circles illustrated earlier.

METHOD

Follow the general instructions for tie dye given on pp. 99–100, but prepare the fabric as follows:

1. Press overlapping pleats in a graduated shingle effect.
2. With a needle and strong thread make short, even running stitches through the folded section of the pleat for the desired width of fabric, which is usually from selvedge to selvedge. In the first example, half ovals have been stitched in a horizontal brick pattern. In the second example, straight horizontal lines have been stitched on the pleat to produce a tunnel just large enough to insert the wooden sticks with a snug fit.
3. There are several ways to accomplish the next process, gathering:
   a. *side to side*—knot the threads used for the running stitches at one side of the fabric and simply pull them from the other side. As each thread is pulled, it is knotted to hold the gathers in place.
   b. *sides to center*—place a weight such as a book or clean brick in the center of the running stitched fabric. Now pull gently on the thread while pushing the fabric toward the weighted center. When gathered, knot the thread to keep the folds in place and repeat the operation on the remaining side. In either case the gathers will fall evenly in place if some vertical tension is applied. This is best done while gathering the fabric but can also be done after gathering is finished.
4. No binding is needed in the second example, but if it is to be applied as in the first example it is done at this point. Notice the consistency of the binding and the way in which it produces the small white horizontal lines in the finished fabric. The binding must be very tight to accomplish this fine line effect.
5. Wet the fabric and proceed with dyeing.

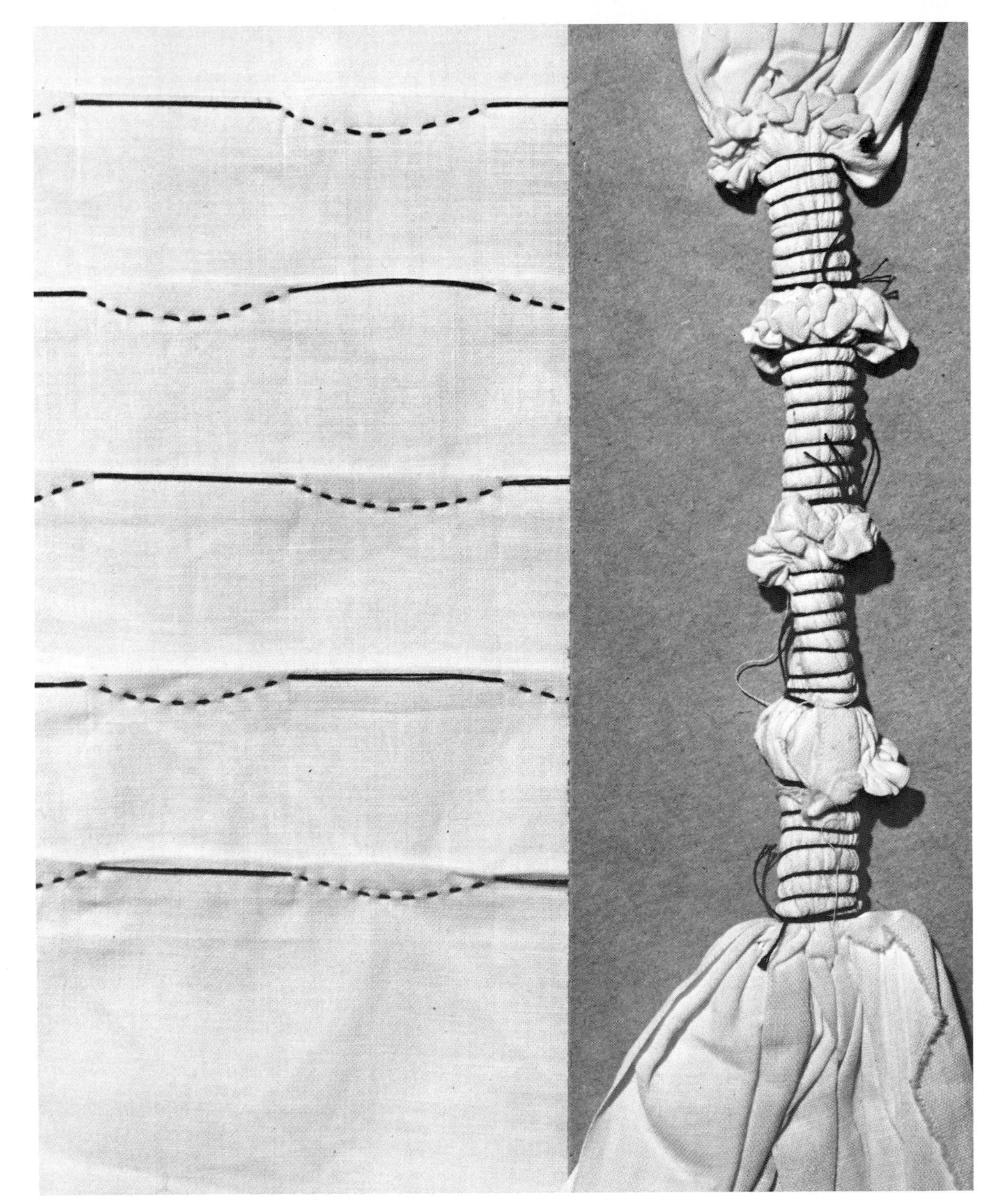

The stitched and bound fabric has been dyed and the threads released.

Left: *Running stitches in pleated fabric.* Right: *Fabric has been gathered on the running stitches and bound in the interspaces.*

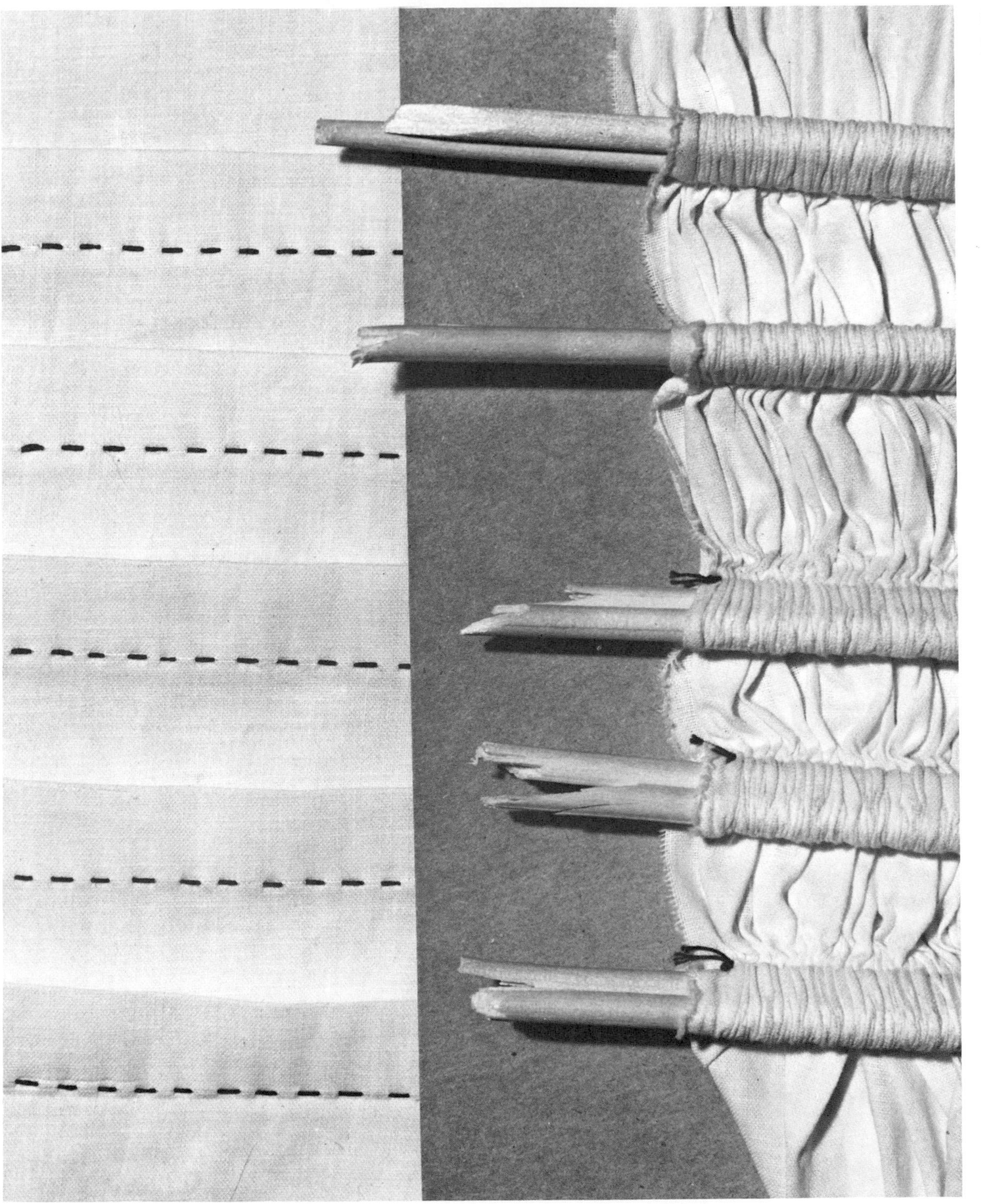

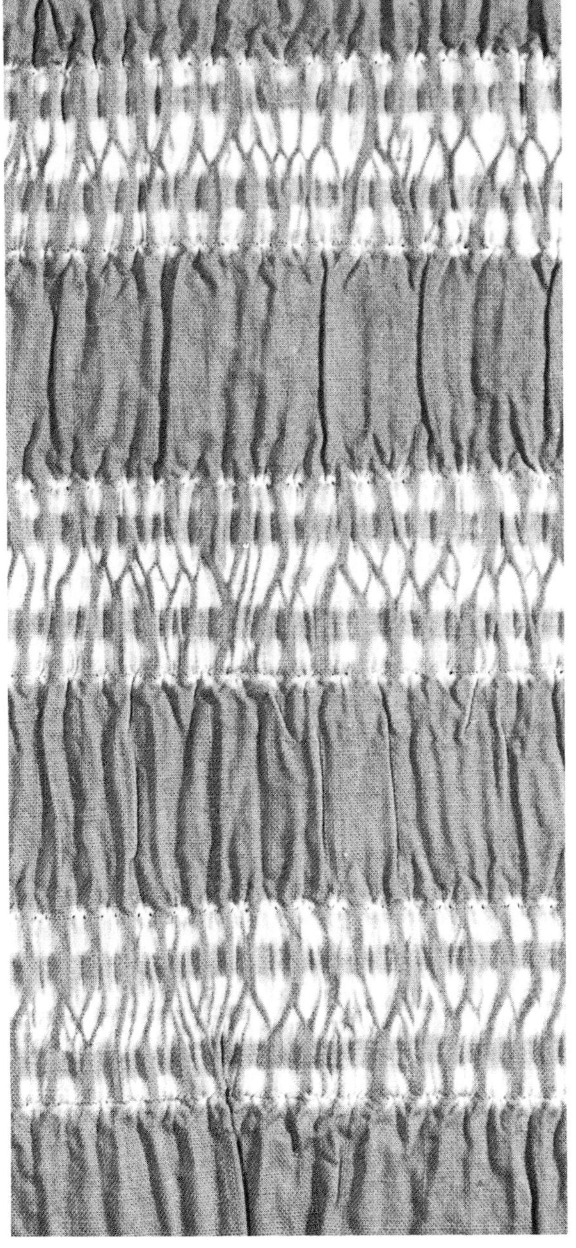

Left: *Running stitches have been made in the overlapped pleats to form narrow casings. Sticks have been inserted in the casings and the fabric has been gathered.* Above: *The fabric has been dyed and the sticks and threads removed.*

RESIST DYEING WITH CLAMPED BLOCKS

As we have seen, tying, sewing, and wrapping produce very characteristic dye resist effects involving tonal gradations and often sharp lines. In these processes the resist shapes are generally bound one at a time. Resist dyeing with clamped blocks differs in both effect and working procedure. The effect is always repetitive and seldom linear, though the tonal gradations resemble conventional dye. The procedure is slightly simpler in that the resisting is done all at once since the blocks are clamped in place.

MATERIALS

Fabric to be dyed
Plywood—3/8 inch or thicker.
Saw—Coping, jig, or band.
C-clamps—One or more depending on the project.
Dye and dye equipment—Must be compatible with fabric to be dyed. Suggestions will be found in chapter 3.

METHOD

1. Wash and press the fabric to be dyed.
2. Transfer the design to the plywood with carbon paper, remembering to mirror image the drawings. For most projects plywood of about 3/8 inch is satisfactory. Very large blocks require thicker plywood.
3. The plywood blocks may be cut by hand with a coping saw, or with an electric jigsaw or bandsaw.
4. If the blocks have appendages or poorly supported sections, it is a good idea to cut a pair of backing or support boards to even out the pressure. Boards may be attached to the blocks with glue or may be left loose.
5. Fold the fabric to the desired shape. Keep the folds as neat and even as possible. Pressing with an iron as the folds progress is sometimes necessary. The folded bundle should be just a bit larger than the plywood block.
6. Sandwich the fabric between the blocks, making certain that they are perfectly aligned. Add support boards now if required.
7. Apply one or more C-clamps to the bundle. The number of clamps depends on the size and shape of the blocks and to some extent on their thickness. The objective is to produce very firm even pressure.
8. Wet the fabric thoroughly and allow to drain. At this stage and also during the dyeing which follows it is helpful to knead heavily folded protruding edges periodically to assure even penetration of the liquids.
9. Dye the fabric according to the instructions in chapter 3 for the dye you have chosen.
10. If a single color is being dyed, the process ends here with a final rinse and a pressing of the fabric. A number of interesting overdye options might be tried.
    a. A graded halo effect results if you refold the fabric on its original folds and sandwich the fabric between smaller blocks of the same shape as the original block prior to overdyeing.
    b. Same as *a*, but go to a larger block of the same shape as the first.
    c. Same as *a*, but offset the original block to one side before overdyeing. In other words, intentionally misregister the blocks.
    d. For a complex appearing but relatively easy process showing overlapping transparency, refold the once-dyed fabric on a different but related grid system. Then sandwich the fabric between the original blocks and overdye.
    e. Same as *d*, but use a different pair of blocks.
    f. Use the once-dyed fabric as a basis for embellishment with conventional tiedye, direct printing, or any of the other techniques featured in this book.

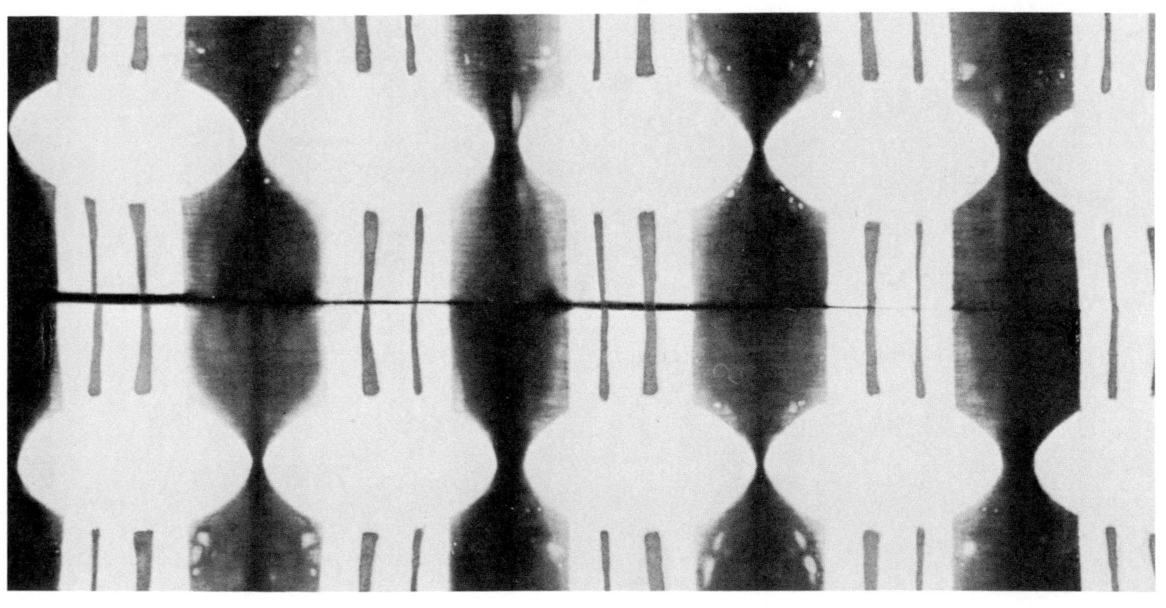

Block and clamp resist dyed fabric. Reactive dye on cotton.

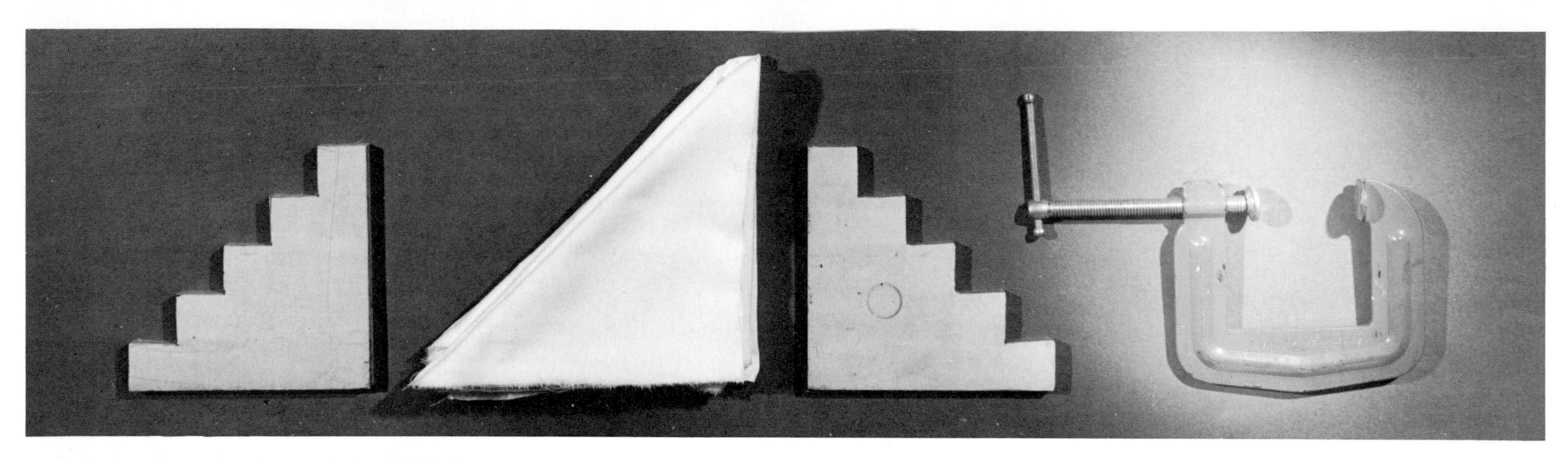

Materials required for resist dyeing with clamped blocks.

Materials assembled and ready for dyeing.

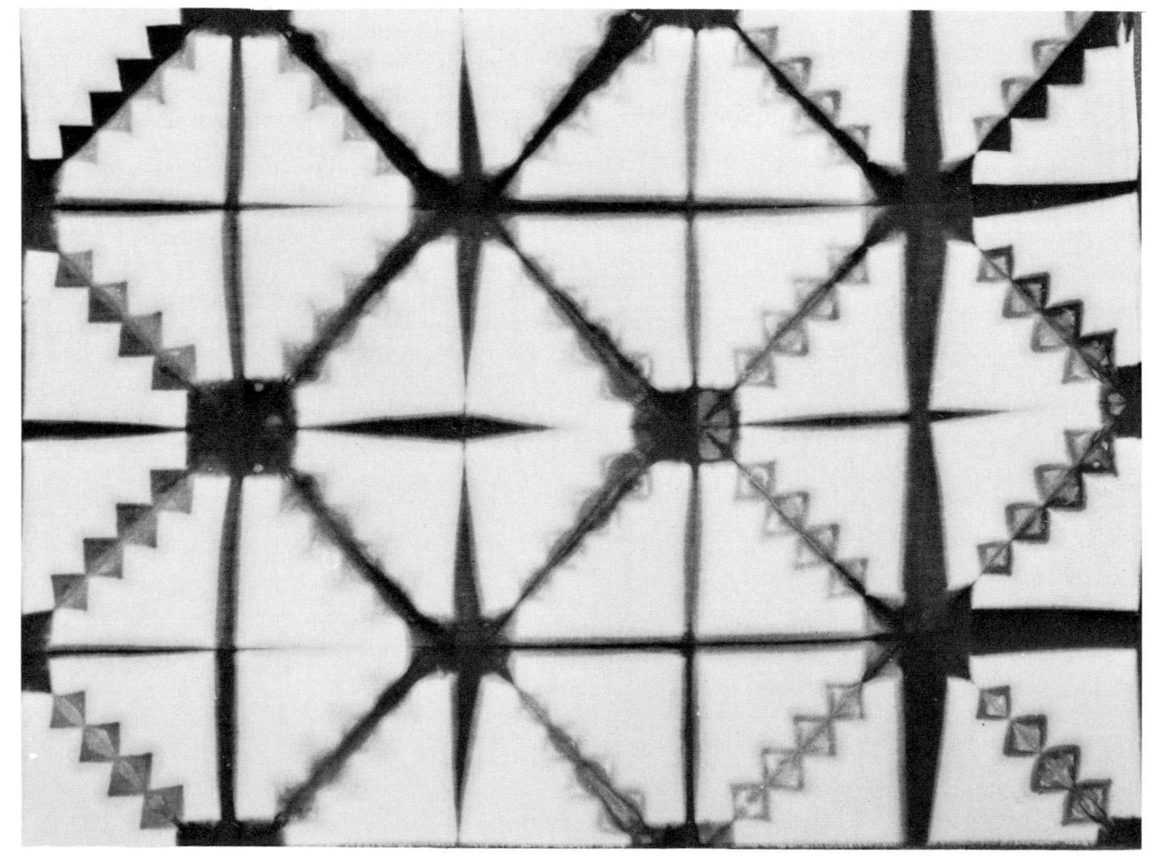

The finished block and clamp resist dyed fabric. Reactive dye on cotton.

TIE DISCHARGE AND DYE WITH WAX RESIST

In the discharge process, a dark fabric, generally black cotton, is bound and bleached. The bindings retain the original dark fabric color and waxed areas and lines are likewise preserved. With some areas lightened and the resist binding released it is a simple matter to apply more wax and brush dye color. A very handy and effective sequence is outlined below.

MATERIALS

Dark bleachable cotton or viscose rayon—Preferably black. Take a small jar of bleaching solution (half water and half bleach) to the fabric store and test a swatch before purchasing in quantity. The fabric should lighten in one or two minutes.
Light chalk
Binding material—Crochet cotton or button and carpet thread.
Wax resist materials and equipment—See chapter 5.
Discharge materials and equipment—See chapter 3, under "Discharge Substances."
Inko brand prepared vat dye for cotton—Or substitute dye paste.
Small plastic pans for mixing dye
Dye brush
Iron

METHOD

1. Wash and press the dark fabric.
2. Sketch the composition or a few proportional guidelines on the fabric with a light-colored chalk.
3. Stretch the fabric on a frame.
4. Apply melted wax as desired with brush or tjanting. Wax resist instructions are given in chapter 5 if a review is needed.
5. When wax is cool, fabric is removed from the frame and the desired areas are bound with crochet cotton or carpet thread.
6. Discharge the waxed and bound fabric to a light or medium color in a solution of one part chlorine bleach to three parts water as described in Chapter 3.
7. Rinse the fabric well in running water for three to five minutes.
8. Release binding material, rinse a second time, and allow the fabric to dry flat.
9. Restretch the fabric on a frame.
10. Additional wax may now be applied if some of the light discharged fabric is to be retained.
11. Inko brand prepared vat dye is now brushed into the desired areas. Detailed instructions for this dye are given in chapter 3. If the sun happens to be shining at this point, expose the dyed fabric to it until the colors develop, usually in three to five minutes. If not simply proceed to Step 12.
12. Place the fabric between absorbent paper and press with a hot iron. This will serve two purposes. First, it will remove most of the wax and second, it will develop the Inko dye if sunlight was not available for Step 11.
13. Residual wax may be left in the fabric or removed by dry-cleaning.

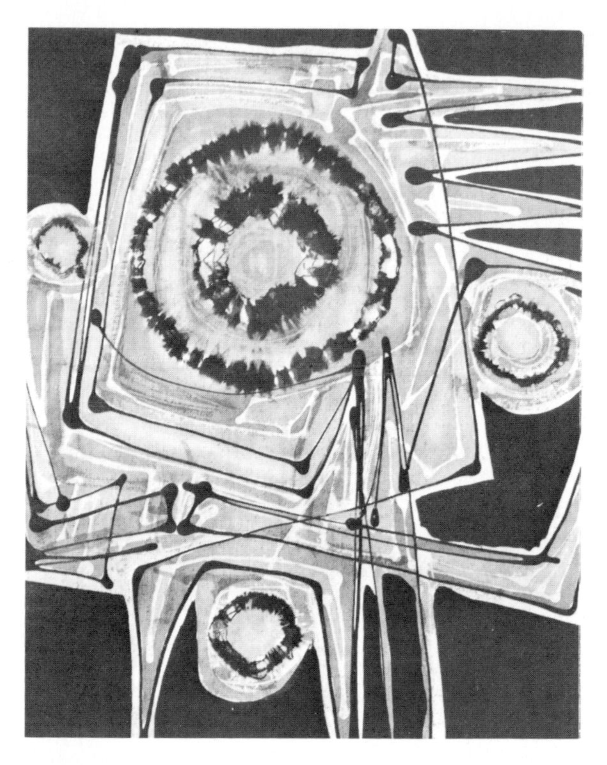

Above: *This piece began as black fabric. Melted wax as well as binding were used to resist the action of bleach in the discharge process. Gray lines show where a second application of wax will preserve the lightest hue.*

Below: *Finished composition. Tie discharge and dye with wax resist. Inko vat dye on cotton.*

Examples of Bound Resist Dyeing

Left and Right: *Indian turban cloth. Rajastan State, Jaipur. Virginia and Prentice Bloedel Collection, Costume and Textile Study Center, University of Washington.*

Above: *Indian Wedding Sari (detail), dyed at Bhuj (Gujarat). Fine handwoven cotton. Elizabeth Palmer Baley Collection, Costume and Textile Study Center, University of Washington.*

Left: *Royal cloth. Stitch resisted cotton cloth dyed with indigo. Western grassland area, Bum group, African Cameroon, 72" x 216" (182 x 549 cm). Collection of Mr. and Mrs. Paul Gebauer, McMinnville, Oregon.*

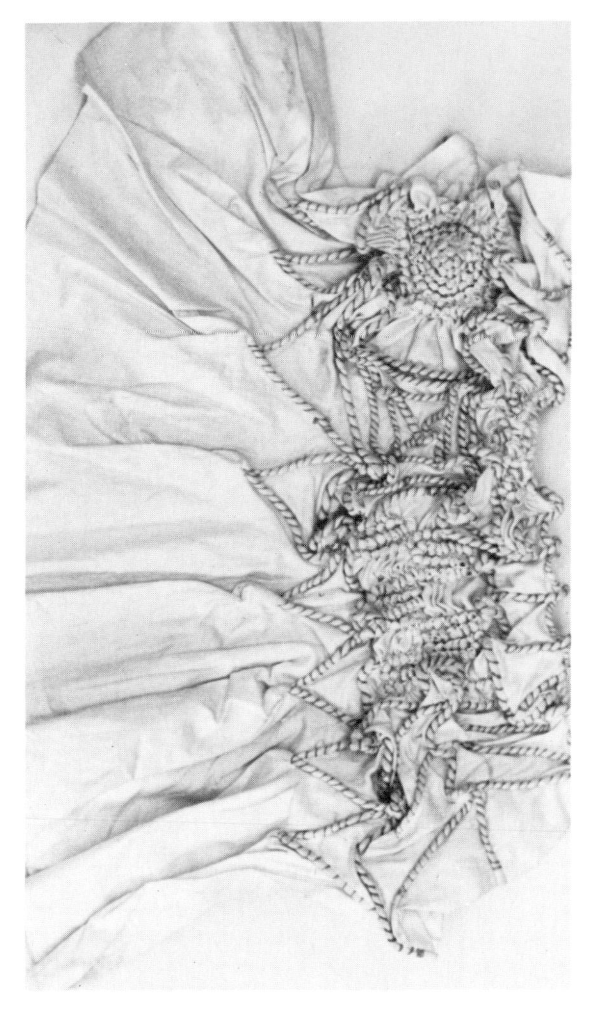

Right: *Tritik, or stitch resist dyed cloth. Indigo on cotton. Yoruba, Nigeria, West Africa. Collection of Simon Ottenberg, Seattle, Washington.*

Above: *Tie dye or tritik in progress showing the manner in which the carefully stitched linear elements will resist the dye. Yoruba, Abeokuta, Nigeria, West Africa. Courtesy of the Lowie Museum of Anthropology, University of California, Berkeley.*

Left: *Marian Clayden. Detail of a very long tie dyed silk banner used in the Los Angeles production of* Hair. *Private collection, Langley, Washington.*

Right: *Kimono fragment. Silk, Japanese, middle of Edo period, about 1750, L. 26″(66 cm). Eugene Fuller Memorial Collection, Seattle Art Museum.*

Far right: *Bustle sash or obi-age. Contemporary Japanese, light blues on white silk damask, 12″ x 46″(30.5 x 177.5 cm). Gift of Miss Blanche Payne, Seattle Art Museum.*

7. Direct Printing

Direct printing is probably the oldest and simplest method employed to produce a repeated image. The process involves the application of color to an object or block and the careful placement of it on fabric or fabriclike material. The color is transferred, producing a characteristic mirror-image impression. The potato printing most of us enjoyed as children is a form of direct printing.

Stamps or blocks are the usual objects used for direct printing. Linoleum is most commonly selected for block printing because it yields gently to carving tools but holds up well under continued use. The possibilities for design and arrangement are many. The choice of placement is unlimited, as are the possibilities for detail and effect. Any relief surface, whether etched, engraved, carved, or built-up, can be inked and printed. The carving of a block can be one of the most appealing aspects of this process, and more than one such block has become a treasured object when no longer in use.

Block-printed fabric has a unique handmade look which is seldom confused with other textile art forms. This look results from the slight irregularities in inking, pressure, and placement. Unavoidable characteristics such as these provide a feeling of vitality and movement impossible to achieve by mass production.

Tools for Direct Printing

Most art supply stores or mail-order houses stock the tools necessary for block printing. Most are modest in price.

Sculptors' mallet for printing pressure—A rubber automotive bodywork mallet is favored by some as it is less noisy.

Gouges for carving wood or linoleum blocks—Several kinds are available, including a Speedball set having a single handle and interchangeable gouge tips.

X-acto or other sharp-pointed knife—For carving small areas and sharp corners. It may also be used to score and cut sheet linoleum.

Pallet knife—For mixing printing paste.

Soft or semisoft rubber brayers for transferring dye paste to the printing block.

Dye pastes or paste paints (block printing inks) as required—Dye pastes and paste paints are both discussed in chapter 3.

A perfectly flat nonporous surface—On which to spread the printing paste with the brayer. A 12 by 18 inch sheet of glass, metal, or plastic is ideal, but a tray or cookie sheet will do.

Appropriate solvent—For oil base inks, mineral spirits or paint thinner is required.

Printing table—A smooth table covered first with a blanket and then with vinyl fabric or oilcloth will usually serve the purpose.

Pins or tape—To secure the printing fabric in place.

Techniques for Direct Printing

PRINTING FOUND OBJECTS WITH OIL BASE INK

Printing with readymade or found objects is deceptively simple. The process sometimes masquerades under the dubious title of "junk printing." It is indeed possible to print with junk, but the exciting challenge is to combine simple, common elements in new contexts. In addition to whatever artistic value it may have, object printing becomes an intriguing game of visual economy in which more is achieved with less.

Repeat designs printed with eraser block. All are fiber-reactive dye on cotton.

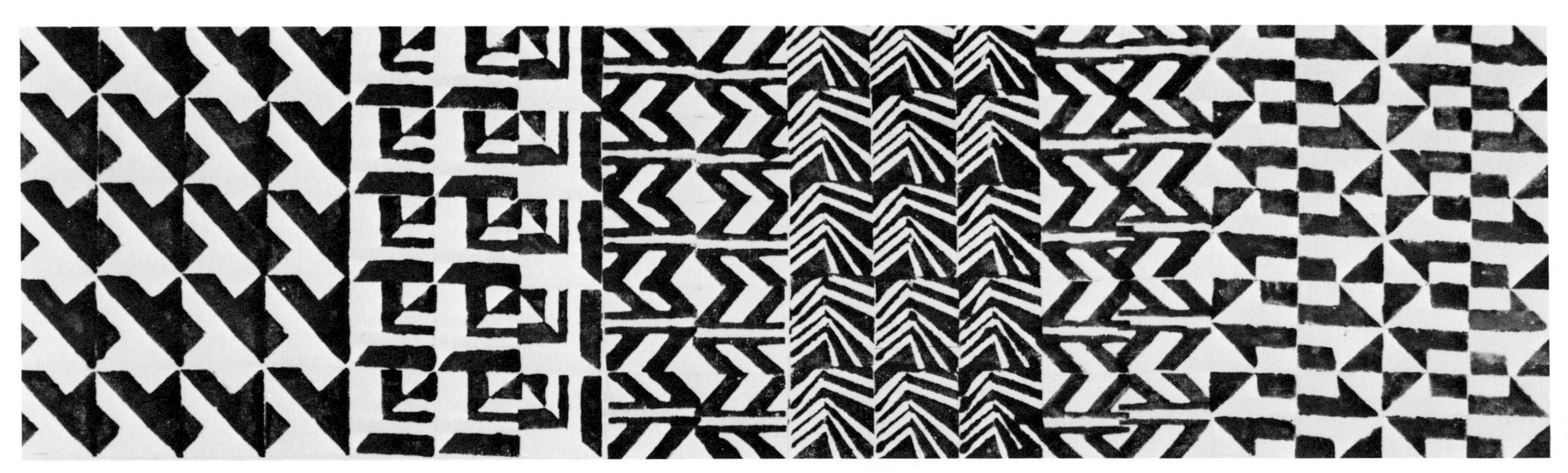

MATERIALS

Rigid or noncrushable textural objects—Might include tools, gadgets, or natural forms.
Oil base block printing ink
Brayer—Preferably soft rubber.
Inking tile—A smooth flat nonporous surface for the even application of ink.
Lightly padded printing surface—A screen printing table is ideal, but a smooth table covered first with a blanket and then with vinyl fabric or oilcloth will do.
Fabric to be printed
Drying area or clothesline
Tape or pins—For attaching fabric to the printing table.
Appropriate solvent—Usually mineral spirits, and clean-up supplies.

METHOD

1. Stretch washed and pressed fabric in place on the printing table and secure it with pins or masking tape.
2. Prepare the ink by spreading several inches of it on top of the tile. Small amounts of artists' oil color for an expanded color range or additives such as dryers and/or transparent extenders may be mixed with the ink at this point. Roll out enough of the ink to coat the brayer and roll it several times diagonally as well as back and forth. When rolling the ink out on the tile, lift the brayer at the end of every other stroke so that contact points vary. This will produce an even coating of ink.
3. Roll the inked brayer several times and if possible in several directions over the ridges or high parts of the found object.
4. Printing is achieved by simply stamping the object on the fabric surface. If the object is flat, downward pressure will be adequate, but if it is convex a slight rolling motion will be necessary. Concave objects are generally not suitable for direct printing.
5. Printed fabric should be allowed to dry thoroughly. A warm, arid atmosphere will speed drying, but some colors are naturally slower than others. Hand or machine wash gently and do not dry-clean.
6. Clean-up is best achieved with mineral spirits (paint thinner), rags, and hot, soapy water.

Two blocks were used to print this pattern derived from the capital of a painted Egyptian column.

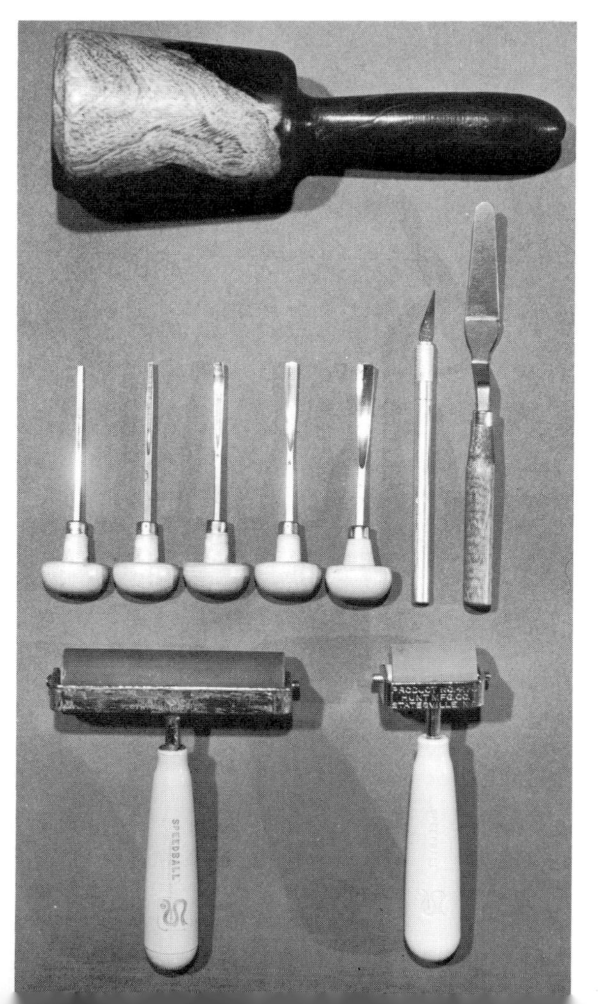

Tools for direct printing.

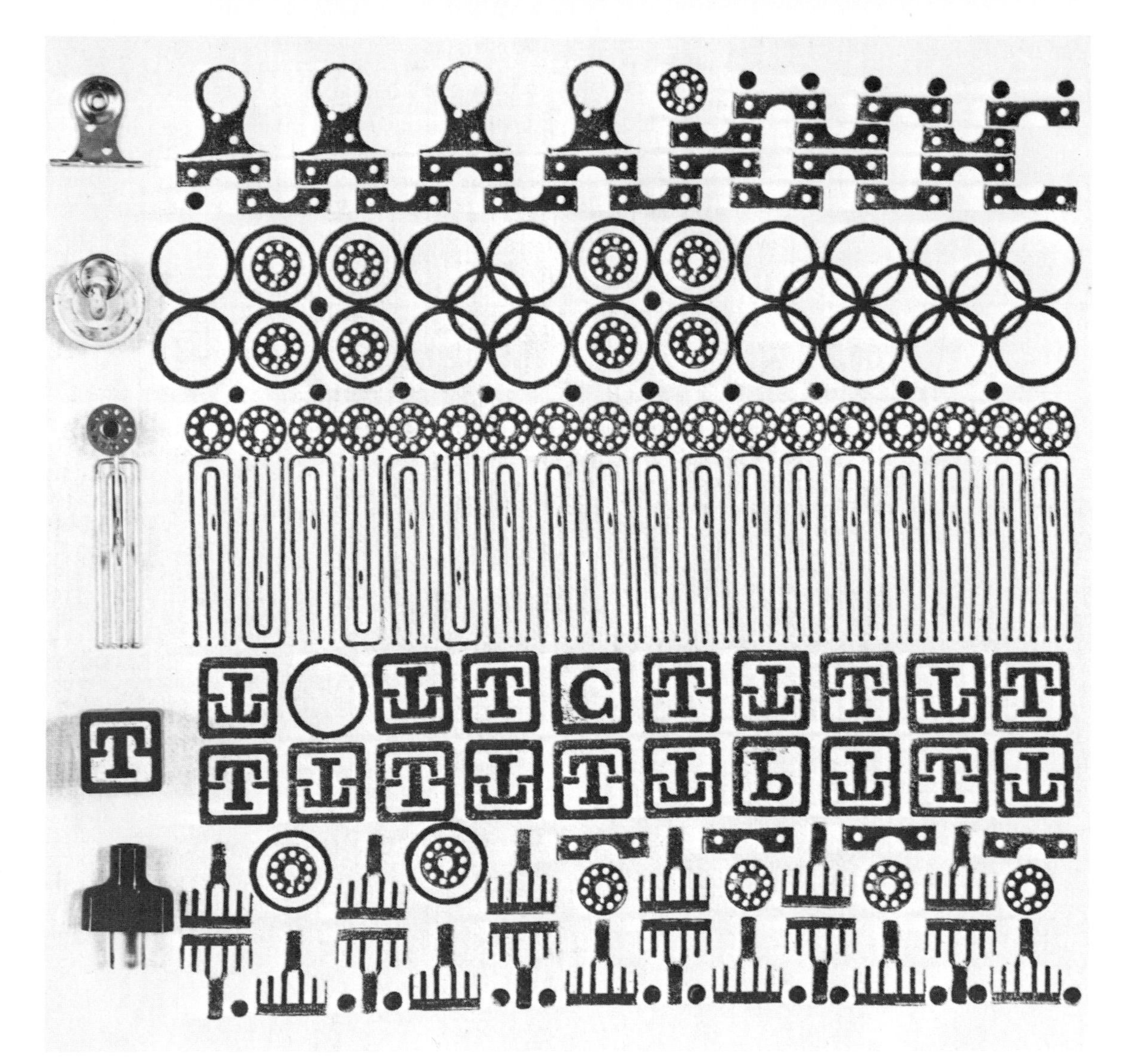

Common household objects have been used to stamp print this sampler. Oil-base block printing ink on unbleached cotton muslin.

PRINTING WITH CARDBOARD

It is possible to cut shapes from cardboard, coat them with dye or ink, or paste, and print them. Results are obtained quickly, simply, and economically. Some detail is possible but it is best to keep the shapes relatively bold and simple. Since the blocks are easy to make, several interchangeable or modular shapes may be employed.

MATERIALS

Cardboard—Tablet backing, matboard, or chipboard.
Sharp knife or utility scissors—For cutting cardboard.
Dye paste or paste paint
Roller or brayer—For dye paste a short nap paint roller is best, and for ink a soft rubber brayer is recommended.
Shallow pan or tile—The former for dye, the latter for ink.
Printing surface, lightly padded—A smooth table covered first with a blanket and then with vinyl fabric or oilcloth.
Fabric to be printed–For dye be certain to check affinity of dye to fiber, for ink the fiber content is irrelevant but fabrics treated with soil-release additives should be avoided.
Appropriate solvent and clean-up supplies

METHOD

1. Secure the washed and pressed fabric to the printing surface with tape or pins.
2. Prepare dye or ink. Place dye in a shallow, nonmetallic pan, or the ink on a large tile.
3. By means of paint roller or brayer, transfer the dye or ink directly to the surface of the cardboard as necessary.
4. Carefully lift the block and place it ink side down on the fabric.
5. Apply pressure to the back (clean) side of the cardboard with simple hand pressure or by means of a rolling pin or similar cylindrical object. The first few impressions may be uneven so it is best to make them on scrap material. If the problem persists, overprinting is usually the solution.

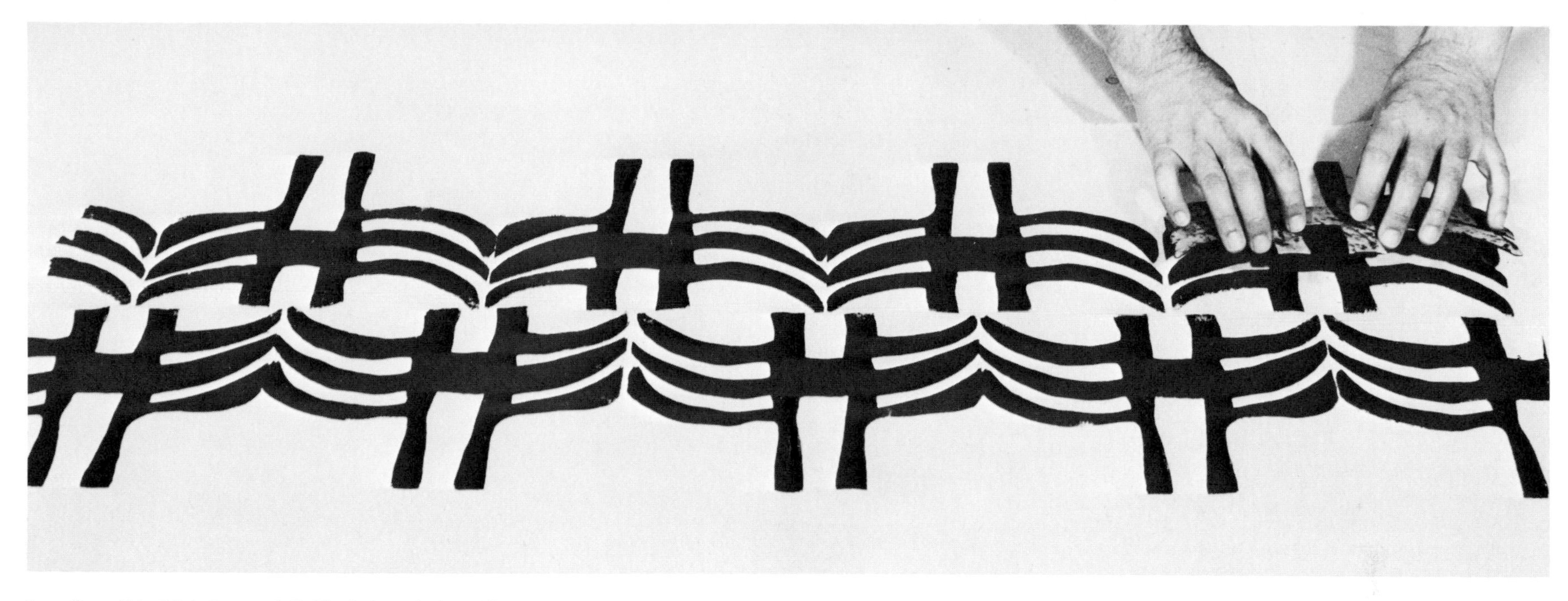

A cardboard block is being carefully lifted after printing with simple hand pressure. Textile paint on cotton. Paint was applied to the block with a small housepainters' roller.

6. Repeat Steps 3 through 5 the desired number of times.
7. Allow fabric to dry and perform whatever fixing or finishing is required.
8. If the block is to be reused, clean it as quickly as possible and with a minimum of water. A cardboard block will dry flat if wrapped in absorbent paper and weighted overnight. If, however, a cardboard block breaks down from moisture it is easy to cut a duplicate shape.

PRINTING DYE WITH CUT AND MOUNTED FELT

Felt is an inexpensive, readily available material with excellent dye absorption capability. Since it may be cut with scissors, it is particularly easy to use. Felt shapes provide an excellent means of creating bold simple shapes which may later be overprinted with some other form of printing or even direct dye application. The possible combinations are countless.

MATERIALS

Felt—Try to locate felt that is approximately ⅛ inch thick.
Sharp scissors
Waterproof glue
Plywood—Scraps will do. The thickness is irrelevant, although ¼ inch or ⅜ inch is easy to cut and handle.
Dye paste
Brush or felt pad in a dish or pan—The choice here depends on application method.
Printing surface, lightly padded–A smooth table covered first with a blanket and then with vinyl fabric or oilcloth.
Fabric to be printed–Be certain that the dye and fiber content have an affinity for each other. The fabric should be washed and pressed.
Clean-up supplies

METHOD

1. Cut felt shape or shapes with sharp scissors. If only thin felt is available, two layers may be bonded together by means of a thermoplastic adhesive such as Stitch Witchery.
2. Glue the cut felt to plywood blocks of appropriate size. The glue should not be water soluble when dry. Allow glue to dry thoroughly.
3. Secure the washed and pressed fabric to the printing surface by means of tape or pins.

4. Prepare the dye paste to the approximate consistency of heavy cream and proceed by either of the following methods. In either case, it takes a bit of experimentation to determine the exact amount of dye required for a good image so a practice piece is recommended.
5. *Method A.* Apply the dye to the felt surface with a brush, and stamp the block on the fabric in the desired location. Simple hand pressure should be sufficient for a clear print.

   Method B. Prepare a simple printing pad by placing a piece of felt in a shallow dish or pan. Saturate the pad with relatively thin dye paste. Press the felt surface of the printing block to the pad several times and print as in Method A. Large blocks may require more than hand pressure. In this case a mallet may be used, or when printing on a smooth floor, foot pressure with body weight will usually suffice.
6. Allow printed fabric to dry and set the dye according to the manufacturer's instruction.

Above right: *Dye paste is being applied to the block for printing.*

Right: *The block is being pressed into a felt pad saturated with dye. This method is similar to the familiar rubber stamp process.*

PRINTING WITH GLUE-COVERED BLOCKS

Relief printing involves a built-up surface. The application of ordinary white glue is one of the simplest and most direct means of creating a relief printing block. Since the dry glue is smooth and hard, the block is best printed with oil base ink or a viscous paste paint. It is best to cover the entire surface of the block with patterns of lines and dots so that the inked brayer is unable to deposit color on the base material of the block.

MATERIALS

Plywood, hardboard, or masonite blocks
Casein-base white glue in a squeeze bottle
Oil base printing ink
Fabric to be printed—The fiber content is irrelevant, but fabrics treated with soil-release additives should be avoided.
Inking tile or substitute
Soft rubber brayer
Printing surface, lightly padded—A smooth table first covered with a blanket and then with vinyl fabric or oilcloth.
Appropriate solvent and clean-up supplies

METHOD

1. Cut the plywood to the desired shape.
2. If the design has been worked out ahead of time it may now be transferred to the block either freehand or with carbon paper.
3. Using a plastic squeeze bottle, apply generous lines or dots of glue to pattern. Work slowly and be prepared for a slight settling or puddling of the glue.
4. Allow the glue to dry thoroughly. It should be hard and no longer milky in color.
5. Stretch the washed and pressed fabric in place on the printing surface and secure it with pins and tape.
6. Prepare the inked tile by spreading several inches of ink at the end of the tile farthest away from you. Small amounts of artists' oil color may be added to the printing ink for an expanded color range. Additives such as dryers or transparent extenders may be thoroughly mixed with the ink. Next bring most of it toward you with the brayer and roll it several times diagonally as well as back and forth and lift the brayer at the end of every other stroke so that contact points vary.
7. Roll the inked brayer several times in several directions over the bumps and lines produced by the dry glue. Make an effort not to get ink on the plywood itself unless a flat tone or woodgrain effect is desired.
8. Printing is achieved by simply stamping the block on the fabric surface. Experiment to determine if hand pressure is sufficient or whether a mallet or even foot pressure is necessary for a clear image.
9. Printed fabric should be allowed to dry thoroughly. A warm arid atmosphere will speed drying, but some colors are by nature slower in drying than others. Fabric may be gently washed by hand or machine. Do not dry-clean.
10. Clean-up is best achieved with mineral spirits (paint thinner), rags, and hot, soapy water. Do not soak the glue block in water for more than a few moments though since the casein glue may dissolve. Coating the block with spar varnish or shellac after the glue is dry will make it impervious to moisture in the clean-up process.

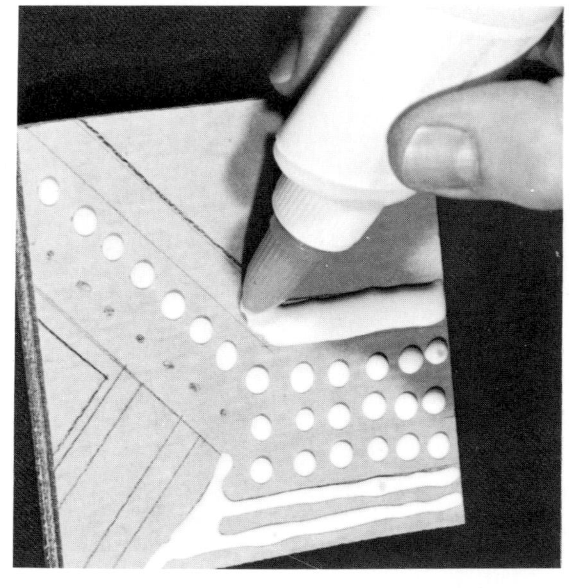

White glue is being applied directly to the plywood block.

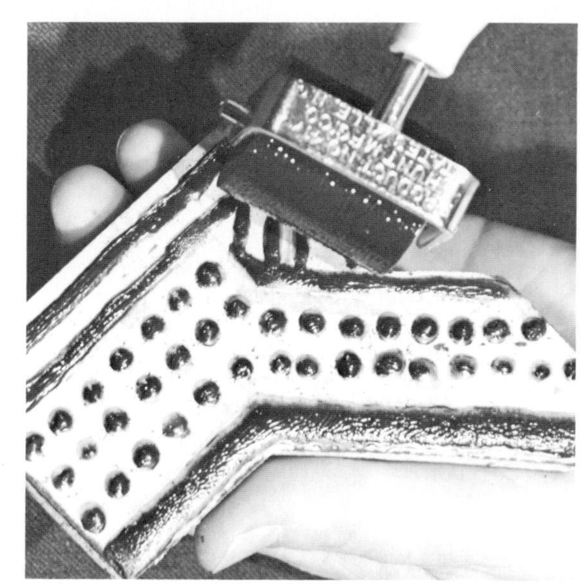

The thoroughly dry, glue-covered block is being inked with a small soft rubber brayer. Note that some of the unnecessary plywood has been removed.

The finished fabric showing one of many repeat design possibilities for the block.

STAMP PRINTING WITH CARVED ERASERS

The common, soft rubber eraser is easily carved and may be used to print either a dye paste or a paste paint. Due to scale limitations, the process is ideally suited to printing small fabrics such as apparel accessories, embellishing larger forms, and decorating fabric or paper.

MATERIALS

Erasers—Either the art gum or soft rubber variety is best.
Knife or single-edge razor blade for a carving tool
Small soft brush
Dye paste or paste paint
Fabric to be printed—For dye paste, be certain to check affinity of dye to fiber content. For paste paint, the fiber content is irrelevant, but fabrics treated with soil-release additives should be avoided.
Printing surface—A flat smooth space covered with several layers of newspaper works well.
Solvent and clean-up supplies

METHOD

1. Apply guidelines to the eraser with a soft pencil.
2. Carve away areas or lines which are intended not to print.
3. Place washed and pressed fabric on newspaper-covered printing area.
4. Brush dye or paint on to the carved eraser. Note that some brushstroke effect may be visible.
5. Stamp the block on to the fabric with firm but gentle pressure. Remember that art gum erasers will crumble if treated roughly.
6. Allow fabric to dry, and fix or finish dye process according to the manufacturer's recommendation.

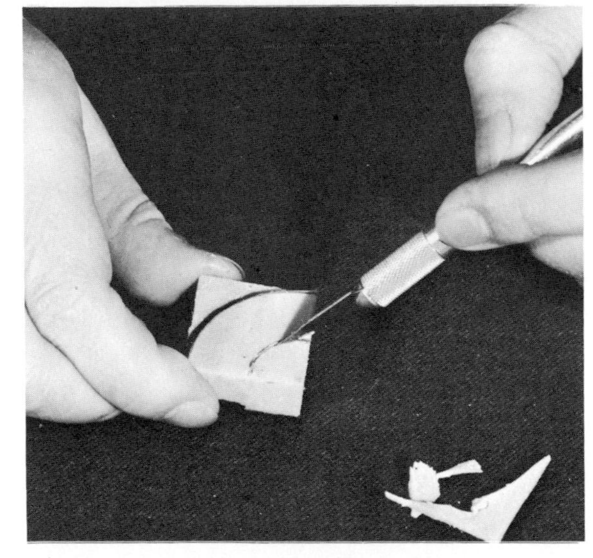

A small art gum eraser is being carved.

The eraser block is being stamp printed with simple hand pressure.

Dye paste (Procion) is being brushed onto the carved eraser block.

PRINTING DYE WITH A FLOCKED BLOCK

A dense surface such as plywood or hardboard can be made to absorb dye by first coating it with several layers of flock. This is the simple principle involved in this method of direct printing.

MATERIALS

Wooden block
Spar varnish
Varnish brush
Flock
Flour sifter
Dye paste
Paint roller, small with short nap
Printing surface, lightly padded—A smooth table first covered with blanketing, then covered with vinyl fabric or oilcloth works well.
Fabric to be printed—Be certain to check the affinity of dye class with fiber content.

METHOD

1. Saw the wooden block to the desired shape. An electric jigsaw is most convenient for complex shapes, but a handheld coping saw would serve the purpose. In the example shown here a backing piece has been cut in order to protect the more fragile parts and to insure even pressure in printing. If a backing is required, it should be glued with a waterproof adhesive and allowed to dry thoroughly.
2. Brush varnish on the face of the block.
3. Using the flour sifter, apply a thick but even coating of flock. Adhesion will be improved if a weighted board is placed on top of the flocked surface while drying. When thoroughly dry, apply an additional coat each of varnish and flock in the same manner.
4. Secure the washed and pressed fabric to the printing surface with pins and tape.
5. Prepare the dye paste to the approximate consistency of thick cream and pour a small quantity in a flat shallow pan, preferably of glass or plastic.

Flock is being dusted onto the varnished block with a flour sifter so that it will absorb dye paste.

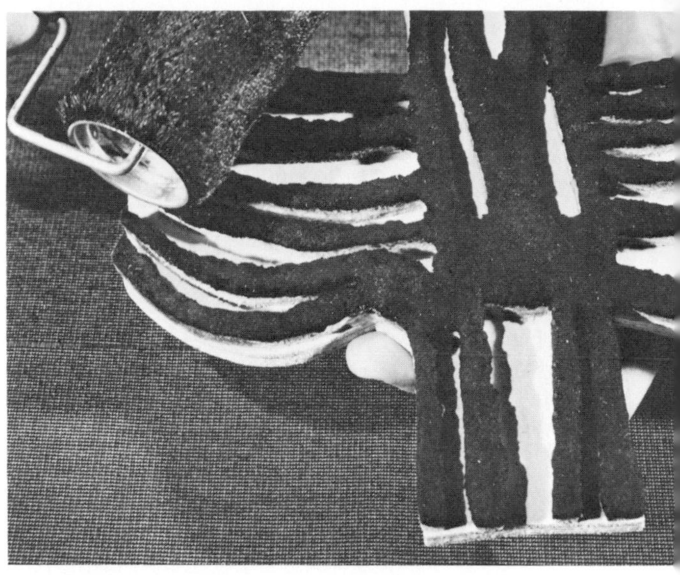

Dye paste is being applied to the flocked block with a short nap paint roller.

Section of printed fabric, prepared vat dye on cotton.

6. With a small, short-nap paint roller, apply an even coat of dye from the pan to the printing block as shown.
7. Printing is achieved by stamping the block in the desired position on the fabric. For small blocks, hand pressure is usually enough, but large or irregular shaped blocks may require a few strokes with a mallet.

PRINTING WITH A LINOLEUM BLOCK AND OIL BASE INK

MATERIALS

Linoleum—It is best to purchase linoleum-covered wooden blocks manufactured specifically for printing. Unmounted battleship linoleum is an alternate choice and offers greater flexibility on size but is difficult to find. In either case it must be soft enough to carve easily. Good printing linoleum will yield slightly to fingernail pressure.

Carbon paper—For transferring design to the linoleum block.

Gouges—Several sets are available. One type provides five different interchangeable blades and a single handle, while others have fixed handles.

Fabric to be printed, washed, and pressed—Fiber content is a matter here of personal choice since oil base ink can be printed on almost anything. Fabrics with soil-release additives should be avoided.

Tailors' chalk or similar marker—For making registration guidelines.

Large tile for inking—Any flat, smooth nonporous surface about 12 by 18 inches will serve the purpose.

Oil base block printing ink

Artists' oil colors (optional)

Drying agents and/or transparent extenders (optional)

Palette knife (optional)

Mineral spirits (paint thinner) and other clean-up supplies as needed

Above: *Linoleum is being gouged from areas that are not intended to print, as described in Method step 2.*

Below: *White oil-base block printing ink is being rolled onto the block with a soft rubber brayer as described in Method step 7. Note that the ink on the tile has been rolled in several directions as in Method step 6.*

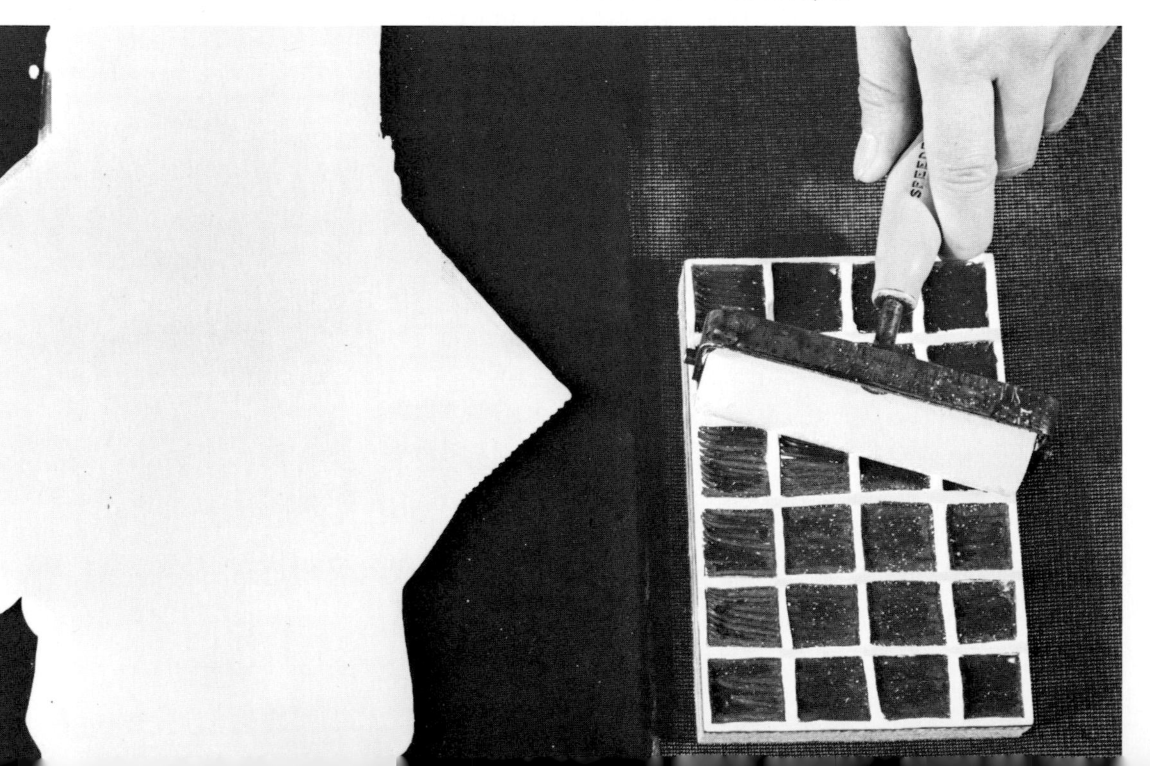

METHOD

1. Transfer the design to the linoleum surface using carbon paper or similar means. Remember that the finished print will be a mirror image of the block, not its duplicate.
2. The recommended procedure for carving is as follows:

   With a small *u*- or *v*-shaped gouge, outline all areas that are to be removed. Always carve away from yourself for safety reasons. If the linoleum crumbles or releases with a rough uneven edge, the gouge is being pushed too deep or it is very dull. It is safer and neater to make two shallow cuts than to attempt one deep one.

   Select a larger *u*-shaped gouge and remove the nonprinting areas outlines in the first step.

   Make a few sample prints, or "proofs" as they are correctly called. This may be done with water base ink for greater ease in clean-up. The proofs will show what areas need to be carved deeper, and whether there are any problems with line up in the case of repeat designs. Also, if you are in doubt about removing an area of linoleum, leave it in and proof the block a few times to judge the effect. It is simple to remove a section or line, but virtually impossible to replace once it is carved away.

   Make any necessary corrections or add final details.
3. Linoleum blocks may be cut to any shape and are often easier to register if this is done.
4. Secure the fabric in place on the printing surface with masking tape or pins.
5. Guidelines for registering the block while printing may be added now with a water soluble marker if desired.
6. Prepare the ink by spreading several inches of it on top of the tile (away from you). When rolling the ink out on the tile, lift the brayer at the end of every other stroke so that contact points vary. Small amounts of artists' oil color may be added to the printing ink for an expanded color range. Additives such as dryers or transparent extenders may be mixed with the ink at this point. An artists' palette knife is a handy mixing tool. Next, bring most of the ink toward you with the brayer rolling it several times diagonally as well as back and forth. This will produce an even coating of ink.

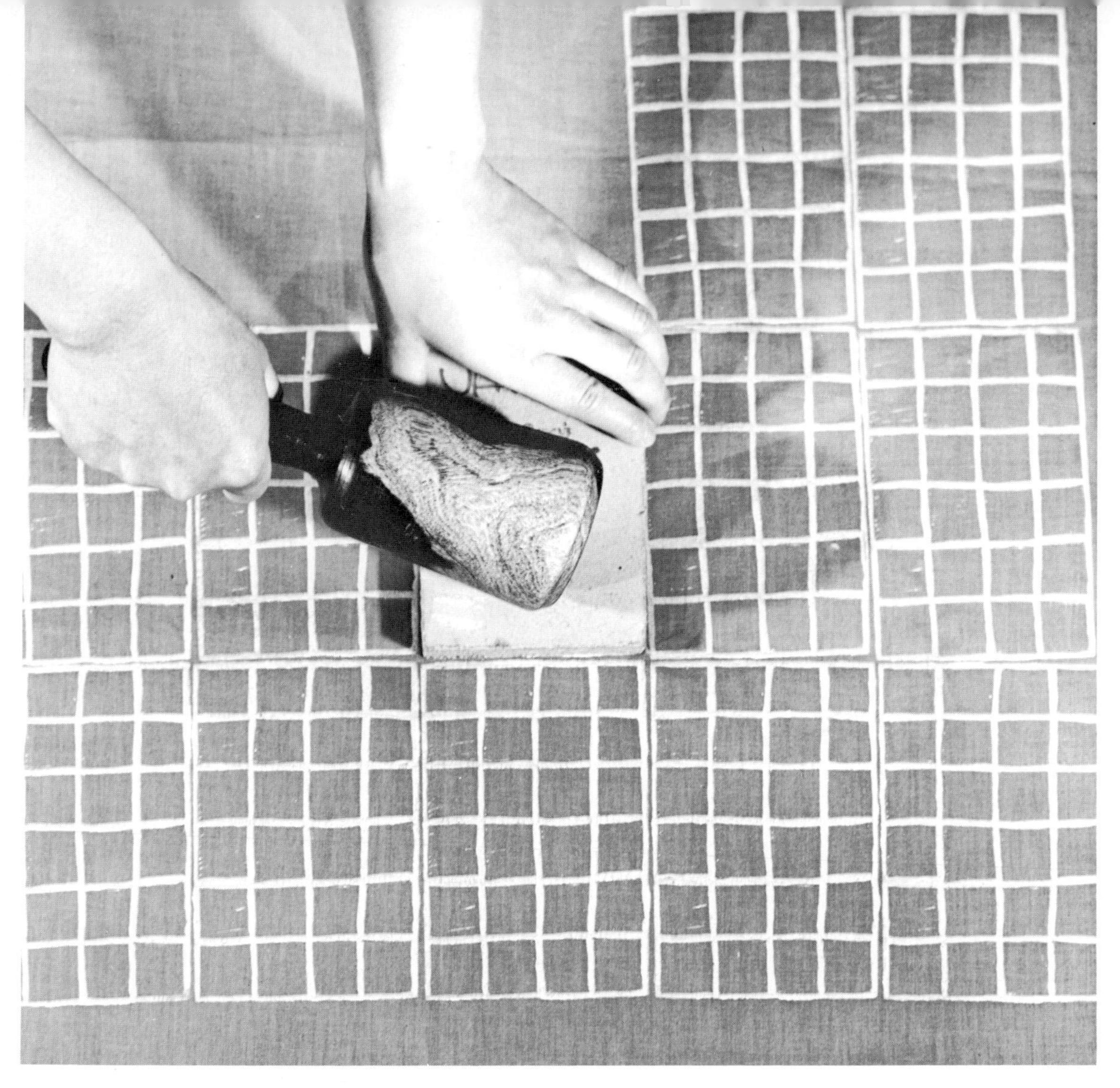

The block is being printed with the assistance of a sculptor's mallet.

7. Roll the inked brayer several times in several directions over the ridges of the linoleum block. If fine, detailed lines become clogged with ink during printing, they may be periodically cleaned with a toothpick or similar object.
8. Printing is accomplished by setting the block ink side down on the fabric and striking it several times with a mallet or heavy object. If printing is done on the floor, foot pressure works equally well and has the advantage of being silent.
9. A warm dry atmosphere will speed the drying process, but some colors dry faster than others. When fabric is thoroughly dry, it may be washed gently to remove registration marks and pressed on the back side. Do not dry-clean.

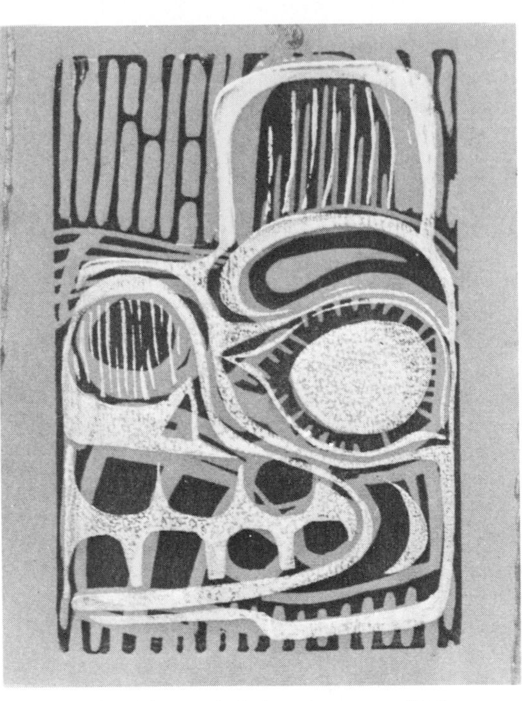

A pair of carved linoleum blocks. The one on the bottom is shown overprinted on the other, as follows:

A. Mid-value fabric with dark underprint and light overprint.
B. Mid-value fabric with dark underprint and even darker overprint.

C. Rubbing effect.
D. Combined techniques; batik and block printing. Acid dyes and oil-base ink on silk.

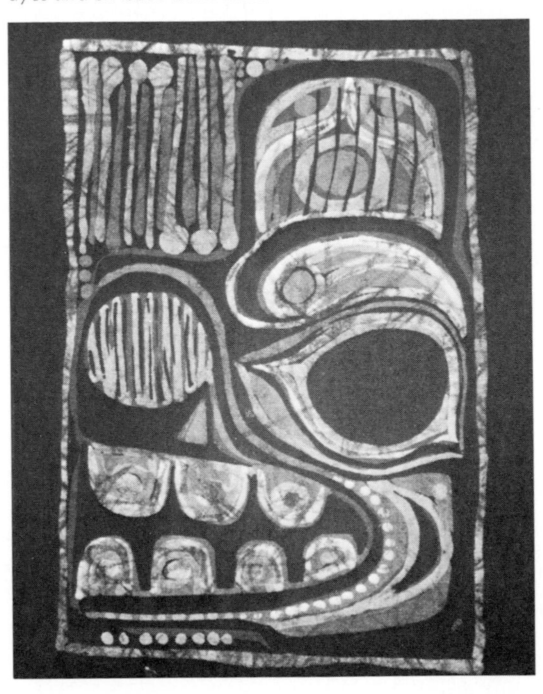

VARIATIONS IN LINOLEUM BLOCK PRINTING

Multiple Blocks

Multiple blocks are a set of blocks carved for printing adjacent to each other. The shapes may be identical, modular, or even dissimilar. Multiple blocks may also be used where the body of a fabric is printed in a repeat design but where special blocks are designed for borders and endings, such as in an Indian sari.

Overlapping Blocks

Overlapping blocks may be two or more blocks designed and carved to be printed directly on top of each other.

Rubbing Effect Printing

When a carved block, or any textured surface for that matter, is placed face up under the fabric and a lightly inked brayer is rolled gently over the fabric, an image resembling a rubbing is produced.

Printing with Dye

If a linoleum block is carved deeply and if the shapes are relatively simple it may be coated with flock for printing with dye rather than ink.

Ombré Effects with Oil Base Printing Ink

The term *ombré* refers to the soft gradation of one color into another. This is easily accomplished with oil base printing inks by squeezing two or more colors at the top of the inking surface or tile. Move the ink-coated brayer back and forth to blend the colors, keeping the brayer in the same position. Only squeeze out small amounts of ink at one time. Relatively simple blocks with more positive spaces than negative ones will emphasize the ombré effect.

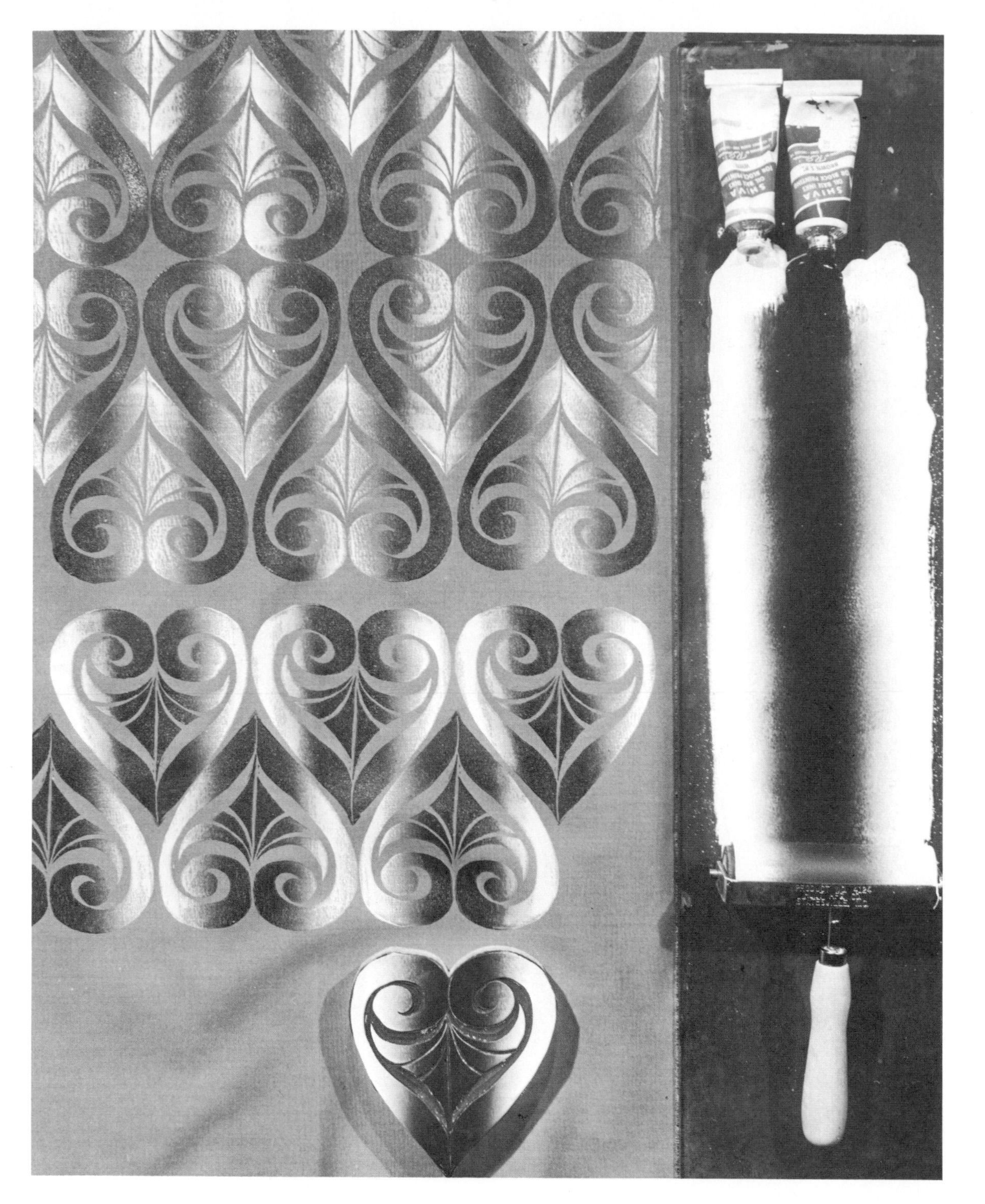

Ombré effect with oil-base block printing ink on cotton.

Examples of Direct Printing

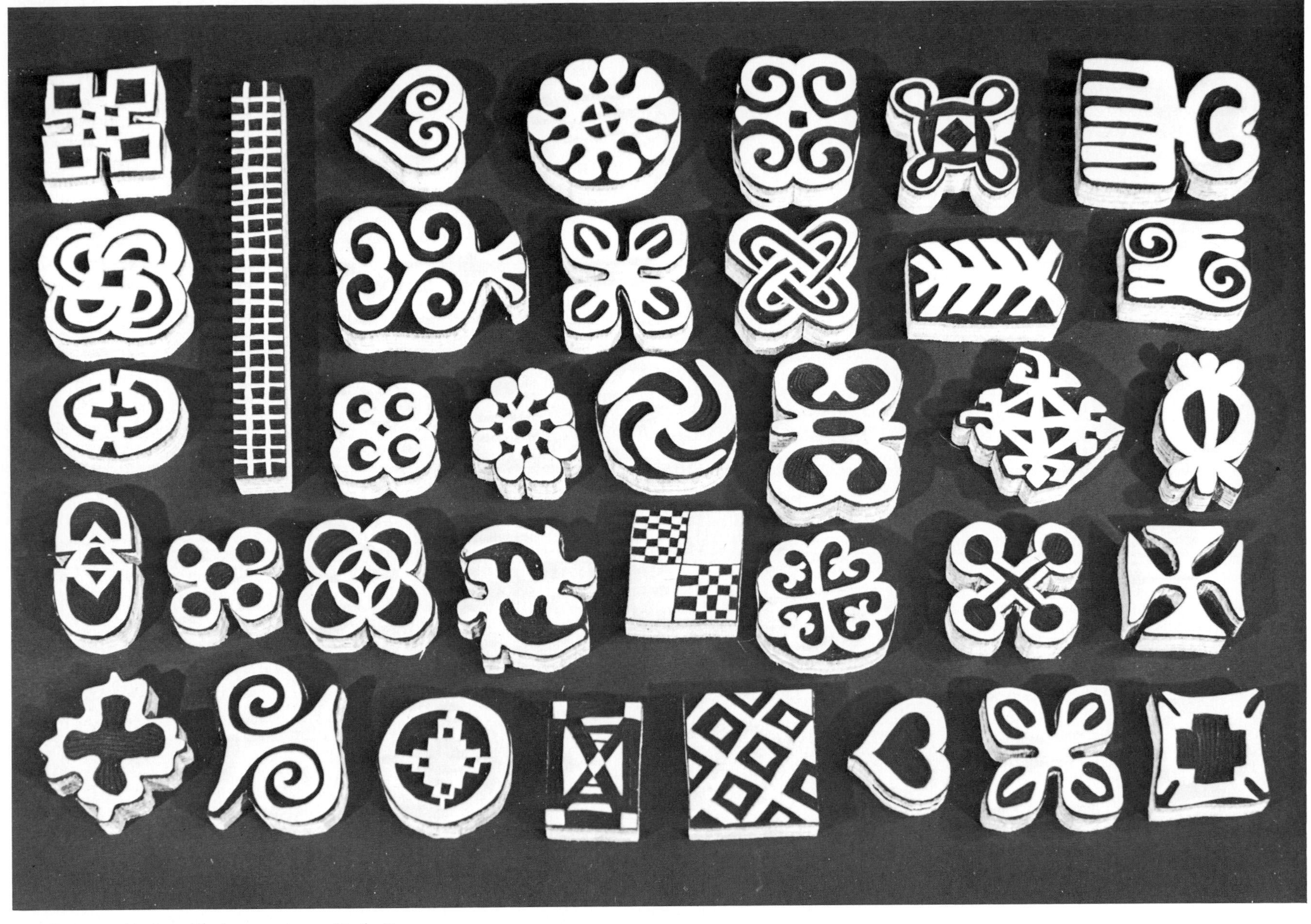

Jennifer F. Lew. Linoleum blocks cut and carved in the "manner of" Adinkra stamps. Average size 2½" to 3" (6 to 8 cm). The linoleum is mounted on ¾ inch plywood.

Right: *Jennifer F. Lew. Adinkra improvisation quilt. Dark brown oil-base ink on cotton strips of various widths sewn together and quilted, ca. 60" x 84" (152 x 173 cm).*

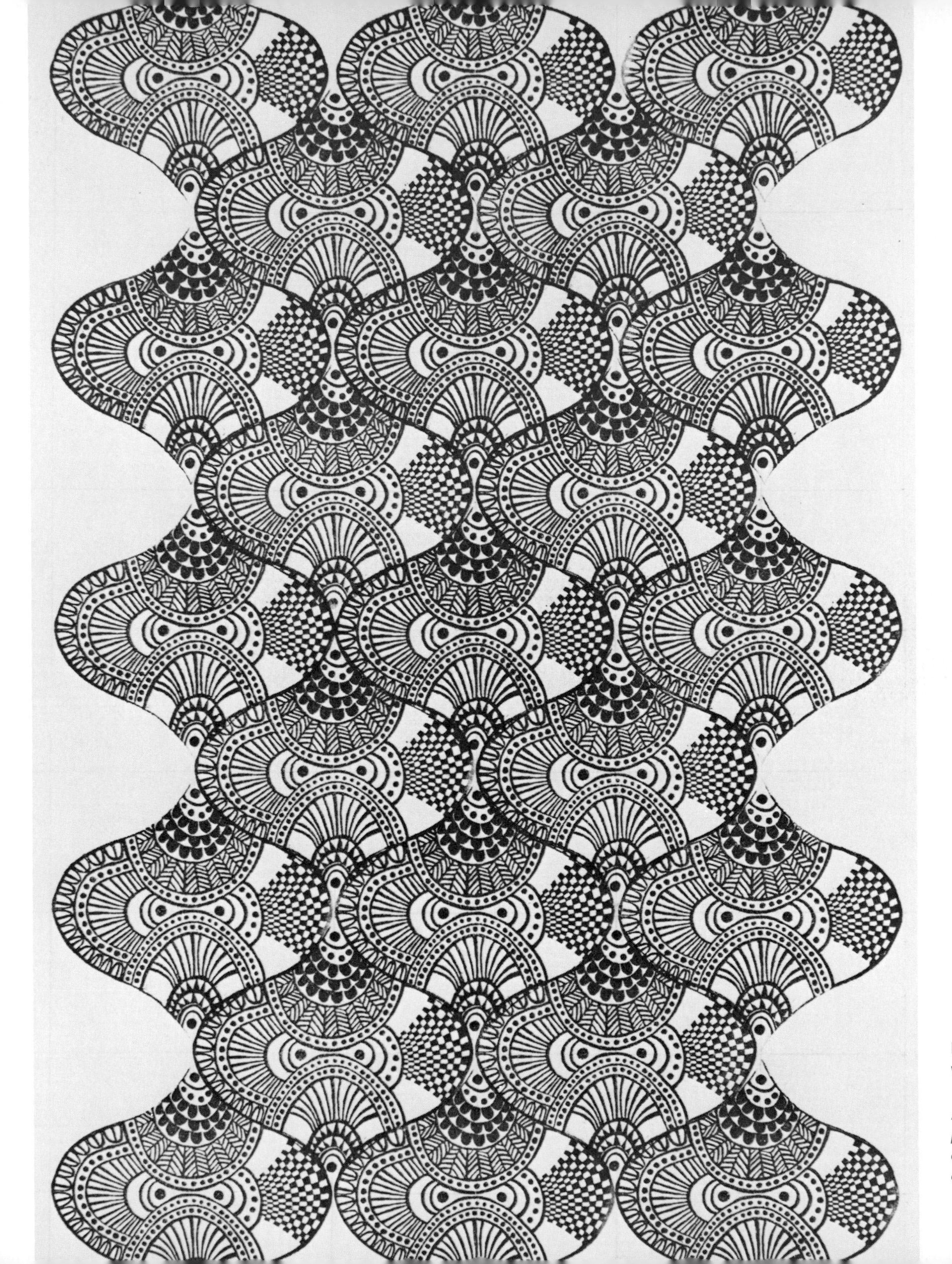

Left: *Jennifer F. Lew. Ogees. Oil-base ink printed on cotton with carved linoleum block, ca. 24″ x 36″ (61 x 91 cm).*

Above: *Richard Proctor. Three rows of feather motifs were printed in alternate directions. Based on a native American carved wooden duck from the Northwest Coast, H. ca. 5″ (12 cm).*

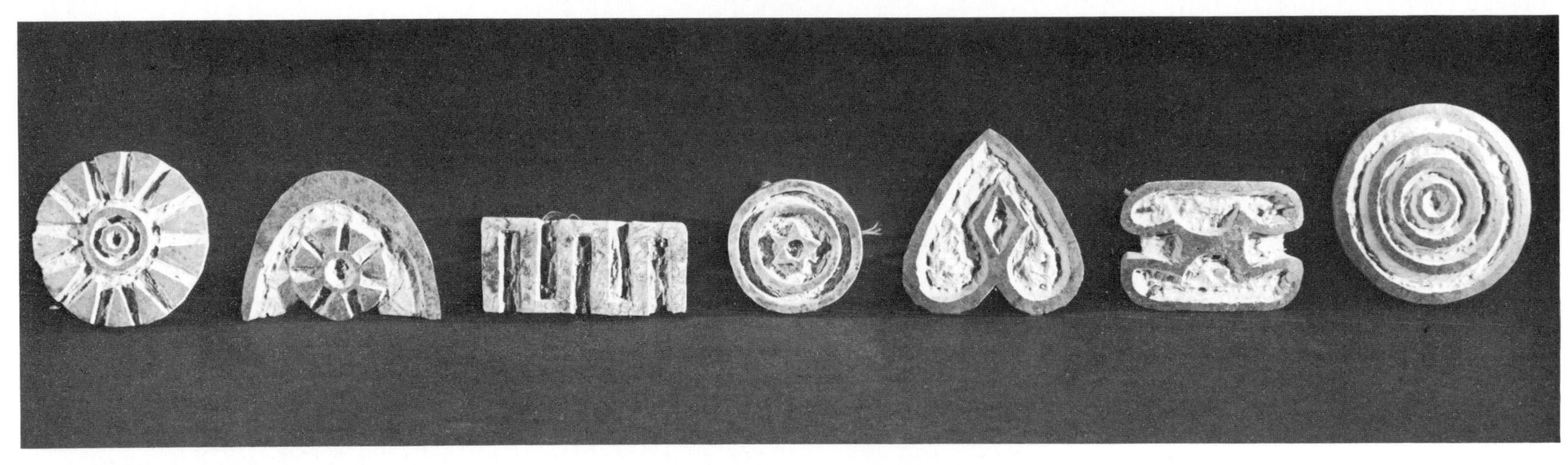

Above: *Adinkra stamps carved from Calabash rind and used for printing cloth. The photograph shows the slightly convex printing surface but not the bamboo handles. Courtesy of Gallery Nimba, Seattle, Washington.*

Below: *Ashanti Adinkra cloth. Ghana, West Africa. Pigment stamped cotton strips joined with decorative stitches, Courtesy of the Field Museum of Natural History, Chicago, Illinois.*

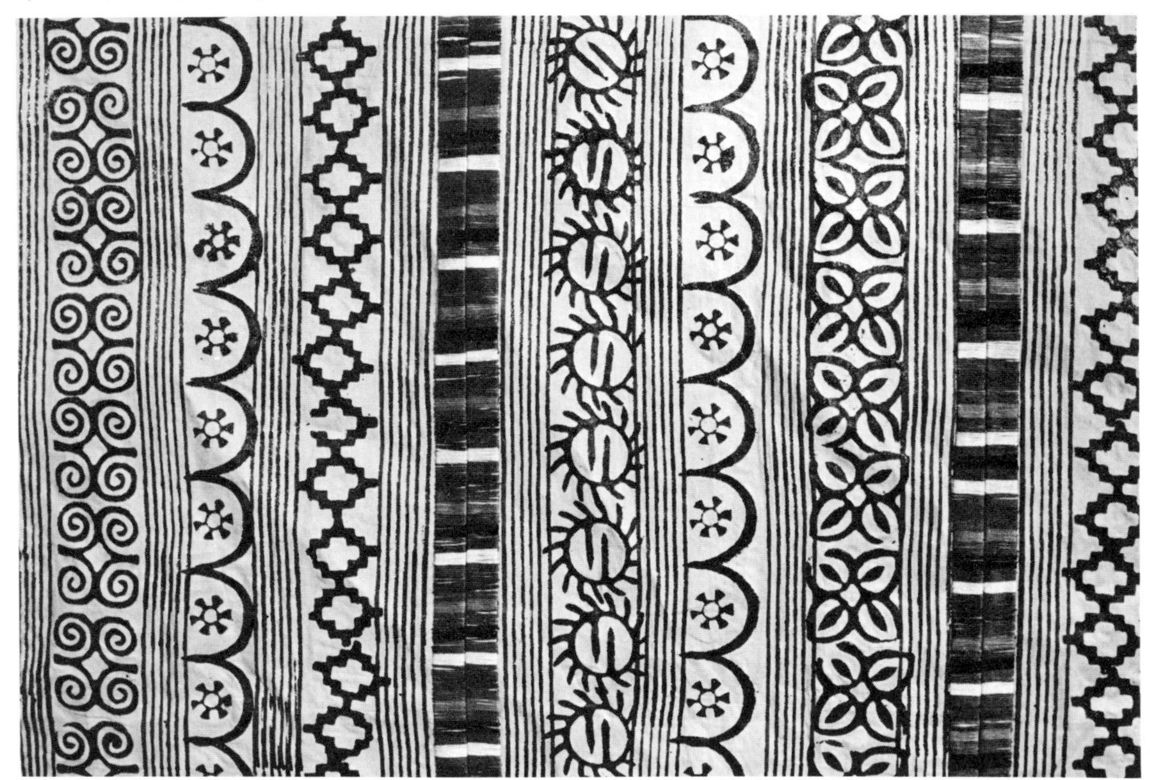

8. Stencil Printing

The two basic types of stencils to be discussed in this chapter are loose or unsupported stencils, and stretched or supported stencils. Those of the first type are usually made of cut paper, and color is applied through the cut-out portion with a brush, spatula, or spray equipment. Stencils of the second type may be composed of any of several materials adhered to a fine mesh fabric held taut by a frame. The screen printing process uses this type of stencil, which prevents the pressure-spread color from penetrating the mesh. A printed image is produced when color penetrates areas of open mesh and is absorbed by the material being printed.

Tools for Stencil Printing

Only a few necessary tools for stencil printing are specialty items. Those that are not readily available may be had from the sources of supply listed in Appendix 2.

Rubber screen printing squeegee—For forcing the printing paste through the screen fabric. Available in standard sizes or by the inch. A common rubber-bladed window washing squeegee is a marginally acceptable substitute.

Screen printing frame—The printing fabric is stretched over this frame. It should be of straight grain, kiln-dried wood such as clear fir or white pine. Mitered corners are not necessary, but the frame must be perfectly squared and level. Very large screen frames are sometimes manufactured of metal.

Rubber spatula—A convenient tool for mixing and transferring the printing paste.

Stencil brushes—Designed for hand application of dye or ink to unmounted stencils.

Gwen-lin Goo. Cadenza. Detail of a large, complex two-layered fabric composition that zigzags along a wall. Both the opaque cotton back layer and the sheer silk organza front layer are printed with detailed geometric patterns, producing the effect of a very dramatic moiré, 18" deep, 42" high, and 90" long (46 x 107 x 229 cm).

Swivel-head stencil knife—A very handy tool for cutting curves in lacquer film stencils.
X-acto or similar pointed knife—For cutting various kinds of mounted or unmounted stencils.
Staple gun—For attaching the stretched screen fabric to the wooden frame.
Dye pastes or paste paints—See chapter 3.
Appropriate solvents—For printing paste and for the stencil itself if the screen is to be reclaimed. Printing paste solvents are discussed in chapter 3. Stencil reclaiming solvents are discussed with each of the stencil techniques in this chapter.
Screen fabric—A variety of fabrics are available. They are discussed later in this chapter.
Tapes—Masking, duct, or gummed kraft paper as required.
Newspaper for clean-up
Water source
Scrap fabric for testing
Rags or cotton waste for screen cleaning
Registration devices—As required by the project.
Covercloth—Usually muslin fabric, which protects the printing table pad.A cover cloth may not be necessary depending on the weight and density of print cloth.
Additional materials—Each of the stencilmaking processes is unique and may call for particular tools and materials.

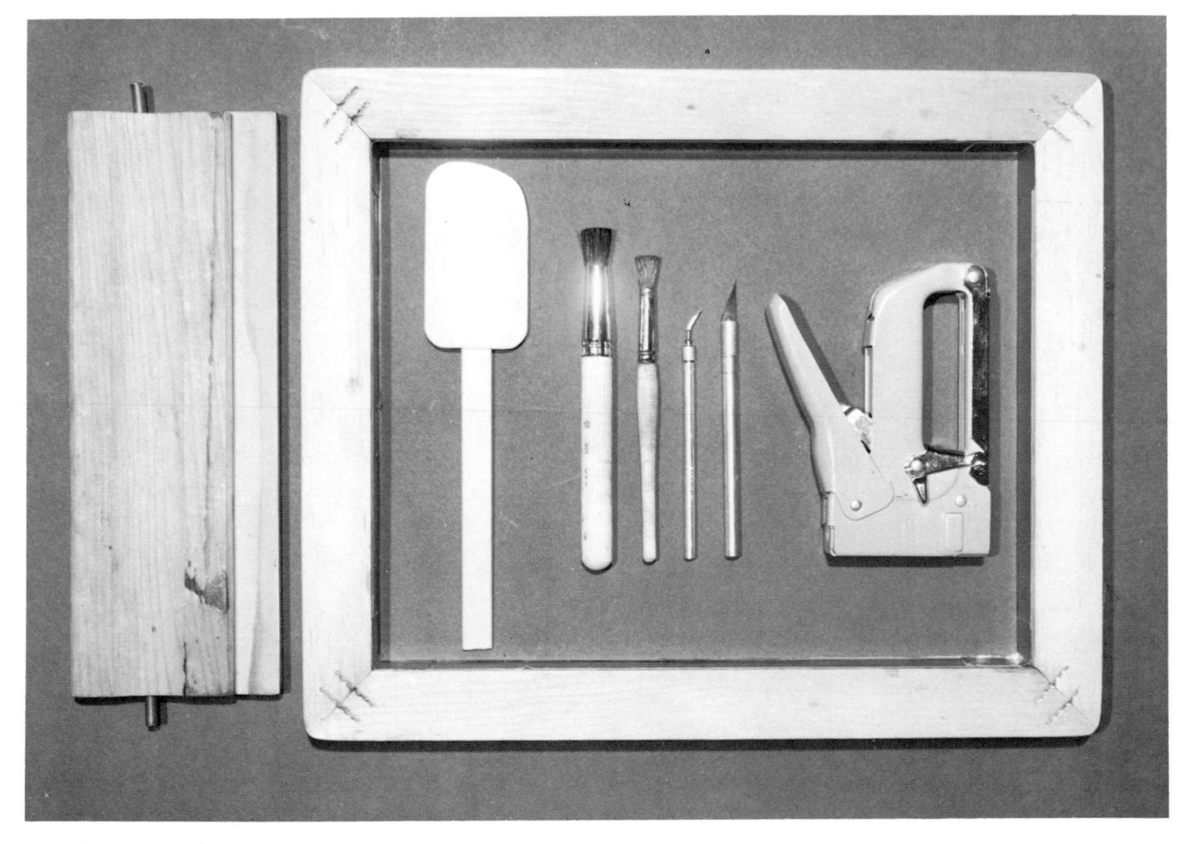

Stencil printing tools.

Techniques for Stencil Printing

BRUSH STENCIL PRINTING

The paper stencil is a convenient, inexpensive, and highly portable means of repeating a design on fabric. The process is simple and consists of brushing dye, pigment, or a resist paste in the openings of the cut stencil. When used without the support of a stretched mesh, as in screen printing, the paper stencil tends to be fragile and floppy, necessitating paper "bridges" between remaining lines or shapes. In Japan this problem has been ingeniously solved by attaching strands of thread once thought to be human hair to bridge the gaps between shapes.

Stencils are most often used to decorate fabric, but with the appropriate choice of coloring agent are equally successful on vinyl, leather, and paper.

MATERIALS

Stencil paper—Special nonabsorbent papers designed for this purpose are available in several weights. Tagboard coated on both sides with polymer emulsion would be a good substitute.
Stencil knife—Any sharp pointed knife or even a single-edge razor blade will do.
Stencil brush—Special stencil brushes work best, but any round stiff bristle brush will serve the purpose.
Work surface—Clean and paper-covered.
Fabric to be printed—If an ink or paste paint is to be used, the fiber content is not important, but if a dye paste is to be used the fabric must have an affinity for it. Consult the dye chart in chapter 3. The fabric should be washed and pressed.
Dye paste, paste paint, or ink—A textile paint such as Versatex would be a good choice since it is manufactured to the correct consistency and cleans up with water. If Procion dye is used, the thickener should be stiff rather than runny.
Appropriate solvent if needed and clean-up supplies

METHOD

1. Transfer the design to the stencil paper. This may be done by tracing or by the use of carbon paper.
2. With the sharp pointed knife cut around the shapes that will be printed.
3. Spread the fabric on the smooth, flat paper-covered worktable. It may be taped in place if desired.
4. Guidelines or registration marks are optional, but if they are to be used they should be applied at this time.
5. Prepare the paste paint, dye paste, or ink. The consistency should be that of cold cream.
6. Secure the stencil to the fabric with tape so that it will not move during the brushing operation.
7. Dip the stencil brush in the paint, ink, or dye, and apply it to the fabric in the cut out spaces of the stencil. Work slowly and deliberately from the edge to the inside of each shape. If the stencil tends to move, it may be held in place with a free hand.
8. When all of the spaces are filled in on the first unit, remove the tape, and carefully lift the stencil. Check the underside of the stencil for damp color and remove with a paper towel if any is present.
9. Tape the stencil to the fabric again and proceed as in Steps 7 and 8. In the case of an all-over repeat in which the shapes of the units touch each other, it is best to stencil every other unit first and later fill in the blanks. This avoids the problem of setting the border of the stencil in damp color.
10. When stenciling is complete there may be a few small gaps between units or possibly an uneven area or two. It is a simple matter to touch these up with direct application of color and a small brush.
11. Allow fabric to dry and then fix or finish as required.

Above: *Stencil paper is being cut with a sharp pointed knife in preparation for printing.*

Below: *The paper stencil has been taped in place, and textile paint is being applied with a stencil brush.*

SPECIAL EFFECTS

1. A resist paste may be stenciled instead of a coloring agent. The process is the same except that dye is not applied until the paste is dry and the darks and lights will be reversed. Paste recipes and instructions will be found in chapter 5 on Liquid Resists.
2. Another method for producing light areas in the open stencil zones is to apply a discharge paste in place of a coloring agent. Discharge paste information is given in chapter 3.

STENCIL PRINTING WITH AN AIRBRUSH

Most airbrush techniques that we associate with paper are applicable to fabric with only minor modification. Stencils, or masks as they are more correctly called, prevent the airbrush spray from contacting the fabric and assure a clean, crisp edge. Although the airbrush can apply flat uniform color, its greatest asset is its unique ability to produce soft gradations, spotlight effects, and the illusion of dimension on a flat plane.

From a compositional standpoint, there are three types of stencils or masks: positive, negative, and edge. With the positive or external mask, color is applied around and outward from the mask resulting in a corona or halo effect. With the negative or internal mask, color is applied around and inward from the mask often implying volume. Edge masks, often simple straight or curved partial templates, are more versatile than either the positive or negative stencil forms. They may be used individually or in combination, or they may be arranged symmetrically, asymmetrically, or as repeat patterns.

Airbrush composition by Richard Proctor illustrating the use of positive shape, negative shape, and edge masks or templates.

METHOD

Directions for basic airbrush operation are given in chapter 4. Refer again to this information and remember in particular that at the beginning of a stroke the hand begins to move, the control lever is depressed slightly for air release, and the control lever is pulled back to release the color. The hand remains in motion and the stroke is concluded by reversing these three essential steps. Beginning and ending splotches will be avoided if the first two steps are accomplished just "off stage" in a masked-out area.

Nonporous stencil paper is probably the best masking material because it may easily be blotted and reused. It must be adhered securely to the fabric so that none of the spray is blown under its edges. This is easily accomplished by stretching the fabric over Celotex or corkboard and securing the stencil with small pins or map tacks.

As with most techniques involving complex equipment, experimentation is imperative, since every project, every pigment, every dye, and every fabric will create unforeseen variables. Feel free to try a variety of masking materials and approaches to airbrushing. Only a few are suggested below.

1. Create stripe effects with masking tape.
2. Try masking with pressure-sensitive papers from a stationary or hardware store.
3. Create interrupted effects by carefully pleating the fabric prior to masking or airbrushing. Apply color, pleat again in a different direction, and apply a second color.
4. Try airbrushing through several layers of sheer, gauzelike fabric.
5. Combine airbrushing with one or more other fabric techniques. A simple tape-masked grid might form an ideal ground for a series of block or stamp prints.

KATAZOME WITH RESIST PASTE

Katazome is the traditional Japanese technique for applying a resist paste with the aid of a stencil. Along with tsutsugaki, in which paste is applied directly in a freehand manner (see chapter 5), katazome is more generally classed as a norizome process. As previously noted, we were introduced to norizome by the Japanese master dyer Shizuo Okawahara when he was visiting professor of art at the University of Washington. The section that follows is based on experience gained under his careful tutelage.

In Japan, katazome is used chiefly for producing long, narrow lengths of kimono fabric, but carrying cloth, quilt tops, and assorted wrapping fabrics are also decorated with this process. Sometimes too, both freehand and stencil techniques may be combined in the same piece.

MATERIALS

Stencil paper—This is called katagami or shibugami, and is a brown paper made from mulberry bark. It has been waterproofed by treatment with tannin containing persimmon juice and by exposure to smoke. This results in a tough, but easy-to-cut, resilient stencil material. Sheets about 22 by 36 inches are available in three weights.

Stencil knife—This is called an into and is a sharp, narrow bamboo-handled knife. The narrow blade allows the cutter a nearly unobstructed view as work progresses. A small X-acto knife may also be used.

Dot punch (optional)—This is called a panchu and is a bamboo or plastic-handled, hollow-tipped tool for punching round holes in the stencil paper. Twenty sizes are available.

Silk gauze (optional)—This is called sha and is an organdy weight silk used to reinforce or support floating or "island" areas of a cut stencil. They are adhered to the stencil paper with clear lacquer or shellac. Threads are sufficiently fine that when the stencil is removed, the paste or nori settles where they were and no resist is formed. Close and open weaves are available.

Tracing Paper—Usually this is a thin, fine rice paper on which the design is applied with a water soluble tint or perhaps with a pencil. Regular tracing paper is a possible substitute.

Layout wax—A sticky wax used to adhere the tracing paper to the stencil paper prior to cutting. Similar to graphic designers' paste-up wax.

Stencil cutting board (optional)—A special, soft plastic cutting board that yields to the knife and does not dull the tip. Available in several sizes from large commercial art supply stores. They are expensive but are a good long-range investment for anyone who cuts many stencils.

Japanese squeegee—This is called a hera and is a wooden spatula used to gently force the paste or nori through a stencil's open areas onto the fabric. They are available in at least three sizes with or without a narrow rubber blade. Many modern practitioners prefer the rubber blade, and most traditional artists use the solid wooden model.

Framed screen mesh (optional)—This is a coarse metal screen not unlike our window screening that is attached to a rectangular 1 by 1 inch wooden frame. The frame should be several inches larger than the stencil.

A large, flat working surface that will accommodate the fabric

Fabric as required

Rice flour resist paste—This is a special form of nori (recipe follows).

Large sink or tub and water to wash up

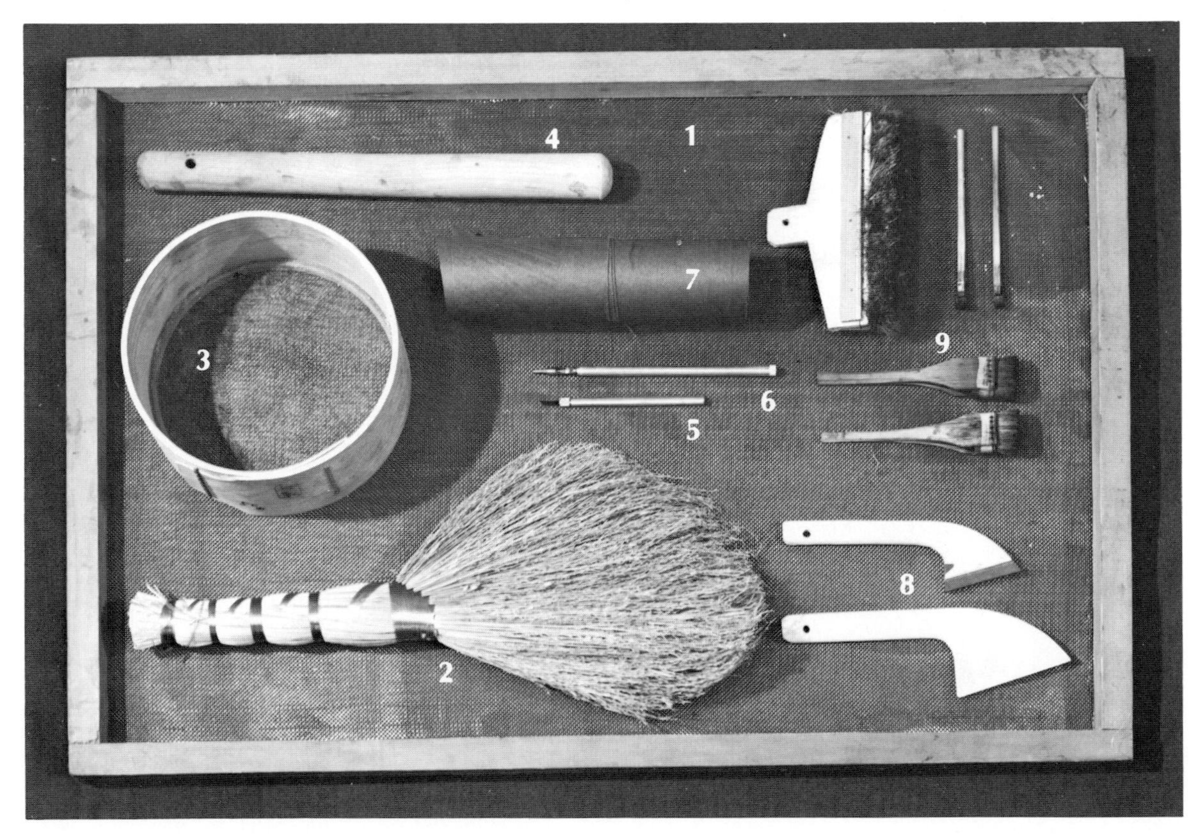

Materials for katazome: (1) mounted screen for supporting stencil; (2) hoki or straw broom; (3) sifter for ogakuzu or sawdust; (4) pestle for mixing nori or rice paste; (5) stencil knife; (6) panchu or dot punch; (7) katagami or shibugami or stencil paper; (8) hera or Japanese squeegee; and (9) Japanese dye brushes.

Nori for Katazome by Steam Method:
The following recipe will yield about 2½ cups of stencil paste. Refer to the discussion of steamed tsutsu-nori in chapter 5 and follow the directions given there, substituting the following recipe.

1¼ cups mochiko
1¼ cups komon nuka
4–7 Tbsp. salt
2–3 Tbsp. Calx
¾ cup water

Katazome stencil. Japan, late 19th or early 20th century. Collection of Dr. and Mrs. Stanley Gartler, Seattle, Washington.

METHOD

1. Prepare the stencil paper. First apply the design to the tracing paper. This may be done freehand or with the aid of a pattern. The design is applied with a pencil, fine marking pen, or with a pointed brush dipped in a dilute solution of water soluble pigment. Next rub a thin coat of layout wax on the mulberry stencil paper and position the tracing where desired. Finally burnish the tracing paper surface to insure good adhesion. Select the appropriate weight of stencil paper. Light is for delicate or intricate patterns, especially repeats. Medium is for designs of intermediate complexity. Heavy is for large bold designs or heavily used stencils.
2. Cut the stencil. Use a sharp knife or punch to remove all sections of the stencil that are to be printed with resist paste. Work slowly and carefully avoiding soft or torn spots. A crisp stencil will produce a clear, clean printed edge. If a small paper "bridge" is torn or cut by accident it may be replaced with a silk thread attached at either end by lacquer, shellac, or nail polish. Larger "islands" of stencil floating in a resist area may now be permanently positioned by spreading silk gauze or sha over the stencil and coating the affected stencil with lacquer, shellac, or nail polish.
3. Prepare fabric for printing. Clean, pressed fabric may be stretched over a perfectly flat table surface and secured with tape or pushpins. For production work in Japan, narrow yardage is pasted to a long board by first spreading the board with thin layers of diluted nori and then carefully spreading the fabric taut. The paste-covered board is dampened with a water brush, or shime waoshi hake, prior to laying out the cloth. Stenciling may begin when board and fabric are dry.
4. Soak the stencil. Place the stencil in a flat pan of water for about five minutes and then blot with absorbent paper.
5. Pour nori in a large open bowl or flat pan.
6. Position the stencil and spread with nori. There are at least two techniques for handling the stencil at this point. The first, the unsupported technique, involves nothing more than the paper stencil and is mostly used for registered repeat designs. The second, screen-supported technique involves the use of a wire mesh window-screenlike frame and is used primarily for single image stencils such as crests or calligraphy.

   For the unsupported stencil technique, position stencil as required. Hold stencil in place with one hand. Dip squeegee or hera in nori and drop a dollop of it near the center of the stencil. Hold the hera at about a 45 degree angle and gently spread an even layer of the paste over the stencil. Continue to spread the nori until the layer is even and the grain of the fabric is no longer visible. This will take some practice so it is wise to experiment on scrap fabric. Remove the stencil by lifting a clean corner or edge of it *very slowly*. If you have been careful there will be nori only on the top surface of the stencil and it may be repositioned for the second image. The stencil must be soaked clean before proceeding if any nori has gotten on the back surface. If you wish to print a continuous repeat from left to right down a length of fabric, then the left solid edge of the stencil must now be folded upward to that it will not rest on the previously finished print. In this case the stencil must be repositioned with great care and attention to alignment. It is probably better to leave a slight gap between prints than to allow the left underedge of the stencil to come in contact with the right edge of the previously printed nori. This gap may be filled in with a cone or tsutsu after the stenciling is complete. The entire process requires a light touch and great care must be taken not to tear or stress the stencil with the hera as the paste is being applied.

   For the supported stencil technique, again position the stencil as required. Place a screen over the stencil with mesh downward and flush with the stencil surface. The frame must be several inches larger than the stencil. Dip the hera in the nori and drop a dollop of it near the center of the stencil. Hold the hera at about a 45 degree angle. With medium pressure, spread the nori over and through the screen until the paste is even and the fabric is no longer visible. The paste thickness will be about ⅛ inch. Lift an edge of the frame *very slowly*. The stencil will adhere to the mesh, and the paste-covered fabric will slowly settle on the work surface. When frame and stencil are free of the fabric, they may be repositioned for an additional print if desired. If any nori has gotten on the underside of the stencil or the frame, they must be soaked clean before proceeding.
7. Soak stencil and/or frame. Cleaning is accomplished simply by soaking everything in clean water for 10 minutes or until the paste can be easily rinsed away. A scrub brush may be used on everything except the stencil. Blot the clean stencil and allow it to dry between absorbent paper which may be weighted lightly.
8. At this point check the image for flaws. Very small overflows of paste may be carefully lifted with a toothpick or a small pointed object. Gaps or thin spots may be corrected with paste applied with a cone or tsutsu as described in chapter 5.
9. From this point onward the paste-resisted fabric is treated in exactly the same way as tsutsugaki fabric. Turn to page 90 and follow steps 8–15.

SCREEN PROCESS PRINTING

Many effects are possible with screen process printing, but the essential purpose and characteristic of the technique is orderly repetition of an image in an efficient manner. Mass production as we commonly think of it may or may not be the goal, but limited production is the usual objective.

When compared to the other fabric design techniques, screen process printing would have to be described as indirect. The printing itself is relatively swift, but numerous preparatory steps must precede this operation to insure well-crafted and satisfying results. The following processes must be accomplished when printing on fabric or fabriclike material: design; preparing the printing frame, including stretching the screen mesh; making the stencil and fixing it to the screen; selecting and preparing the fabric for printing; preparing the printing table and securing the fabric to it; preparing the printing color; determining the printing sequence and registration system; printing; cleaning the printing equipment; drying the fabric; overprinting or printing additional colors if required; and fixing or finishing as required. Throughout the remainder of this section on stencil printing, each of these twelve steps will be explained. There is nothing particularly difficult or mysterious about any of the steps, but they must be followed in order with a reasonable amount of advance planning.

Design

Regardless of whether the image is to be realistic, abstract, or nonobjective, or whether it will be repeated on a block, brick, or halfdrop network, there are important design considerations that must be made. Specifically, it must be determined if the units are to touch each other, and if so will they merely touch or will they nest into each other, overlap each other, or possibly combine more than one of these systems.

In addition, practical factors such as fabric width, printing table size, screen frame size, and the availability of a helper (as in the case of full-width screens) all have a bearing on the design. There are probably as many technical as aesthetic decisions to be made in screen process printing, but neither component may be left to chance.

The following are the repeat systems most commonly used.

Random printing. Units are printed so that there is no formal repeat. This method may not be suited to fabrics that will have to be cut and joined. The advantage is that no registration system is necessary and the results can be very flowing with irregular clusters, directional movements, and dappled, all-over effects.

Spaced printing. Each unit is surrounded by unprinted fabric and each appears to float. This system is very forgiving of minor flaws in registration.

Butt joint. Units are tangent on all sides and the number required to cross the width of the fabric may vary from one (selvedge to selvedge) to any number, with four being the usual maximum. This system is applicable to both the square and the half-drop network.

Dovetail, top and bottom. This system requires a large screen on which the full width of the fabric is printed at one time. Usually two printers are required. It is the most commonly used system in production printing because the repeat lines on top and bottom image borders may be skillfully disguised and integrated with the design.

Dovetail, all sides. In this system, sometimes called the jigsaw puzzle system, it is impossible to tell where one unit begins and another ends. Perfect registration is required and the process is a bit tricky; however, good, all-over coverage is possible with screens of a convenient size.

Combinations. Many combinations of the above systems are possible to accommodate specific design requirements. A few include butt sides with dovetail tops and bottoms, dovetail sides with spaced tops and bottoms for horizontal band effects, and systems incorporating intentional overlaps for increased pigment density.

Random printing.

Spaced printing.

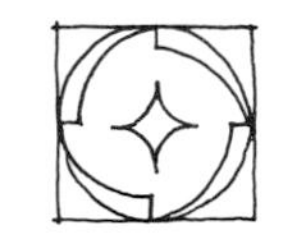

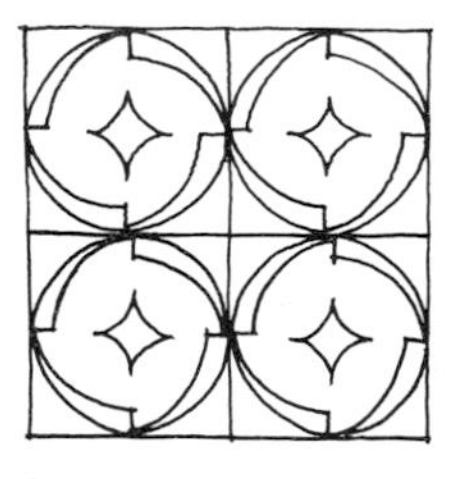

Butt joint.

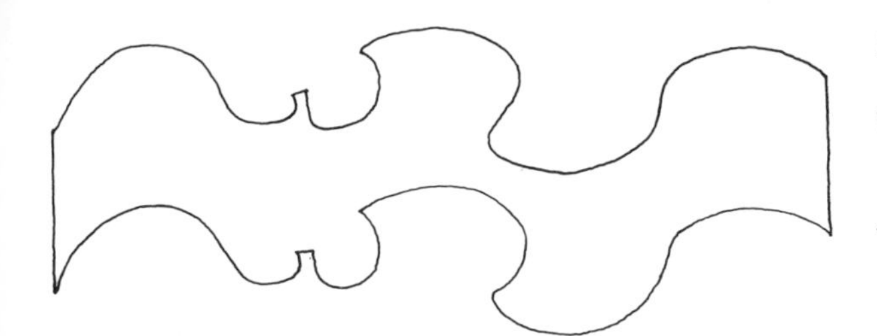

Top and bottom dovetail unit.

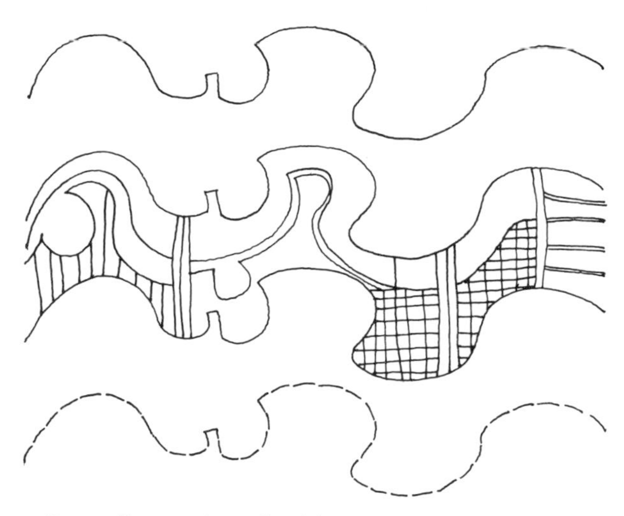

Top and bottom dovetail unit in repeat.

Dovetail, all sides.

HINTS AND SUGGESTIONS

Wherever possible try to avoid lines, especially fine lines which must connect perfectly and continue from one unit to the next.

The spaced print is the easiest system for the beginning printer with a small screen to use. The second easiest is the top and bottom dovetail, but it requires a very large screen and usually a helper.

It is usually easier to create a design for a repeat system than it is to adjust a given design to a specific system.

Preparing the Printing Frame

The best advice we can offer to the beginning printer is to buy a well-crafted prestretched screen consisting of a mitered, wooden, wobble-free frame and a polyester screen fabric. This may be more expensive than a homemade version, but the novice may gain experience and become familiar with the best attributes of a screen before constructing one. Regardless of whether the screen is purchased or handbuilt it will consist of two parts: the mesh screen fabric and the outer frame.

Constructing a screen frame. For screens up to 24 inches in their greatest dimension, 2 by 2 inch lumber may be used. For larger screens we suggest that 2 by 3 or 2 by 4 lumber be selected. It should be straight, clear, and dry. Green wood that has not been kiln-dried is subject to warping. The exact species of wood is less important than its condition, but it should be soft enough to allow staples to enter with relative ease. Birch, cedar, fir, mahogany, pine, redwood, and spruce are frequently used.

The corners are usually mitered and joined firmly with a corrugated fastener or a screwed down steel angle bracket. A solvent proof glue may be used for additional strength. For very large screens a more sophisticated joining system such as the tongue-and-groove joint may prove useful. The simple butt joint may be used for small screens but must be well reinforced since it is more fragile. Use a rafter square or similar device to be certain that all angles are a perfect 90 degrees.

When the frame is complete, sand any rough spots and give it one or two coats of clear shellac. This will prevent the absorption of water and will also facilitate clean up. However, if the screen is to be masked with paper tape, the shellac should be applied after the tape is adhered.

Choosing the screen fabric. Very finely woven silk, polyester, and stainless steel are the three most common fiber choices. For many years silk was the only suitable mesh fabric available and it is still popular for its weave consistency, durability, tensile strength, and ability to reproduce fine detail. However, silk is relatively expensive, stains readily, and is destroyed by the chlorine bleach necessary to reclaim direct emulsion screens. Polyester is the most frequently used screen fabric today. It is reasonably priced, strong, stable, uniform, and resistant to chlorine bleach. Stainless steel fabric is favored by industry for its exceptional durability and ability to reproduce the fine detail necessary for such items as printed electronic circuits. It is costly and vulnerable to denting or bending if handled carelessly.

Nylon monofilament mesh fabric is also available but is not suitable for most stencils that must be adhered with solvents. Screen fabric is available in a variety of densities, each having a different number of threads per inch. This thread count is identical for both the warp and the weft since screen fabric must be perfectly regulated balanced weave. It is also available in three weights with medium or "double extra" (XX) by far the most common and generally suitable. For most purposes we prefer 10XX or 12XX polyester screen fabric.

Stretching the screen fabric. The usual method of attaching fabric mesh to the frame is with staples driven by a hand-operated staple gun and set closely in double parallel rows or diagonally.

There are numerous stretching sequences to choose from and several kinds of stretching pliers as well. We will present here a simple, accepted technique that requires only hand pressure. Readers are directed to books devoted exclusively to screen process printing for alternate techniques. The objective is to stretch the fabric as tightly as possible with manual pressure. The fabric is grasped between the thumb and index finger with the latter supplying the leverage.

METHOD

1. Cut the fabric one or two inches larger than the exterior dimensions of the frame.
2. Staple the first corner, corner A, in place.
3. Making sure the grain of the fabric is straight, pull very taut at corner B and secure it with three or four staples.
4. Staple from corner A to corner B. Side 1 is now complete.
5. Apply pressure at corner C by pulling against corner B and secure corner C with several staples.
6. Staple from corner B to corner C, thus completing side 2. Again, be certain that the fabric is as straight as possible.
7. Now stretch the fabric diagonally from corner B to corner D and secure it with several staples.
8. Staple side 3 from corner C to corner D, pulling directly away from side 1 as each staple is driven in. Side 3 is now complete.
9. Next staple side 4 pulling against side 2 as the fabric is attached.
10. If any staples are not flush with the wood, they should now be pounded all the way in.
11. Trim excess fabric with a knife or single-edge razor blade.

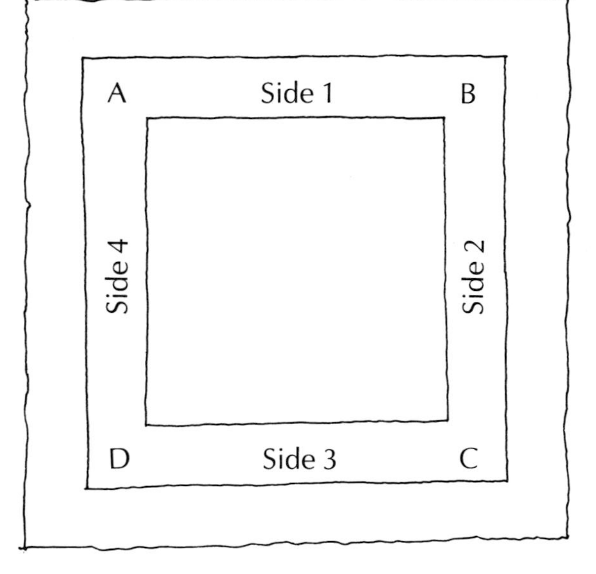

Sequence for stretching a screen fabric.

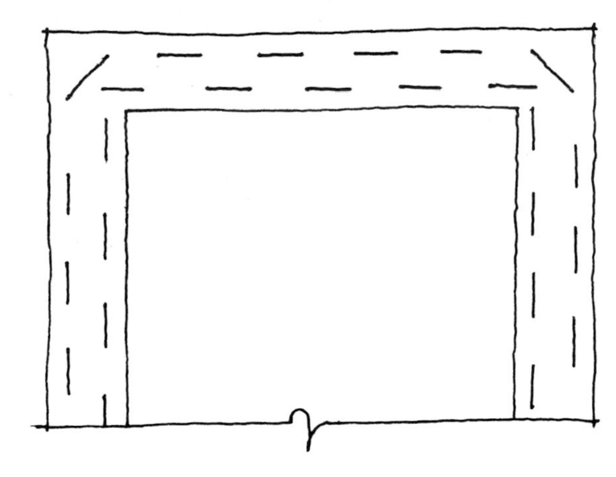

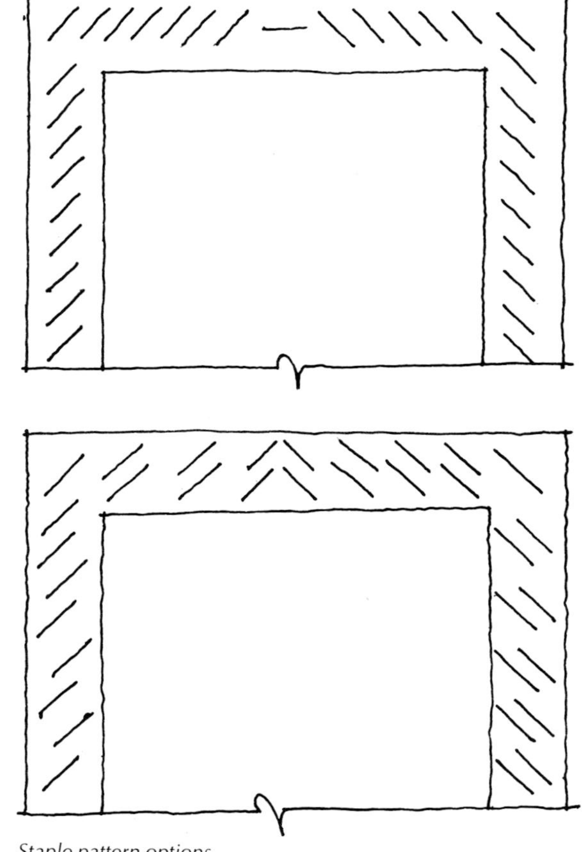

Staple pattern options.

Many screen supply houses now stock special wooden screen frame components that are premitered and have a shallow groove on their bottom surface. These are available in pairs of numerous lengths. The fabric is stretched by forcing a cord into the groove. Instruction sheets are available wherever this handy and efficient system is sold.

Masking the Screen. If there is no masking or covering at the juncture of the fabric and the frame, printing paste will seep in and create leakage problems. Furthermore, some sort of masked area is necessary as a reservoir for the printing paste. The two basic choices are tape or liquid masks. Gummed paper tape which is later coated with shellac is by far the most common masking device. It is economical, permanent, and efficient. If only a few images are to be printed, other tapes such as masking, duct, or gummed cloth tape may be adhered, but be certain to select one that is solvent proof.

METHOD

To tape the bottom or outside of the screen:

1. Invert the screen so that the staple side is facing upward.
2. Cut 4 strips of 3 inch gummed paper tape 2 inches longer than the length of the frame. Cut 4 strips 2 inches longer than the width of the frame.
3. Beginning with the long sides, moisten and apply tape strips that extend 1½ or 2 inches onto the fabric. The additional inch at each end of the tape should be brought down onto the outside of the frame.
4. Repeat process for the short sides of the frame, but this time bring the tape 3 or 4 inches onto the fabric. This additional allowance will later provide a reservoir for the printing paste.
5. Crease the remaining 4 strips of tape at 1 inch from their long edges so as to resemble the letter "L." Make a 1 inch cut on the crease at each end of the four tapes. These tapes will be attached with 2 inches covering the staples or the previous tape and 1 inch covering the sides of the frame. If the two tapes will not overlap, an intermediate strip should be applied at this time. This will probably be necessary at the reservoir ends.
6. Moisten and attach the four L-shaped tapes, folding the corner tabs neatly as you proceed. The outside of the screen is now masked.

To tape the inside of the screen:

1. Turn the screen over so that the inside is upward and the finished fabric side is downward.
2. Cut 4 pieces of tape 2 by 2 inches. Fold each square in half twice to produce four 1-inch quadrants. On one of the folds cut 1 inch into the center of each square and overlap the tabs with the gummed side out. As you see this produces a three-surfaced corner protector.
3. Moisten the corner protectors and place one neatly in each inside corner of the frame.
4. Tape the sides and ends of the inside of the frame, bringing the tape 1 inch up onto the inside wall of the frame. Be sure inside strips match up with the previously applied outside or bottom strips of tape. This process completes the inside masking.
5. Apply two coats of clear shellac to the tapes and the frame allowing the shellac to extend about ⅛ inch onto the mesh fabric.

As you proceed, keep the following hints in mind:
Practice with scrap material to determine how much moisture to use on the tape.
Use a clean, dry rag to burnish the tape and force the moist gum well into the fabric and the wood grain.
Do not shellac the frame before applying paper tape. If this has been done, it should be roughened slightly with sandpaper or steel wool.
Be sure the tape is perfectly flush with the wood and the fabric and that no air bubbles remain.

Liquid Maskouts. Many liquid maskouts are available on the market and it is important to select one that is not soluble in any component of the printing paste or its clean-up solvent. Liquid maskouts are applied with miniature squeegees made from small squares of stiff cardboard. They are dipped in the liquid and lightly scraped across the fabric while held in a perpendicular position. The solution should be applied evenly and not drip through to the opposite side. The same surfaces should be covered as described in the tape method.

Final Cleaning. Scrub both surfaces of the screen well with an abrasive kitchen cleanser and rinse several times with running water before use. If you are planning a direct emulsion or photo film stencil on a polyester screen, it is necessary to scrub it additionally on the stencil side with ½ teaspoon or more abrasive kitchen cleansing powder and a wet rag. Many printers do a final degreasing of the fabric by scrubbing on both sides with a brush and trisodium phosphate on both sides followed by a hot water rinse.

Screen-printed fabric panel from Inko direct screen emulsion stencil. A flocked version of this design appears later in this chapter.

Stencil Making for Screen Process Printing

There are many successful and highly inventive methods of creating a screen printing stencil. The technique should be chosen that will be in harmony with the design idea. Carefully study the following processes and note that each design has in some way taken advantage of the unique potential afforded by the chosen stencil technique. We have attempted to explain these processes in order of increasing complexity, but if all steps are followed, none is especially difficult.

Direct Wax Crayon Stencils

Direct wax crayon stencils work on the underside or outside of the screen. The mesh should be backed with a smooth hard surface. Wax crayon is then applied with considerable pressure. The objective is to force the wax well into the screen mesh. The wax deposits create the stencil and prevent dye or ink from passing through the screen onto the print cloth. Fine lines tend to be a little fuzzy, and solid areas may be slightly toned but these qualities seem perfectly natural. Crayon stencils are not as durable as most of the others. To remove the stencil, press the screen between two sheets of absorbent paper with iron. Any remaining wax may easily be removed with mineral spirits.

Wax Crayon Rubbing Stencil

The textured element used to create a wax crayon rubbing stencil may be a found object or a custom designed surface. In the example shown here twine of several weights was soaked in diluted white glue and applied to a stout cardboard backing. As with the direct crayon method, work proceeds on the underside or outside of the screen. When the glue is thoroughly dry, the plate is raised to the height of the screen mesh with something like a stack of magazines. The screen frame is then inverted so that the inside surface of the mesh is firmly in contact with the texture. The texture is then rubbed with a wax crayon. Considerable pressure is needed to insure a well-defined print. Durability and stencil removal are similar to the direct crayon method.

Textural composition made by twine glued to cardboard.

Wax crayon is being applied to the outside of the screen fabric as the texture rubbing progresses.

Above: *Screen prepared for printing with two crayon stencil techniques. The wax crayon stencil on the left utilizes both line and mass to play an organic shape against a geometric background. On the right is a wax crayon rubbing stencil. Note that the screen is masked only with light duty tape suitable for proofing or printing a very short run.* Below: *A sample print has been made of the two crayon stencils. They exhibit a textural quality characteristic to this technique.*

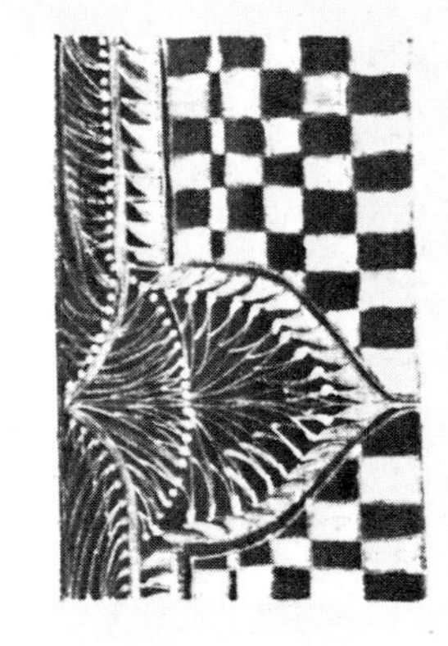

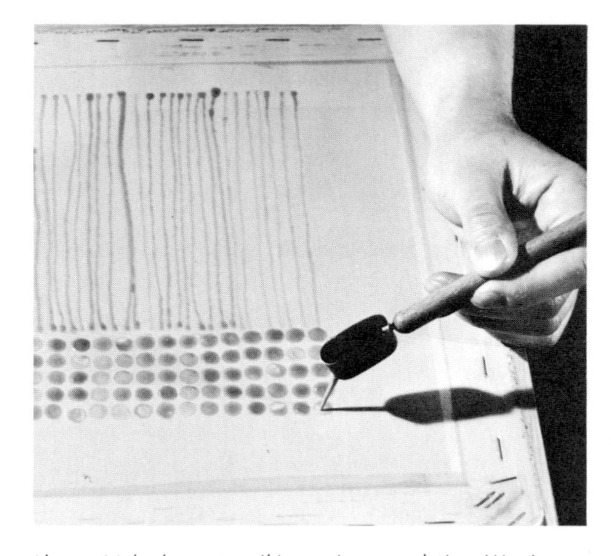

Above: *Melted wax stencil is nearing completion. Wax is applied with a small tjanting designed for batik work.*

Below: *A sample print from the melted wax stencil that has a strong batiklike quality.*

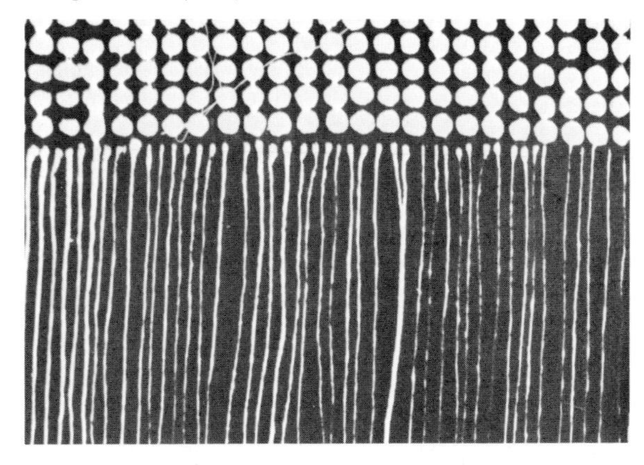

Melted Wax Stencils

Melted wax may be applied to the screen mesh in the same method and with the same tools as for batik. The only drawback with this method is that bumps of melted wax are frequently formed on the inside of the screen which can interfere with the smooth operation of the printing squeegee. We have had good results removing these wax bumps with an artists' palette knife. In all other respects melted wax stencils are similar to crayon stencils except that the former are more durable.

Both of the stencils on the above screen have been made from commercial press-apply materials. The one on the right is of contact paper; this variety is plastic coated and intended to be used as shelf covering. The stencil on the left is composed of pricetag stickers, gummed reinforcements, signal dots, graph tape, and contact paper. Sample prints are shown below.

Stencils from Press Apply Materials

Very satisfactory screen printing stencils may be made quickly and practically from the vast array of pressure sensitive items currently on the market. The working method is quite simple. Shapes are peeled from their backing sheet and carefully set in place. Tweezers or stamp collector's tongs may be helpful in arranging small or fragile shapes. For optimal adhesion, the stencil should be burnished with something smooth and hard, such as the flat side of a fingernail.

A direct block-out stencil is in progress. A product called block-out black is being directly applied to the screen fabric with a small bristle brush. The design for this stencil with its "bridges" between lines is reminiscent of a paper stencil but far too complex to be handled without the support of a stretched screen.

Detail of a strike-off print from the direct block-out stencil described above. Versatex textile ink on cotton.

Direct Block Out Stencils

Screen printers' supply houses carry a wide variety of premixed liquids that may be applied with a brush directly to the screen. These products may be called "block outs" or liquid stencils. It is very important to ascertain that the printing paste does not contain any of the solvent for the selected block out.

Resist Techniques

There are several resist techniques for making stencils. One of the most common is the tusche–glue technique. Tusche, an ink soluble in mineral spirits, is applied to the screen with a brush, or a special tusche crayon is used. A water-soluble glue base product is spread over the entire screen and allowed to dry. The tusche is then dissolved with solvent, leaving open areas in the mesh which will print. This is satisfactory for oil, plastic, lacquer, or vinyl inks but not for dye pastes containing water. Glue stencils are not suitable for long production runs.

A much more practical resist technique for the fabric artist is to substitute Inko Direct Fillin for the tusche and Inko Lacquer Proof Maskout for the glue. By so doing a stencil is produced which is more durable and can be used with standard inks and dye pastes except vinyl ink.

MATERIALS

Prepared screen
Brush for applying fillin
Inko Direct Fillin Resist
Inko Lacquer Proof Maskout
Inko De-Stencil for reclaiming the screen

METHOD

1. Center the original drawing or design under the screen and set the registration guides.
2. Trace the drawing on the inside surface of the screen mesh with a soft pencil.
3. Raise the screen slightly at one end so that the Direct Fillin will not seep through onto the drawing.
4. Using a sable show card or similar brush, paint the design on the mesh with Direct Fillin. Wash out mistakes with water.
5. When the Direct Fillin Resist is dry, apply Lacquer Proof Maskout to the entire surface of the screen. Using a squeegee or a piece of cardboard held vertically to the screen, draw a thin coat of Maskout across the entire inside surface over the Direct Filllin. Allow to dry. If open areas remain, apply a second thin coat of Maskout perpendicular to the first coat.
6. Wash out the resist from the underside of the screen with water, rubbing gently with fingernail or stiff brush. The Maskout will remain where there was no resist, but it will wash out where the resist prevented the Maskout from contacting the mesh.
7. Check the stencil for pinholes by holding it up to the light. Stubborn areas that did not wash out cleanly may be scrubbed with a bristle brush or scraped with the fingernail. Touch up holes or defects with Maskout. Block out any remaining open area from the stencil to the edge of the frame with Maskout or blockout tape.
8. The stencil is now ready to print.
9. After printing, the screen may be reclaimed by removing the Maskout with Inko De-Stencil.

Lacquer Film Stencils

Lacquer film stencils are perhaps the most popular and frequently used forms of screen printing stencils. With only a little practice, the beginning printer can produce highly durable and even intricate stencils capable of rendering clear crisp images on fabric.

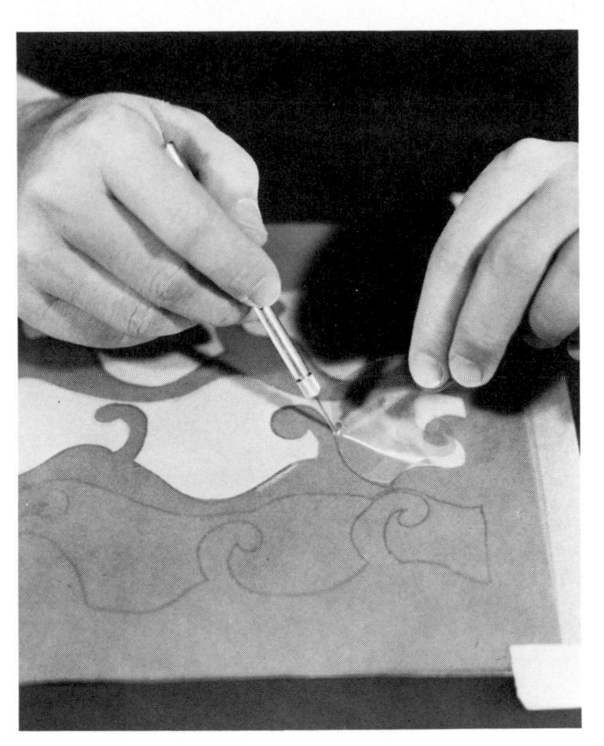

Above: *A lacquer film stencil is being cut. In this photograph the translucent film is being peeled away. Areas shown in white will be printed and the gray or film portions will resist the flow of printing paste. The original outline drawing is clearly visible underneath the still supported lacquer film.*

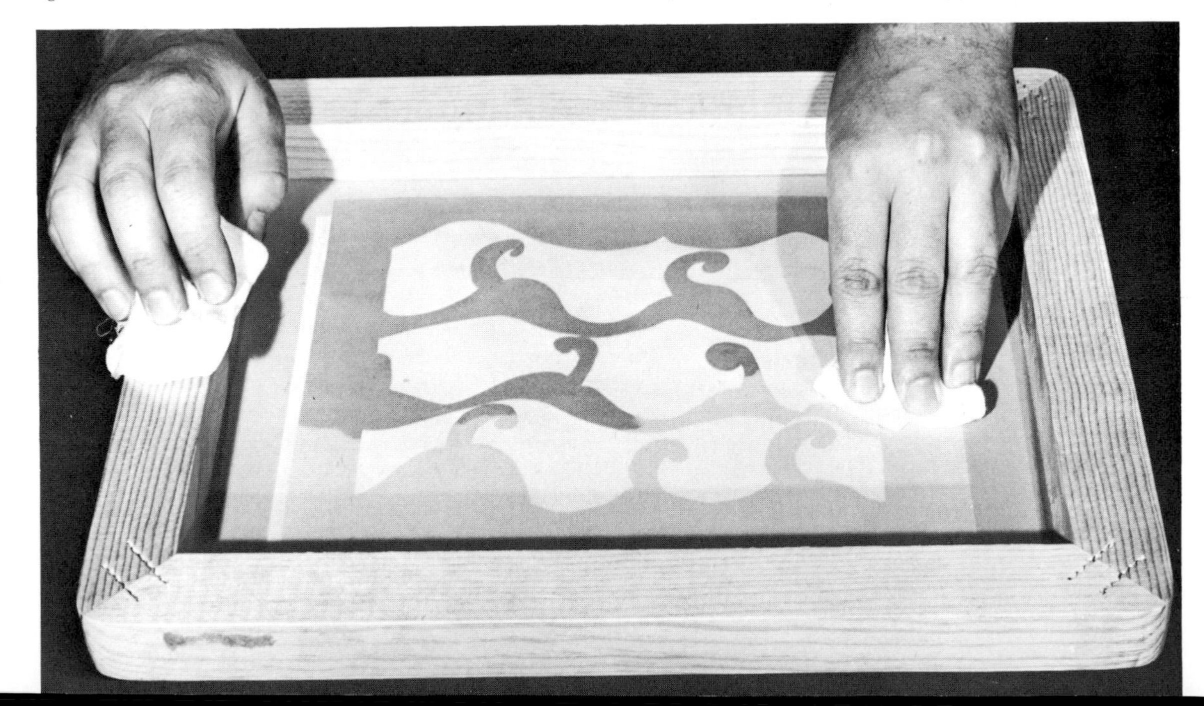

Below: *Adhering a lacquer film stencil requires two rags: one saturated with adhering fluid, and one that is dry for burnishing. Small areas are worked at a time.*

The screen has been remasked with duct tape and is being printed "checker" fashion on a simple grid system without any mechanical registration device. Blank spaces will be printed as soon as the printing paste is dry. The grid has been overemphasized for the camera.

MATERIALS

Stencil knife—An X-acto knife with a long pointed blade is a good choice, but special stencil knives are available. A particularly handy one is a swivel knife for cutting smooth curves. There are also loop cutters for fine lines of consistent width and an adjustable biline cutter for cutting two perfectly parallel lines simultaneously.

Lacquer film—The film consists of a backing paper or other backing material such as vinyl or polyester coated on one side with a thin even film of lacquer which is generally amber or green in color.

Adhesive fluid—Lacquer thinner is often used but is generally less satisfactory than the fluid designed specifically for this purpose.

Prepared printing screen—May be of silk or polyester.

Clean rags or cotton waste

De-Stencil Fluid—For reclaiming the screen when stencil is no longer needed.

METHOD

1. Plan the design, taking into consideration that at least 3 inches at the top and bottom and at least 1 inch at the sides will be required as space for surplus printing paste. For example a 9 by 12 inch printing image will require a screen with minimum *inside* dimensions of 11 by 18 inches.
2. Place the drawing face up on a firm smooth surface and secure the corners in place with tape. Place the film on top of the drawing lacquer side up and secure it gently with tape. Note that paper-backed films are dull on the paper side and glossy on the lacquer side, but the reverse may be true of polyester or vinylbacked film.
3. If this is your first experience with lacquer film, it would be advisable to make a few sample cuts on scrap film. The objective is to cut only the lacquer and never the backing. Furthermore, try to avoid making any grooves or embossed lines on the backing. With the tip of the knife, very gently lift the corner of one of the shapes you wish to print. It is a good idea to save most of these little lacquer film shapes since they may be useful later. Proceed until all of the print shapes have been removed.
4. To adhere the film, place the stencil with its lacquer side up on a level stack of absorbent paper such as newsprint. Position the screen right side up on top of the stencil, that is, with the screen mesh downward. Be certain that the stencil is positioned accurately and that the contact is snug. Have two small clean rags or pieces of cotton waste handy and saturate one of them with adhering fluid. It should be quite moist but not dripping wet. With a circular motion, apply the damp rag to a small area no larger than your fist. Set this rag aside and immediately rub the area with the clean dry rag. Use a circular motion as before and exert considerable pressure. This action forces the softened lacquer well into the mesh and helps to insure a crisp image. Continue to adhere adjacent zones until the task is complete. You may work in a spiral direction from the center out or in rows from end to end, but remember to do small sections with the least possible overlap.
5. Allow the stencil to harden for at least fifteen minutes. In the meantime make a small batch of correction fluid which will be handy should your

stencil have any pinholes or fuzzy edges. To do this place 1 or 2 tablespoons of adhering fluid in a small lidded jar and add some of your reserved lacquer scraps. Stir them around and they will dissolve. Keep adding scraps until you have an easily brushed lacquer solution.

6. Remove the backing sheet. Begin in a corner and very carefuly pick up the backing and double it back on itself so that you may observe the adhesion of the lacquer as you gently pull the sheet away. If by any chance the stencil clings to the backing rather than the mesh you should stop and repeat step 4 for the area needing attention, wait an additional fifteen minutes, and proceed.
7. Mask and tape the screen as directed on pp. 138-39.

Photographic Stencils

Most of the available sheet film products for screen process printing produce stencils that are water soluble. This of course means that dye pastes of fiber-reactive and vat dyestuffs cannot be used with them. For this reason we prefer the use of a direct screen emulsion. Inko Direct Screen Emulsion will produce a tough and durable all-purpose photographic stencil directly on the screen. Any type of screen may be used: polyester, nylon, stainless steel, or silk. All screens except silk may be reclaimed for reuse. Direct Screen Emulsion differs from photostencil films in that it is resistant to all types of inks, including water base inks and dyes. Because the emulsion is embedded in the mesh and not merely adhered to the bottom of the screen, the finest detail is held firmly in position and there is no danger of damaging the stencil during repeated washups. Processing is simple, the temperature of water washout is not critical, and the finished stencil will withstand long production runs.

MATERIALS

Prepared screen—Polyester or stainless steel.
Photo positive—Suggestions follow.
Sodium dichromate (also called bichromate)
Inko Direct Screen Emulsion
Squeegee or special emulsion coater
Light source high in ultraviolet rays—See chart below.
Source of tepid or cool running water—Preferably with a spray or shampoo attachment.
Electric fan (optional)
Chlorine bleach, acetone, or denatured alcohol—For reclaiming the screen. This treatment destroys silk.

METHOD

1. Prepare the photo positive by one of the following methods:
   a. Locate flat opaque objects which when sandwiched between the screen and a sheet of glass will make a desirable arrangement and still permit a snug fit. Try items such as yarn, fan coral, opaque foliage, skeletonized leaves, paper doilies, lace, paper clips, and washers.
   b. Purchase a piece of frosted or treated acetate and paint the desired design on it with Grumbacher's Patent Black, a very dense opaque product created especially for this purpose. The substance is very dense and may need to be thinned slightly with water. Work on the matte side of the acetate and check your work for pinholes of light. By using a very small brush, such as size O, extraordinary detail is possible.
   c. Cut a film positive using Rubylith, a red, light-blocking film laminated to a thin clear plastic backing sheet. This film is cut and peeled in the same manner as lacquer base stencil film. All lines or shapes of the red Rubylith in the design will eventually become the areas that will print and the shapes or lines of clear plastic backing will become the closed stencil areas. Be careful not to pierce or cut the plastic backing sheet.
2. Prepare the sensitizing solution by dissolving 4 ounces sodium dichromate in 1 pint of water (for a very small amount dissolve 6 grams dichromate in 5 teaspoons water). This solution will keep indefinitely if kept in a closed amber glass bottle. Now prepare the screen coating mix by combining 1 part sensitizing solution with 4 parts emulsion. Prepare this mixture under ordinary incandescent light. One tablespoon (½ fluid ounce) of coating mix will coat 1 square foot of screen area.
3. Clean the screen, new or used, with trisodium phosphate (TSP) solution, rinse with hot water, and wipe dry. Coating of the screen is done under subdued incandescent light. Pour the prepared coating mix across one end onto the outside of the screen. Using a squeegee, coat the entire screen with the emulsion. Continue to squeegee back and forth both on the inside and the outside of the screen until the emulsion is spread on both sides. Allow to dry. Drying time may be reduced by using a cold air fan, but do not use heated air. Excess sensitized coating will keep for two weeks if protected from sunlight. The screen must be exposed and washed out within a few hours after being coated. Do not wait overnight.
4. Inko Direct Screen Emulsion may be exposed with any light source high in ultraviolet intensity. Be absolutely sure that there is intimate contact between the glass, the positive, and the coated screen. It is also most important that the opaque areas of the positive be absolutely opaque. The use of a piece of foam rubber against the inside of the screen and weights against the glass will help provide the good contact between the positive and the screen necessary to retain fine detail. The chart below gives starting point exposures for various ultraviolet light sources. It is always wise to make an exposure test strip. If the estimated exposure is 12 minutes, make tests varying from 6 to 24 minutes, and choose the optimum exposure. The distance from the lamp to the screen should be approximately equal to the diagonal of the screen. If the glass becomes heated during exposure, cool with a fan.

Light Source	*Exposure at 15 inches*	*Exposure at 30 inches*
Single carbon arc	3 min.	10 min.
Twin carbon arc	1 min.	3 min.
New photo flood No. 2	5 min.	20 min.
Used photo flood No. 2	8 min.	30 min.
Sunlamp	6 min.	25 min.
Sunlight	3 min.	
Black light fluorescent tubes (at 4 inches)	3 min.	

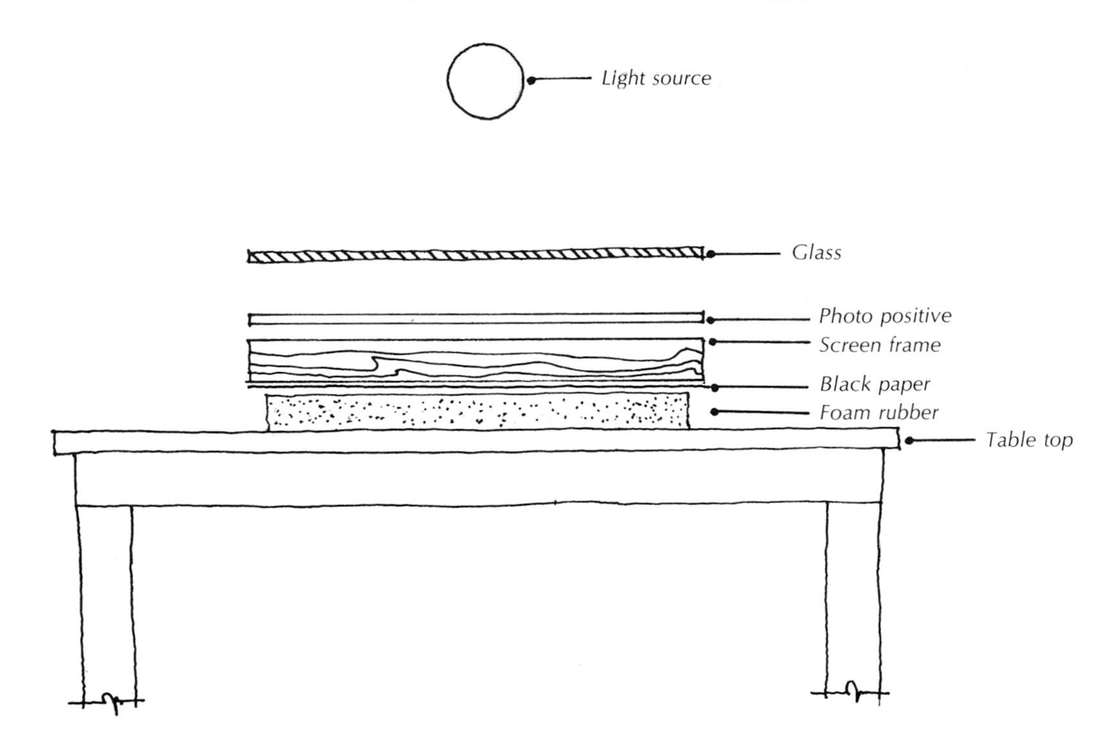

5. Tepid or cool water may be used to wash out unexposed areas of the screen. Wet both sides of the screen with a shampoo type spray appliance. If available using a short bristle brush such as a stencil brush or fitch, scrub out the detail, and then stop. Continued scrubbing will destroy the detail as the stencil is not tough at this stage. Blot off excess water. Let dry overnight.
6. Keep Inko Direct Screen Emulsion in a closed lightproof or amber container. Protect from freezing. The emulsion will keep indefinitely.
7. To remove the emulsion from the screen, first remove all traces of ink with the proper solvent. Now wet both sides of the screen and let soak for 10 to 15 minutes in fresh household bleach. Immerse in a tray or use paper towels to keep the stencil wet. If bleach does not remove the stencil, follow with a 10 minute soaking in acetone or denatured alcohol. Then scrub both sides of the screen with a brush and rinse with water.

Inko Direct Screen Emulsion is available in quart and gallon plastic bottles. Sodium dichromate sensitizer is packaged in ¼ and 1 pound jars. The ¼ pound size is enough sensitizer for ½ gallon of emulsion. Also available, for testing or for small jobs, is a 4 ounce jar of emulsion with the required amount of sensitizer. To prepare this size, dissolve the 6 gram package of sensitizer in 5 teaspoons of water and then combine 1 part sensitizer solution with 4 parts emulsion as needed.

Selecting and Preparing the Fabric

The print fabric should be selected with technical and aesthetic considerations in mind. First, it must have an affinity for the printing paste, and in most cases it must be free of finishes, especially soil-release finishes. Mercerized or untreated fabrics of natural fiber content are the most frequently used, and several excellent mail-order sources for them are listed in Appendix 2.

The aesthetic considerations of fabric selection are somewhat more complex as they involve matters of scale, texture, pattern, and color. Essentially we must adjust the weight, texture, and color of the fabric to the style and relative complexity of the image to be printed. There are certainly no rules, but we offer a few guidelines.

Medium to large shapes and/or lines	Nearly any weight or texture
Large bold patterns or stripes	Heavier fabrics such as duck, canvas, and terry-cloth are suitable, as well as smooth surface fine grain weaves lighter in weight
Small patterns and/or lines Complex designs with fine detail	Smooth surface fabrics of medium to light weight
Any design with extremely minute detail	Fabric with fine uniform pile such as velveteen

Beware of fabrics that are rich or complex in their structures, since printing often confuses rather than enhances their characteristics. Such fabrics as rib weaves, heavy tussah silks, brocades, and fabrics with pronounced variations in texture, may be printed but they do present design challenges that the beginner may wish to avoid or at least postpone.

Dye printers generally prefer a white base fabric as it has the greatest reflective quality, but there is no reason that a precolored base fabric may not be used. It is likewise possible to print on fabric woven of different colored yarns, such as stripes, checks, or plain weave fabrics with warp threads of one color and filler (weft) threads of a second color. Other novel effects may result from overprinting a patterned fabric. All-over batik crackle and simple tie dye stripes for instance may provide rich surface treatments for screen overprinting.

Finally, the fabric should be washed, pressed, and kept rolled on a cardboard tube until ready for use. Washing preshrinks the fabric and removes the sizing present making it more receptive to the printing paste. Ironing removes creases and wrinkles, which can cause serious imperfections in printing.

Preparing the Printing Table

The top of a good printing table consists of three layers: the foundation, the padding, and the covercloth. The actual materials may vary according to budget, space available, volume of operation, and to some extent the nature of the fabric and printing paste.

The foundation is usually plywood with a good smooth top surface. Masonite or a plastic laminate may be used to cover plywood that is not perfectly smooth. The foundation should be about an inch thick and the smallest work table size should be the standard 4 by 8 foot size in which plywood sheeting is marketed. Special widths of plywood may be ordered for commercial operations or for printing extra wide fabric.

The padding is most commonly of felt and should be roughly ⅜ inch thick. Several thin layers may be used to reach this thickness if heavy felt is not easily available. Other substitutes are foam rubber, melton cloth, rug padding, thick cotton flannel layers, or even an old army blanket.

The covercloth may be of medium-weight cotton canvas since it is readily available in several widths and is easily washed and restretched. When a nonporous material is desirable as a covering, we recommend oilcloth, or better still, one of the newer vinyl materials many of which are felt-backed or lightly padded.

To assemble the layers, first spread the padding evenly out on the backing surface and spot press with a steam iron if necessary. If the padding has overhang, it should be lightly stretched and secured with staples to the sides or bottom of the foundation. If the padding has no overhang, it may be secured with a small amount of white glue at the very edges but not in the center. When the padding is secure it is then topped with the covercloth which is likewise stapled to the sides or bottom of the foundation.

This procedure is relatively standard for printing fabric that is secured to the table with pins and/or tape. In some special instances the fabric to be printed is entirely adhered to the table surface by means of a special adhesive or a natural gum. In this case tables are usually covered with neoprene, rubber, or vinyl.

Preparing the Printing Color

For all practical purposes there are only two types of printing color: dyes and inks, often referred to as dye pastes and paste paints, respectively. Both are discussed fully in chapter 3. The color accuracy, paste consistency, and the quantity required, that is, the approximate coverage must now be determined. The only safe method for making these determinations is testing and, of course, learning by experience.

To determine the color accuracy, test the dye or ink on a sample swatch of the fabric to be printed and be certain to complete all of the fixing and finishing steps as they may affect the final color.

When determining the paste consistency, keep in mind that coarse fabrics and those with pile or napped surfaces generally require a less thick printing paste than the average, smooth-surfaced fabric. Screens of finer mesh or stencils with fine lines or dots also require a less thick printing paste.

An exact prediction of the quantity required is impossible without testing, but one pint will cover an average of one yard of fabric. Some of the variables are the number of squeegee strokes, the number and the size of open stencil areas, the consistency of the printing paste, and the relative absorption rate of the fabric. Obviously, with mixed colors it is crucial that the batch be sufficient as it is nearly impossible to make an exact remixture. With a commercially manufactured color it is likewise crucial to have enough on hand. If two containers of the same color may be needed it is wise to mix them together in a large container, especially if the factory batch numbers are dissimilar or absent. It is generally helpful if the printing paste is poured into a spouted container such as a two-cup or quart Pyrex measuring cup or pitcher.

Determining the Registration System and Printing Sequence

Registration involves the precise positioning of the screen frame on the fabric for the orderly repetition of the image. It is generally achieved by mechanical means. Study the various systems and decide on the one best suited to the proposed design and the limitations of the print table.

The Collage System

The collage system is well suited to screens that will be repeated two or more times across the width of the fabric and to situations where mechanical registration devices are not readily available.

1. With a dark value printing paste, run off between nine and twelve prints on white construction paper and allow them to dry. Construction paper is inexpensive and has a low shrinkage ratio.
2. Clean the screen thoroughly and allow it to dry.
3. When the paper prints or "strike sheets" are dry, assemble them exactly as you want them to appear on the fabric. Use a ruler and triangle and tape them either to each other or to a large sheet of butcher paper depending on the relative space between images. Be as accurate as possible.
4. By looking through the open mesh of the stencil, set the screen directly on one of the strike sheet images. When it is perfectly superimposed draw an outline of the frame directly on the strike sheet collage. Move to the neighboring image and make a second outline. Proceed in this manner until each image has a frame line. This network of lines is a master grid which indicates the correct screen placement for a regulated all-over repeat.
5. With the aid of tracing paper transfer this grid to the fabric. Be sure to use a nonindelible mark. The tracing is of course moved and realigned a number of times in order to cover the entire length of fabric. If desired, the outline grid may be converted to small L-shaped marks corresponding to the frame corners.
6. The fabric is now ready to print.

The Sliding Cross Bar System

Like the collage system, the sliding cross bar system is best suited to registering small screens requiring three or more repeats across the width of the fabric. No elaborate equipment is required.

1. Attach the fabric to the printing table and neatly run a strip of masking tape down both selvedges. This tape has three functions: it covers any pinheads if they are used; it provides a neat print edge or mask; and it allows the printer to make measured registration marks down the entire length of the table.
2. Run four or more strike sheets as on the previous system or make as many tracings of the original design.

3. Tape them together in such a way that a grid is constructed indicating the outline of the printing frame. Refer to steps 3 and 4 of the collage system.
4. Measure the distance between vertical repeats of the top *or* bottom of the frame and mark these points continuously down both of the selvedge tapes making sure the marks are directly opposite each other.
5. Construct the sliding cross bar from perfectly straight, clear 1 by 6 inch wood such as fir or pine. The cross bar is simply a T-square with a second end resembling the letter "H." The end pieces should fit the sides of the printing table snugly, yet allow the bar to slide with relative ease. Sand any rough spots to prevent snags and assure smooth movement.
6. Apply a strip of masking tape to the top surface of the cross bar. It should run the full length of the bar and be flush with one of its edges.
7. Measure the distance between the horizontal (selvedge to selvedge) repeats of the right *or* left sides of the frame and mark these points continuously across the bar.
8. Place the taped bar edge on the first pair of the selvedge tape marks. Set the screen on the fabric aligning one of its edges with the proper mark on the cross bar. When this unit is printed the screen is moved to the second or third cross bar mark depending on the printing sequence. If desired the cross bar marks may be converted to lines corresponding to a mark or a key point on the printing frame.

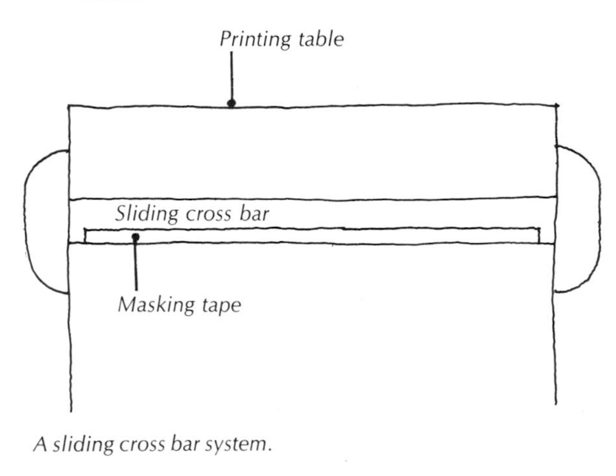

A sliding cross bar system.

The Single Rail System

The single rail provides an efficient production system, which employs one large screen that crosses the full width of the fabric from selvedge to selvedge. Of necessity the frame will have to be large and heavy, and the aid of a second printer may be necessary. Two exceptions where smaller screens could be utilized with a single rail system would be selvedge border prints and narrow width specialty fabric woven for such items as towels and traditional kimonos.

By studying the diagram shown here you will note that four mechanical aids are required. They are the rail, adjustable rail stops, the frame stop, and the vertical edge adjustment screws.

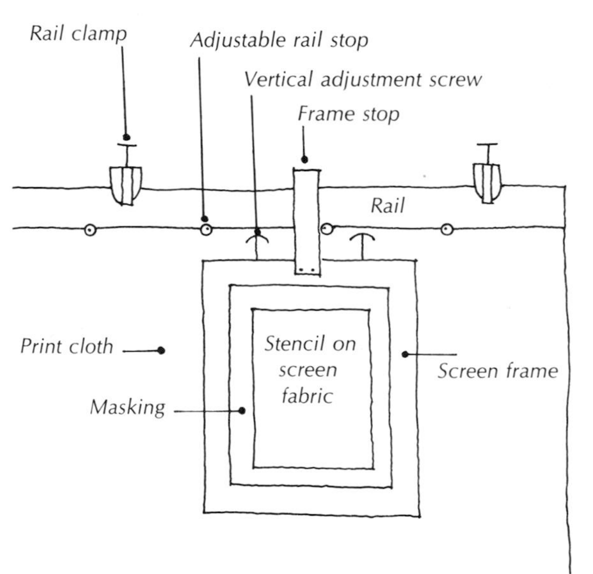

A single rail registration system.

The rail is usually L-shaped in section and of metal angle stock. It must be perfectly straight and run the full length of the printing table. The rail may be drilled and secured with screws for semipermanent installation or with large C-clamps if the rail is to be portable. The clamps may be welded to the rail if desired. The height of the rail must not exceed the height of the screen frame.

The adjustable rail stops are small metal clamps that firmly grasp the rail at carefully measured intervals. The best ones have thumb screws and are especially fabricated for this purpose. Very small C-clamps may be used provided that they will not wobble when in contact with the frame stop.

The frame stop may be a small metal bar or bracket in the shape of an "L," "T," or simply a straight line. Its longest leg should extend about three inches from the top midpoint of the frames rail adjoining side. It must be secured with two or more screws to prevent the possibility of misalignment. Reinforcing brackets from a hardware store make excellent printing frame stops.

The vertical edge (side) adjustment screws are a pair of adjustable round-headed screws near the top and bottom corners of the frame's rail adjoining side. Their dual function is to assure accurate consistent spacing between the rail and the frame and to assure that the stencil image is squarely on the fabric. Round-headed wood screws of the necessary length are most often used. Especially fabricated threaded metal plates are sometimes attached to the frame to receive the proper adjusting screws. In this last case the frame must be predrilled to permit entry.

METHOD

1. Secure the rail to the printing table.
2. Attach the fabric to the table. The selvedge and the rail must be parallel. The space between them is determined by measuring from the inside rail surface to the nearest edge of the stencil image. Include allowance for the adjustment screws. If the fabric is pinned to the covercloth remember to place tape over the pinheads.
3. Square the frame to the rail and install the vertical edge adjustment screws. This is a simple operation provided that the stencil has been adhered squarely on the screen mesh and that the screen frame is also square. A large rafter square, T-square, or triangle is set against the rail extending well onto the printing table and the adjustment screws are tightened or loosened as needed to assure that the frame is at a perfect right angle to the rail and the correct parallel distance from it.
4. Attach the frame stop and the adjustable rail stops. One edge of the frame stop should be midway between the top and bottom of the frame and extend

at a right angle about 3 inches from it. When properly aligned, the frame stop must slightly overlap the top of the rail. Measure the exact distance between repeats and install the adjustable rail stops so that the *same* edge of each stop is equidistant from the *same* edge of every other stop. Recheck all measurements and be certain that the stops are secure.
5. Check registration and alignment by printing a five-image strikeoff. Place the frame on the fabric so that the frame stop touches either edge of the first rail stop and print the first image. Lift the frame and reposition it so that the frame stop touches the *same* edge of the third rail stop that was used for the first rail stop. Print the fifth image in the same manner and allow one, three, and five to dry or cover them carefully with paper. Complete the five-image strikeoff by printing images two and four. Study the result and make any necessary adjustments.

The Double Rail System

The double rail system is identical to the single rail system except that there is a second rail with identical stops. The frame likewise has two sets of screws and stop bars. It is generally more efficient to relocate the frame stop bars to the top edge of the screen frame for easy contact with the rail stop prior to setting the frame on the fabric.

The Modified Double Rail System

This system is very convenient since it utilizes a smaller and more manageable screen than does the double rail system. The screen must however be sufficiently large that the stencil will reach from a selvedge to the center of the fabric.

METHOD

1. Fit the screen with matching pairs of frame stops and adjusting screws.
2. Attach the rails and fabric so that the rails are parallel and that the fabric is centered between them.
3. Adjust the screws so that the stencil will reach midpoint when the screws on the right touch the rail on the right and likewise on the left.
4. Secure the rail stops at identical mirror image intervals on both rails.
5. Run a strikeoff of ten images by printing images 1, 3, and 5 with the left rail. Walk around the table and, using the opposite frame stop, print images 2 and 4 with the right rail. Allow these to dry, or cover with paper and print the alternate images taking care not to rotate the screen.
6. Study the strikeoff and adjust as necessary.

Further modifications are possible by designing a stencil that will produce different effects when inverted, half-dropped or even checkered with another screen.

It would be very handy to start the printing sequence at one end of the fabric and print every consecutive image in order until the other end was reached, and under special circumstances this can indeed be done. The problem, however, is that some of the moist printing paste will usually adhere to the bottom of the screen where it overlaps. If this occurs, it will be redeposited on the fabric, resulting in an unwanted ghost image fragment. This can be avoided by a careful prearrangement of the printing sequence or by masking the fresh images.

When printing full-width screens, the usual technique is to print images 1, 3, 5, 7 and the remaining odd images, allowing these to dry on the printing table. Then the alternate images are printed. Another method is to print the odd-numbered images, then mask them with carefully precut sheets of clean newsprint paper. The paper masks will prevent smudges and substantially reduce the printing time.

When printing two or more images across a width of fabric, printers usually work on a checkerboard principle using square paper towels to mask the corners of the preceding row. Alternately they may print 1, 3, 5, etc. across row 1, skip row 2 entirely, and print 1, 3, 5, etc. across row 3 and all other odd rows, returning later to complete the checkering, and still later to complete the job.

In planning a printing sequence several things should be considered: What is the average drying time? How rapidly is the printing paste absorbed by the fabric? If the fabric is allowed to dry on the table will it shrink enough to cause a misregister, and how heavy is the deposit of printing paste? These and other questions are best answered by printing a strikeoff on the actual fabric or one known to have its behavior properties.

Printing

Producing a consistent series of clear screen print images takes both dexterity and practice. If the angle of the squeegee or pressure on it is incorrect, too much or too little paste will be deposited. Other variable factors are the amount of padding on the table, the density and porosity of the fabric, the density of the screen mesh, the consistency of the printing paste, the relative flexibility or shape of the squeegee blade, and finally, the number of squeegee strokes. By first running a strikeoff as suggested in the previous section, the printer can substantially reduce the variables and be properly prepared for the best possible results with the finished fabric.

The squeegee. The best, all-purpose fabric printing squeegee has a blade with slightly rounded edges. A perfectly sharp right-angle blade produces a very thin deposit on the screen fabric and is suitable only for very sheer or lightweight fabrics or for working with very thin printing paste. Conversely, a rounded squeegee will produce a heavy deposit of paste and should be used only with very heavy, porous fabric or with a very stiff printing paste. The squeegee should be only slightly shorter than the inside width of the printing frame. A pair of nails or extension bars protruding from each end of the squeegee handle will prevent it from accidentally falling into the frame.

An assistant or second printer. The beginning printer will find an assistant very useful for holding the frame in place. The printer's hands will then be free to operate the squeegee and replenish the printing paste. A second pair of hands may also be helpful for the careful lifting and accurate repositioning of the screen. The more experienced printer with a full-width screen will find an assistant on the opposite side of the table invaluable since each person may squeegee toward themselves in alternation. This motion of pulling the squeegee only toward yourself is by far the smoothest and most efficient method. Successfully pushing the squeegee directly away requires practice and often results in uneven pressure and its attendant problems of skipping and having streamers of paste follow the squeegee. If you will be printing alone or if the screen is small, it is best to design a stencil that can be printed with a side-to-side stroke, that is with the frame running lengthwise on the table.

Preparing to print. Prepare an area near the printing table with several layers of newspaper the size of the screen or larger, and in a convenient place have clean rags, solvent, a rubber spatula, the pitcher of printing paste, and some masking tape for emergency mending of small leaks should they occur. Next, set the screen on the pad of newspaper, and squeegee some printing paste onto the paper. If the print seems uneven, do this a second time. This operation serves to wet the open mesh and assures that the first fabric image will be as clear as the succeeding ones.

Single-hand printing. Place the screen on the fabric and lower the squeegee into place about two inches from the left end of the frame. The handle will be facing right and the nails or extension bars will prevent it from contracting the screen. Pour a line of printing paste in the well between the blade and the frame. Hold the frame in place with the left hand and with the right hand in the center of the squeegee back track slightly, and at about a 50 degree angle draw the paste as smoothly as possible across the mesh. Now lift the squeegee, engaging the transported ridge of paste and draw it back to the left of the screen. If you are left-handed, you will probably be more comfortable reversing the operation. Special vertical metal peg handles are available, and some printers find them an advantage for long production runs in single-hand printing.

Two-hand printing. When working alone this method assumes that the frame will be large or heavy enough to remain perfectly in place while both hands are used for printing. The operation and objective is identical to the single-hand technique except that when stroking from left to right the right hand is at the far end of the squeegee, and when stroking from right to left the right hand is at the near end of the squeegee.

Four-hand printing. Depending on the proportions of the screen, this may be done in either of two ways. The paste may be drawn from selvedge to selvedge with each printer pulling the squeegee toward their side of the table in alternation. In the second technique the printers stand on either side of the table and with equal pressure stroke the paste back and forth on the lengthwise direction of the table. This latter technique is preferred by most large-scale production printers.

Lifting the Screen. Freshly printed fabric has a natural tendency to follow the screen as it is lifted. This condition is more pronounced with inks than dye pastes and with stencils that print massive areas rather than fine lines, dots, or textures. Sheer and stretch fabrics are especially prone to lifting. To minimize this problem, always gently lift one end of the screen first then follow through gracefully with the remaining portion. A helper with clean hands may also be enlisted to hold the fabric in place as the printer lifts the screen.

Clean Up

If your screen frame will fit into your studio sink and if you have been using a water soluble paste, then clean up is blissfully simple. Clean up out of doors with a garden hose is also ideal. However, in many instances the above conveniences are not available, so the following procedure is recommended and it may be modified to suit any situation. You will need newspaper, clean rags or cotton waste, water, soap, or detergent and a rubber, nylon, or soft plastic kitchen spatula.

1. With spatula remove as much paste as you can from the screen and squeegee and deposit it in a suitable closed container.
2. Arrange a stack of newspaper about ½ inch thick the size of the screen frame and place the screen on the paper with the mesh touching the paper.
3. Pour a small amount of solvent onto the mesh and scrub with a rag. Invert and similarly clean the back. Remove the top layers of newspaper and repeat the process on fresh paper.
4. Again with the spatula, remove as much paste as possible from the squeegee and clean it with a rag saturated with solvent.
5. Finally wash everything with warm, soapy water. Use the bucket and sponge method if a sink is not available.
6. Rinse and dry the equipment, double-checking the screen for traces of dried printing paste. New mesh, especially if it is silk may take on the color that was being printed but this will not affect the future performance of the screen.
7. If the screen is to be reclaimed by removing the stencil from the mesh it is done at this point. Essentially the process involves scrubbing the screen with the appropriate solvent followed by a detergent bath. Reclaiming agents are discussed in the section of this chapter on stencil making, pp. 139-46.
8. A word of caution: papers and rags that have been soaked with flammable solvents must be disposed of immediately and should not be allowed to stand in open, nonmetallic containers.

Drying the Fabric

If at all possible the fabric should be allowed to dry in place right on the table. This is especially true if it is to be overprinted with an additional color or colors demanding precise registration. However, in small studios or crowded classrooms this is not always feasible. The fabric should instead be carefully lifted with the aid of a helper and hung to dry on an improvised clothesline or lines. Special care will be needed to prevent the fabric from touching itself.

Overprinting or Additional Colors

Overprinting is a process for the application of an additional color or colors. In most cases it involves different stencils, however, overprinting may be achieved by offsetting, rotating, or in some way repositioning the original screen. When working with transparent dye pastes overprinting has the special advantage of producing a third or "bonus" color if the second stencil is printed over a portion of the original image. Paste paints are usually semi-opaque and overprinting nearly blocks out the under color, but many transparentizing agents or extenders may be added to approximate the effect of dye overlap.

Transparent, colored tissue paper is frequently used as a design tool for visualizing overprint possibilities. Simply cut an image approximately the same color and shape as the original print and attach it to a sheet of white tissue. If the ground fabric is a color rather than white, then attach the image to a tissue that corresponds to that color. Next cut an image that approximates the color and shape of the prospective overprint, attaching it as before. Now hold the composition so that light passes through it and you will have a close idea of the compound effect. This process may be repeated for additional color shapes and by rearrangement, numerous design variations may be tested.

When the overprint screen is ready, it may be registered by any method previously described. However, the problem with overprinting by a fixed mechanical system is that all too often the first printing will cause some shrinkage and as the second screen is printed down a length of fabric the resulting misregistration compounds itself. To avoid this problem we suggest the following matboard or picture frame overprint registration technique:

1. Cut a 2 inch wide cardboard mat the outside dimensions of which are exactly the same size as the printing frame.
2. Cut a piece of good quality tracing paper slightly larger than the opening in the cardboard frame.
3. Secure the tracing paper in the opening with tape. It should be taut but should not distort the cardboard.
4. Position the prepared overprint screen carefully, aligning edges and corners.
5. Print the image on the tracing paper with any mid-value printing paste that is handy and allow the print to dry thoroughly, or trace the outline with a pencil.
6. Have the previously printed fabric stretched in place on the printing table.
7. By looking through the still translucent parts of the tracing paper, it will be easy to align the new image with the original image on the awaiting fabric.
8. Mark any two convenient corners of the cardboard mat directly on the fabric with lines that will later wash out. Special pencils of this type may be found with sewing notions at fabric or department stores.
9. Reposition the cardboard mat and again mark the same two corners. Repeat this process until all images have been marked.
10. The marked pairs of corners from step 8 of course correspond to the corners of the printing frame and will allow you to position the frame with ease and precision. With the aid of these marked corners continue printing.

This system is applicable to any number of overprints the project requires. Clear or frosted acetate, tissue paper, clear vinyl, or sheer fabric may be substituted for tracing paper.

Fixing and Finishing

Every class of dye and even different products within the same dye class may require different applications of heat, light, and/or pressure for fixing. It is essential to obtain this information when the dye is purchased. Pigment pastes generally require only heat, but different products and different fabrics again will vary. Dye-printed fabric usually requires a final wash out to expel the thickener, but pigment prints generally do not need this final step.

Even if you are using one of the products covered in this book, it is wise to check the manufacturer's instructions since formulas can change and improved procedures are constantly being developed.

Flocking

Flocking produces a suede or velvetlike surface and is a two-process technique. First, the surface must be printed with an appropriate adhesive; and second, the flock must be evenly applied to the adhesive while it is still wet. The adhesive we prefer is Inko Flocking Base, a dense, opaque, pigmented ink that remains flexible and is thoroughly washable. Our experience with flocking is limited to the Inko Washfast Rayon Flock, which consists of millions of tiny strands of rayon fiber. Both products are available in a variety of colors and it is advisable to match them as closely as possible.

Applying the Flock Adhesive. The flock adhesive may be screen printed through a 6XX or 8XX mesh, although brushing, rolling, or stamp printing are possible methods of applying the flocking base. Clean up is achieved with mineral spirits or with Inko #17 Screen Wash.

Adhering the Flock. While the base is still wet, the flock is applied with a flour sifter or a special flock gun. Apply about ⅛ to ¼ inch of flock to the base printed areas, but allow some of the flock to settle on the unprinted areas as well. The flocked fabric may be allowed to dry in place for twelve or more hours. This method produces a surface that resembles felt. There are two alternate methods that produce a velvetlike surface since the flock fibers can be made to stand up rather than lay down.

For the first method, with the help of an assistant, gently lift the freshly flocked fabric while the base is still wet and *gently* shake the fabric, causing the flock to dance around on the surface. Carefully set the fabric back down to dry on a clean, paper-covered surface. Excess flock may be reclaimed when adhesive base is dry.

The second method assumes that a covercloth has been laid down prior to printing and flocking. Detach the covercloth all arond the table by removing any pins or tape. Next slide a 1 by 1 inch square or hexagonal wooden or metal "beater bar" under the covercloth extending slightly beyond the selvedges of the cloth. This bar is then rotated down the length of the printing table causing the flock particles to dance and become attached on end. The purpose of the cover cloth is to prevent the ink (base) from smudging on the underside of the fabric and may not be needed if the fabric is heavy enough. Excess flock may be dusted off when adhesive base is dry.

Detail of a flocked fabric panel. Values are very close. Yellow rayon flock on sheer white ground fabric.

Examples of Stencil Printing

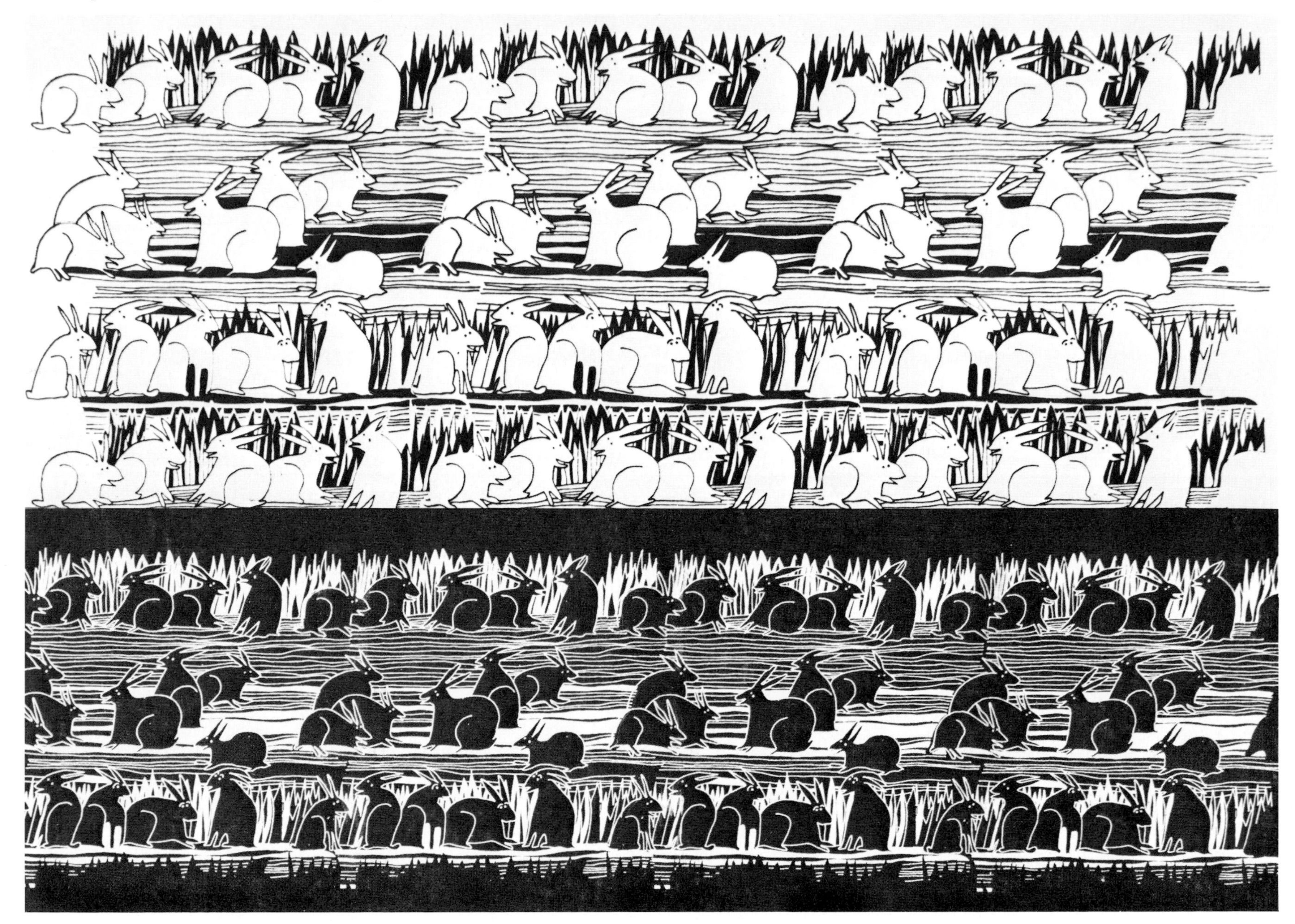

Hazel Koenig. Rabbits. *An excellent example of how four-sided dovetail units interlock with their neighbors. The top sample is black dye on white cotton; the bottom sample is white ink on black cotton.*

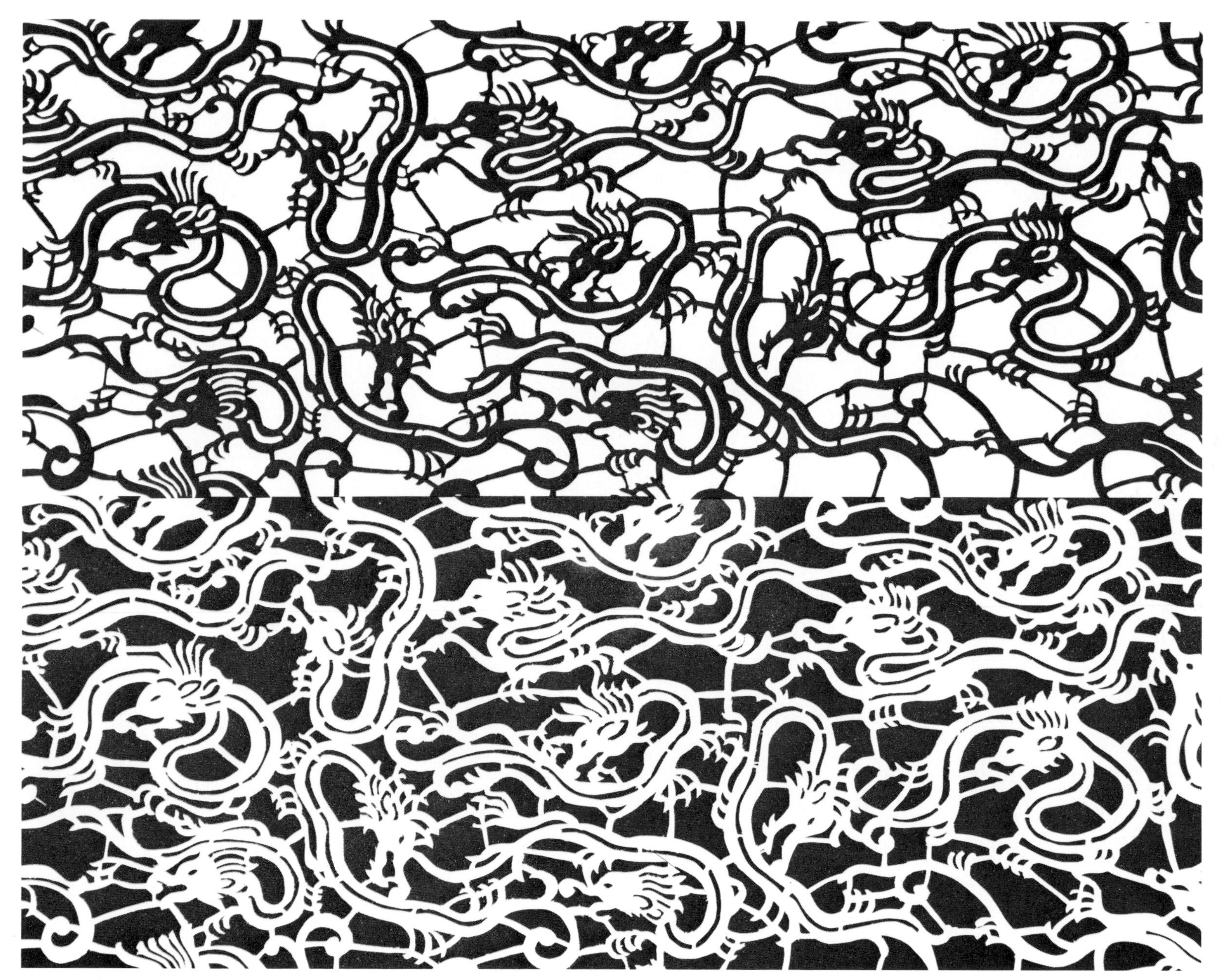

Cut paper dragon stencil by Jennifer F. Lew, ca. 10" × 24" (25 × 61 cm), shown as cut (bottom) *and as reversed photographically* (top).

Cut paper ornament from Peoples' Republic of Poland, ca. 8"x 8"(20 x 20 cm).

Example from Chinese Papercut Pictures *by Nancy Kuo. Courtesy of Academy Editions, London.*

Detail of contemporary Mexican white tissue-paper stencil commemorating the Day of the Dead, ca. 18"x 24" (46 x 61 cm).

Nigerian stencil printed fabric in "Oloba" or jubilee design honoring England's King George and Queen Mary, who appear in the center detail. Indigo dye on cotton.

Chinese resist paste and stencil printed cotton fabric. Brown and white, first half of 20th century. Costume and Textile Study Collection, University of Washington.

Left: *Marmara, a flocked sheer fabric from Jack Lenor Larsen, Inc. Based on a drawing by Connecticut artist Sewell Sillman and first shown at the 13th Milan Triennale.*

Right: South China Sea *(homage to Jim Thompson). Printed with discharge dyes to create a negative image in off-white. Courtesy of Jack Lenor Larsen, Inc.*

9. Needlework

The term *needlework* encompasses many varied processes. In this chapter we will emphasize only the three fundamental techniques of embroidery, appliqué, and quilting. Each of these creates a three-dimensional change. Embroidery often produces raised linear effects or textural changes resembling satin, fine pile, or knotting. Appliqué is an additive process resembling collage in which shapes, textures, or lines are applied to the fabric surface. It involves layered effects as well as the inventive use of stitches and edge treatment. Quilting develops three-dimensional effects through changes in relief. These may be dramatic sculptural changes or subtle indentations of dots or lines. Although the effects of these techniques are quite unique, the use of the needle is common to each.

Needlework is both functional and decorative. In a piece of clothing, for example, once the functional concerns of joining and fitting are satisfied, the need to embellish, personalize, decorate, or create symbols ensues and finds expression in applied design. Through a common vocabulary of stitches or techniques, each needleworker develops a personal style and quality of hand.

Nirmal Kaur. Rare Fishies. *Mixed media composition with beads and embroidery, 12″ x 15″ (30.5 x 38 cm).*

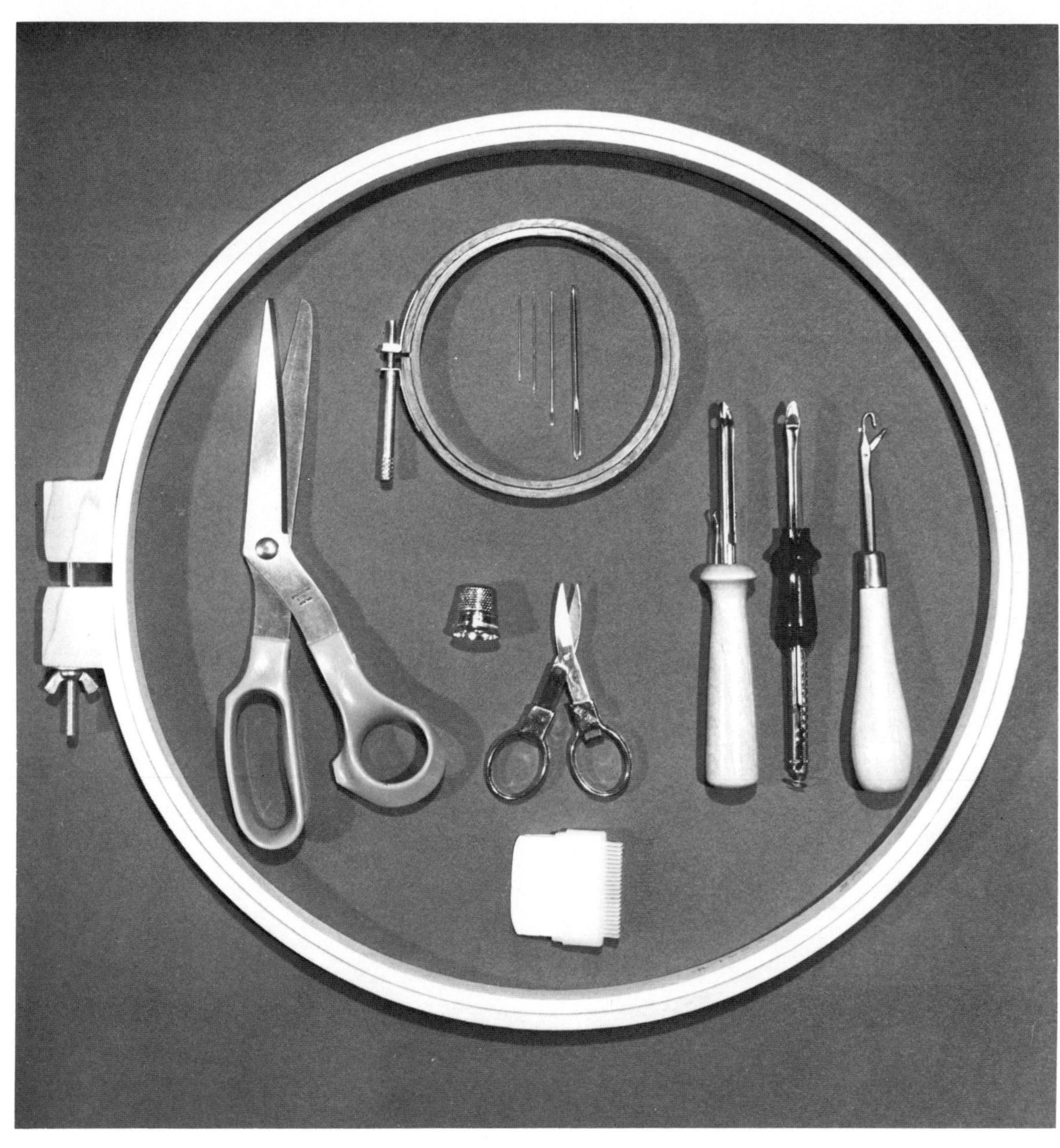

Tools for needlework.

Tools for Needlework

Needlework tools, equipment, and supplies are readily available and generally low in cost. They are found in fabric and yarn shops, the notions departments of variety stores and numerous specialty mail order supply house catalogs. Several excellent suppliers are listed in Appendix 2.

Large embroidery hoop—This style is used for large pieces, for heavy fabric or for rug techniques. In most cases a rectangular wooden frame or artist's stretcher bars may be substituted.
Fabric scissors—Many excellent scissors of this type are available in right- and left-handed models.
Thimble—An optional tool available in many sizes and types. Leather thimbles for the side of the finger are now on the market.
Dressmakers' chalk—This product has recently been surpassed by a totally water soluble, soft-tip fabric marker from Japan.
Embroidery scissors—Small, sharp-pointed scissors for cutting thread or yarn. The model illustrated is collapsible.
Embroidery hoop—These round or oval hoops are available in wood, metal, and plastic.
Assorted needles—Described at length on page 161.
Rug needle A—This style is somewhat adjustable and may be used for rug yarn only.
Rug needle B—This style adjusts for a variety of pile depths and comes with a second tip (not shown) for less bulky yarn.
Latch hook—This tool is used to knot precut lengths of yarn to a special rug mesh.

Techniques for Needlework

EMBROIDERY BASICS

The three physical requirements for embroidery are fabric, a needle, and thread or yarn. With the possible exceptions of an embroidery hoop or stitching frame and a good pair of small scissors, nothing else save a knowledge (or book) of stitches is necessary.

Fabrics for Embroidery

Nearly any fabric is suitable so long as its weight and density are reasonably adjusted to the size and type of needle and/or yarn. Chapter 2 deals with fabric characteristics and should be helpful in selecting the best fabric for the embroidery project at hand. Beginners will usually find medium-weight opaque fabric of a balanced weave the easiest to use, especially if it is held in place with an embroidery hoop and worked with six-strand embroidery floss or No. 5 pearl cotton through a No. 5 crewel or a No. 18 tapestry needle. Good fabric and yarn stores often stock a range of special fabrics for hand embroidery. An experienced salesperson at such an establishment can provide excellent advice on choosing fabric, yarn, and needle.

Sewing Threads

Sewing threads are specialized yarns, designed to be of uniform diameter, and maximum strength. Some threads are intended both for hand and for machine sewing, while others have highly specialized functions. If thread is being selected for a piece that will be laundered, or dyed at a later time, it is very important to select one of the same fiber content.

Mercerized cotton thread. This is the most useful hand sewing thread available and is equally suited to machine use. The coarsest thread is size 8 and the finest is size 100. Size 8 is available in black and white only, and size 100 in white only; but the color range in the most popular size 50 thread numbers around 150 different colors.

Button and carpet thread. A very strong hand sewing thread generally of mercerized cotton designed for attaching buttons, binding rugs, and working with heavy furnishing fabrics. The color range is limited to about ten colors.

Silk sewing thread. A good choice for small decorative hand sewn works or other pieces that do not require frequent laundering. It is available in about 100 colors and is relatively expensive.

Silk buttonhole twist. Designed for edging of buttonholes and also for attaching buttons. This strong and beautiful thread is also excellent for embroidery and may be used in multiple strands for greater display of color or as a single strand for quilting, top stitching, or detail work. Because this thread looses its twist during sewing, it is best to work with relatively short strands. Close to 100 colors are available.

Synthetic threads. Polyester, nylon, and cotton-wrapped polyester are the most common synthetics. The color variety is outstanding and these threads behave very well for machine sewing. As a group they tend to be somewhat elastic, which makes them ideal for sewing knits and stretch fabrics. For hand sewing, however, the synthetics have an annoying tendency to snarl and twist around themselves.

Specialty thread. Larger fabric shops and sewing notions departments stock an interesting and challenging variety of novel and special threads. There are color variegated threads, opalescent threads, monofilament nylon or "invisible" threads, metallic threads, and waxed threads for quilting, beading, and leather work to name only a few.

Yarn for Embroidery

Pearl cotton. This yarn is composed of three strands of cotton yarn plied with a relatively high twist. It is readily available in a good color range and in three common sizes: 8 fine, 5 medium, and 3 heavy. Other sizes are rare but are measured with higher numbers indicating finer threads. Pearl cotton is smooth with a very slight luster making it pleasant to work with. Stitches tend to be crisp and defined.

Six-strand embroidery floss. Cotton floss is by far the most common embroidery thread, but with a bit of searching it can also be found in rayon and silk. The rayon floss has an exceptionally high luster, and the silk floss has a characteristic sheen of great richness. Any floss may be used since it comes from the skein with all six strands or the strands may be separated. Special effects may be achieved by recombining strands. For example, a very rich six-strand yarn could be easily created by threading two strands of blue-violet, two strands of blue-gray and two strands of blue-green through the same needle.

Crochet cotton. An exceptionally strong three- or four-ply yarn of medium luster and twist. It is available in a good range of color and size.

Crewel or Persian yarn. These are most often three-stranded yarns, each consisting of a twisted two-ply yarn. They are designed for embroidery and needlepoint. The yarn has a medium luster and may be stitched as it comes from the skein or separated in the same fashion as six-strand embroidery floss. It is available in bales, skeins, or small portions wrapped around cards.

Tapestry yarn. A four-ply yarn roughly equivalent in weight to four-ply knitting worsted, the most common knitting yarn on the market. It cannot be separated and must be used as it comes from the skein. About 100 colors are available in small skeins of modest cost.

Miscellaneous yarns. Larger yarn shops and especially weaving supply shops carry a seemingly endless variety of domestic and imported yarns, threads, strings, twines, roving, and fibrous materials that certainly have their place in contemporary needlework.

Garment appliqué, presumably of European origin, early 20th century. Courtesy of Leather and Things, Gastown, Vancouver, British Columbia, Canada.

Many heavy and irregular yarns are unsuitable for threading through a needle but may be effective textural elements if couched or attached with a thinner, more consistent yarn.

Yarn Effects

Several important and often overlooked factors dictate the effect stitches will have in a composition. In selecting yarns and threads for decorative or functional embroidery, take into account their color, luster, twist, and elasticity. Yarns that are light in value show the texture and definition of the stitches much more clearly than dark yarns. Yarns that have some reflective quality show their dimensional characteristics regardless of color. Highly twisted but not kinked yarns have greater definition than soft, loosely twisted yarns. Rigid, nonelastic yarns show the stitches clearly, while stretchy yarns tend to distort the fabric surface and the structure of the stitches.

Needles

Sharps. These are general purpose needles of medium length with rounded eyes. They are sized from 1 to 10, with 1 the largest and 10 the finest.

Betweens. Very short needles designed for fine stitches and ideal for quilting, sometimes packaged as quilting needles. Relative sizes are graded from 1 to 10 as with the Sharps.

Milliners'. Very long and slender needles designed to hold several stitches as in smocking, shirring, and basting. Again, these needles are graded from 1 to 10.

Crewel or embroidery needles. These pointed needles are of medium length with long oval eyes. The sizes are from 1 (large) to 10 (small). Within this range it is possible to stitch with a very wide variety of flosses, threads, and yarns. The long eye makes them easy to thread. They are probably the most useful family of needles for decorative stitching.

Tapestry needles. These are sturdy, blunt-ended, large-eyed, needles designed for penetrating loosely woven fabric or canvas. Needlepoint or canvas work utilizes tapestry needles, and they are also used for lacing, whipping, or threading yarns through standard embroidery stitches.

Wendell Brazeau. Standing Figure. *Jute ground with simple satin and running stitches, ca. 9"x 12"(23 x 30.5 cm). Courtesy of Mrs. Elizabeth Brazeau.*

Embroidery Stitches

From hundreds, perhaps thousands of different embroidery stitches we have selected eleven which we feel are basic, versatile, useful, and representative of linear, space filling, edging, and texture producing functions. Most of our stitches are shown in their simplest form and in many cases interesting variations exist. The bibliography gives the titles of several excellent books devoted to embroidery stitches.

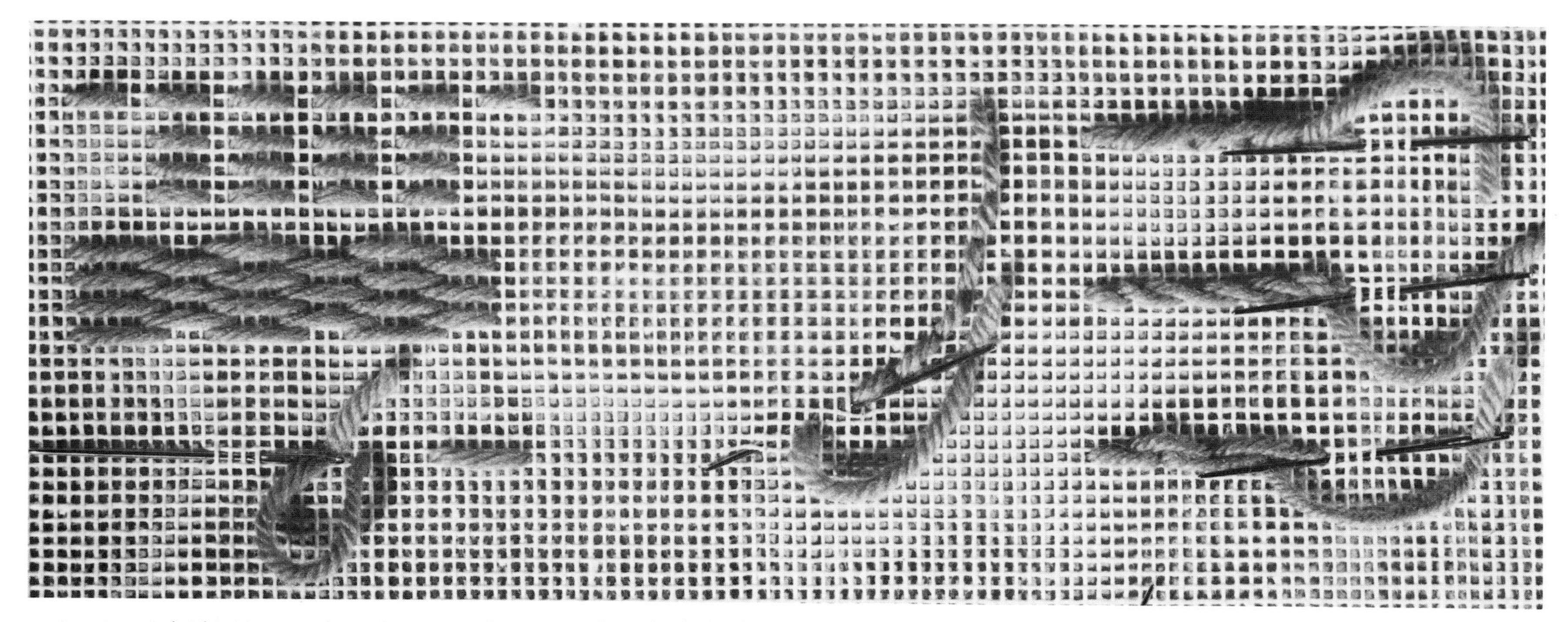

Running stitch. This is a versatile stitch creating a linear effect with stitches and spaces of equal or consistent lengths. Run needle in and out of fabric, making stitches even in size and in desired length. This may be used as an outline or filling stitch.

Back stitch. The back stitch produces a very neat almost solid line. Bring the needle through the fabric from back to front, pierce the fabric about ⅛ of an inch to the right, bringing it up again about ¼ of an inch to the left. Repeat this procedure in a left to right progression, remembering that the thread travels under the fabric twice the distance that is visible from the top surface.

Stem, outline, and cable stitches. These closely related stitches offer crisp delineation of textural filling possibilities. The outline stitch, the stem stitch, and the cable stitch are slightly diagonal lapped stitches repeated on a line and vary only in whether the thread is held above (outline) or below (stem) the needle. In the cable stitch, the thread is alternatively held above and below the needle. Work from left to right.

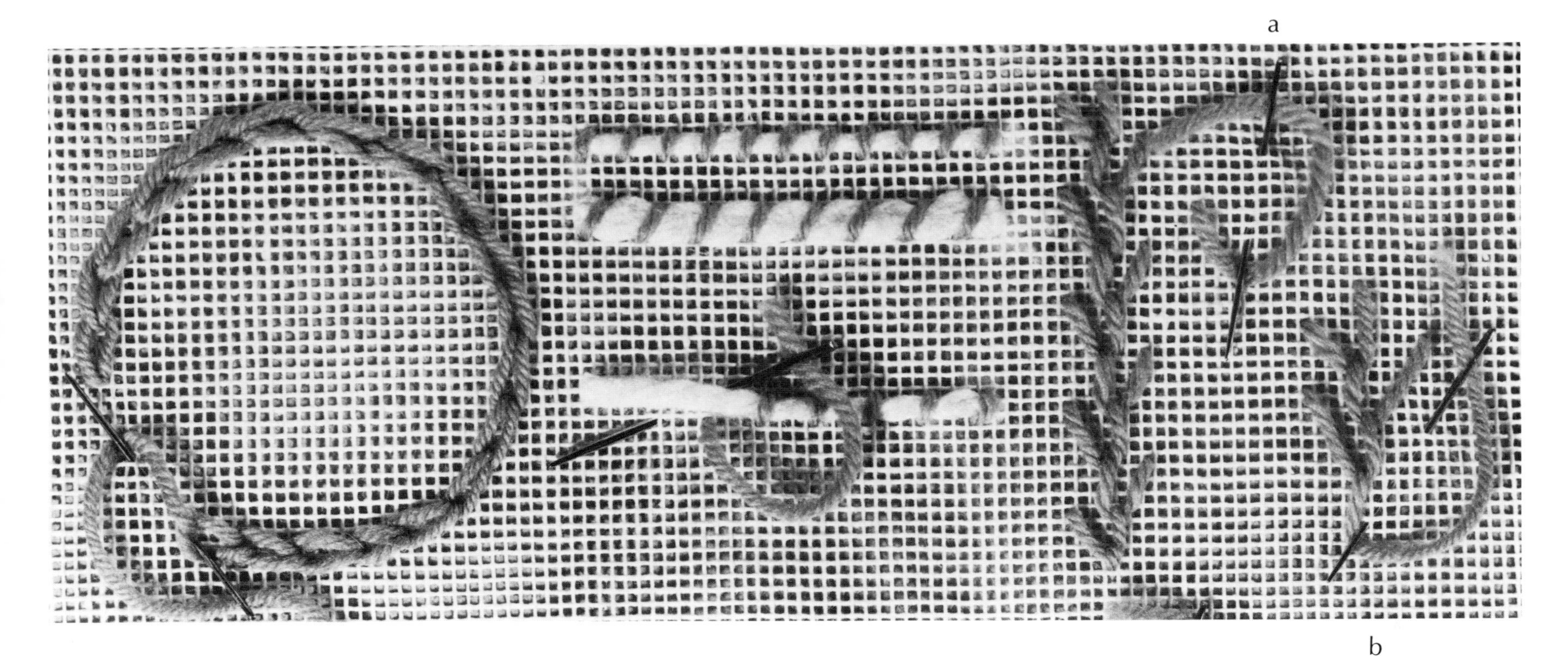

Chain stitch. The chain stitch is a linear, linked stitch perfectly reflecting its name. It is often used as a space filling stitch and has several variations. Bring needle to right side of fabric on line, take a stitch looping thread under needle. Repeat, putting needle inside first loop close to where thread came out. For ladder or square chain stitch (not shown), slant the needle and insert it to the right of each stitch. Stitches should not be drawn so tightly that the fabric is distorted.

Couching. This process stitch consists simply of sewing one yarn or thread in place with small even stitches of the same or another yarn. The effect can vary considerably according to the number, color, and texture of the couched thread.

Feather stitch. This is a looped branchlike stitch that always proceeds in the direction of the loop (downward in our example). Bring thread to right side. Holding thread on left and toward you, take a short diagonal stitch down and to the left (step a.) passing needle over thread. Draw to form a loop. Hold thread at right and take a short diagonal stitch a little below the previous one slanting it to the right. Hold thread at the left and make another diagonal stitch (step b.) Variations of the stitch can result from taking two or more stitches to the right or left alternately.

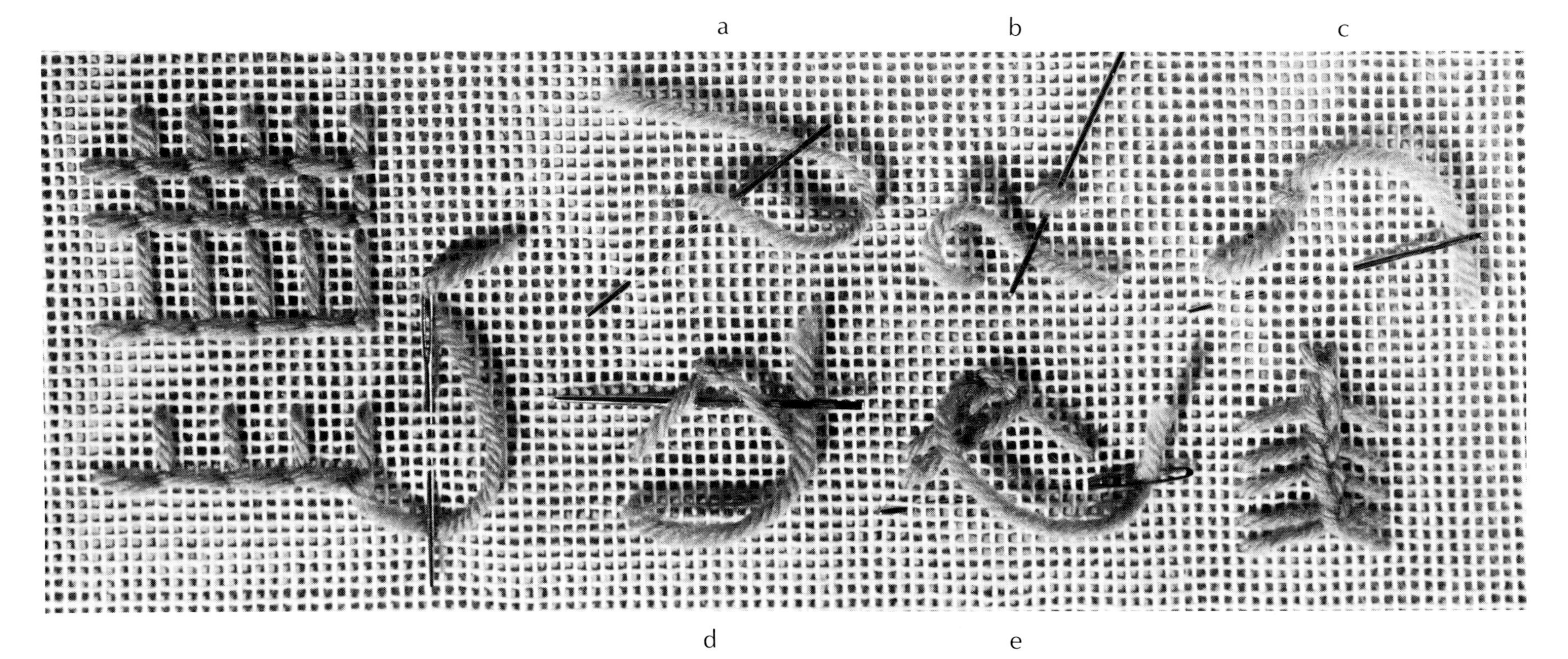

Blanket stitch. This may be used as an edge finishing stitch or as a decorative surface stitch. In our example it is shown in a straight line but it is very effective for curves or outlining circular forms. Work from left to right. Bring needle to right side on lower line. Hold thread down and take a stitch toward you with thread under needle. Stitches may be short or long and grouped or spaced in different ways for varied decorative effects. The buttonhole stitch is structurally identical to the blanket stitch, but stitches are closer together forming a solid line.

Vandyke stitch. This stitch gives a distinctly raised surface effect and depending on the relative length or regularity of the "legs" can be made to resemble rope, fishbones, or foliage veins. For our version bring the needle to the right side of the fabric and make a small horizontal stitch bringing the needle through again below and to the left (step a.) Thread the needle through this stitch (step b.) and insert it below and to the right in line with the first "leg" (step c.). The needle is brought through just below the first "leg" and without piercing the fabric is threaded from right to left under the uppermost part of the two "legs" (step d.). The thread is now gently pulled down and to the right, where the needle is inserted just below the right "leg" and brought through just below the left leg (step e.). Steps d and e are repeated for the desired distance.

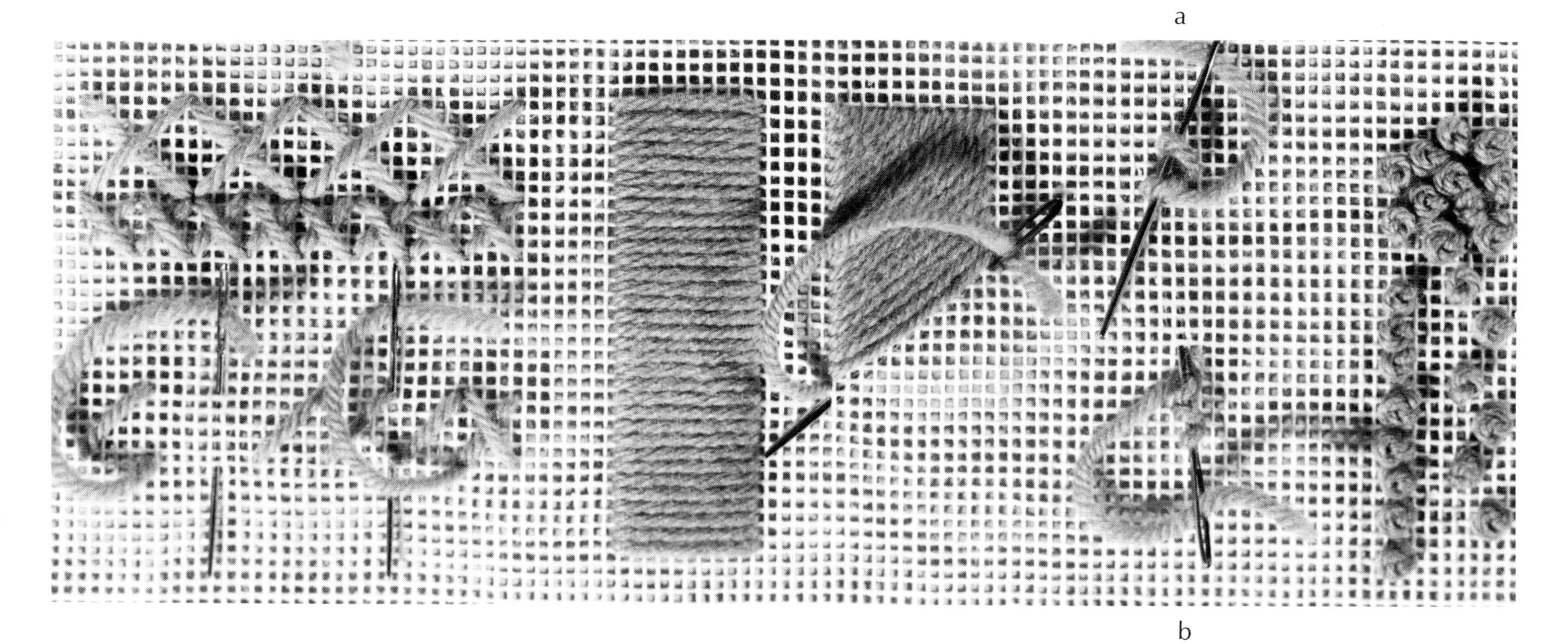

Cross stitch. Traditionally, the familiar cross stitch is worked on a canvas ground in which the threads are easily counted so that each completed stitch fits within a perfect square. It may be used by itself or in concert with a variety of other stitches. Rows may be worked from right to left or from left to right but it is considered desirable to have all of the tip or overcrossing threads point in the same direction. Form the first half of a row of cross stitches by making a row of 45 degree slanting stitches (step a) to complete the row; work back over the previous row in the opposite direction (step b).

Satin stitch. This is a smooth, space filling stitch occasionally worked over other stitches or filler to produce a padded effect. If the yarn or thread has a natural sheen such as silk or rayon then considerable luster can be generated with this simple stitch. Try to keep edges neat and avoid excessively long stitches which are easily snagged.

French knots. These are very useful knotted stitches which may be used in clusters, lines, or as embellishment for other stitches. Used by themselves in carefully selected colors, French knots can achieve impressionistic color effects similar to pointillism. Bring the needle to the right side of the fabric. Wind thread around the needle three times (step a.). Insert needle close to where it came out (step b.) and draw thread through forming a knot on the fabric surface. If the wraps are too snug the needle may be difficult to operate, and if the wraps are too loose the knot will lack definition.

NEEDLEPOINT AND CANVAS EMBROIDERY

The term *needlepoint* refers to a vast family of stitches worked on canvas-ground fabric. The canvas mesh has a balanced weave, and the regularity of the stitches depends upon counting warp and weft threads as the work proceeds. Needlepoint stitches cover the mesh entirely, while the term *canvas embroidery* refers to a broader family of counted thread stitches, a few of which expose the ground fabric.

Needlepoint nomenclature is related to the scale of the canvas mesh. Quickpoint is worked on the coarsest mesh with up to seven threads per inch, grosspoint has between eight and fifteen threads per inch, and petitpoint has sixteen or more threads per inch.

Needlepoint canvas may be woven with single threads or with pairs of threads. Single thread canvas is called "mono," and double thread canvas is called "Penelope." Both are heavily sized and generally are made from cotton. Mono canvas is slightly easier to work, but Penelope with its double sets of threads enables the needleworker to do both grosspoint and petitpoint (or quickpoint and grosspoint) on the same canvas. This is a special advantage when a few areas of greater detail, such as facial features, are needed in a composition. It is a good idea to protect the cut edges of the canvas from unraveling with a lengthwise fold of masking tape. Furthermore, two inches beyond the working area should be allowed for blocking and finishing.

Three-ply Persian yarn is most often used and it is available in precut strands or in skeins. Other yarns may also be useful depending on the design requirements or the limitations of the canvas. It is possible and in fact often desirable to use fewer or more than the three standard strands of Persian yarn. Unusual color blending effects may be created by stitching with strands of several colors.

Blunt tapestry needles, available in a variety of sizes, are most often used for needlepoint. The needle is threaded with a length of yarn about twenty-four inches long. As the first stitch is made several inches at the end of the yarn should be left free. This loose end may later be threaded on a needle and worked into the back of several completed stitches. Hereafter all ends should be worked in and clipped short avoiding knots.

Contemporary needlepoint pillow. Tent stitch. Designed by Frank Danner, worked by Kay Danner.

Needlepoint Stitches

Needlepoint has enjoyed very high popularity in recent years, and books, pamphlets, and instructive literature on the subject are widely available. For this reason we have elected to present only a few basic yet versatile stitches for the beginner to experiment with. Several excellent needlepoint and canvas embroidery texts are listed in the bibliography.

Scotch stitch. A very easy stitch to work that produces a checkerlike pattern. Colors may alternate or they may be monochromatic. Squares may be of any practical size but should be kept small for utilitarian pieces subject to abrasion or snagging. The Scotch stitch is especially effective for slightly textured background areas.

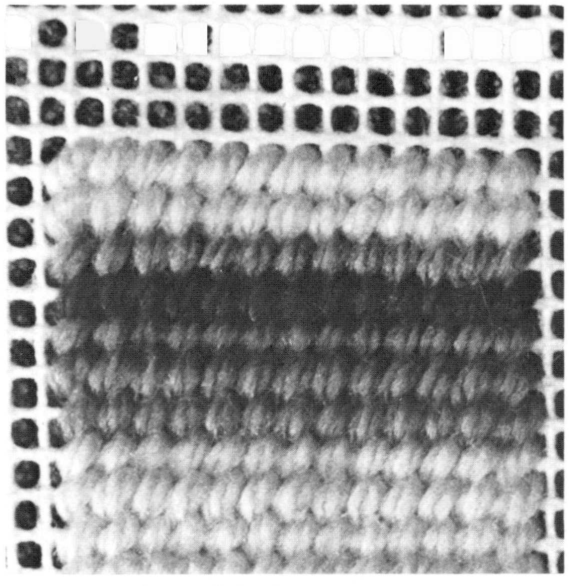

Continental tent stitch. This common stitch is best used in small areas or for relatively narrow lines since it has a strong tendency to distort the shape of the piece if used to fill large areas. This is due to its diagonal stress on the canvas. It is, however easy to work and is very useful if its limitations are respected.

Continental tent stitch, reverse side.

Basketweave or diagonal tent stitch. The most stable and nondistorting form of the tent stitch. Its surface is identical to the Continental but the back produces a neat durable basketweave pattern. This is an ideal stitch for large areas of solid color and for functional objects. Considerable practice is needed before it becomes second nature but it is well worth the initial effort.

Basketweave on diagonal tent stitch, reverse side.

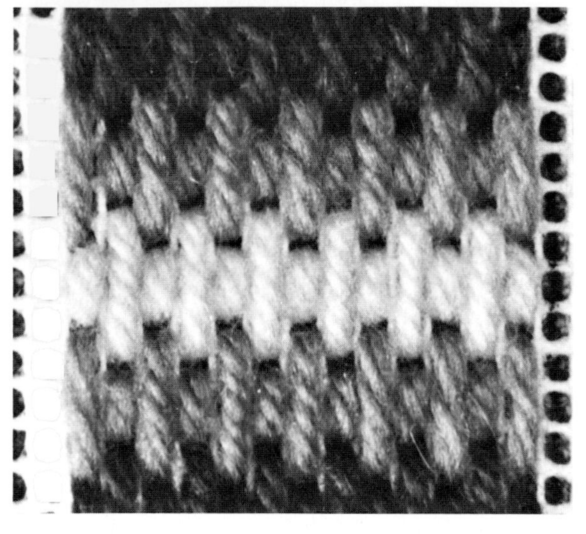

Parisian stitch. Another easy stitch that creates a soft stripe effect. It is a durable stitch and is most effective when worked in gradations of hue, value, or intensity. Our example shows three equidistant values of the same yarn color.

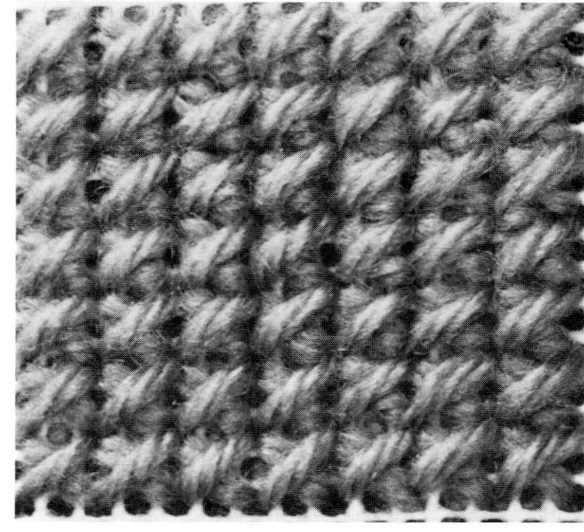

Cross stitch. This is of course the same cross stitch used in conventional embroidery but in this case it is worked with counted thread canvas. It produces an attractive allover textural effect when worked in one color but may be worked in two colors for a more pronounced contrast.

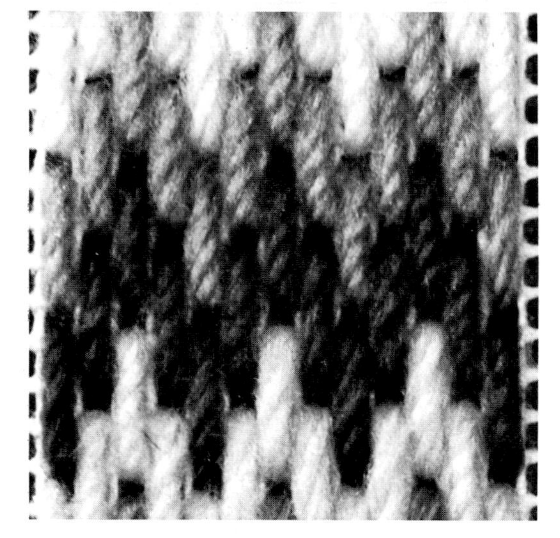

Florentine stitch. This vast family of stitches also known as Bargello, Flame Stitch, and Hungarian point is well known and recently has been the subject of numerous books. All of the stitches have a zig-zag effect and are most effective when worked in graduated colors of yarn. Our comparatively simple example involves only three values.

Smyrna or double cross stitch. A beautiful compact stitch composed of the regular diagonal cross stitch crossed by a second upright cross stitch. We feel that it is most effective when the second cross is of slightly different color.

Cubed cross or leviathan stitch. This is a very textural stitch worked over four squares of canvas and reminiscent of the hobnail surface common to pressed glass. Because of the longer float thread and raised effect it is more suitable for decorative than for functional pieces.

Leaf stitch. This distinctive foilagelike stitch is not difficult but depends upon a very accurate counting of threads and stitches. Due to its strength of form and outline this is one of the few stitches that can retain its character if worked with variegated yarn.

APPLIQUÉ

Appliqué refers to the process of sewing or attaching elements, usually pieces of fabric, to a base or ground, again, usually a fabric. It may also refer to a finished work created by this process or it may refer to an ornamental or emblematic "patch" created by some other means such as embroidery or beading that is expressly intended to be attached or appliquéd to a secondary backing.

We might say that appliqué is to needlework what collage is to two-dimensional art. Certainly appliqué and collage may exist in a pure form, that is, void of other techniques but just as collage has found its way into contemporary painting, drawing, and printmaking, so too has appliqué been successfully combined with the other fiber arts.

Appliqué lends itself an incredible range of unusual impressions and effects. See the section of examples at the end of this chapter.

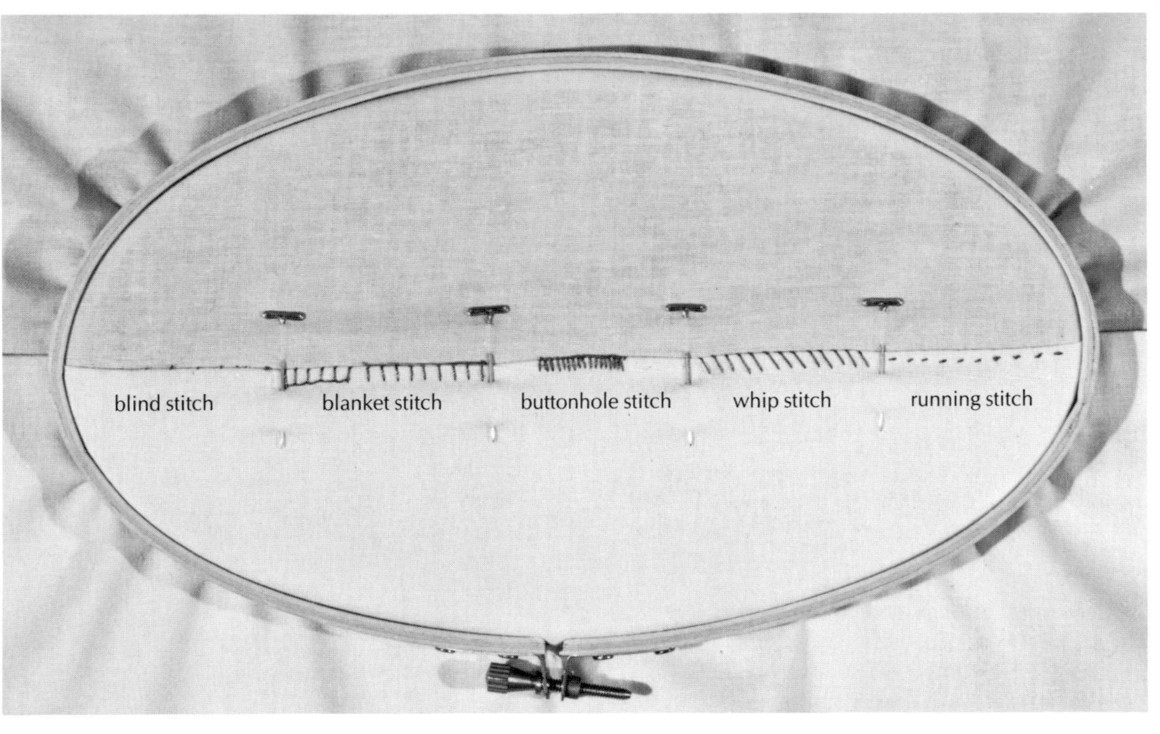

Appliqué techniques.

Detail of an autograph or album quilt top made for Mary H. Taylor, Morristown, N.J., 1842–44. Courtesy of the Division of Textiles, National Museum of History and Technology, Smithsonian Institute.

Appliqué Techniques

Appliqué, like all of the fabric arts discussed in this book, may be handled in traditional or nontraditional modes. In this short section we offer several of the accepted appliqué stitches. These represent only a few of the possible hand sewing techniques and in addition we must mention the possibility of creating appliqué with studs, staples, grommets, iron on fabrics, glue, fusible gauze, and of course the sewing machine.

Blind stitch. As its name implies, this attaching stitch is nearly invisible and tends to raise the appliquéd fabric slightly. Unlike the stitches that follow, emphasis is on the fabric rather than on the stitch. Untreated light- or medium-weight cotton is the best choice for blind stitching as it holds the thread concealing crease very well. Baste the shape in place. Edge creases may be ironed prior to basting or they may be turned as the work progresses. Knot a single thread and bring the needle up so that it appears from inside the edge crease. Next pick up one or two threads of the base fabric and reinsert the needle into the edge crease bringing it out about ¼ inch away taking another minute stitch of the base fabric similar to the first. Proceed until the shape is attached.

Blanket stitch. This attractive and ornamental stitch may be worked with the legs reaching from figure to ground or vise versa. Instructions appear on page 164.

Buttonhole stitch. The buttonhole stitch is nothing more than the previous stitch worked very close together. The technique is identical but a very strong outline results.

Whip stitch. The whip stitch is possibly less ornamental than many, but it is very strong and especially suited to heavier fabric. The needle and thread are brought up through the background and the appliqué fabric a fraction of an inch inside the edge crease. The needle is then inserted down through the background at the edge of the appliqué shape and slightly to the left. This forms the first slanting stitch. Subsequent stitches are formed in the same way.

Running stitch. The running stitch is easy and sturdy, and it creates a rhythmic indentation or pucker, thus adding surface interest. This stitch is particularly effective in felt appliqué.

Reverse Appliqué

In reverse appliqué several layers, usually three, of differing colors but similar fabrics and identical size are basted together on all four sides very close to their edges. With the aid of a sharp pair of scissors, shapes are then removed from the top layer and their edges secured with a row of stitches. Traditionally smaller replicas of the first shapes are then cut in the newly exposed second layer and the cut edges of the second layer are also secured with a row of stitches. The molas or blouse panels made by the Cuna Indians of the San Blas Islands are complex and refined demonstrations of this technique.

The blind stitch is most often used in reverse appliqué as it retains a clear edge quality and raises the fabric slightly. Other stitches may be effective in other situations and the technique may be combined with conventional appliqué and, of course, with embroidery.

Beginners may wish to make design experiments using color construction paper cut with an X-acto knife or razor blade prior to working in fabric. Another quick method for experimenting with this technique is to work with felt. It cuts easily, comes in a magnificent range of colors, and is easy to secure with running stitches or with French knots.

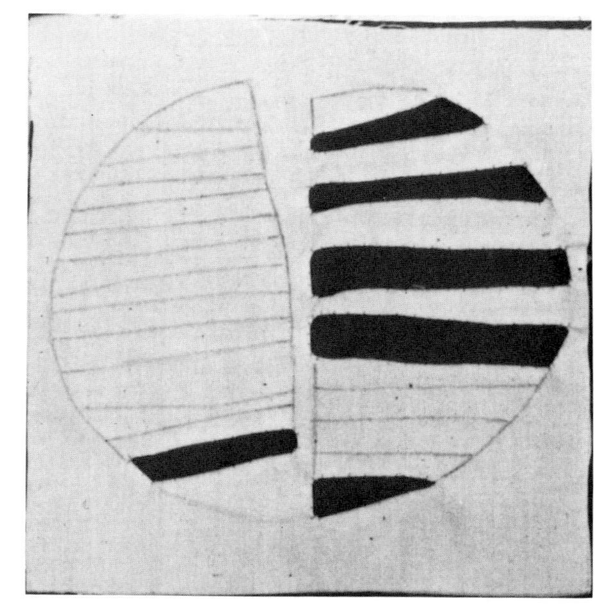

Reverse appliqué sample showing use of the blind stitch.

"Mola" or women's blouse panel in the geometric style, contemporary, Cuna Indian, San Blas Islands. Reverse appliqué technique, cut and turned edges are secured with blind stitches, all cotton. Collection of Jennifer F. Lew.

Nancy Clark. Toucan Quilt *(detail). Dye painted cotton velveteen with outline quilting.*

QUILTING

The term *quilting* generally refers to stitched fabric constructions with a raised surface having three essential layers: a backing or lining, a filler layer, and a top layer that is usually decorated. The earliest quilts were actually a form of insulation used to seal doors and windows as well as to retain body heat. Quilted jackets of present day attest to the efficiency of this three-layered construction. The great resurgence of interest in quilting is due in part to its practicality but predominantly to its extraordinary range of decorative possibilities.

Quilting lends itself decoratively to tailored geometrics as well as to compositions that are organic, classical, floral, graphic, or Pop. The uses for quilting are equally varied; apparel, hangings, bedcovering, table linen, soft sculpture, and even such mundane items as movers' blankets, tea cozies, and hot pot holders are in fact "quilts." Very large quilts, particularly quilted wall hangings, have a secondary function, that is, sound dampening, which is only beginning to be explored by architects and designers.

Quilt Nomenclature

The nomenclature of quilting is somewhat confusing because quilts may be described either by the technique used to decorate the quilt top or by their stuffing or surface raising technique. Actually they should be described by both and in some cases by more than two terms as it is common to use several decorative and/or construction techniques in the same piece.

The Quilt Top

Quilt tops may be of two types: continuous, or pieced. Continuous tops may themselves be devoid of decoration and serve as monochromatic sculptural surfaces subservient to the filler or stuffing. The well-known all white "bridal quilt" is a good example of the monochromatic continuous top. Next in order of complexity is the continuous polychrome top in which color has been added to a single surface skin by means of dye, ink, appliqué, embroidery, or a combination of techniques.

Pieced tops are generally of two types: symmetric and asymmetric. Collectively called patchwork, pieced tops originated chiefly as a decorative and functional means of utilizing precious sewing scraps in an era when most fabric was costly or imported. Another reason for piecing was that wide fabric, such as that in our modern bed sheets, was not available. Symmetric pieced quilt tops may be bold and simple, but more often they are rich and complex compositions of small joined geometric patches, as in the American "log cabin" quilt.

Asymmetric pieced quilt tops may be simple, bold nonrepeating geometric or pictorial compositions or they may be seemingly random admixtures of countless tiny pieces. This latter type is of course the crazy quilt so popular in the Victorian era.

Surface Raising Techniques

Although there are hybrids and offshoots, we recognize only three surface raising techniques. In each case the same technique that raises the surface also joins or confines the three essential layers—backing, filler, and top—making them one. Remember, this holds true in all cases regardless how the quilt top is decorated.

Conventional quilting. In conventional quilting the three layers are temporarily secured by long, relatively loose basting stitches and the design is worked with simple running stitches. The thread pierces all layers and may be contrasting or it may be the same color as the quilt top, but in either case a puckered line will be produced. Stitches should be made straight down and straight up, never at an angle. Our modest sample shows a continuous monochromatic top but conventional quilting may also be used to outline color shapes derived from dye, ink, appliqué, patchwork, or embroidery. The sewing machine is a real time saver, but its linear qualtiy is dull and hard by comparison to careful hand stitching. Nevertheless it may be effective for large pieces intended to be viewed at some distance.

Cord quilting. This interesting two-part process sometimes called Italian quilting may be used by itself in combination with either or both of the other two surface raising techniques. In the first step a parallel double outline is produced with the running or back stitch. These stitched rows pierce the top and the backing fabrics and then a filler yarn is inserted or threaded in the interspace. The distance between the rows may be determined by the diameter of the filler yarn, or conversely, the number or type of filler yarns may be determined by the distance between the rows.

Filler yarn is threaded on a large-eyed needle. A blunt needle is preferable, but a sharp one may be used if the fabric is too closely woven to permit entry by a blunt point. Working on the back side and leaving about a ½ inch tail, the needle is threaded through a channel until a corner or sharp curve is encountered. When this happens, bring the needle out on the back surface and reinsert it in the same opening but pointed in the new direction and proceed as before. It is best to leave a small loop when reinserting the filler yarn. This loop is later clipped, thus preventing the ends from working their way back into the channel. Synthetic knitting worsted yarns are ideal fillers since they are washable, shrink resistant, inexpensive, lofty, and easy to use in multiples if required.

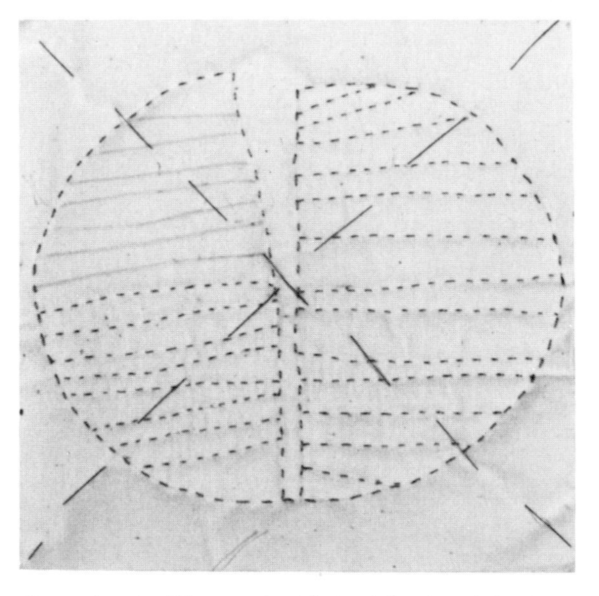

Conventional quilting sample with simple basting stitches intact.

Trapunto. Trapuntolike cord quilting is a two-step technique in which the raised elements, in this case shapes rather than channels, are first outlined with a row of stitches connecting the top layer to the backing fabric. Also, like cord quilting, the filler is later added from the back surface of the work. This is very simply achieved by making a small slit in the backing fabric, inserting a filler such as cotton batting, or polyester fiberfill and sewing the slit closed again. A small wooden meat skewer or a slightly sharpened chop stick is a handy tool for arranging the filler and especially for reaching pointed corners.

Quilting Hints

In conventional quilting large pieces are best worked on a frame because the needle *must* be inserted at right angles to the surfaces.

Baste layers together carefully to avoid shifting as work proceeds. For small quilted pieces a pair of basted lines may cross diagonally in the form of the letter "X". Larger projects should also be basted with a second pair of lines crossing in the center but parallel to the edges. The outside edges may also be secured with a row of basting an inch or so inside the border. Work from the center toward the edges to equalize tension using long loose stitches. Check the back of your work for unsightly puckers and adjust if necessary.

Seek out specialty quilting items such as short needles, waxed threads, and lightweight adjustable frames.

Polyester fiberfill is available in two basic forms. Loose fill is very suitable for soft sculpture, small pillows, trapunto, and small compact objects. Large quilts and quilted hangings require a more stable filler for which we recommend the polyester fiberfill that has two fused surfaces. It is far less fragile and holds up very well in laundry or dry-cleaning.

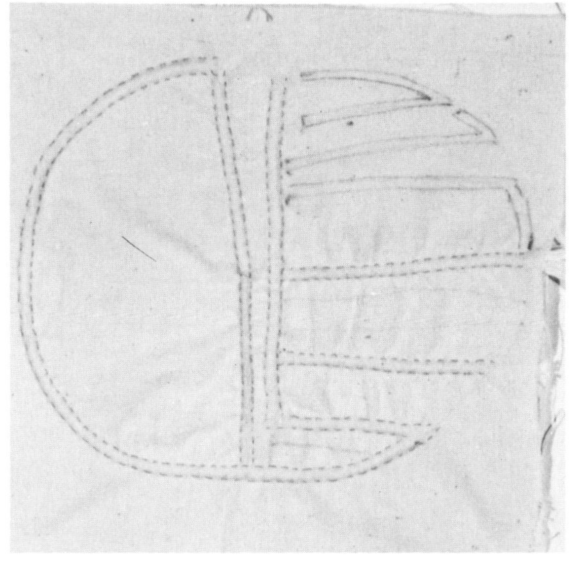

Cord quilting sample (top view).

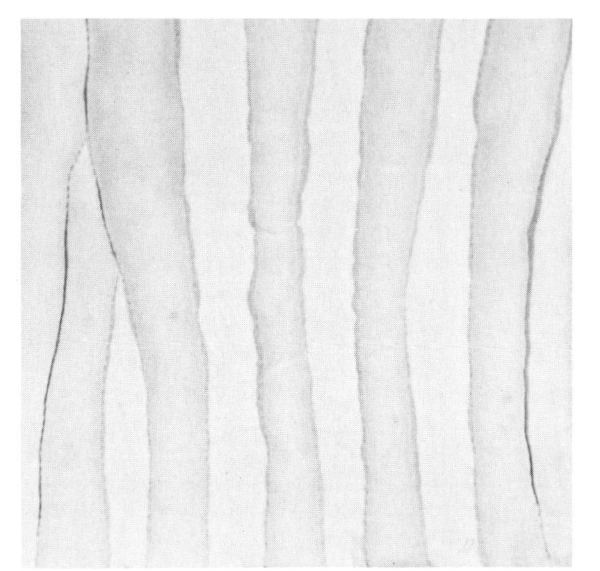

Trapunto sample (top view).

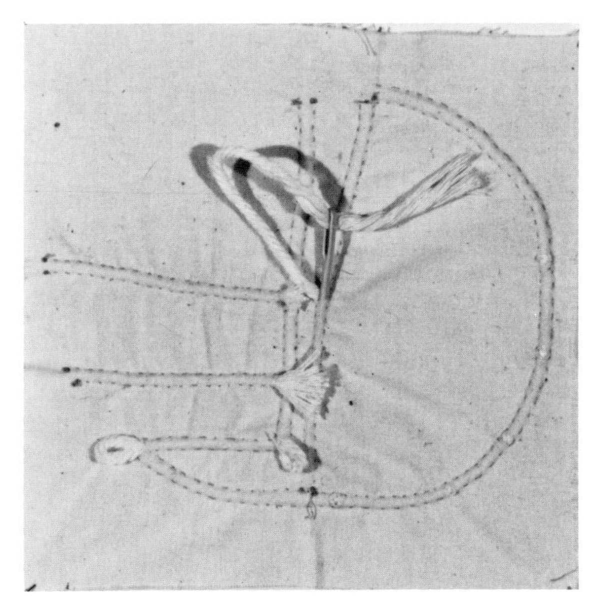

Cord quilting sample (underside) *with threaded plastic needle about to complete a raised line.*

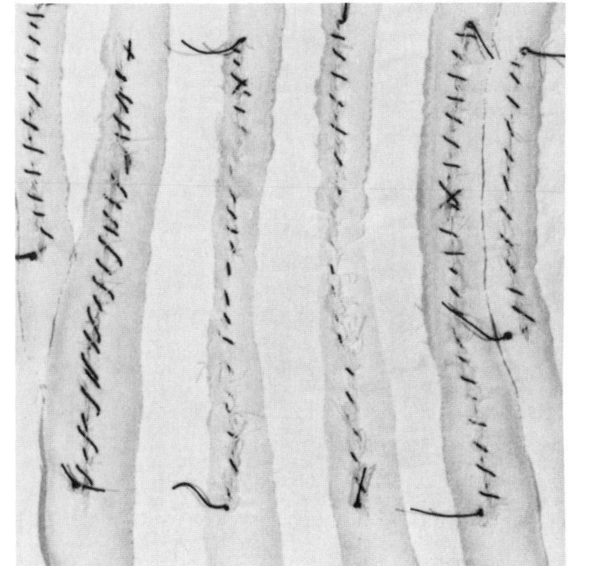

Trapunto sample (underside) *showing simple closure stitches.*

Quilting techniques including machine quilting have been used to create this richly textured fabric collage. Other techniques include tearing, weaving, smocking, pleating, twining, sculpturing, and plaiting. A class team project, University of Washington.

YARN PILE SURFACES

Pile techniques afford the fiber artist a multitude of possibilities for creating rich textural surfaces unattainable by any other means. The most familiar, of course, is the hooked rug, but simple pile techniques may also be used in sculptural forms, hanging, and even in apparel fabric.

We will cover two basic pile methods: in the first precut lengths of yarn are secured to a backing with a latch hook, in the second a continuous length of yarn is secured to a foundation fabric through a hollow needle. In the first method the surface is a velvetlike plush, and in the second method a looped surface results which may be left as is or cut to produce a plush texture.

In selecting yarn for either technique, remember that cut pile absorbs light and looped pile reflects light therefore the same value of yarn will appear darker if cut and lighter if looped. The same holds true to some extent for intensity: a strong red will by comparison appear slightly muted in a cut pile.

Latch Hooking Technique

MATERIALS

Latch hook
Rug backing
Masking tape
Permanent felt-tip marker
Rug yarn—May be precut or in a skein. If rug yarn is not desirable two or even three strands of less bulky yarn may be treated as a single strand of rug yarn.
Yard cutter—If yarn is not purchased precut, a method must be devised for cutting uniform lengths. We feel that the simplest tool is a block of wood or a piece of stout cardboard and a pair of scissors.

METHOD

1. With a folded strip of masking tape, cover the cut edges of the rug backing to prevent unraveling.
2. Apply the design to the backing with felt-tip marker. It is vital that the marker be waterproof and smudgeproof. Tracing the design from a full-scale cartoon is easily accomplished because of the holes in the backing.
3. Cut the yarn to desired length by wrapping the yarn around a strip of wood or cardbord of appropriate size and cutting it with scissors or a sharp knife.
4. Attach yarn with latch hook as shown in photograph.
5. Tighten the knot by pulling the cut ends with equal pressure.
6. To prevent secured yarn from getting tangled in the latch as it closes it is best to work from right to left. It is possible to work from left to right, but in this case the latch should be on the right. There is also less likelihood of hook interference if work progresses from bottom to top.

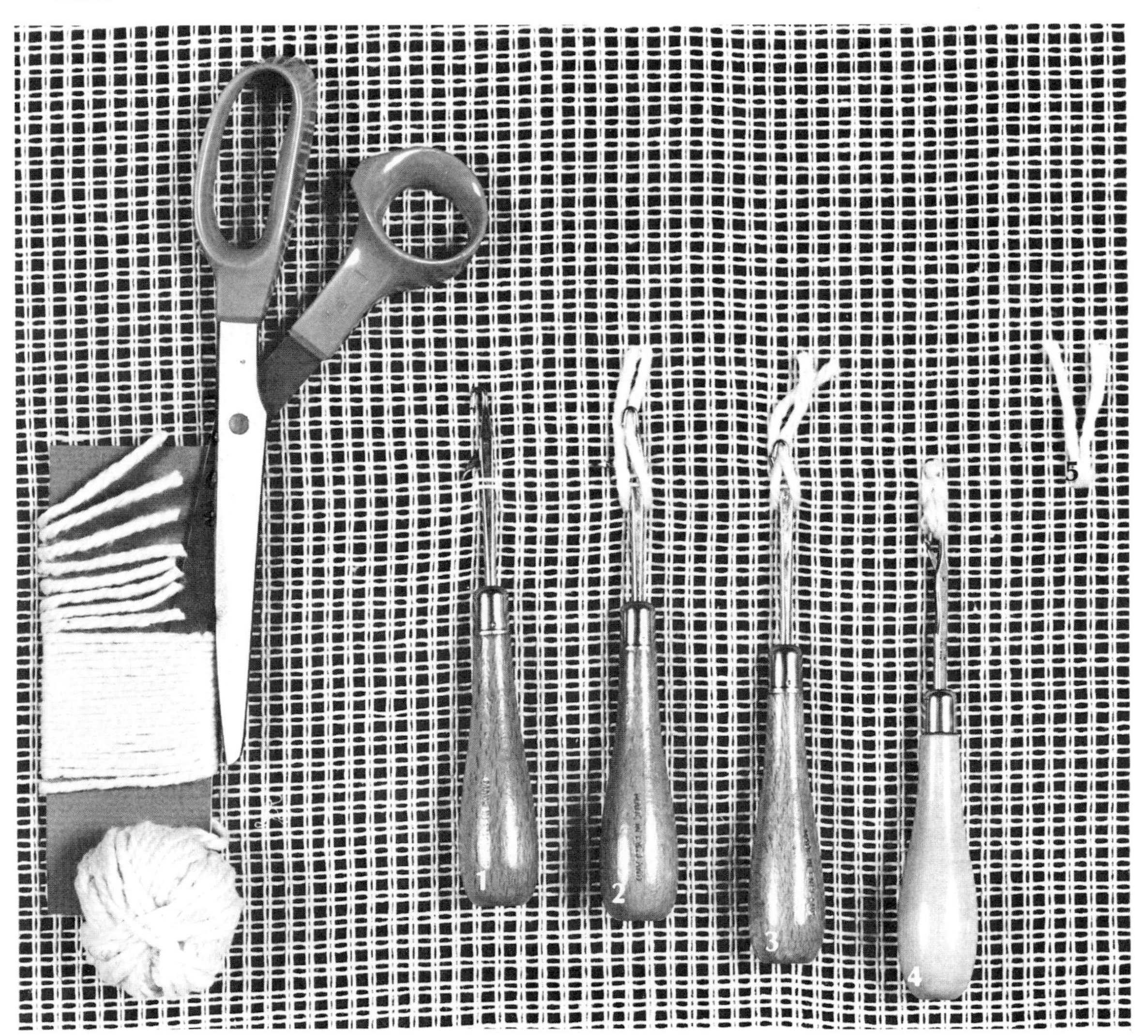

Five steps for attaching yarn with a latch hook (left to right): *1. With latch open insert the hook in a large hole and bring it up in the next large hole above; 2. Secure a length of yarn by looping it under the shaft of the hook with its ends through the hook, leaving the latch device is still open; 3. Gently but firmly pull the handle toward yourself, which will close the latch against the hook and draw the cut ends through the shaft loop; 4. Continue to pull until the ends are free; 5. Tighten the knot by pulling the cut ends with equal pressure.*

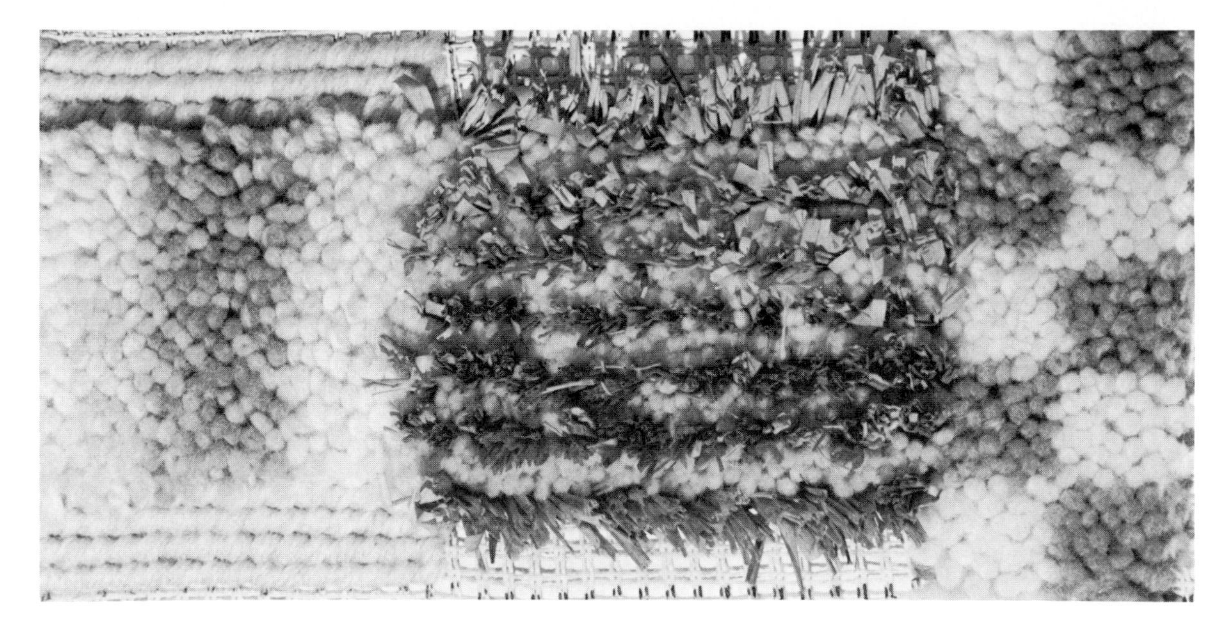

Latch hook rug sample showing (left) *color gradation,* (center) *texture by the addition of raffia and* (right) *contrasting checks.*

SUGGESTIONS

Sculpture the surface by using yarns of different length. Alter the texture by using yarns of different diameter, twist, or fiber content.

Combine the pile surface with blocks, shapes, or stripes of needlepoint stitches worked with a double strand of rug yarn.

Finish raw edges by folding an inch of backing over and hooking slightly longer strands through the doubled thickness. This is a bit tedious but results in a well-crafted edge treatment.

Create irregular or oversize shapes by slightly overlapping aligned sections of backing, basting them in place, and hooking through their double thickness as in the suggestion above.

Hollow Rug Needle Technique

MATERIALS

Hollow rug needle—Two types are shown on page 159. The wooden handled model has a wire loop to adjust pile length. The black plastic handled model has a calibrated pile adjustment on its shaft and comes with a thinner needle component (not shown) for less bulky yarn.

Foundation fabric—Burlap is traditionally used but it is less permanent and also less pleasant to handle than the special cotton foundation fabric designed for this purpose.

Wooden frame—There are special furniturelike floor frames for large projects but a simple picture frame, a set of four artists' stretcher bars, or a large embroidery hoop like the one shown on page 159 will serve the purpose. The frame, regardless of type, should be a bit larger than the finished piece.

Staples and staple gun (optional)—A means of attaching foundation to the frame. Pushpins or tacks may be used but they can snag the yarn.

Laundry marking pen or a permanent felt-tip marker—The ink must be waterproof.

Rug yarn—The yarn must pass with ease through the hollow needle yet be relatively snug. Skeined yarn must be rolled into a ball or wrapped on a large spool unless it is marketed as a "pull skein."

Large-eyed yarn needle

Scissors

METHOD

1. Apply the design to the *back* surface of the foundation fabric with laundry marker. If there are important directional elements in the design, especially letters, be certain to reverse the cartoon or the image will emerge backwards. Leave 1½ to 2 inches hem allowance for finishing your work.
2. Attach the fabric to a frame. This may be done with staples, tacks or with tension in the case of the large embroidery hoop. Another method involves padding the stretcher bars with fabric and then stitching the foundation to the padding. In any case the tension should be even but need not be drum tight.
3. Thread the needle through the shaft and out the small eye near the tip or according to the manufacturer's instructions. Leave a yarn extension of about 2 to 3 inches.
4. Set the pile adjusting device as desired. If you are not sure of the setting, make a few stitches at a medium length and re-adjust as needed. Stitches pull out easily, too easily in fact, so this experiment may be made right on the foundation.
5. Place the ball of yarn where it can unwind with an absolute minimum of resistance such as in a stainless steel mixing bowl or perhaps a coffee can. It is very important throughout all steps that the least possible resistance be on the yarn as it passes through the needle—in fact the tool works best when it simply takes up slack yarn.
6. Hold the needle with the hole and the tail pointing upward and make the first stitch straight down through the foundation until the needle stops. Slowly draw the needle out but *only* until the tip is

free and reinsert it about ¼ inch *below* the first stitch. Proceed in this manner until the perimeter of the color shape is reached. At this point turn the needle so that it points upwards and proceed in a like manner.

7. Work all loose ends of yarn through to the front surface with a yarn needle and trim them flush with the pile.

SUGGESTIONS

Work most shapes from the center to the edges or from side to side not from the edges inward.

To help maintain tension it is usually best to begin somewhere near the center of the design and work outward finishing the edges last.

Try to position the frame in such a way that you can slip one hand underneath to assure that proper loops are being formed. This is especially important with the first few stitches after threading the needle.

If you are trying to produce an extra compact pile your free hand will be needed to force the previous row of loops out of the way of the needle. A word of caution here however that large areas of extra compact pile will almost certainly distort the backing material.

Loops are very vulnerable to snags and of course unravelling. This may be prevented to a large degree by painting the back of the finished work with a rubber like liquid non skid carpet coating made for this purpose.

West African marriage bed or dowry cloth, Niamey, Niger. A splendid example of satin stitching in which two of the crocodiles are partially worked with variegated embroidery floss. Collected by Harriet Boyce.

West African marriage bed cloth (detail).

Linda McFarland. Vestigial Pocket Series. *Dyed, stitched, and stuffed cotton gauze appliquéd to linen ground fabric.*

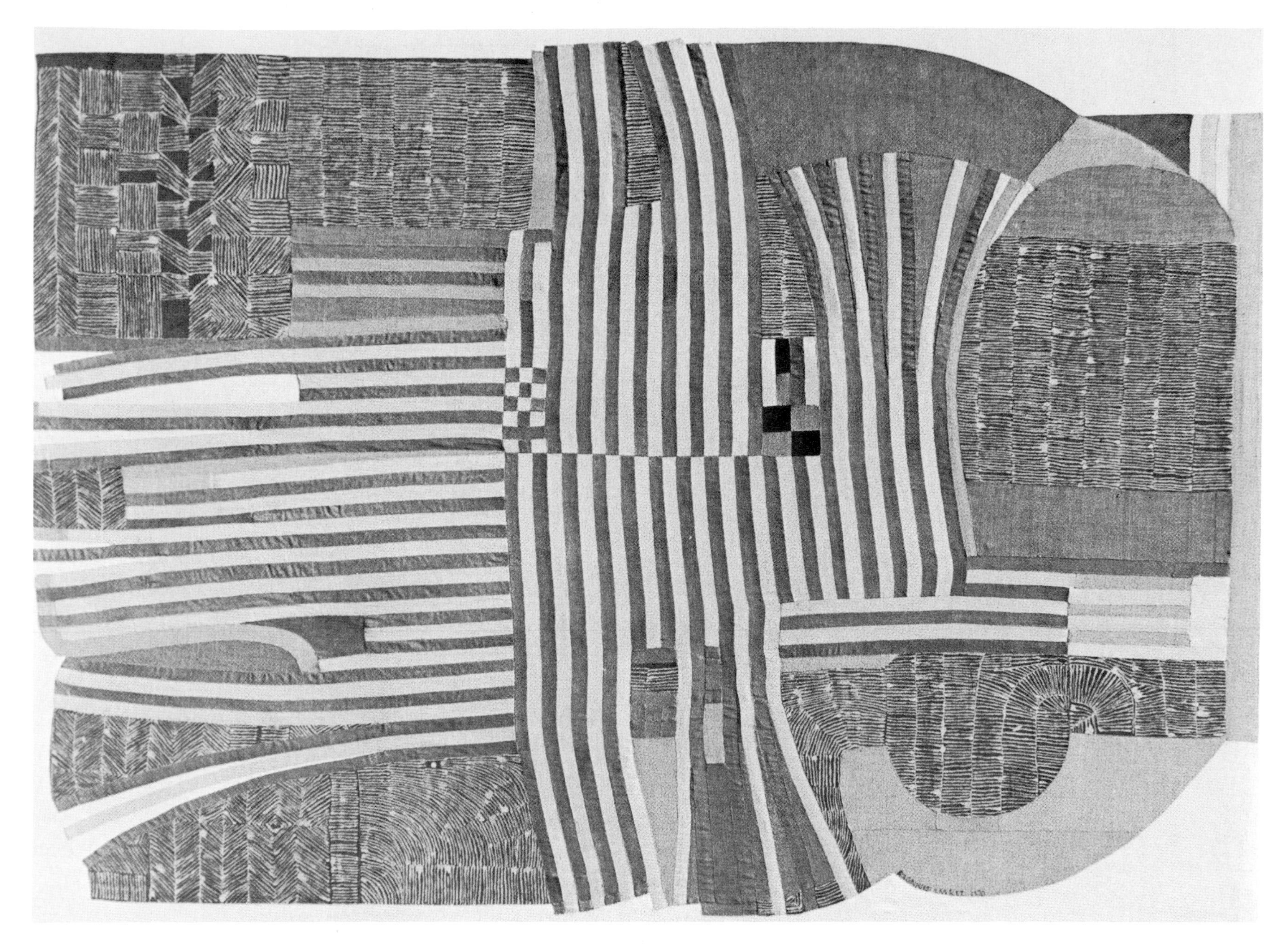

Ragnhild Langlet. New Palouse, *1966-70. Stretched appliqué wall piece of resist vat dyed linen. 70" x 50" (177 x 127 cm).*

Assorted garment appliqués in a variety of hand and machine techniques. Presumably of European origin, early 20th century. They are included here for their beauty and their remarkable combinations of stitches and decorative elements. Courtesy of Leather and Things, Gastown, Vancouver, British Columbia, Canada.

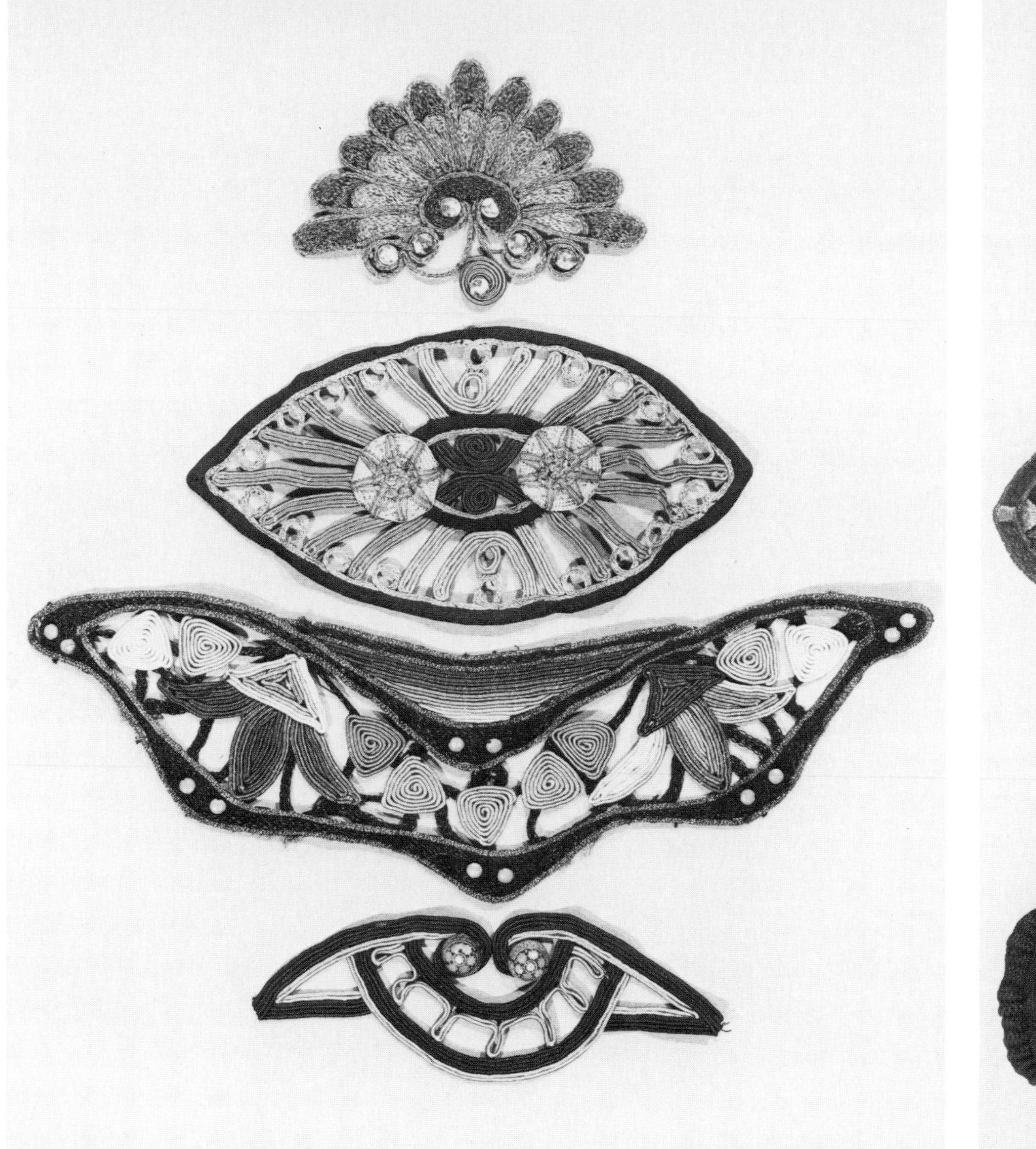

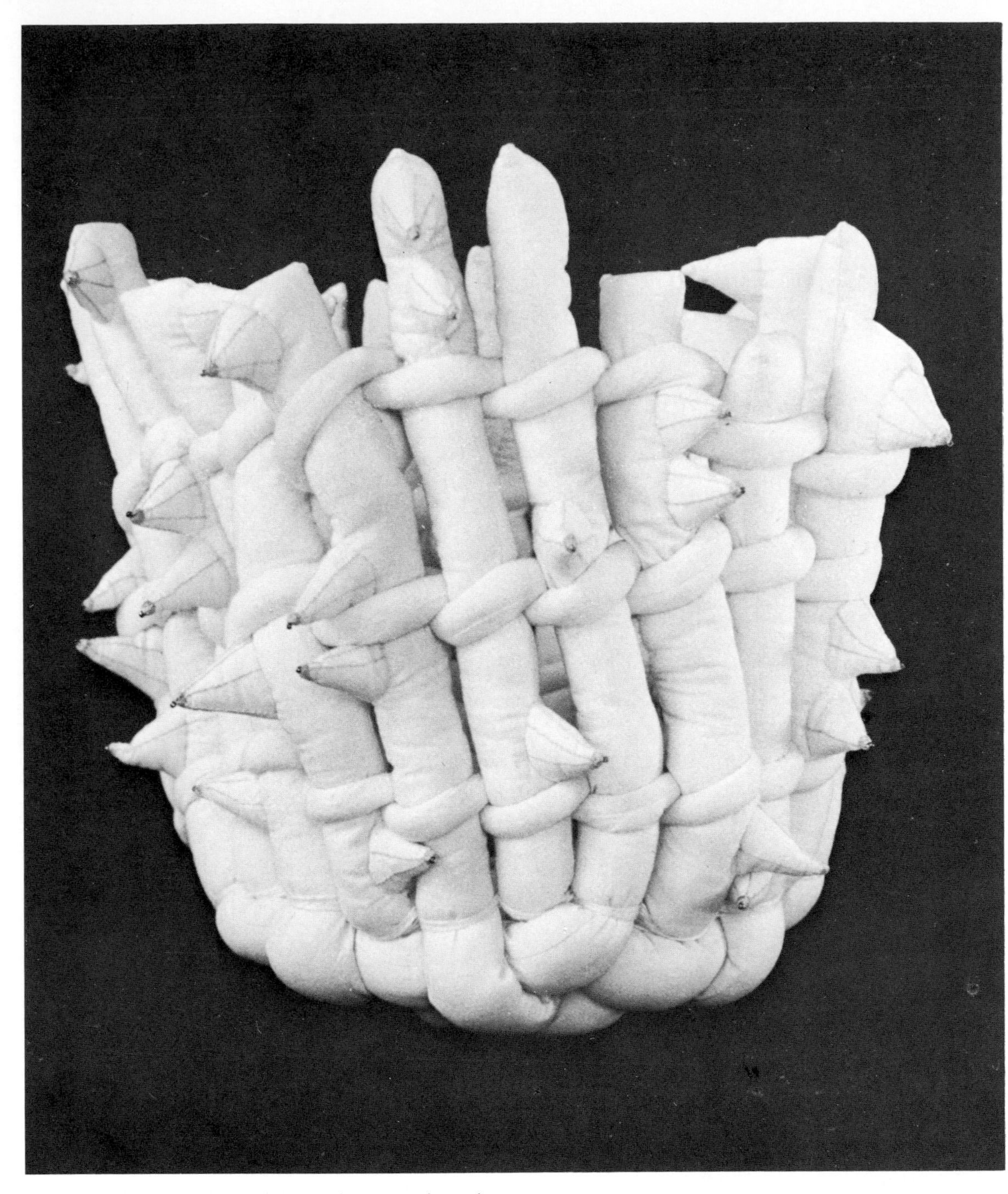

Ashby Carlisle. Thorns/Sprouts. *A twined container form of stuffed, embroidered cotton elements. Each thorn tip is finished with a small glass bead, 12" x 12" (30.5 x 30.5 cm).*

Ashby Carlisle. Thorns/Sprouts *(detail)*.

Appendix 1: Finishing

A beautiful fabric, well designed, superbly crafted, and tastefully presented with simplicity, grace, and apparent ease is a great pleasure to see. From experience, we have observed, often painfully, that fabric artists may have fewer problems with their design, color, and technique than with the finishing and presentation of their work. This final chapter may help to remedy this problem by suggesting ways in which the fabric artist may strike an appropriate balance between the art work itself and its finishing details and/or support system. We will emphasize decorative rather than utilitarian treatments.

The most common finishing pitfall of emerging and even experienced fabric artists is the unfortunate tendency of focusing too much viewer attention on the mounting and not enough where it belongs—on their art work. So often otherwise beautiful works are virtually upstaged by heavy frames, aggressively colored borders, overscaled dowels, and unnecessary fringes, pompoms, tassels, finials, or that worst of all offenders, driftwood. When it comes to finishing and mounting, the simplest solution, the one that competes visually the least with the work, is the best solution.

A major characteristic that sets fabric apart from other materials is its tendency to be soft and fluid. If we are to preserve the integrity of the fabric it would seem reasonable whenever possible to retain this primary characteristic. We enjoy seeing fabric move as we walk by or having it respond to a gentle breeze. There are however instances where fabric movement could be annoying or unsafe.

In most cases, site limitations will determine whether a piece should hang as "soft goods" or whether it should be stretched or in some way restrained. Wherever possible however, we feel that fabric should be allowed to retain its flexible nature as honestly as possible. This is not especially difficult with large, free-hanging pieces, but small fabrics present special scale-related problems and are usually displayed to their best advantage with some form of matting or separation from the wall. Very often, small textiles have eccentric edges or nongeometric borders and may resemble ancient textile fragments in their irregular shape.

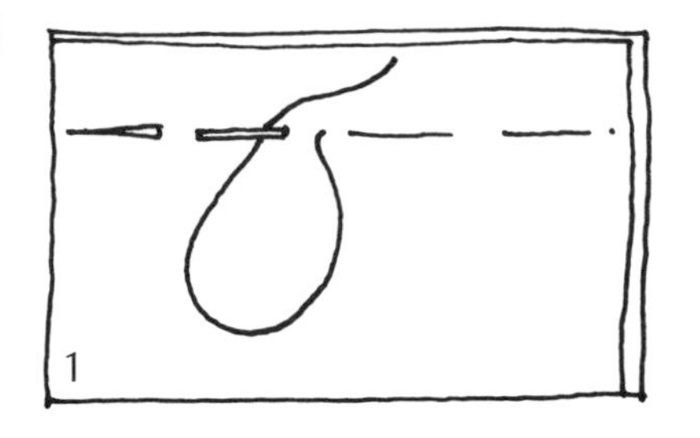

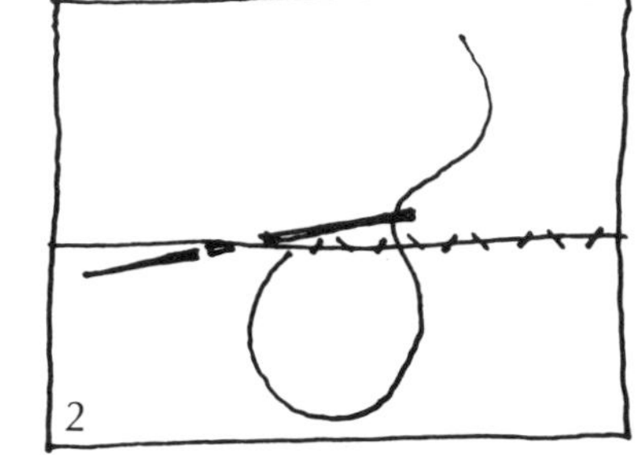

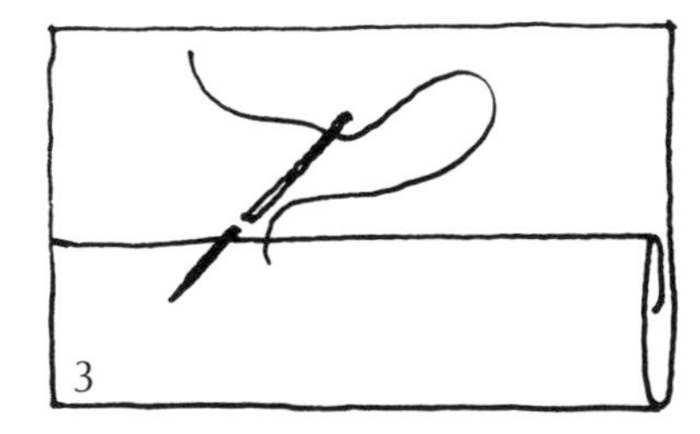

It is essential to the character of these works that their irregularity be preserved. This is often achieved by mounting the pieces to shaped board or "foam core" and causing them to project slightly from the ground panel or wall resulting in a subtle shadow line separation. The Plexiglas box or deep frame has become the standard means of protecting small or fragile fabrics.

The following pages illustrate a broad range of possibilities for finishing, mounting, and hanging your work.

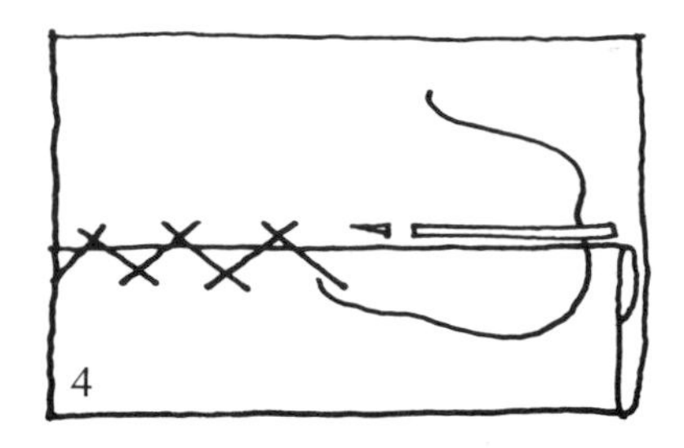

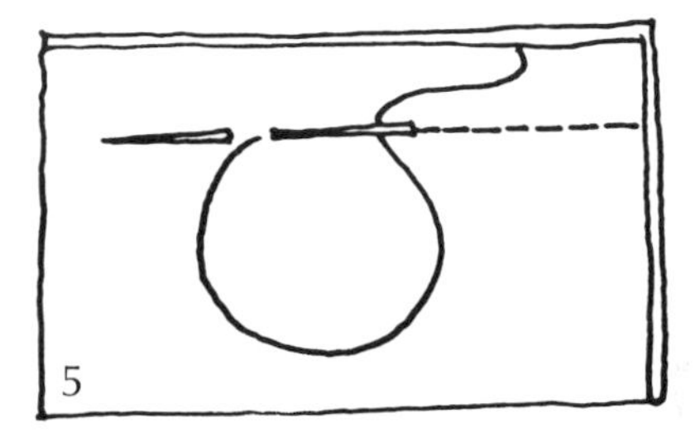

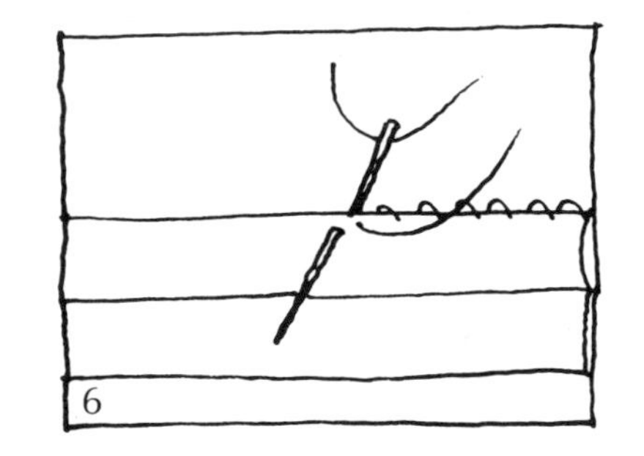

HANDSEWING EDGES
1. Basting: used to hold fabric in position while permanent stitching is done.
2. Slipstitch: used for holding folded edges together.
3. Hemming: used for holding a folded edge.
4. Catchstitch: suitable for curved edges.
5. Backstitch: handsewing substitute for the machine stitch.
6. Overcasting: use this stitch to neaten raw edges.

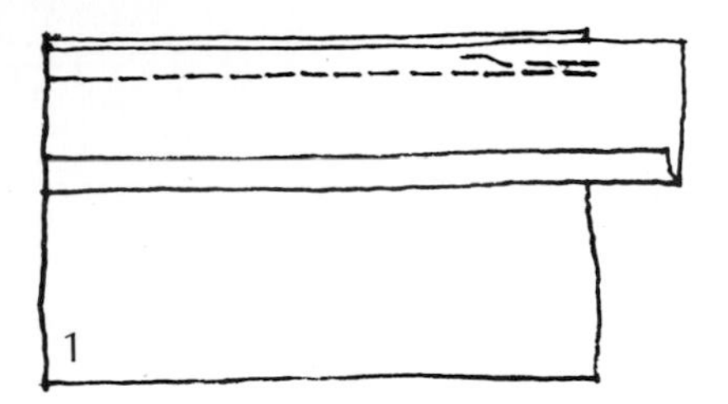

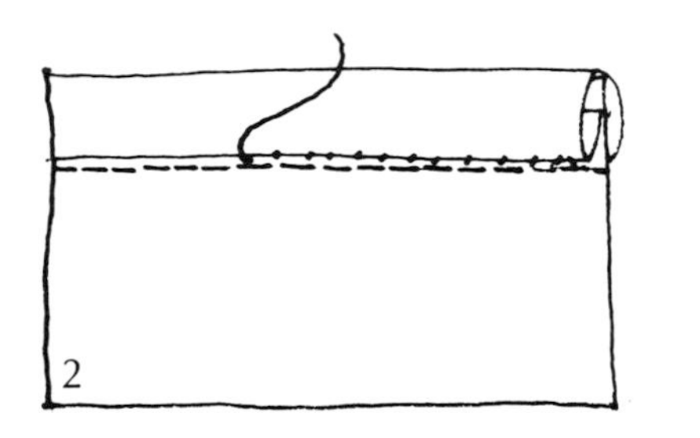

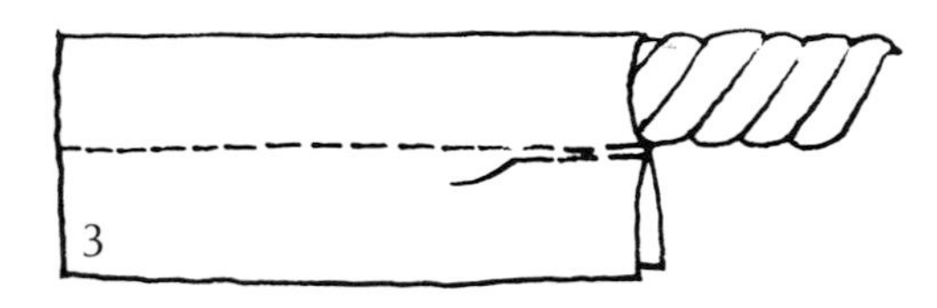

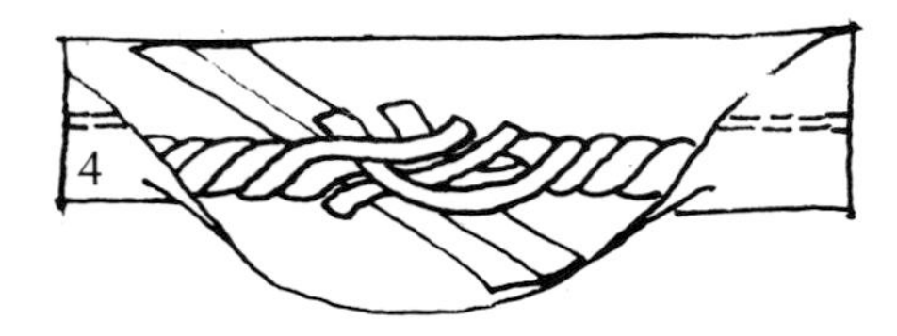

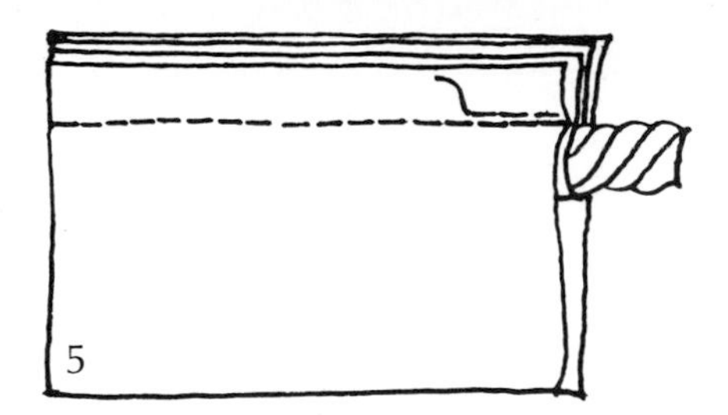

CORDING

1. Stitch binding to right side of fabric.

2. Turn to wrong side and slipstitch along turned edge.

3. Stitch down strip as close to the cord as possible.

4. Join piping to form a continuous piece.

5. Piping is sandwiched in the middle and is sewn through two pieces of fabric. Wrong side of fabric is shown.

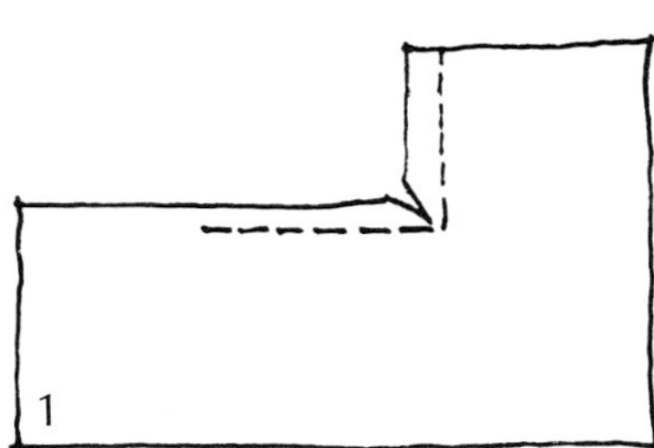

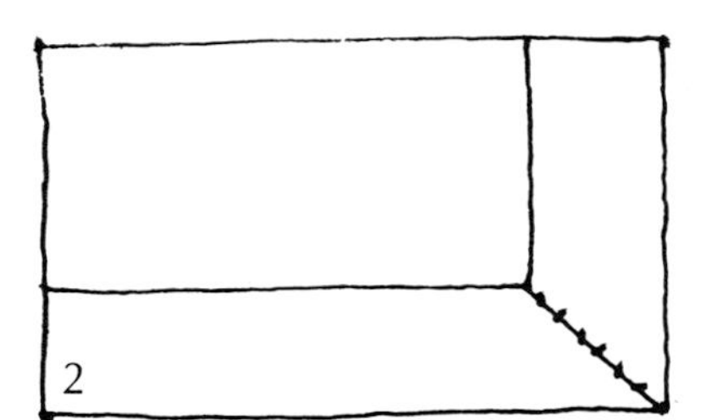

MITRING

1. Mitring on an outward corner by folding in hems and slipstich edges. This technique neatens fabric ends at corners.

2. Mitring on an inward corner by stay-stitching foldline of hem around corner to be mitred. Clip into the turning at corner. Then turn in hems and stitch.

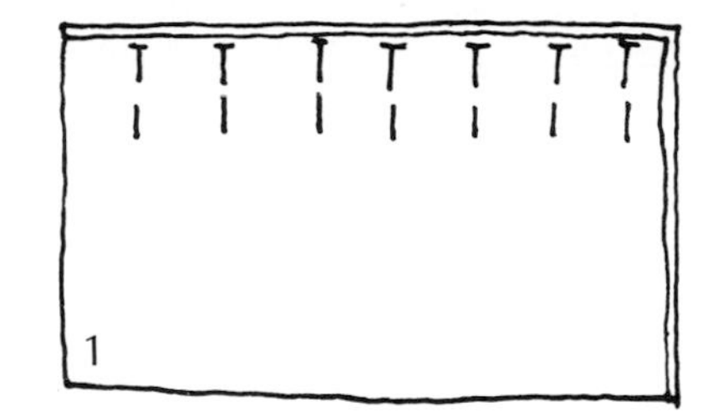

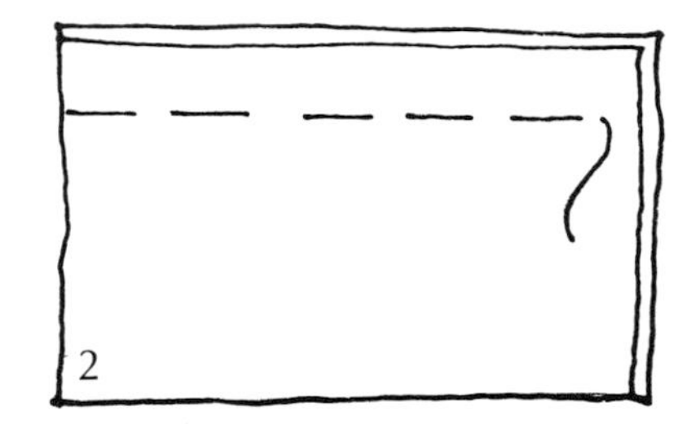

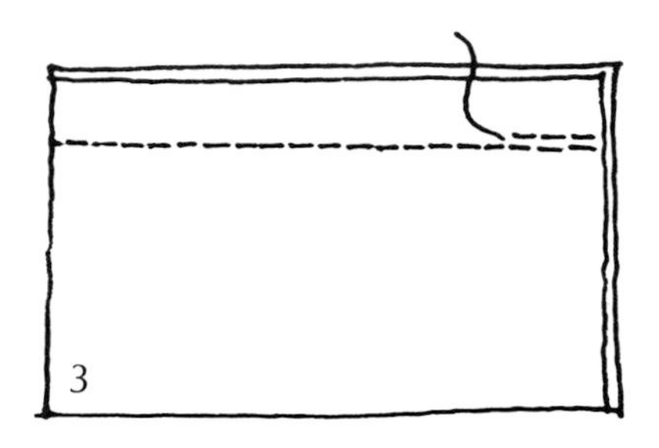

SEAMS

1. Flat seam. Pin fabric together with right sides facing inward.

2. Baste seamline down.

3. Secure seam ends using the backstitch. Removing basting and press seam open.

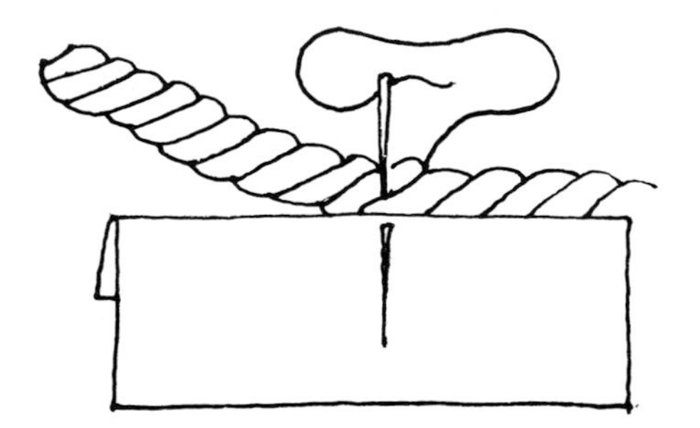

APPLYING CORD

Stitch through the cord to attach using small stitches on fold of seamline.

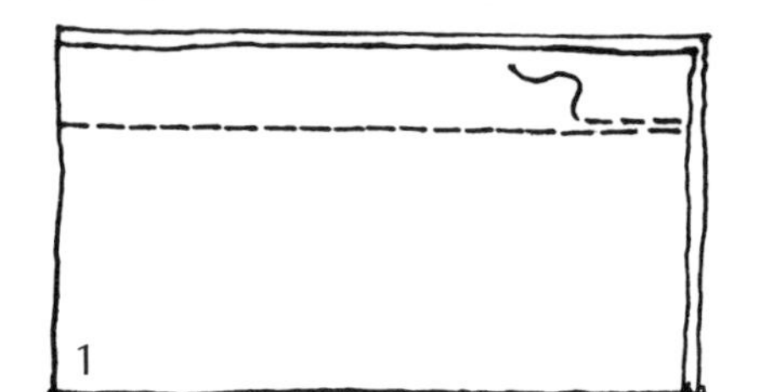

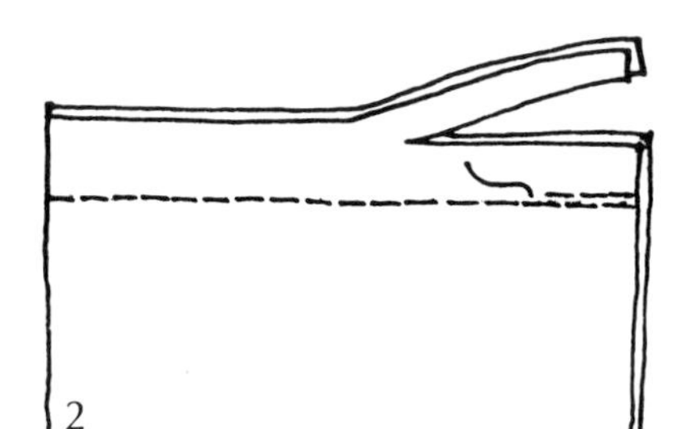

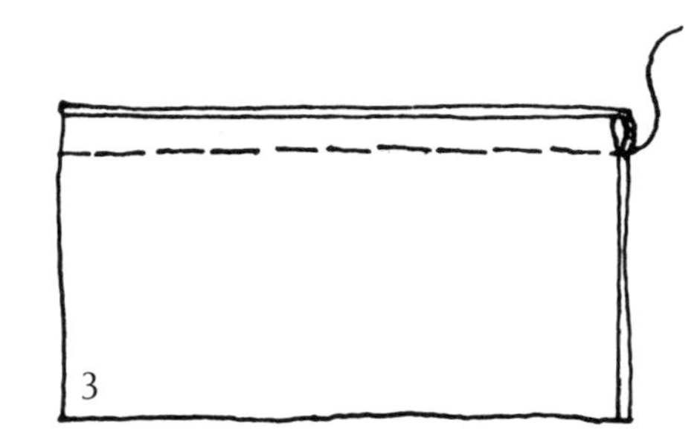

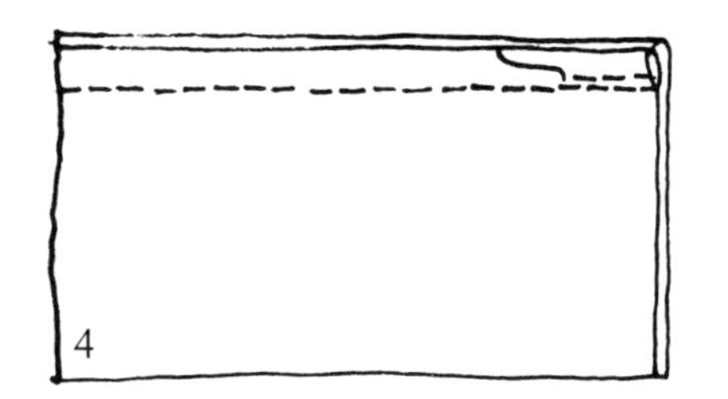

FRENCH SEAM
1. Join fabric wrong sides together.
2. Reduce bulk by trimming seam.
3. Turn fabric to right side and baste ⅜" from seamline.
4. Machine stitch, enclosing raw edges as indicated. The French seam produces a totally enclosed finish with no seamlines showing on the right side of the fabric.

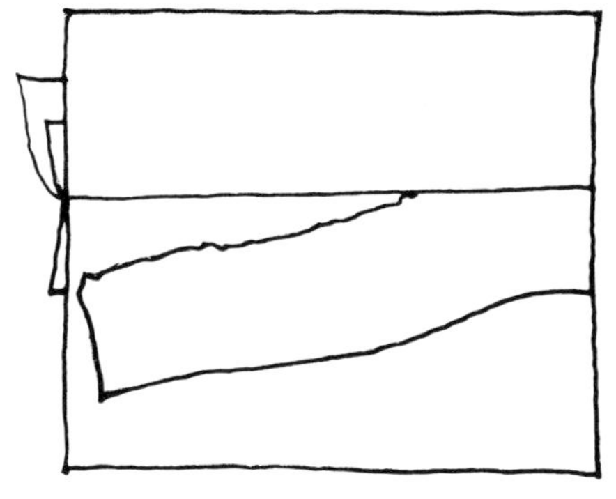

SEAMS FOR SPECIAL FABRIC
1. Use tissue paper strips along seamline and stitch the seam with a layer of tissue paper between two pieces of fabric. Use this method for fine slippery fabrics such as silk.

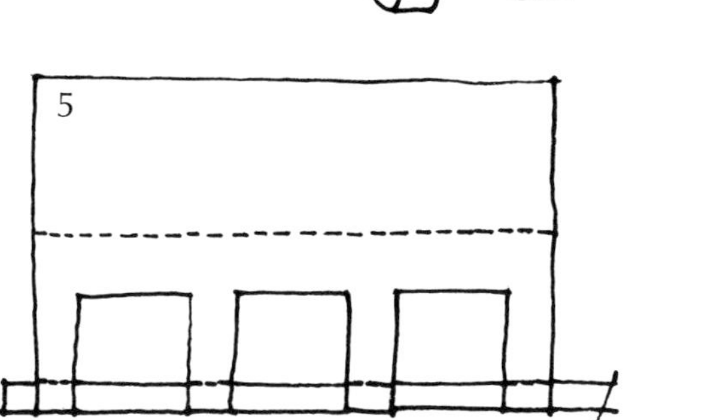

DECORATIVE EDGINGS
1. Stitched batten casing.
2. Stitched dowel casing.
3. Glue is spread on wrong side of fabric. Roll up to enclose batten in casing.
4. Shaped casing.
5. Rod or dowel pushed through casing.

Appendix 2: Resources

Mail-Order Sources of Supply

Aiko's Art Materials
714 N. Wabash Ave.
Chicago, IL 60611
(Dyes, pigments, supplies)

Cerulean Blue, Ltd.
P.O. Box 5126
Seattle, WA 98105
(Full range of supplies, fabrics, and norizome supplies)

Color Craft
P.O. Box 936
Avon, CT 06001
(Dyes and pigment colors)

Dharma Trading Co.
P.O. Box 916
San Rafael, CA 94902
(Surface design suppplies)

Earth Guild
Hot Springs, NC 28743
(Dyes and equipment)

Fab Dec
3553 Old Post Rd.
San Angelo, TX 76901
(Dyes, pigments, and fabrics)

Fezandie and Sperrle Inc
103 Lafayette St.
New York, NY 10013
("Fezan" dyes)

H.T.H. Publishers
P.O. Box 468
Freeland, WA 98249
(Textile books and monographs)

Ivy Crafts Imports
6806 Trexler Rd.
Lanham, MD
(Surface design supplies)

N-K. Tex Inc.
468 Park Ave. South
New York, NY 10016
(Untreated fabrics by the bolt)

Rupert, Gibbon and Spider
470 Maylin St.
Pasadena, CA 91105
("Deka" dyes and inks)

Screen Process Supplies Manufacturing Co.
1199 East 12th St.
Oakland, CA 94606
("Inko" dyes and screen printing supplies)

Straw Into Gold
5533 College Ave.
Oakland, CA 94618
(Dyes, pigments and other supplies and specialty items)

Sureway Trading Enterprises
826 Pine Ave., Suites 5 & 6
Niagara Falls, NY 14301
(also 111 Peter Street, Suite 212
Toronto, Canada M5V 2H1; Silk and French silk dyes)

Testfabrics
P.O. Drawer "0"
Middlesex, NJ 08846
(Untreated and "Print ready" fabrics, excellent variety)

Textile Book List
Box C-20
Lopez, WA 98261
(Books)

Textile Book Service
Box 907
144 East Second St.
Plainfield, NJ 07060
(Books)

Textile Resources
3763 Durango Avenue
Los Angeles, CA 90034
(Dyes, fabrics, books, supplies)

Thai Silks
393 Main
Los Altos, CA 94022
(Silks and cotton fabrics)

The Unicorn
Box 645
Rockville, MD 20851
(Textile and craft books)

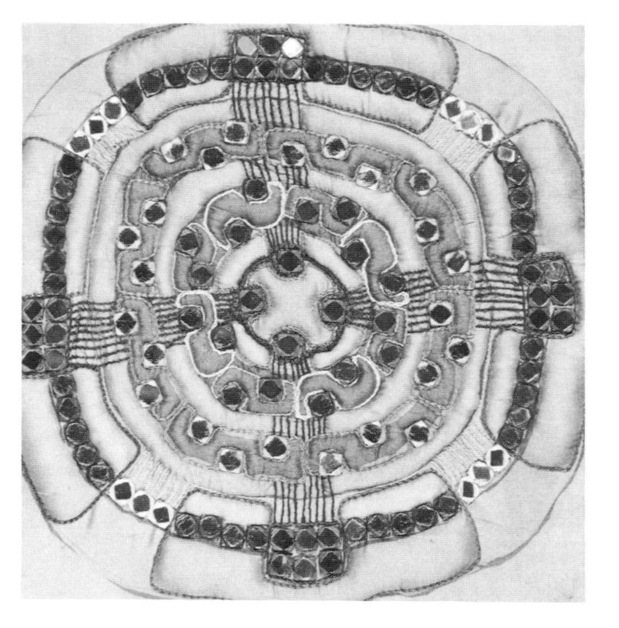

Ronald Childers. Wall piece. Resist dyed silk shantung with trapunto, conventional quilting, embroidery, and fiber attached mirrors, 15"x 15"(38 x 38 cm).

Surface Design Association, Inc.

The Surface Design Association grew out of the first national textile printing and dyeing conference, Surface Design Conference I, held in Spring 1976 at the University of Kansas. Since then national conferences have been held every two years with several regional conferences being organized on alternate years. Our express concern is to improve communication among artists, designers, industry, and teachers working in surface design on textiles and related media.

The purposes of the Surface Design Association, Inc. are to stimulate, to promote, and to improve education in the area of surface design; to encourage the surface designer as an individual artist; to improve communication and distribution of technical information concerning professional opportunities in surface design through galleries, studios, workshops, industry, small business, and teaching; to provide opportunities for the surface designers to exhibit their work; and to provide a forum for exchange of ideas through conferences and publications.

The *Surface Design Journal* is published four times a year and contains regional news, technical information, commentary, criticism, history, book reviews, exhibition, and educational opportunities as well as advertisements for equipment and supplies.

Membership is open to all persons interested in the creation, production and promotion of all phases of surface design. For current membership and subscription information consult a recent issue of the *Surface Design Journal* at your local library.

Tropic of Capricorn. *A complex and skillfully blended combination of geometric and organic imagery often seen on the kimonos of Japan. The light value lines of the ground fabric provide unity. Courtesy of Jack Lenor Larsen, Inc.*

Bibliography

For anyone seriously seeking complete bibliography material on the full range of fiber and fabric arts, we highly recommend two companion publications of the American Craft Council: *Bibliography: Fiber-Knotting, Stitchery, and Surface Design* and *Bibliography: Fiber-Weaving and Off Loom Weaving,* both 1979. A.C.C. librarian, Joanne Polster, compiled and updated these unusually thorough and well-organized listings. Contact the American Craft Council, 22 West 55th St., New York, N.Y. 10019 for availability and current price.

Technical Books

Belfer, Nancy. *Designing in Stitchery and Applique.* Worchester, Ma.: Davis Publications, 1972.

Biegeleisen, J.I. *Screen Printing.* New York: Watson-Guptill Publications, 1971.

Bruandet, Pierre. *Photograms.* New York: Watson-Guptill Publications, 1974.

Clarke, W. *An Introduction to Textile Printing.* London: Halsted Press, 1974.

Coats and Clark's One Hundred Embroidery Stitches. New York: Coats and Clark, Inc. 1975.

Collingwood, Peter. *Techniques of Sprang.* New York: Watson-Guptill Publications, 1974.

Constantine, Mildred, and Jack Lenor Larsen. *Beyond Craft: The Art Fabric.* New York: Van Nostrand Reinhold Co., 1973.

Corbman, Bernard P. *Textiles: Fiber to Fabric.* New York: McGraw-Hill, Inc., 1975.

A Dictionary of Textile Terms. Danville, Va.: Dan River, Inc. (current edition).

Dean, Beryl. *Ideas for Church Embroidery.* London: Charles T. Branford Co., 1968.

Emergy, Irene. *The Primary Structures of Fabrics: An Illustrated Classification.* Washington, D.C.: The Textile Museum, 1966.

Enthoven, Jacqueline.*The Stitches of Creative Embroidery.* N.Y.: Van Nostrand Reinhold Co., 1974.

———. *Stitches with Variations.* San Ramon Ca.: Sunset Designs, 1976.

Frew, Hannah. *Three-Dimensional Embroidery.* New York: Van Nostrand Reinhold Co., 1975.

Gostelow, Mary. *A World of Embroidery.* New York: Charles Scribner's Sons, 1975.

Grae, Ida. *Natures Colors: Dyes from Plants.* New York: Macmillan and Co., 1974.

Granich, Ronald B. *Japanese Paste-Resist Dyeing.* Seattle: Cerulean Blue Ltd., 1979.

Hanley, Hope. *The A B C's of Needlepoint.* New York: Charles Scribner's Sons, 1973.

Harvey, Virginia I. *Macrame, The Art of Creative Knotting.* Van Nostrand Reinhold Co., 1967.

———. *Color and Design in Macrame.* Van Nostrand Reinhold Co., 1971.

———. *Techniques of Basketry.* Van Nostrand Reinhold Co., 1974.

Hayward, John. *The Stevens Fabricopedia.* New York: J.P. Stevens & Co. 1970.

Held, Shirley. *Weaving: A Handbook of the Fiber Arts.* New York: Holt, Reinhart and Winston, 1978.

Hurlburt, Regina. *Left Handed Needlepoint.* New York: Van Nostrand Reinhold Co., 1972.

James, Michael. *The Quiltmakers Handbook.* New York: Prentice Hall Publishers (Spectrum Books), 1978.

Johnson, Meda Parker, and Glen Kaufman. *Design on Fabrics.* New York: Van Nostrand Reinhold Co., 1967.

Johnson, Pauline. *Creative Bookbinding.* Seattle: University of Washington Press, 1963. Techniques for decorative papers.

Karasz, Mariska. *Adventures in Stitches.* New York: Funk and Wagnalls Co., 1959.

Krevitsky, Nik. *Batik: Art and Craft.* New York: Van Nostrand Reinhold Co., 1964.

———. *Stitchery: Art and Craft.* New York: Van Nostrand Reinhold Co., 1966.

Laliberte, Norman, and Sterling McIlhany, *Banners and Hangings: Design and Construction.* New York: Van Nostrand Reinhold Co., 1966.

Lantz, Shirlee. *A Pageant of Pattern for Needlepoint.* New York: Atheneum Publishers, 1973.

Larsen, Jack Lenor, et al. *The Dyers Art: Ikat, Batik, Plangi.* New York: Van Nostrand Reinhold Co., 1976.

———, and Jeanne Weeks. *Fabrics for Interiors: A Guide for Designers, Architects and Consumers.* New York: Van Nostrand Reinhold Co., 1975.

Laury, Jean Ray. *Applique Stitchery.* Van Nostrand Reinhold Co., 1966.

———. *Quilts and Coverlets: A Contemporary Approach.* Van Nostrand Reinhold Co., 1970.

Mackenzie, Clinton D. *New Design in Crochet.* New York: Van Nostrand Reinhold Co., 1972.

Mailand, Harold F. *Consideration for the Care of Textiles and Costumes.* Indianapolis: Indiana Museum of Art, 1980.

Maile, Anne. *Tie and Dye as a Present Day Craft.* rev. ed. London: Mills and Boon Ltd., 1969.

Maurello, Ralph S. *The Complete Airbrush Book.* New York: Wm. Penn Publishings Corp., 1955.

Meilach, Dona Z. *Contemporary Batik and Tie-Dye,* New York: Crown Publishers, 1973.

———. *Soft Sculpture and Other Soft Forms.* New York: Crown Publishers, 1974.

Miller, Joni, and Lowry Thompson. *The Rubber Stamp Album.* New York: Workman Publishing, 1978.

Morgan, Mary, and Dee Mosteller. *Trapunto and Other Forms of Raised Quilting.* New York: Charles Scribner's Sons, 1977.

Moseley, Spencer, Pauline Johnson, and Hazel Koenig. *Crafts Design.* Belmont, Ca.: Wadsworth Publishing Co., 1962.

Pearson, Sina. *Textile Glossary.* New York: Brickel Associates Inc., 1980.

Perrone, Lisbeth. *The New World of Needlepoint.* New York: Crown Publishers, 1972.

Phillips, Mary Walker. *Step by Step Knitting.* New York: Van Nostrand Reinhold Co. 1967.

———. *Step by Step Macrame.* New York: Golden Press, 1970.

———. *Creative Knitting: A New Art Form.* New York: Van Nostrand Reinhold Co., 1971.

Polakoff, Claire. *Into Indigo.* New York: Anchor Books, 1980.

Putnam, Dyes Inc. *The How to Dye Book.* Quincy, Ill.: Putnam Dyes, Inc., 19 (P.O. Box 40, Quincy, IL 62301).

Readers Digest Complete Guide to Sewing. New York: Readers Digest Assn Inc., 1976.

Reichman, Charles. *Transfer Printing Manual.* New York: National Knitted Outerwear Assn., 1976.

Robinson, Stuart. *A History of Dyed Textiles.* Cambridge, Ma.: M.I.T. Press, 1969. *A History of Printed Textiles,*

———. *A History of Printed Textiles.* Cambridge, Ma.: M.I.T. Press, 1969.

Rossbach, Ed. *Baskets as Textile Art*. New York: Van Nostrand Reinhold Co., 1973.
———. *The New Basketry*. New York: Van Nostrand Reinhold Co., 1976.
Schwalbach, Mathilda, and James Schwalbach. *Screen-Process Printing for the Serigrapher and Textile Designer*. New York: Van Nostrand Reinhold Co., 1970.
Simmonds, Max. *Dyes and Dyeing*. Van Nostrand Reinhold Australia Pty., Ltd., 1978.
Simplicity's Needlework Plus. New York: Simplicity Pattern Co., Inc., 1980.
Skowronski, Hella, and Mary Reddy. *Sprang: Thread Twisting, A Creative Textile Technique*. New York: Van Nostrand Reinhold Co., 1974.
Snook, Barbara. *Needlework Stitches*. New York: Crown Publishers Inc., 1963.
Storey, Joyce. *The Thames and Hudson Manual of Dyes and Fabrics*. London: Thames and Hudson Publishers, 1978.
Thiel, Philip. *Visual Awareness and Design*. Seattle: University of Washington Press, 1981.
Valentino, Richard, and Phyllis Mufson. *Fabric Printing: Screen Method*. San Francisco: Bay Books, 1975.
Wilcox, Donald J. *Modern Leather Design*. New York: Watson-Guptill Publications, 1969.
———. *New Design in Stitchery*. New York: Van Nostrand Reinhold Co., 1970.
Wilson, Erica. *Erica Wilson's Embroidery Book*. New York: Charles Scribner's Sons, 1973.
Woodsmall, Annabel Whidney. *Contemporary Appliqued Beadwork*. Freeland, Wa.: H.T.H. Publishers, 1980.

Design and Resource Books

Albers, Josef. *Interaction of Color*. New Haven: Yale University Press, 1963; paperback editions, 1971.
Bates, Kenneth F. *Basic Design*. Cleveland: World Publishing Co., 1960.
Bossert, Helmuth T. *Folk Art of Primitive Peoples*. New York: Frederick A. Praeger, 1955.
Bourgoin, J. *Arabic Geometrical Pattern and Design*. New York: Dover Publishing, 1973.
Clark, Fiona. *William Morris: Wallpapers and Chintzes*. London: Academy Editions, 1973.
Collier, Graham. *Form, Space, and Vision: Discovering Design through Drawing*. rev. ed. Englewood Cliffs, N.J.: Prentice Hall Inc., 1967.
Day, Lewis F. *Pattern Design*. New York: Taplinger Publishing Co., 1979; reprint of 1906 edition.
Encyclopedia of World Art. (15 volumes) London: McGraw-Hill Publishing Co. Ltd. 1968.
Itten, Johannes. *The Art of Color*. New York: Van Nostrand Reinhold Co., 1961.
Jefferson, Louise E. *The Decorative Arts of Africa*. New York: The Viking Press inc., 1973.
Justema, William. *The Pleasures of Pattern*. New York: Van Nostrand Reinhold Co., 1968.
Kent, Kate P. *West African Cloth*. Denver: Denver Museum of Natural History, 1971.
Kepes, Gyorgy. *Vision and Value Series*. 6 vols. New York: George Braziller, 1966.
Lubell, Cecil. *Textile Collections of The World*. 3 vols. New York: Van Nostrand Reinhold Co., 1975, 1976, 1977.
Lauer, David A. *Design Basics*. N.Y.: Holt, Reinhart and Winston, 1979.
Proctor, Richard M. *The Principles of Pattern for Craftsmen and Designers*. New York: Van Nostrand Reinhold Co., 1969; paperback edition, 1971.
Racinet, Albert. *Polychrome Ornament*. London: Henry Southeran, 1877.
Scott, Robert Gellam. *Design Fundamentals*. New York: McGraw-Hill, 1951.
Sieber, Roy. *African Textiles and Decorative Arts*. New York: Museum of Modern Art, 1972.
Thoss. *Design and Color in Islamic Architecture*. Washington, D.C.: Smithsonian Press, 1968.
Vilimkova, M. *Egyptian Ornament*. London: Allan Wingate Ltd., 1963.

Periodicals

American Craft (formerly *Craft Horizons*). American Craft Council, 22 W. 55th St., New York, N.Y. 10019.
American Fabrics and Fashion. Doric Publishing Co., 24 East 38th St., New York, N.Y., 10001.
Art Hazards News. Center for Occupational Hazards, 5 Beekman St., New York: N.Y., 10038.
Fiberarts. 50 College St., Asheville, N.C., 28001.
The Flying Needle. National Standards Council of American Embroiderers, 826 Lincoln Ave., Winnetka, Ill., 60093.
Needle Arts. The Embroiderers Guild of America. 6 East 45th St. New York, N.Y., 10017.
Sew News. 1008 Western Ave. Suite 520, Seattle, Wash. 98104.
Shuttle, Spindle and Dyepot. Handweavers Guild of America, 65 LaSalle Road, West Hartford, Conn., 06107.
Surface Design Journal. Surface Design Association Inc., ℅ Sonya Whiddon, Art Dept., North Texas State University, Box 5098, Denton, Tex. 76203.
The Textile Book List. A quarterly review of new titles in the fields of textiles clothing, costume, dyeing, textile crafts and technology. R. L. Shep, Box C–20, Lopez, Wash., 98261.
Textile Museum Journal. The Textile Museum, 2320 S. St. N.W., Washington, D.C., 20008.

Brush dyed folded fabric. Acid dyes on silk crepe.

Richard M. Proctor. Cross. *Batik with acid and basic dyes on silk, constructed of seven panels, overall size ca. 48″ x 60″ (122 x 152 cm). Collection of Mr. and Mrs. Charles D. Hills, Seattle, Washington.*

Index